THE BRITISH GENERAL ELECTION OF 1997

The British General Election of 1997

David Butler
Fellow of Nuffield College, Oxford

Dennis Kavanagh
Professor of Politics, University of Liverpool

First published in Great Britain 1997 by
MACMILLAN PRESS LTD
Houndmills, Basingstoke, Hampshire RG21 6XS and London
Companies and representatives throughout the world

A catalogue record for this book is available from the British Library.

ISBN 0–333–64775–0 hardcover
ISBN 0–333–64776–9 paperback

First published in the United States of America 1997 by
ST. MARTIN'S PRESS, INC.,
Scholarly and Reference Division,
175 Fifth Avenue, New York, N.Y. 10010

ISBN 0–312–21079–5

Library of Congress Cataloging-in-Publication Data
Butler, David, 1924–
The British general election of 1997 / David Butler, Dennis
Kavanagh.
p.   cm.
Includes bibliographical references and index.
ISBN 0–312–21079–5 (cloth)
1. Great Britain. Parliament—Elections, 1997.   2. Elections–
–Great Britain.   3. Great Britain—Politics and government—1997–
I. Kavanagh, Dennis.   II. Title.
JN956.B8683 1997
324.941'0859—dc21   97–27660
                                                         CIP

This book is printed on paper suitable for recycling and made from fully managed and sustained forest sources.
10   9   8   7   6   5   4   3   2   1
05   05   04   03   02   01   00   99   98   97

Printed and bound in Great Britain by
J. W. Arrowsmith Ltd, Bristol

Contents

List of Tables

List of Illustrations

List of Plates

Preface

This is the fifteenth in the Nuffield College series of election histories. It is the seventh undertaken jointly by the present authors. We are saved from the anxiety about becoming stale in repeating the same enterprise by the continuous change in the personnel and the practice of British politics. It is arguable that the 1997 contest was the most innovative since 1959. We have certainly found it as fascinating as any that we have observed.

This book, like its predecessors, ends with the counting of the votes. Political life in Britain continued busily after 1 May 1997; the principal actors in the election became preoccupied with mastering the intricacies of government or with electing a new party leader and adjusting to the frustrations of opposition. As we asked them, in our post-election interviews, to reflect on what was well or ill done during the past five years, or during the campaign, their enthusiams had moved on. But their memories were sharp and critical. This book is written without the longer perspectives of history but it does, we hope, escape the instant judgements, made in the heat of the campaign.

The Nuffield series of election studies was designed by its instigator in 1945, R. B. McCallum, 'to find immortality in the footnotes of others' and to prevent myths growing up about the nature of a campaign as they did after 1918 and 1924 and 1931. This work tries, once again, to pursue that honourable goal.

1997 provided a landmark election. It was not just that, for the first time in 18 years, it led to a change in government. It was also because the way in which it was conducted marked a change in style on a scale unmatched in any post-war election except one. In 1959 the advent of intensive television coverage, of large-scale advertising, of press conferences, and of private polls transformed the nature of campaigning. In 1997 the Labour Party brought to an altogether new pitch, the sophisticated presentation of its messages, nationally and locally. The six weeks of the campaign did not, of course, decide the outcome but the three years of disciplined preparation and the final assault must have had a substantial impact on the scale of the majority.

In addition to the two authors on the title page, another five are named in the table of contents. But there are many more contributors to this work. Journalists covered the election more exhaustively than ever before and many of our insights are drawn from them. The parties were immensely cooperative, allowing us access to their activities and giving us many hours of their time in interviews. Party leaders generously granted interviews, and some key participants commented on parts of our draft; we cannot embarrass them by naming them, but they know how grateful we are.

Vernon Bogdanor, Michael Hart, Paul Martin, Peter Riddell, Marc Stears, John Taylor and Anthony Teasdale are among those who made comments on particular chapters; other helpful critics remain anonymous. We are deeply indebted to all those who have saved us from error of fact or interpretation or infelicity of style. We must also thank Nuffield College and the Department of Politics and Communications at the University of Liverpool for all sorts of practical assistance, and the Leverhulme Trust for so generously providing financial support.

Our work was greatly lightened by our Research Assistant, Ian St John of Nuffield College, and Marian Hoffmann and Yvonne Janvier did a vast amount of our typing. Martin Range had a major role in the production of the statistical appendix and Steve Moyle helped with the maps. Our wives once again tolerated the burdens imposed by our psephological enthusiasm.

David Butler
Dennis Kavanagh

August 1997

1 The Longest Parliament, 1992–97

On 9 April 1992 the Conservative Party won its fourth successive victory. This brought immense exhilaration to the party; but in fact it heralded a long slide to disaster. For most of the next five years the government appeared to be under siege.

For many Conservatives, though not for John Major, the outcome was unexpected. The economy had been in poor shape and none of the opinion polls had suggested a working majority. In fact the actual lead – 21 seats – was 41 less than might have been anticipated from an 8 per cent margin in votes.[1] At their first working meeting John Major and Chris Patten had a sense of foreboding. They realised that the 21 majority contained several potential dissenters and would not suffice to carry the government through the difficult times ahead.

A short wave of Conservative euphoria and Labour despair did follow the election. Were the Conservatives to be in power for ever? Had Labour thrown away its last chance? Was Britain to become, like Japan, a one-party democratic state as it moved towards 18 years of continuous Conservative dominance?

Mr Major was not given long to savour his triumph. In October 1990, in the last days of Margaret Thatcher's premiership, Britain had entered the European Exchange Rate Mechanism (ERM) at what proved to be an unrealistically high level (a mid-point of DM2.95 to the pound). Speculative pressure and demands for a realignment of currencies grew during August 1992. By 13 September sterling was bumping against its permitted floor of DM2.87. The Chancellor of the Exchequer, Norman Lamont, desperately sought backing from the Bundesbank and other sources. £10bn of British reserves were spent in efforts to prop up sterling. However, Britain was not popular in key circles in Europe; the compromises insisted upon at the 1991 Maastricht summit and afterwards had dented any will to help. Extreme measures on 'Black Wednesday', 16 September 1992, including raising the bank rate to 10 per cent and then to 15 per cent in the space of hours, proved insufficient to save the pound, and Norman Lamont had to announce that the country was unilaterally pulling out of the Exchange Rate Mechanism.[2]

For good and ill this event coloured all the politics of the parliament. Membership had been enthusiastically backed by the Labour and Liberal Democrat parties, but it was the Conservatives who collected the odium for the failure of the policy. For the government the positive side was that devaluation provided a great boost to British exports (the pound had fallen to 2.43 to the Deutschmark and to 1.43 to the dollar by December 1992); moreover, since sterling no longer had to be kept within the ERM bands, there was greater freedom to reduce interest rates. These two developments lay at the heart of the economic recovery of the mid-1990s. Yet the fact remained that the forced exit from the ERM shattered the government's economic strategy. This had been explicitly grounded upon tight fiscal and monetary policy as a means of ensuring Britain's competitiveness at the fixed exchange rate and squeezing inflation. The attempt to do this had failed, seriously compromising the Conservatives' reputation for economic competence. It also fatally damaged the standing of John Major. Only six days earlier at Glasgow he had stated that leaving the ERM would be a betrayal of Britain's future. The Gallup poll, following 'Black Wednesday', showed a halving in public satisfaction with Mr Major, with the government's record, and in optimism about the economy. Mr Lamont did not resign, taking the line that the responsibility was at least as much John Major's as his. For a time John Major's self-confidence was dented, and he even discussed resignation with one or two colleagues.

Another economic problem to confront the government in the months following the election was the rapid growth in the Public Sector Borrowing Requirement. It became apparent in early 1993 that on current trends government borrowing was set to reach £50 bn in 1993–94 – equivalent to 8 per cent of national income. This deficit was a consequence of the 1990–92 recession, which reduced tax revenues and increased spending on unemployment and other welfare benefits. In addition, the government had entered into significant spending commitments before the election. The party which had won the 1992 election by stressing that tax rises were inevitable under a Labour government now had to impose its own increases by raising national insurance contributions. Most significantly, Norman Lamont, in his Budget of 16 March 1993, imposed Value Added Tax on domestic fuel. (This was the last March Budget, the decision having been taken in future to combine the presentation of the government's revenue and spending decisions in a November Budget.)

During the first by-election of the parliament, at Newbury in May 1993, the domestic fuel tax loomed large as an issue. Mr Lamont memorably reported that he sang in his bath 'Je ne regrette rien'. The complacent comment did little to restore Mr Lamont's tarnished image; it struck entirely the wrong note at a time when living standards were being squeezed for many people. The by-election was overwhelmingly lost and on 27 May Mr Lamont (John Major's campaign manager in the 1990 leadership race) refused a move to Environment Secretary and resigned from the government. Few critics were appeased; they considered that Mr Lamont's continuance in his post reflected the government's lack of an apology for its mistakes.

Kenneth Clarke took over at the Treasury and, during the next four years, presided over a steady recovery in the country's economic fortunes. Unemployment, which stood at 2.9 million early in 1993, declined month by month and dropped below 2 million by the end of 1996. Inflation stayed under 3 per cent, except in 1995. Interest rates fell with devaluation and the Chancellor, in a celebrated confrontation on 5 May 1995, resisted pressure from Eddie George, the new Governor of the Bank of England, to raise them. The rate of growth moved up to 3 per cent in late 1993 and to 4 per cent by late 1994. House prices began to rise again and the number of home-owners suffering from negative equity gradually declined. The Conservatives could legitimately claim that Britain was setting an example to Europe and the world as a model of prudent and sustained economic growth. By 1995 John Major and Michael Heseltine were constantly inserting into interviews a mantra – the highest rate of growth, the lowest unemployment, and the lowest inflation in the European Union. Kenneth Clarke tried to reclaim the party's reputation for tax cutting by reducing the basic rate of income tax by 1p in his 1995 Budget and by a further 1p in his 1996 Budget, but he commented, 'We're only clearing up our own mess', and Labour could continually tease the government with '22 tax increases since 1992'.

Neil Kinnock's immediate response to the 1992 defeat was to resign the Labour leadership. John Smith easily won the fight for succession, defeating Bryan Gould in the electoral college by 91 per cent to 9 per cent. Mr Smith, with the help of an impassioned speech by John Prescott, narrowly persuaded the 1993 Party Conference to accept 'one member, one vote' (OMOV) for candidate selection and other constituency decisions, thus curbing trade union influence. He had been accepted as a widely admired leader when he died suddenly on 12 May 1994 at the start of the Euro-election campaign. Tony Blair, after some quick manoeuvring with his friend, Gordon Brown, and with Robin Cook, declared his candidacy and defeated John Prescott and Margaret Beckett for the leadership, securing large majorities in each section of the electoral college.

Mr Blair rapidly made his mark on the party, acting boldly to secure repeal of the Clause Four commitment to nationalisation and modifying the party constitution in other ways. Under him, party organisation and relations with the media were transformed (see Chapter 3). He moved fast in the sphere of policy to sanitise Labour, distancing the party from old shibboleths and associations alienating to middle Britain. He promised real change but, as Labour policies seemed to edge closer to the Conservatives, the most obvious

Table 1.1　Economic and political indicators, 1992–97

		(1) Real personal disposable income (1990 =100)	(2) Weekly earnings (1990=100)	(3) Retail Prices (1987=100)	(4) Year on Year inflation (%)	(5) Unem- ployment (UK)(%)	(6) Days lost in strikes (OOOs)	(7) Gross domestic product (1990=100)	(8) Balance of Payments (£m)
1992	1	100.7	113.4	136.2	4.1	9.1	115	96.9	-2025
	2	103.1	113.7	139.1	4.1	9.5	85	97.1	-2325
	3	103.7	114.9	139.0	3.6	9.7	161	97.6	-2492
	4	103.7	116.4	139.6	3.0	10.1	175	98.0	-3291
1993	1	103.4	117.1	138.3	1.8	10.5	194	98.5	-3114
	2	104.0	117.9	140.9	1.3	10.4	199	99.0	-2327
	3	103.6	119.0	141.2	1.7	10.3	77	100.0	-2411
	4	103.7	120.2	141.6	1.6	10.1	180	100.7	-2443
1994	1	104.3	121.7	142.0	2.4	9.9	14	101.8	-1140
	2	104.5	122.7	144.3	2.6	9.6	118	103.1	-519
	3	105.6	123.7	144.3	2.3	9.3	91	104.1	-106
	4	106.1	124.9	144.8	2.6	8.9	54	105.0	110
1995	1	107.2	126.0	145.9 .	3.4	8.6	70	105.4	587
	2	107.6	126.7	148.2	3.5	8.3	101	105.8	-1653
	3	107.7	127.7	148.5	3.7	8.2	76	106.4	-1354
	4	110.2	129.1	149.0	3.2	8.1	168	107.0	-1252
1996	1	110.9	130.5	150.1	2.8	7.9	102	107.6	-1206
	2	111.8	131.4	152.4	2.2	7.8	262	108.2	689
	3	112.7	132.8	152.8	2.1	7.6	713	108.9	-426
	4	114.0	134.5	153.8	2.6	7.2	226	109.7	508
1997	1	113.7	136.4	154.4	2.7	6.5	72	110.8	1459

Sources: 1–5, 8, 12–13 *Economic Trends*; 9–11 *Financial Statistics*; 6 *Employment Gazette*; 14–15 MORI.

innovation lay in the separation of the Labour Party from its past. Indeed, when more positive proposals, such as the creation of a 'stakeholder society', failed to strike a chord with the party and country, they were allowed to fade into the background.

During a parliament that saw Britain more closely linked to the continent by the opening of the Channel Tunnel, relations with Europe repeatedly bedevilled Conservative politics. The party, which under Edward Heath had, on the whole unitedly, led Britain into the Common Market, seemed to fall apart over the issue. Sir Teddy Taylor, Bill Cash, and a number of other high-profile back-benchers, maintained a militant anti-Maastricht Treaty position. The solid core of the Conservative Party at Westminster and in the constituencies became increasingly Euro-sceptic. Lady Thatcher made her hostility plain and the possibility of an outburst from her was a continual worry.

Ministers themselves stretched collective Cabinet responsibility to the limit with their anti-European remarks; a comment by John Major, publicly

(9) FTSE 100 Share Index (1 Jan 1984 = 1000)	(10) US$ to £	(11) Sterling Exchange Rate Index (1990=100)	(12) Interest rates (%)	(13) House prices (1993 = 100)	(14) MORI State of the Economy Poll': Net Optimists	(15) MORI polls (voting intention) Con Lab LD
2521	1.77	99.4	10.5	NA	+1	40 40 17
2618	1.81	101.2	10.2	101.7	+12	43 38 16
2413	1.90	99.4	9.7	102	−27	39 43 15
2692	1.58	87.7	7.3	98.1	−32	34 46 15
2842	1.48	86.6	6.0	98.6	−15	34 46 16
2847	1.54	88.7	6.0	99.4	+3	30 45 22
2966	1.50	90.2	6.0	101.5	+1	28 43 25
3183	1.49	90.2	5.7	99.6	−7	29 46 22
3344	1.49	90.7	5.3	100.7	−10	28 47 21
3066	1.51	89.1	5.3	102.1	−5	26 48 22
3119	1.55	87.9	5.4	103.8	−6	24 54 19
3081	1.59	89.1	5.9	103.1	−9	24 58 15
3045	1.58	87.2	6.6	102.2	−20	25 57 14
3283	1.60	84.3	6.8	103.3	−15	26 57 15
3482	1.57	84.3	6.8	104.2	−19	26 54 15
3627	1.56	83.5	6.7	102.8	−17	27 56 13
3728	1.53	83.5	6.2	104.3	−15	28 56 13
3758	1.52	84.8	5.9	104.4	−6	29 53 14
3841	1.55	85.5	5.8	108.5	−3	29 52 13
4052	1.64	91.4	6.0	108.6	−3	30 52 12
4298	1.63	96.9	6.0	NA	+1	30 52 12

overheard in July 1993, about the 'bastards' being 'the source of the poison' plainly referred to colleagues such as Michael Portillo, Peter Lilley and John Redwood. The pro-Europeans in the Cabinet were on the whole silent and, after Douglas Hurd left the Foreign Office in 1995, Kenneth Clarke was exposed as the only vocal advocate of closer union. Although Michael Heseltine, also a committed pro-European, gave strong backing to Kenneth Clarke in Cabinet, Mr Clarke, as Chancellor of the Exchequer, was inevitably embroiled in EU discussions and thus had a much higher profile on Europe than the Deputy Prime Minister. The latter, moreover, was determined to demonstrate loyalty to John Major.

The ratification of the Maastricht Treaty hung over the 1992–93 session. The Danish rejection of Maastricht in their first referendum on the Treaty (2 June 1992) led the British government to postpone the question until the Danes had voted again. John Major looked back on this as the greatest 'if only' of the parliament. The passage of the Treaty would have been so much easier had they embarked on it at the beginning of the parliament. After the

Danish vote President Mitterrand announced that France would also hold a referendum. These steps emboldened the Euro-sceptics in the party and the press. On 4 November 1992 a paving motion to proceed with the committee stage only passed, with Liberal Democrat support, by a majority of three; 26 Conservatives voted against the government, although John Major had indicated that it was a resigning issue. When the ratification bill was debated in the summer of 1993 filibustering by Euro-sceptics took up many hours of parliamentary time. On 22 July the government lost a key vote by 326 to 318, with 27 Tories defying a three-line whip. Mr Major had to call a confidence vote the next day which, thanks to the Unionists, he won comfortably.

Although Mr Major suggested that the party had 'drawn a line in the sand' under its European divisions, they continued unabated and Mr Major knew that on some issues he was actually leading a minority government. On 28 November 1994 eight Conservative MPs abstained on the European Communities (Finance) Bill. The whip was promptly withdrawn from them and Sir Richard Body volunteered to join them. There was no precedent for the withdrawal of the Conservative whip on such a scale – apart from Rupert Allason in 1993, the whip had not been taken from any Conservative MP since 1942. The 'whipless nine' continued to make trouble until, on 25 April 1995, the whip was restored – without any assurance of improved behaviour. Since John Major had pushed for the original withdrawal of the whip, the climbdown only reinforced the impression of weak leadership.

Europe remained a contentious issue right up to the end of the parliament, as the date confirmed by EU leaders at the Madrid summit in December 1995 for the commencement of the projected Single European Currency (1 January 1999) approached. In October 1995 Sir James Goldsmith announced the formation of a referendum party whose sole object would be to force a referendum on Britain's relations with Europe. This caused some alarm in Conservative circles, with a number of individuals, notably Lord Archer, worrying publicly about losing key marginals through split votes.

On 2 April 1996 the government promised to hold a referendum if a future Conservative administration decided to join the single currency. John Major did not like the idea, but had signalled his willingness to consider the device in an interview with David Frost in January. Within a week Sir James announced that he would run Referendum Party candidates against sitting MPs in the general election. Michael Heseltine had worked hard to sell the referendum idea to a reluctant Kenneth Clarke, who in turn insisted that collective responsibility would be imposed on Cabinet ministers. This agreement just managed to hold until 1 May 1997. It was widely known that Mr Clarke would resign if further concessions were made to those who

On the single currency... ...we are *unequivocally*...

...*committed to being*... ...*equivocal*.

Peter Brookes, *The Times*, 5 December 1996

wanted an outright declaration that the government would never enter a single currency or would rule it out for the lifetime of the next parliament. He was irritated by Central Office briefings that a change to a more Euro-sceptical line was likely. The agreement to keep the options open was his line in the sand.

Opinion polls suggested that the public was 2 to 1 against Britain entering the single currency, and Mr Clarke was increasingly portrayed by the sceptics as the only barrier to John Major ruling out entry. Motions for the party conference showed the party to be increasingly hostile to European integration and even monetary union. The Cabinet became steadily more Euro-sceptic over the course of the parliament. John Major's thinking, however, was coloured by the knowledge that Kenneth Clarke's views found favour with a sustantial body of MPs and ministers. It was also coloured by his calculation of the national interest. He did not like the single currency; he had been scarred by the experience of the ERM, and, if it had not been started, he would have worked to oppose its creation. However, he knew that France and Germany were determined to achieve monetary union, and if he was to negotiate with authority then he could not rule out membership now; moreover, the scheme

CHRONOLOGY OF EVENTS, 1992–97

1992

9 Apr.	General election. Clear Con. majority of 21
10 Apr.	Reshuffle. J. Patten, Bottomley, Shephard, Portillo and Mayhew enter Cabinet
13 Apr.	Kinnock announces resignation
24 Apr.	Chris Patten appointed Governor of Hong Kong
7 May	Local Government elections
2 Jul.	Danish referendum rejects Maastricht
18 Jul.	Smith elected Lab. Leader (Smith 91%; Gould 9%). Beckett Deputy Leader
18 Aug.	Troops sent to Bosnia
3 Sep.	Government uses £10bn to support sterling
16 Sep.	'Black Wednesday'. Britain withdraws from ERM. Parliament recalled
24 Sep.	Resignation of Mellor
29 Sep.	Smith's first conference speech as Leader
13 Oct.	Closure of 31 pits announced; temporarily reprieved after furore
4 Nov.	Commons pass Maastricht paving motion 319–316
4 Nov.	Clinton elected US President
10 Nov.	Scott Inquiry set up after Matrix-Churchill case

1993

1 Jan.	Start of Single Market
26 Jan.	Base interest rate cut to 6%, lowest since 1977
5 Feb.	Con. Central Office cut 61 jobs as a result of £19m debts
12 Feb.	Inflation rate of 1.7%, lowest since 1968
17 Mar.	Budget raises taxes, including fuel VAT
31 Mar.	Labour's Plant Report on electoral systems published
6 May	Lib. Dems win Newbury by-election. Con. lose control in 15 County Councils
27 May	Clarke replaces Lamont as Chancellor. Howard becomes Home Sec.
1 Apr.	'Care in the Community' programme launched by government
21 Jun.	Heseltine heart attack in Venice
30 Jun.	Lab. decide on all-women shortlists
1 Jul.	E. George appointed Governor of Bank of England
20 Jul.	Redistribution of Seats Act passed, accelerating redistribution of seats

22 Jul.	23 Con. MPs vote against Maastricht Bill. Government defeated 324–316
23 Jul.	Government wins confidence motion by 40 votes
25 Jul.	Leak of Major's 'bastards' comment on colleagues
28 Jul.	Lab. abandons 1992 tax proposals
29 Jul.	Lib. Dems win Christchurch by-election
7 Sep.	At TUC conference Smith commits Lab. to full employment and union rights
27 Sep.	Lab. conference votes for minimum wage and reaffirms commitment to Clause Four. One member, one vote accepted for election of parliamentary candidates. Benn loses seat on NEC
8 Oct.	'Back to Basics' conference speech by Major
5 Nov.	Bill to privatise railways passes through parliament
30 Nov.	First unified Budget
15 Dec.	Anglo-Irish Downing St Declaration

1994

1 Jan.	Stage 2 of EMU process begins
5 Jan.	Yeo resigns (scandal)
9 Jan.	Earl of Caithness resigns (scandal)
24 Jan.	International disarmament body sets out N. Ireland principles
29 Mar.	Britain accepts Ionnanina compromise on blocking minority in EU Council of Ministers
29 Mar	Marlow openly calls on Major to resign
5 May	Severe Con. losses in local elections
6 May	Opening of Channel Tunnel
7 May	M. Brown resigns as government whip (scandal)
12 May	Death of John Smith
23 May	European Manifestos
9 Jun.	European Parliament elections. Lab. 62; Con. 18; Lib. Dems 2
9 Jun.	Lib. Dems win Eastleigh by-election
30 Jun.	Lab. narrowly hold off SNP in Monklands E. by-election
10 Jul.	Cons. MPs Riddick and Tredinnick accused of accepting 'cash-for-questions'
15 Jul.	Britain agrees to Santer as President of the EU Commission
20 Jul.	Cabinet reshuffle. MacGregor, J. Patten, Lord Wakeham leave. Shephard to Education. Cranborne to lead Lords. Hanley replaces Fowler as Con. Party Chairman
21 Jul.	Blair elected Lab. Leader. Prescott Deputy Leader
4 Aug.	Gallup poll gives Lab. record 33% lead over Con.

31 Aug.	IRA announce cease-fire
18 Sep.	Lib. Dem. conference. Ashdown urges 'common cause' with Lab.
6 Oct.	Lab. conference rejects change to Clause Four
13 Oct.	Swedes vote to join EU (21 Oct. Norwegians vote No)
14 Oct.	Loyalist cease-fire in N. Ireland
20 Oct.	Lab. Shadow Cabinet reshuffle. Cook to Foreign Affairs; Straw to Home Affairs; Blunkett to Education
21 Oct.	Tim Smith resigns following failure to disclose payments from al-Fayed
24 Oct.	Borrie Report on social justice published
25 Oct.	Neil Hamilton resigns following allegations of undeclared payments. Appointment of Nolan Committee
14 Nov.	Lottery launched
20 Nov.	Chief Executive of Br. Gas gets 75% pay increase
28 Nov.	Government wins confidence vote on EU bill 330–303. Whip withdrawn from 8 Con. rebels
29 Nov.	Budget
2 Dec.	Blair's son to go to grant-maintained school
6 Dec.	Government defeated on proposal to raise VAT on fuel from 8 to 17.5%
15 Dec.	Lab. win Dudley West by-election

1995

1 Jan.	Austria, Finland, and Sweden join EU
11 Feb.	C. Wardle resigns over immigration rules
22 Feb.	Framework Document launch, Belfast
6 Apr.	Scottish Local Gov. elections. Only 81 Con. Councillors elected
20 Apr.	Two Tory MPs suspended over cash for questions
24 Apr.	Whip restored to 8 Con. Euro-rebels
29 Apr.	Lab. membership endorses new Clause Four
4 May	Local elections. Cons lose 1800 seats
5 May	Clarke over-rules Bank of England on interest rate rise
11 May	First Nolan Report
25 May	SNP win Perth and Kinross by-election
14 Jun.	Commons approves new parliamentary boundaries for England
22 Jun.	Major resigns to seek re-election as Leader
26 Jun.	Redwood resigns to fight Major
4 Jul.	Major re-elected Leader 218–89 (22 abstaining)
5 Jul.	Reshuffle. Heseltine becomes Deputy PM. Rifkind replaces Hurd at Foreign Office

27 Jul.	Lib. Dems. win Littleborough by-election
15 Aug.	Major allows early civil service–Lab. transition talks
8 Sep.	Trimble succeeds Molyneaux as U. Unionist Leader
7 Oct.	Howarth switches from Con. to Lab.
10 Oct.	Con. conference. Portillo attacks EU and affirms independence of UK defence policy
16 Oct.	Howard sacks Director of Prison Service
28 Oct.	Budget. 1p tax cut
27 Nov.	Goldsmith launches Referendum Party
29 Dec.	Emma Nicholson switches from Con. to Lib. Dems

1996

8 Jan.	Labour's women-only shortlists declared illegal
21 Jan.	Row over Harman's choice of school
24 Jan.	Mitchell Report and N. Ireland election scheme
9 Feb.	Canary Wharf bomb ends IRA cease-fire
15 Feb.	Scott Report on 'arms to Iraq'
22 Feb.	Thurnham resigns Con. whip
26 Feb.	Government escapes Scott censure 319–318
13 Mar.	Massacre at Dunblane
20 Mar.	Link between BSE and CJD admitted. Worldwide bans on Br. beef
14 Apr.	Goldsmith announces plan for campaign
2 May	Local elections
9 May	District Auditor surcharges Westminster City councillors £31m
31 May	N. Ireland assembly elections. Unionist majority
2 Jun.	R. Richards resigns (scandal)
10 Jun.	MPs vote themselves 26% pay increase
10 Jun.	All Party Talks begin in N. Ireland
11 Jun.	78 Con. MPs support referendum on Europe
15 Jul.	Prince of Wales and Princess Diana divorce
22 Jul.	Heathcoat-Amory resigns over Europe
30 Nov	Budget. 1p off income tax
16 Dec.	Willetts resigns (misleading committee)

1997

20 Jan.	Cabinet publicly agrees EMU entry in 1999 'unlikely'
20 Jan.	Brown accepts Con. spending limits for next two years
27 Feb.	Lab. win Wirral South by-election
18 Mar.	Election announced

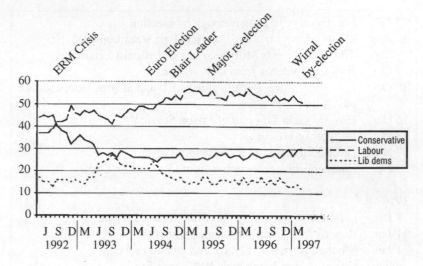

Figure 1.1   Opinion poll trends, 1992–97
(average of nationally reported polls asking 'How will you vote?')

might succeed and membership prove to be in the national interest. Though he occasionally flirted with ruling out membership, he never came seriously near to doing so.

The government's popularity never recovered from the 'Black Wednesday' debacle. The Conservative Party, which had enjoyed a 7 per cent lead in the polls in June 1992, plummeted to a 20 per cent deficit by December 1993, and, on average, Labour led by more than 20 per cent for the rest of the parliament. This inevitably bolstered opposition morale and depressed ministers. John Major's satisfaction ratings were the lowest recorded for any prime minister since Gallup first asked the question 50 years earlier. Voters liked Mr Major as a person, but found him weak and ineffectual as a leader.

Right-wing Conservatives could look to Lady Thatcher and Lord Tebbit for support and, within the Cabinet, to Michael Portillo, Michael Howard, John Redwood and Peter Lilley. They advocated tax reductions, spending cuts (although often being vague on where these should fall) and resistance to further European integration. For a brief time this wing of the party was inspired by the success of Newt Gingrich's 'Contract with America' which helped the Republicans to do so well in the 1994 mid-term elections. Mr Major, however, was determined to hold a balance between the pro- and anti-Europeans and to keep open the option of joining the single currency; he rejected the choice between tax cuts and spending cuts, wanting both lower taxes and more spending on key public services.

All the electoral omens seemed bleak. In each of the eight constituencies where a Conservative died, the opposition won – the first time a government had lost every by-election in the course of a parliament. Four seats went to the Liberal Democrats, three to Labour, and one to the Scottish Nationalists (see p. 292). In three cases the Conservative candidate sank from first to third place. The swing to the Liberal Democrats in Christchurch (35 per cent in July 1993) and to Labour in Dudley West (25 per cent in December 1995) were all-time records.

In local government elections, too, the story was disastrous. Good results in May 1992 were followed by appalling ones in each of the next four years. By the end of the parliament the Conservatives had a clear majority in only one county (Buckinghamshire), five London boroughs and eight shire districts. There were a mere three authorities outside the Home Counties where they remained in control. After the 1996 elections there were only 4700 Conservative councillors nationwide compared to 5100 for the Liberal Democrats and 10,800 for Labour.

The one nationwide test came with the European elections on 9 June 1994. The campaign was low key and it was overshadowed by the death of John Smith. Although the Conservatives were relieved to survive with 18 of the 87 seats, they were near to defeat in 14 of those, and the Liberal Democrats, winning their first two Euro-seats, were tantalisingly close in five more. Their share of the mainland vote, at 29 per cent (compared with Labour's 44 per cent and the Liberal Democrats' 17 per cent), was the lowest the Conservatives had ever registered in a national election. Labour's 62 MEPs offered them a significantly widened regional base and gave a stronger voice to Europe in the party's counsels.

Due to by-election attrition, the government's clear majority, 21 in 1992, had sunk to 11 by the end of 1994. It virtually disappeared for six months while the nine Euro-sceptics were denied the whip. It was further dented when Alan Howarth crossed the floor to Labour, and Emma Nicholson, followed by Peter Thurnham, went over to the Liberal Democrats. Finally, when Barry Porter died in Wirral South on 3 November 1996, Mr Major ceased to have a majority.

To the surprise and disappointment of Conservative Central Office, the economic recovery failed to feed through into support for the government. Voters' economic optimism, the 'feel-good factor', was slow to rise. For this there were several possible reasons. The recession had been severe, and many people continued to be afflicted with problems such as anxiety over the security of their job or the negative equity of their house. It was only in 1996 that unemployment fell below 8 per cent. There remained a general sense of economic insecurity. As Spencer and Curtice observed, the recovery was marked by low inflation, more flexible and short-term work, and declining or only slowly rising property prices. As a result voters felt less secure and optimistic than during previous economic recoveries.[3] Further, it was recognised that the Conservatives had broken the promises on tax made at the election, and that recovery had only commenced once the government had been forced to abandon its initial policies. The Conservatives failed to regain their standing as the party of low taxes and competent economic management. They progressively lost the support even of the Conservative-inclined newspapers.

In any case, the economy was not the only factor to affect the government's popularity. It quite soon began to attract a reputation for incompetence, with the mishandling of a series of sensitive issues. There were three outstanding examples.

As a prelude to the privatisation of the declining mining industry, plans to close 30 pits were announced in September 1992 by Michael Heseltine (who had revived the ancient title of President of the Board of Trade when he moved to the Department of Trade and Industry in the new government). The abruptness of the decision produced a notable explosion of public indignation, not confined to the mining areas. In December it was declared 'unlawful and irrational' by the High Court. In due course ten of the threatened pits were given the opportunity to prove themselves viable – even though most of these were later closed. During the parliament the number of miners (700,000 in 1950) fell from 43,000 to less than 7000.

The second issue concerned the Child Support Agency. This body, set up in 1991 with the laudable intention of making fathers who had left home pay for the support of their children, was grossly mismanaged at its inception and MPs' postbags were flooded with stories of injustice and maladministration. In due course the situation was partially remedied but it continued to be used as an illustration of a harsh and uncaring government.

The third issue was more serious and expensive. On 20 March 1996 the Health minister, Stephen Dorrell, had to announce that there was evidence that 'mad cow' disease could spread, to humans, through the eating of beef, causing a particularly horrible death through Creutzfeld-Jacob disease. His statement produced widespread panic and a sharp drop in beef consumption.

The European Union immediately placed a ban on all beef and cattle exports from the United Kingdom. In the vehement reaction to this John Major promised obstruction to all European decisions that required unanimity until the ban was modified. A deal of a sort was reached at the Florence summit in June 1996, but it was not implemented as Britain failed to fulfil the necessary conditions. There were recriminations about the belated banning in 1990 of the cattlefeed that was the cause of the trouble. Farmers suffered severely and the National Farmers Union became more and more critical of Douglas Hogg, the Minister of Agriculture, as he sought vainly, and perhaps undiplomatically, to secure an easing of the European ban. He survived a confidence motion in the Commons on 17 February 1997 by 320 to 307, helped by Ulster Unionist abstentions.

Mr Hogg and his predecessor, William Waldegrave, had already been mauled over the export of live animals, which in the summer of 1995 had provoked some notable humanitarian and middle-class blockades at ports and airports, but the most spectacular demonstrations were the work of environmentalists, protesting against new by-pass roads, most notably at Newbury.

As important as the impression of ineptitude, an atmosphere of 'sleaze' and decadence began to surround the government – with perhaps more damaging consequences. Comparisons were frequently drawn in the media with the Profumo Affair and the last days of Macmillan's administration. Press mentions of sleaze and related terms, covering the conduct of Conservative ministers and MPs, mushroomed. In 1994–95 the term appeared more frequently than in the previous nine years put together.[4] This image of sleaze was built up over a number of issues.

Policy resignations

11 Feb. 95	Charles Wardle (immigration policy)
26 Jun. 95	John Redwood (to fight for the leadership)
22 Jul. 96	David Heathcoat-Amory (European policy)

Resignations over personal conduct

22 Sep. 92	David Mellor (acceptance of foreign hospitality)
24 Sep. 93	Michael Mates (link to Asil Nadir)
7 May 94	Michael Brown (domestic scandal)
20 Oct. 94	Tim Smith (cash for questions)
25 Oct. 94	Neil Hamilton (cash for questions)
7 Jan. 95	Tim Yeo (domestic scandal)
11 Jan. 95	Earl of Caithness (domestic scandal)
8 Feb. 95	Allan Stewart (violence in a demonstration)
6 Mar. 95	Robert Hughes (domestic scandal)
5 Jul. 95	Jonathan Aitken (to fight libel action)
2 Jun. 96	Rod Richards (domestic scandal)
16 Dec. 96	David Willetts (conduct before Standards Committee)

First, the popular image of privatisation became tarnished as the privatised industries seemed to lead the field in raising salaries and benefits for senior executives and directors – the so-called 'fat cats'. There was particular indignation when it was revealed that the Chief Executive of British Gas, Cedric Brown, had enjoyed a 75 per cent salary boost in November 1994. This came at the same time as a rogue trader, Nick Leeson, lost £700m in the futures market and brought down Barings, the City's oldest merchant bank. This, and the continuing problems with Lloyds insurance, helped to discredit capitalism at a time when the City of London was being spectacularly successful as a world financial centre, contributing hugely to keeping down the balance of payments deficit.

Second, there were more ministerial resignations than in any previous parliament this century. Most were due to private scandals; only three were explicitly over policy. A number of Parliamentary Private Secretaries also resigned over policy or, more often, after some personal peccadillo.

This casualty rate among ministers, mostly because of unrelated private scandals, reinforced the image of sleaze, and it did not help that in many cases the resignations occurred only after considerable pressure from public opinion and the 1922 Committee. They were particularly embarrassing to a prime minister who had earlier seemed to idealise the family with his 'Back to Basics' call at the 1993 Conservative conference (see p. 18).

Two more substantial public issues focused media attention upon the conduct of government. In July 1994 the *Sunday Times* showed that some Conservative MPs had been ready to accept cash in return for asking parliamentary questions. Graham Riddick and David Tredinnick were compelled to resign as Parliamentary Private Secretaries and were later suspended for their behaviour. There were further charges in the *Guardian* in October about the willingness of certain Conservative MPs to accept unreported hospitality at the Ritz in Paris from Mohamed al-Fayed, the owner of Harrods. This ultimately led to the resignations of two junior ministers, Neil Hamilton and Tim Smith, and the withdrawal of Jonathan Aitken from the Cabinet. The government reacted to these scandals by setting up a Commission on Standards in Public Life under Lord Nolan. Its first report, published in May 1995, prompted the establishment of a new Commons Standards and Privileges Committee. This was to be serviced by a permanent Commissioner, Sir Gordon Downey, and to report on MPs' interests and conduct. One of the first casualties of this committee was David Willetts, the high-flying Paymaster-General, who resigned in December 1996 because of his confusing explanation of the injudicious advice he had given as a whip when these scandals were developing. As the election approached, the Committee was still awaiting Sir Gordon Downey's report on the case of Neil Hamilton (on which consideration had been delayed until, in September 1996, he abandoned his libel action against the *Guardian*).

In October 1992 the prosecution of three businessmen for selling arms to Iraq was suddenly dropped in the light of evidence given by Alan Clark, a former Minister of Trade, to the effect that the exports had tacitly received official approval. The government sought to quell indignant questions by asking Lord Justice Scott to conduct a one-man public inquiry into the whole question of export licences and ministerial accountability to parliament. Sir Richard Scott's report was published on 15 February 1996, after three years of much publicised and much criticised hearings. It made adverse comments on the conduct of various ministers and civil servants, and it concluded that William Waldegrave, Alan Clark and Sir Nicholas Lyell had indeed misled the House of Commons in sundry answers to questions – though not deliberately. However, no one resigned and no one was prosecuted. When the issue was debated on 22 February 1996, the government survived by one vote.

There were also scandals in local government. The most long-running and serious saga concerned the Conservative-run Westminster City Council, which was accused of selling off graveyards for peppercorn fees and of conducting housing policy in a fashion designed to gerrymander Labour voters out of key wards. There was also a less publicised report about the practice of nepotism by Labour councillors in John Smith's Monklands constituency.

As the government remained unpopular, and its majority shrank, divisions within the Conservative Party were accentuated. John Major's leadership was under challenge from 1993 onwards. The discredited Norman Lamont made no secret of his disillusion, stating in his resignation speech that Mr Major gave the impression of being 'in office, but not in power'. On 29 March 1994 Tony Marlow openly called on him to go. The Prime Minister's standing in the polls fell and in the spring of 1995 plans to unseat him were rumoured. It was said that the rebels only just failed to muster the 34 MPs needed to launch a leadership election in November 1994 – in part because eight of Mr Major's most vociferous critics were still deprived of the whip.

Fears that they would be more successful the next November led John Major to announce boldly, in June 1995, that he was seeking immediate re-election as party leader. In announcing his resignation, John Major challenged his critics to back him or sack him, and said he would expect, in future, total support from his parliamentary colleagues. John Redwood, the Welsh Secretary, resigned to challenge him. He clearly represented the right, with his mixture of Euro-scepticism and free market beliefs and he warned MPs: 'no change, no chance'. After a fraught week John Major won by 219 to 89, with 22 abstentions. He could ruefully reflect that, having been elected leader with the votes of the right, he now relied on the centre and left. John Major promptly reorganised his government, making Michael Heseltine Deputy Prime Minister and first Secretary of State, with wide overview powers, and moving Brian Mawhinney to Central Office to take charge of election preparations. Heseltine was also given a major role as a spokesman for the government. Some of Mr Major's right-wing critics found the promotion of Mr Heseltine hard to bear. With Clarke and Heseltine in such key positions, it seemed that Mr Major had clearly ruled out the idea of excluding Britain in advance from the first stage of monetary union. Yet in fact the re-election did not herald a new beginning. Complaints about weak leadership, drift, and division over the European issue continued unabated. John Major's critics argued that although he now had a fresh mandate, he did little with it.

Disunity over Europe persisted. In April and June 1996 two Conservative Euro-sceptics introduced bills: one to curb the powers of the European Court of Justice, the other to hold a referendum on Britain's future relations with the EU. The votes showed that at least a third of the back-benchers were hostile to further integration. Within weeks of John Major's re-election as leader, the party lost the Littleborough and Saddleworth by-election with its vote share halved from 1992. Three MPs defected to other parties, and one, Alan Howarth, became the first Conservative MP to switch to Labour since Oswald Mosley in the 1920s. A possible relief for John Major came in February 1996 when the executive of the 1922 Committee suspended the rules which would have allowed a leadership election in November.

Although John Major went out of his way not to be identified with an 'ism', this did not stop observers from complaining that he lacked a big idea. The fate of the 'Back to Basics' speech at the 1993 party conference illustrated the reasons for Major's caution. The plan was to emphasise the issues of the economy, law and order, and education. But the Policy Unit added the phrase 'Back to Basics', and the speech was given a moralist interpretation that the writers and Major himself had never intended. It also offered free rein to a prurient tabloid press, as ministers became embroiled in scandals and sleaze.

The Prime Minister's leadership victory in 1995 secured his position for the rest of the parliament – but it did not stop the jockeying for the succession. As the opinion polls made a Conservative defeat more and more likely, the media speculated increasingly about the possible leadership candidates, and many of the things said, or not said, by Michael Heseltine, Kenneth Clarke, Michael Portillo, Michael Howard, Malcolm Rifkind, Stephen Dorrell, Michael Forsyth and others were interpreted as positioning for the struggle that would come after the election.

Despite all their adversities, the Conservatives rejected advice to play safe. In the Cabinet there was a debate between the activists and the consolidators. The former pressed for more free market measures; the latter claimed that party supporters were fed-up with constant change and needed reassurance. This was not a left–right division. Kenneth Clarke and Michael Heseltine were prominent activists, and John Major, Tony Newton and Sir George Young were among the consolidators. The government pressed on with its plans to privatise the railways, notwithstanding gibes about 'a poll-tax on wheels,' and by 1997 the whole network had been franchised to private companies. The selling off of the London Underground and of the Post Office were also discussed, and the Labour Party was teased for its ambivalent position over privatisation, but the consolidators were vindicated when enough Conservative MPs blocked the sale of the Post Office.

Further, the Treasury continued to redefine the boundary between the public and private sectors by developing the Private Finance Initiative. Companies were invited to bid to deliver services to the public sector, either after taking control of existing public sector assets or by constructing new ones. Instead of contracting for the delivery of assets (or inputs), the public sector was to contract for the services (the output from those assets), with payment made in return for satisfactory performance, typically over the life of the assets in question. A number of new prisons and roads were among the first services to be provided on this basis. The Conservatives also continued with their efforts to develop an internal market in the Health Service, with fund-holding general practitioners competitively 'buying' hospital treatment for their patients.

The parliament saw extensive local government reorganisation. There was a comprehensive switch to single-tier authorities in Scotland and Wales. Nineteen English areas, too, were taken out of the dual county and borough system. There were complaints of partisan intention but, since none of the new authorities were won by the Conservatives, these could hardly be pressed.

There were interesting efforts to rethink social policy. John Smith sponsored an independent Commission on Social Justice under Sir Gordon Borrie to advise on policy issues, which reported in October 1994. New think-tanks and old tried to face up to the welfare problems of an ageing population, an ever more expensive health service, and a deprived underclass. On the eve of the election Peter Lilley, the Social Security minister, sketched a radical long-term change in pensions policy, and Stephen Dorrell, the Health minister, unveiled plans to reform the care of the elderly. However, the policy innovation that drew most attention was the coming of the National Lottery in November 1994. Its vast success made available large sums for charity and for the increasingly active plans to celebrate the Millennium.

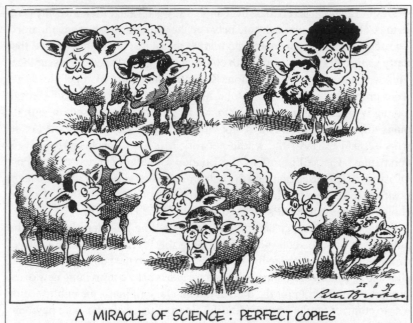

A MIRACLE OF SCIENCE : PERFECT COPIES

Clark/Brown		Shephard/Blunkett
Major/Blair	Howard/Straw	Rifkind/Cook

On 23 February 1997 it was announced that Edinburgh scientists had produced a cloned pair of sheep.

Peter Brookes, *The Times*, 25 February 1997

The Home Office is never an easy portfolio. From May 1993 Michael Howard proved a particularly controversial Home Secretary, pursuing 'law and order' themes in a populist fashion. In October 1995 he dismissed the Director-General of the Prison Service, Derek Lewis, after the Learmont Report into a prison breakout the previous January blamed prison management for the escapes. A number of Michael Howard's immigration and parole rulings were overturned by the Courts, and his Police and Criminal Justice Bills were roughly handled in House of Lords debates – especially by the senior judges. Tony Blair, as Shadow Home Secretary in 1992–94, had sought to free Labour from its reputation for softness with his slogan: 'Tough on crime and tough on the causes of crime'; his successor, Jack Straw, was accused of finally abandoning Labour's humanitarian tradition as he close-marked Michael Howard's hardline pronouncements – particularly when in the last session of the parliament he supported most of the government's proposals on police bugging of telephones and on mandatory sentencing of repeat offenders.

Northern Ireland was an ongoing source of anxiety – but also, for a brief period, of hope. On 15 December 1993, following prolonged negotiations in Dublin and Belfast, the Downing Street Declaration was issued. This led the IRA on 31 August 1994 to announce a cease-fire, and for eighteen months talks – and talks about talks – stumbled on, seeking agreement on the decommissioning of arms. Sir Patrick Mayhew, the Secretary of State for Northern Ireland, aided in due course by the American mediator, Senator George Mitchell, tried desperately to keep any statements or concessions within the limits that would allow the extremists on each side to keep within the peace process. But on 9 February 1996 the IRA exploded a large bomb at Canary Wharf in London's Docklands. On 15 June another was detonated in the centre of Manchester. Talks continued but it became plain that the IRA would not re-establish a cease fire.

On 8 September 1995 David Trimble succeeded James Molyneaux as leader of the nine Ulster Unionist MPs. His flexible style aroused some hope but, flanked by Ian Paisley's Democratic Unionists and by the violent Loyalists, he could do little, especially after the Orangemen's marches, banned and then unbanned in July 1996, had exacerbated tensions.

The British parties maintained a united front on Northern Ireland and there was no point-scoring. It had seemed at one or two moments that John Major might realise his dream of achieving a settlement for the troubled province, but, caught between the intransigence of the Unionists and Sinn Fein, and handicapped by the parliamentary uncertainty, he was in too weak a position to seek heroic solutions.

The period did witness one final legacy of Empire as Hong Kong prepared for its 1997 handover to China and its last Governor, Chris Patten, strove to secure the rights of its citizens.

Apart from Northern Ireland, British forces were involved in policing flights over Iraq and, more conspicuously, in peace-keeping activities in Bosnia. There was some controversy within both parties about how far it was wise to become entangled in Balkan troubles – Paddy Ashdown was notably interventionist. Bipartisanship survived in defence and foreign affairs. It was, indeed, the first full parliament after the fall of the Iron Curtain. News from overseas focused on the coming to power of Nelson Mandela in South Africa, and on the troubles in Somalia and Rwanda, rather than on the old Cold War issues – even though there was full coverage of the shaky rule of President Yeltsin.

The election and re-election of President Clinton also made a mark; his 1992 theme, 'It's the economy, stupid', was much quoted, but so too was his recapture of the centre ground after the disastrous mid-term Congressional elections in 1994.

The Queen described 1992 as a personal *annus horribilis*. Two of her children's marriages broke up, and in November there was a serious fire at Windsor Castle. A government statement that it would meet the costs of restoration prompted further scrutiny of royal privileges; in response it was announced that the Queen would begin paying tax on her personal fortune. This was the first parliament of the century in which republicanism was seriously discussed. The Labour leadership stayed publicly monarchist, but opinion polls showed a sharp fall in support for the institution.

Each party claimed to put education in the forefront among domestic policy issues. The Liberal Democrats continued with their 1992 pledge to earmark a 1p increase in income tax to remedying the ills of the schools. The Conservatives had put forward various unpopular proposals under John Patten. When he was removed in July 1994, the more emollient Gillian Shephard endeavoured (as head of the Department of Education which, from July 1995, was merged with the Department of Employment) to complete the establishment of a national curriculum, with regular testing of students. She was relatively successful in defending her territory in the annual expenditure rounds.

The period saw a change in approach to electioneering. There were precedents for most of the innovations in communications, advertising and press relations, but a difference in degree can be so big as to be a difference in kind. It seemed that there was a move to permanent electioneering. The pace was set by Labour after Tony Blair put Gordon Brown and Peter Mandelson in charge of election preparations. The party's Rapid Rebuttal Unit with the Excalibur computer system was in due course copied by the Conservatives. In both parties spin-doctors became much more prominent, speedily offering journalists the answer to any initiative from the other side. Observers noted the new discipline in the Labour party, as the managers tried to get all their spokesmen to sing from the same hymn-sheet and to reiterate the soundbites best calculated to sell the party's united message. There was also the phenomenon of 'close-marking' by Labour, as it tried to ensure that it was never seen in fundamental opposition to popular government policies. Each party was getting similar messages from its focus groups about what the public wanted or would react favourably to; each therefore tended to find itself saying almost the same thing.

In 1993 the government took steps to accelerate the ongoing redrawing of parliamentary boundaries which was expected to help the Conservatives – by as much as 20 seats, some suggested. Under the Redistribution of Seats Act 1993, the process was to be completed by December 1995. In the end, partly because Labour were more skilful in coordinating their submissions to the Boundary Commissions, the final advantage to the Conservatives was negligible.[5] A consequence of the new boundaries was the much satirised 'chicken run' to safer pastures by MPs whose seats had been abolished or made marginal; among those involved were Brian Mawhinney, Chairman of the party, and two other Cabinet ministers, Stephen Dorrell and Sir George Young; not to mention Norman Lamont and David Amess, the 1992 hero of Basildon.

Because the Conservatives were so far behind in the polls, there was little speculation about an early election. The parliament could last until 1997, and throughout 1996 it was generally assumed that it would do so. But as the Conservative majority in the Commons evaporated there was speculation about the possibility of a forced election following a defeat on a vote of confidence. It was constantly pointed out that the survival of the government was now in the hands of the Ulster Unionists. But the difficulty of getting all the opposition members to Westminster on a given day and into one lobby was widely recognised. After quarrels over pairing arrangements in December 1996 the Labour Party withdrew cooperation with the Conservative whips. This freed them to inflict a surprise defeat on a measure affecting grant-maintained schools on 27 January 1997, but there seemed little steam behind the threats to force a snap election.

The vacancy at Wirral South which necessitated a by-election by February heightened the possibility of an election on 6 March or 20 March 1997, but it was not until mid-February that it became clear that the contest would have to be on 1 May, the last practicable date in what would be the longest peacetime parliament since the Quinquennial Act of 1911.[6]

NOTES

1. D. Butler and D. Kavanagh, *The British General Election of 1992* (1992), pp. 347–51.
2. P. Stephens, *Politics and the Pound* (1996).
3. P. Spencer and J. Curtice, 'Flexibility and the Feel Good Factor', *Kleinwort and Benson Securities*, November 1994.
4. P. Dunleavy et al., 'Sleaze in Britain', *Parliamentary Affairs*, 1995.
5. I. McLean and D. Butler, *Fixing the Boundaries* (1996).
6. Legally, parliament could have lasted three weeks longer than it did, with a General Election on 22 May, but the statutory necessity of holding county elections on 1 May made any later date inconceivable.

2   Conservative Troubles

'Bad luck will be engraved on our tombstone' was the anticipatory verdict of the Chancellor of the Exchequer, two days after John Major announced the date of the 1997 general election. Kenneth Clarke was recalling how John Major's personal mandate on 9 April 1992 had been wasted; for virtually the whole parliament the Conservative government had been on the defensive.

Conservatives had started the parliament on a high note, following such an unexpected election victory. If the party could win in spite of being in office for a long period, facing adverse opinion polls and an economic recession, then its continued dominance seemed assured. The election had again confirmed the Conservatives' flexibility and campaign professionalism, as well as the deep conservatism of the British voters. Within days of the victory Saatchi and Saatchi, the party's advertising agency, produced a paper entitled 'How To Win The Next Election'.

However, the next five years were deeply unhappy for the party. Office proved to be more of a trial than an opportunity. Throughout the entire parliament, the party was bitterly divided over Europe. The uniformly depressing news from the opinion polls, as well as from Euro-elections, by-elections and local elections, affected morale. For no other government in the post-war period, with four years of office remaining, was election defeat so widely anticipated. No governing party had ever trailed the opposition in the opinion polls by such a large margin and over such a long period. Throughout the parliament, many Conservatives showed as little interest in the electorate as Labour had in the early 1980s. In a striking reversal of the two parties' images, it was the Conservatives who were now seen as the more incompetent, divided and mistrusted.

Britain's exit from the ERM on Wednesday 16 September 1992 was a blow from which John Major's government never recovered (see Figure 1.1, p. 12). Some might argue that the 1997 election was effectively lost there and then, although neither John Major or Tony Blair would agree. The Conservative Party had fought the 1992 general election on the basis that membership of the ERM was the cornerstone of its economic policy; the exit was followed by a loss of trust among voters and an immediate collapse in support among many traditionally sympathetic newspapers. There were also large tax increases and cuts in living standards for many supporters. Because the episode raised the issue of 'Europe', it also emboldened Euro-sceptics in the party and the press. The passage of the Maastricht legislation during 1993 was a nightmare for party managers, as Conservative dissidents rebelled

24

and found support in the party and the country. A member of the Prime Minister's staff complained that Europe was a 'poison'; 'From being 80/20 split on Europe, we became 50/50 split.' Within six months the twin themes of the 1992 election success – tax cuts and trust in John Major – had been reversed.

The leadership could be consoled that the ERM exit had occurred early enough in the parliament to allow time for the party to regain the voters' trust. The electorate would, it was hoped, forget 'Black Wednesday' and appreciate the benefits of economic recovery; after all, the Wilson government had restored its electoral standing within two years of the 1967 devaluation, as had the Callaghan government after the 1976 International Monetary Fund intervention. Pessimists could recall, however, that the Labour governments had lost the general elections of 1970 and 1979. Cabinet ministers, Number 10 staff, and Central Office strategists agreed on the virtues of playing it long. If they waited for the economic prosperity to translate into the 'feel-good factor', then the government would recover from the slump in its popularity, Conservative messages would sink in and the Blair honeymoon would end. They waited in vain. As the parliament neared its end, they were puzzled because their expectations that voting would be economically determined had been confounded; they were depressed that they had made so little progress. The comprehensive Wirral South by-election defeat on 28 February 1997 (see p. 77), so near to a General Election, was to be the defining moment for the pessimists.

Central Office gained little credit for the 1992 election victory. Relations had been less than smooth between the Party Chairman, Chris Patten, and some key staff at Number 10 who were not happy with the handling of the campaign. Mr. Patten, who had lost his Bath seat, left Central Office to become Governor of Hong Kong. He was replaced by Sir Norman Fowler who was a former Cabinet minister and had accompanied John Major on the election 'battle bus'. At his first meeting with Central Office staff, Sir Norman announced that the election had been won, not in party headquarters, but on the bus. John Major, like most party leaders before him, was not interested in Central Office, and his brief for Norman Fowler was 'to sort it out'. The new Chairman was unwilling to surrender his business interests; his decision not to take ministerial office, and therefore his inability to serve in Cabinet, severely limited his usefulness as a link between the Prime Minister and Central Office; it also curtailed his ability to defend the government's case in public.

The first problem was party finance. The deficit had accumulated to an alarming £19m by the middle of 1993. Expenditure had outrun income for a number of years and Kenneth Baker's costly refurbishment of party headquarters in Smith Square had imposed further pressures. All this coincided with a downturn in corporate and constituency association contributions. In late 1993 a crisis meeting was held in Downing Street to establish the extent to which John Major, as party leader, was personally responsible for the debt.

The tough measures which Norman Fowler took to tackle the deficit were not calculated to make him popular. The party cut back on many of its activities, but the main savings had to come from downsizing at Central Office and the area offices. Some 70 staff were shed between April 1992 and February 1993, and a further 70 by June 1994. Norman Fowler's standing was not helped by the fact that he, like his immediate predecessors as Chairman, had to make frequent media appearances to explain away Conservative electoral defeats and other misfortunes.

Lord Harris of Peckham, the Queensway carpet manufacturer, proved an energetic fundraiser. Thanks largely to his efforts, the bank overdraft inherited from 1992 was repaid by the summer of 1996, and an election war chest of £20m was promised by October 1996. A revenue deficit of £7.2m at the end of March 1996 was transformed into a surplus of £2m by the end of May 1997. Many of the contributions were long-term loans, on which Central Office gained the interest. The party suffered from the allegations about large payments from overseas contributors, including one or two – notably Asil Nadir – who had had brushes with the law.

An organisational review of Central Office management and finance was conducted by Andersen Consulting immediately after the general election. The new appointments of a Director General and Finance Director and the creation of a Board of Management were part of this process. Andersen recommended the recruitment of a finance man with experience of a blue chip company. In the event, Martin Saunders, who had recently retired as Finance Director from P&O and was a former Conservative Leader on Hertfordshire County Council, was appointed in October. The Treasury Department was brought under the control of Central Office to oversee fundraising and expenditure. The Board of Management contained senior figures from the parliamentary party, National Union and Central Office. It met between four and six times a year; it provided a focus for the different sections of the party and was important in asserting budgetary control.

Financial constraints precluded any opinion polling or advertising and it was not until the European elections in June 1994 that there was any press or poster advertising. In that campaign the party was actually outspent by Labour, the first time this had happened in a national election. The decline in membership continued a trend which dated back at least a decade. In the lifetime of the parliament, membership was halved to about 400,000. MPs noted the low levels of activity and poor morale; journalists accompanying the Prime Minister on his constituency visits commented on how elderly many of the members were, in contrast to the more youthful Labour gatherings. This was part of a larger 'de-energising' of the grassroots party.[1] Some 90 per cent of constituency associations did not pay their financial quotas to Central Office. The devastation of the Conservative Party in local elections greatly reduced the number of party councillors and activists. Little of the disaffection in the local association was related to specific issues, or even to Europe. The controversial deselections of sitting MPs – David Ashby in Leicestershire North-West, Sir Nicholas Scott in Chelsea and Sir George Gardiner in Reigate (see Chapter 10) – were cases where members had overtaxed the patience of the local membership. MPs spoke of party activists feeling 'fed-up' and 'let down'.

Sir Norman Fowler changed a number of senior Central Office personnel. In November 1992 he appointed 43-year-old Paul Judge, a self-made millionaire in the food business, to the new post of Director-General, effectively the chief of staff. Mr Judge called in outside consultants to advise on use of computers and interviewed senior staff about their remits. His appointment was not a success; his lack of political experience was evident. Directors resented having to report to him, and senior staff complained of being distracted by his lengthy meetings on organisational matters.

There was much turnover among those handling communications. Soon after the 1992 general election, Shaun Woodward left his post as Director of Communications and was replaced by Tim Collins, a former Research Department officer and a one-time Special Adviser to Sir Norman Fowler, who had also served on the campaign bus with John Major. Mr Collins left this post to join the Policy Unit at Number 10, and was succeeded by Hugh Colver. Mr Colver had worked in public relations with the Ministry of Defence and British Aerospace and did not see himself as a spin-doctor. Under a new chairman, Brian Mawhinney, he did not feel that he was the right person and resigned after less than six months in the post. His position had been undermined when, at the 1995 party conference, the Chairman appointed MPs to brief the media. Tim Collins then returned as media adviser to the Chairman, an appointment made without Colver's knowledge. On Colver's departure, Tim Collins was reappointed Acting Director until Charles Lewington, political editor of the *Sunday Express*, took the post in December 1995. Conservatives in and out of parliament complained that the party was regularly outscored by Labour spokesmen. Mr Lewington faced the challenge of preparing a strategy and regaining the support of the newspapers which had given up on John Major.

Sir John Lacy retired as Director of Campaigning and Constituency Services soon after the 1992 general election. Constituency Services was created as a separate department by Paul Judge in March 1993; however, it was disbanded two years later, and its activities dispersed to other departments. The two departments were separated and the former was headed by Tony Garrett who had been the chief agent in the 1992 election, and had succeeded Sir John as head of campaigning. He concentrated on organising the central employment of agents and the despatch of direct mail to the marginal seats. The party had experimented with central employment of constituency agents in the early 1970s. The scheme, however, was resented by many associations and expired in 1974. It was revived because of the pressing need to provide a career structure for agents and to ensure that they were concentrated in marginal seats. The service was in decline: there had been a net loss of over 90 agents in the twelve months after the 1992 election. Between the scheme's launch in January 1995 and October 1996, 103 central appointments were made, amounting to a third of all agents.

In July 1994, the appointment of a junior minister, Jeremy Hanley, to succeed Sir Norman Fowler as Central Office Chairman, was a surprise. Some senior figures had been mentioned for the post – at least one was said to have turned it down – and it was assumed that the new appointee would conduct the next general election campaign. Mr Hanley confirmed both the hopes and the fears of observers: he was amiable, popular in the constituencies, and helped to rescue Central Office finances, but his gaffes and visible lack of confidence on the airwaves rapidly encouraged speculation that he would be replaced. 'If you do not win the battle of the media, you are a failure in this game', said one of the Prime Minister's staff. Campaign preparations were dilatory. In March 1995 Andrew Lansley, the Research Director, together with Tim Collins and Tony Garrett, joined Michael Dobbs, a deputy chairman, to prepare a war book for the next general election. This made little progress. Both Mr Lansley and Mr Collins were seeking seats and could be departing soon and, more importantly, staff were waiting on the appointment of a new Chairman, expected to be announced in the summer reshuffle.

There were not many Cabinet heavyweights who could be spared for the Chairman's job. Kenneth Clarke did not want it; anyway he was an obviously successful Chancellor, and his pro-European views would be a handicap with a section of the party. In 1994, Michael Heseltine, as President of the Board of Trade, had embarrassingly pre-empted John Major's options by informing all who would listen that his work at the Department of Trade and Industry was too important for him to move, and he repeated this refrain in 1995. The position was eventually given to Brian Mawhinney, Secretary of State for Transport, after he had played a key role in the Prime Minister's campaign to be re-elected as leader. He enjoyed the friendship and confidence of John

Major and as Chairman he clearly had a grip and fired the enthusiasm of staff. Within a short period he had appointed advertising and polling agencies, a new Research Director and a new Communications Director, and he had taken significant steps to develop a campaign strategy, yet he lacked the media skills and the political weight of such predecessors as Chris Patten and Norman Tebbit. Increasingly, Michael Heseltine, now Deputy Prime Minister, rather than Brian Mawhinney, acted as media spokesman. Michael Trend, Mawhinney's former Parliamentary Private Secretary at Transport, was made Deputy Chairman, effectively chief of staff, and was given fat reducing responsibility for the election campaign arrangements when Paul Judge departed. Throughout the parliament, Conservative attempts to concentrate on the election were stalled by mishaps, often self-inflicted. As noted in Chapter 1, Europe was a running sore; it advertised party disunity, undermining John Major's leadership and overriding news about economic recovery. There were the resignations of ministers due to private scandals or public accusations of sleaze. The BSE affair, with the beef embargo, was clumsily handled by the agriculture minister Douglas Hogg, and echoed throughout the last year of the parliament. The five-volume Scott Report into the 'arms for Iraq' allegations was published in February 1996; in spite of its criticisms of William Waldegrave for misleading MPs and of the Attorney-General for his handling of the Public Interest Immunity Certificates, the government presented the report as a clean bill of health. By-elections, local elections and weekly opinion polls were a regular source of humiliation (see p. 12–13).

In June 1995 John Major tried to reassert his authority by standing for re-election as leader (see p. 17). But his defeat of John Redwood and his reorganisation of the government with Michael Heseltine in a key role did little to still his troubles. The 89 Redwood votes constituted nearly half of the party back-benchers.

The party had to endure attacks by former party officials. Robin Harris, a former Research Department Director and member of Mrs Thatcher's Policy Unit, was unreconciled to John Major's succession. In the *Sunday Times* on 9 July 1995 ('Why the Tories will lose the next election') he praised John Redwood and welcomed the prospect of a general election defeat because this would enable the right wing to take over. Lord MacAlpine, a party treasurer under Mrs Thatcher, was another high-profile prophet of doom. He joined the Referendum Party and regularly used the press to attack his former colleagues. 'Off message' speeches by Cabinet ministers were widely interpreted as bids to succeed to a post-Major leadership vacancy. Hugh Colver, after resigning from his post in Central Office in November 1995, offered an explanation of why the party was so unpopular: 'It is because the

Tory party behaves as if it is in office by divine right that it manages to create public relations disasters, where there should be obvious triumphs. There is a lack of resolute day-to-day leadership in government.'

The party also lost much of its traditional press support. Only one newspaper, the *Express*, backed John Major against John Redwood in the leadership contest in 1995. Since the ERM fiasco the tabloids, along with the Rupert Murdoch and Conrad Black newspapers, which had been so staunchly Conservative in previous elections, poured scorn on his leadership. If they were not anti-Conservative, they certainly were anti-Major and supported the Euro-rebels. Their political agenda no longer coincided with that of the Conservative government. The largest falls in Conservative support in the two years after the 1992 election occurred among readers of the Murdoch-owned tabloids, notably the *Sun* (a fall of 16 per cent according to MORI). There is no doubt that the bad press hurt John Major, both personally and politically. He grew increasingly irritated over the dissent, sleaze and leaks, as well as by the disloyal briefings from senior party figures. He was too easily upset by critical articles, even by junior journalists: 'All this time at the top and he has still not acquired a rhinoceros skin', said a colleague. But some of his supporters felt he could have tried harder to cultivate press proprietors and editors.[2]

After the 1992 election the Research Department had suffered a loss of staff and morale. It was known that Andrew Lansley, the Director, would not be in post for the next election. In the event he did not leave until September 1995. His replacement was Danny Finkelstein, a recruit from the Social Market Foundation think-tank. During the 1992 election he and a number of other Social Democrat colleagues had made a much publicised switch to the Conservative Party. Under Mr Finkelstein the department's work concentrated on political strategy, briefing MPs, and working with party press officers on rebutting Labour claims. Policy making virtually ceased in the department. Andrew Lansley had been a respected campaign strategist but he had a tense relationship with Sarah Hogg and the Policy Unit in the 1992 election. Relations improved markedly when the Number 10 staff changed. Mr Finkelstein worked closely with Howell James, Mr Major's political secretary from 1994 and Norman Blackwell, Sarah Hogg's successor as head of the Number 10 Policy Unit.

The Harris Poll had conducted surveys for the Conservatives in all general elections since its formation as Opinion Research Centre (ORC) in 1965. But in 1994 it moved to new ownership and the relationship with the party was terminated. In January 1996 the party had commissioned from Wirthlin a 1000-sample survey on perceptions of the Labour Party, with questions suggested by Tim Bell and Maurice Saatchi. It also considered working with

Martin Goldfarb, who had been a pollster for Pierre Trudeau while he was Canada's Prime Minister. Central Office found this research expensive and, on the basis of focus groups, insensitive to the subtleties of British politics (one recommendation was that the government should announce British acceptance of the EU's Social Chapter). After considering a number of agencies, in July 1996 the party appointed ICM, run by Nick Sparrow.

ICM had shifted to telephone polling and was the first company to adjust its voting figures after the 1992 general election to allow for under-reporting among Conservatives (see Chapter 7). It conducted all the party's focus groups and polls (although Wirthlin provided one survey); and it tested phrases, slogans and themes which could be incorporated into John Major's speeches and into party literature. Nick Sparrow presented his work every two months in Central Office. His polling was reported to Andrew Cooper, Deputy Director of the Research Department. Mr Cooper also provided weekly digests of the public and private polls which were distributed to key people in Central Office and at Number 10.

It was taken for granted that Saatchi and Saatchi, having been involved in four successive Conservative election victories, would carry out the party's advertising. Although the agency was still owed £2m from the 1992 campaign, it agreed to a lengthy schedule of repayment, on the understanding that it would retain the Conservative account at the next general election. But the agency's declining commercial fortunes led to a shareholder revolt and the departure in 1994 of the brothers, Maurice and Charles. Would the Conservative contract go to the successor company Saatchi Cordiant, or to the new agency created by the brothers, M & C Saatchi? Although Central Office considered presentations from other agencies there was no doubt that John Major wished to carry on working with Maurice Saatchi, who continued to advise him informally and was part of his campaign team for the leadership election in 1995. Saatchi Cordiant's bid for the account may have suffered because it was shorn of most of the Saatchi staff who had worked on earlier Conservative campaigns. Brian Mawhinney, under some obligation, asked Cordiant to consider working with other, unspecified, agencies in the forthcoming election; doubtless Saatchi would have had a role, and Cordiant refused. In January 1996, the party formally left Saatchi Cordiant and approached M & C Saatchi to handle its communications; outstanding amounts from 1992 were settled in full.

The Party Chairman also wished to bring on board Sir Tim Bell, who had handled the Conservative account for Saatchi for the 1979 and 1983 general elections and was close to Mrs Thatcher. He had been kept on the sidelines by Chris Patten and Shaun Woodward in the 1992 election. After the 1995 annual conference it was planned that he and Peter Gummer (soon to be Lord

Chadlington), head of Shandwick Public Relations, would set up an outside unit and provide advice on strategy. That plan was aborted, and the two arranged to work with Lord Saatchi and attended meetings in Central Office. The idea was that the 'three musketeers', as they were soon called, would present a collective view on campaign strategy to Brian Mawhinney. The three men had well-publicised breakfasts in the Connaught Hotel and attended strategy meetings in Central Office on Monday afternoons. Brian Mawhinney was not always comfortable with the persuasive trio, notably with Maurice Saatchi's forceful approach to analysis and strategy formulation. Fearing that he might be having a 1992 election strategy imposed upon him, he drew on other sources of advice. He rarely argued on strategy with the trio, but would convey his doubts by saying, 'it is being said' or 'people are thinking', and rejected advice on the grounds that 'it will not work in the Dog and Duck in Peterborough'.

As ever, there was the challenge of linking the operations of Central Office, the Whip's office and Number 10, to communicate the work of the government. For the first half of the parliament, Central Office directors and Number 10 staff met daily as the Number 12 Committee, so called because it was run by the Chief Whip at 12 Downing Street. The task now fell to the Cabinet's Co-ordination and Presentation committee, known as EDCP, which was established in February 1995 and chaired by David Hunt, the Chancellor of the Duchy of Lancaster. It was essentially a media-orientated operation, meeting weekly or fortnightly to anticipate and coordinate party and government announcements and activities and, if necessary, reschedule them. Under Mrs Thatcher this job had been done by the Liaison Committee. Because Sir Robin Butler, the Cabinet Secretary, recognised EDCP as a Cabinet committee, civil servants provided secretarial support when the agenda clearly dealt with the presentation of government policy but went out when it turned its attention to party matters. David Hunt readily acknowledged the shortcomings of the arrangements, one factor being his own lack of seniority *vis-à-vis* some of the Cabinet ministers. The committee needed a more heavyweight chairman if it was to be effective.

EDCP's work gained in urgency when the Deputy Prime Minister, Michael Heseltine, took over the chair in July 1995. It now met daily and included the Chief Whips in the Commons and Lords and key figures from Central Office and Number 10. David Willetts, then a whip, was brought in to convey the message to other government departments. When he resigned in December 1996 as Paymaster-General and as a member of EDCP, he was replaced by another whip, Michael Bates.[3] The group met for half an hour each morning at 8.30 or at 9.15 and sought to anticipate news items. It also met every Wednesday evening for a two-week forward look. The Number 12 Committee was scrapped.

EDCP had its last meeting on 17 March 1997, when John Major announced the date of the election. The group never achieved the discipline and focus that was evident in the Labour Party. Ministers still went their own way and it was remarkable that so much of the 'good news' on the economy that the Committee wished to promote was lost because of events or unscheduled and controversial activities of ministers and back-benchers.

EDCP's work was reinforced by a brief Monday meeting immediately afterwards in Number 10 between John Major, Michael Heseltine and Brian Mawhinney, as well as the Prime Minister's aides, Howell James and Norman Blackwell. There were some exaggerated media reports of conflict over whether Mr Mawhinney or Mr Heseltine would be the campaign supremo. Much of the reported tension centred on Heseltine's greater media visibility; however, he was clearly the more confident broadcaster, and it could be argued that his public prominence grew out of his EDCP remit. Brian Mawhinney ran the Central Office side of operations and both men respected each other's responsibilities. Effectively, Michael Heseltine was in charge of presentation, and sometimes appeared to have a regular slot on the *Today* early morning radio programme.

After Douglas Hurd left the Cabinet in July 1995, the anti-Europeans turned their fire on Kenneth Clarke. The right, supported by some Cabinet ministers and some staff in Central Office, believed that a clear government declaration that Britain would not join the first wave of a single European currency in 1999 would be a vote winner and unite the party. Mr Clarke, however, was contemptuous of these claims; he thought that too much ground had been given to Euro-sceptics, who simply regarded each concession, such as holding a referendum before entry to a single currency, as the opportunity to make fresh demands. Mr Clarke was a successful Chancellor and Mr Major would not risk his resignation, as well as, perhaps, that of Michael Heseltine. The Euro-sceptics were furious at what they regarded as the Prime Minister's surrender to the Chancellor. Kenneth Clarke also dismissed the political right's demands for large income tax cuts in his 1995 and 1996 Budgets. He thought it was far more important for the Conservative Party to look beyond the next Budget and even the next election. What mattered more for the party's election prospects was that MPs showed more discipline and that the party restored its reputation for economic competence. Any tax cuts had to be sustained in the years to come – they could not risk a repetition of 1992, cutting taxes before an election and increasing them afterwards, so he cut 1p off the standard rate in 1995 and again in 1996.

Strategic thinking for a 1996–97 election lay largely with Danny Finkelstein and Norman Blackwell, with input from Maurice Saatchi and Tim Bell. What emerged at first was a three-stage campaign:

1. to convince the electorate that life was better with the Conservatives;
2. having created a sense of contentment, to warn against the risks of a Labour government; and
3. to counter Labour's appeal of 'time for a change' with a message for the future.

Positive press advertisements were placed at the start of the New Year of 1996 on the theme of life being better in Britain. They pointed to a run of achievements (in particular low inflation, falling unemployment and low interest rates) of which Britain could be proud; they were signed by John Major and did not mention the Conservative Party at all. The impact was blunted by coinciding with media coverage of Emma Nicholson's defection to the Liberal Democrats and the Scott Report on arms to Iraq. Over May and June, 'Yes It Hurt; Yes It Worked' was launched as a poster and press campaign; economic achievements in the areas of employment, inflation and income tax were compared to other major European countries – listed in small print at the bottom of the advertisement. John Major had taken time to be persuaded that ministers should admit, however implicitly, that they had made mistakes. Maurice Saatchi argued that, to have maximum impact, a large-scale press campaign was necessary. It was not forthcoming – Central Office said it did not have the money. Kenneth Clarke vetoed a number of Saatchi claims about the economy on the grounds that they gave hostages to fortune. 'Nit-picking' was the reaction of his critics. Some Tory MPs criticised the 'It Hurt' slogan for being backward looking, reminding people of the broken promises, and showing little awareness that many voters disagreed that 'it' had worked. By 1996 the British Election study panel found a modest recovery among 1992 Conservative voters in the government's perceived economic competence. But this was offset by their dissatisfaction with its record on health and education, while voters discerned few differences between the Labour and Conservative parties on economic issues.

It took the Conservatives some time to come to grips with the impact of Tony Blair in transforming public perceptions of Labour. But by June 1996 it seems to have been agreed that the party would have to focus on the dangers of Labour rather than fight on its own record. The admiration of many Conservatives, and much of the media, for Tony Blair's campaigning skills paralleled the respect extended to Harold Wilson's efforts in 1963–64. As opposition leader he held his own with John Major at PM's Question's, and was clearly in command of his party in a way that John Major was not. Labour dissenters were slapped down – unnamed Labour back-benchers complained of Stalinist management – while Conservative rebels spoke out with impunity and at times were openly dismissive of their party leader. What should the party say about Labour? For much of the time ministers made different charges, some of which lacked credibility and some of which were self-defeating. Addressing a political cabinet in January 1996 Danny Finkelstein illustrated the contradictions in ministers' reactions to Tony Blair's speech in Singapore about stakeholding a few days earlier. Some had claimed that, underneath the public relations veneer, it was the same old Labour party, while others argued variously that Labour was simply stealing their language and policies, that Blair had changed but his party had not, or that the Conservatives were 'the real thing'.

Maurice Saatchi argued that Labour had now stolen so many Conservative policies that voters believed it was safe to vote Labour. The Wirthlin survey (see p. 30) showed that over 70 per cent believed in the sincerity of Labour's change. The Conservatives needed an intellectual response and Saatchi argued that it should begin by acknowledging that Labour *was* new and the challenge therefore was to demonstrate that 'it was newly dangerous in new ways'. There seemed to be an acceptance of the 'New Labour, New Danger' strategy. A version of the party's war book warned in April 1996: 'As a matter of considerable urgency we need to resolve the debate on how to position the Labour Party. We also need to ensure that the chosen line is followed consistently and with discipline by all colleagues.' The battle would centre on the interpretation of the word 'New' – untried and risky, or exciting and innovative? 'Whoever wins that battle will win the election', said Maurice Saatchi.

In the following months it became apparent that many ministers had not actually internalised the strategy. Too many had fought for too long against old Labour using their traditional rhetoric. One forceful dissenter at January's political cabinet was Kenneth Clarke, who dismissed Labour as an empty vessel and claimed that its traditional weaknesses could continue to be exploited. Peter Lilley expressed reservations about whether the strategy could be implemented effectively. Subsequently, other ministers departed from the core message. Blair was dismissed as 'phoney', a 'chameleon', 'full of wind and soundbites' and 'ephemeral'. Michael Heseltine and John Major were prone to talk in terms of the old Labour Party. In private, John Major distinguished Labour's 'head' (Tony Blair and a handful around him) from its 'body and tail' (the rest of the party). Only the 'head' accepted that Britain was a conservative country and that a socialist message was a barrier to being elected. John Major always believed that 'Labour in its instincts does not favour lower taxes, low public spending or privatisation. The old Labour Party is still there.'

TOO MUCH VIOLENCE ON TELEVISION . . .

| Redwood | Lamont | | Gorman | Currie | Cash |
| Heseltine | Howard | | Clarke | | Mawhinney |

The internal Conservative fighting over Europe found an echo in a publicised report on television violence.

Peter Brookes, *The Times*, 11 December 1996

In the summer of 1996, the party launched the 'New Labour, New Danger' campaign and the first of the 'demon eyes' posters, designed to promote suspicion and unease about Labour. This began with a poster showing red eyes peering through a red curtain. This was followed by 'New Labour, New Taxes' (red eyes in a purse), 'New Labour, No Britain' (white flag). The notorious advertisement showing Tony Blair with red demon-eyes appeared once in three Sunday papers – amid great publicity. Until 1993 political advertisements had been exempt from the Advertising Standards Agency (ASA) code of conduct, but in August 1996, following public complaints, the ASA made its first ruling on a political advertisement: it rejected charges that the advertisement was offensive to the public, but ruled against posters using Tony Blair's image on the grounds that his permission had not been granted. However, the advertisement had very high recognition ratings – a consequence, in large part, of the controversy. To Peter Mandelson's delight, his description of it as 'demonic' and 'demonising' stuck. Initially, the campaign had been planned for September, but it was brought forward in response to demands that the party attack Labour more robustly.

NEW LABOUR
NEW DANGER

One of Labour's leaders, Clare Short, says dark forces behind Tony Blair manipulate policy in a sinister way. "I sometimes call them the people who live in the dark." She says about New Labour: "It's a lie. And it's dangerous."

'New Labour, New Danger' was not an electoral success. One of its architects bluntly assessed its impact as 'zero'. At a dinner with John Major and some senior ministers at Chequers in September, Maurice Saatchi presented a progress, or rather a lack of progress, report. He assessed the dangers which party spokesmen associated with Labour against the criteria of being clear, credible and frightening, and he concluded that the attacks had made no impression. What was required was a single danger – a big 'D' – and the best candidate was Europe, specifically the European social model, and the Social Chapter, which Labour wanted to embrace. He suggested a 'True to Britain' campaign, and such slogans as 'Euro Labour, Euro Danger'. Mr Clarke and Mr Heseltine objected that these slogans were anti-European, even xenophobic, and misrepresented the party's position. However plausible the thesis, John Major ruled it out. More decisive than the objections of his two senior colleagues was his own view that this was beneath the dignity of a British prime minister.

The Saatchi advertisements had little impact on two key but overlapping groups – the new Labour voters and the defectors from the Conservative party since 1992. A Gallup poll found that 73 per cent of voters, including 58 per cent of Conservatives, disliked the advertisements. The failure to recover in the polls and the complaints about the advertisements led to growing hostility in the party towards the agency, as well as a fruitless search for alternative messages (see Chapter 12). The problem, however, was not the presentation but the product.

Throughout 1996 Michael Trend convened a Central Office group, known as MSI, to prepare the war book.[4] It covered questions of strategy, key seats operations, timetable options and the mechanics of the campaign. Its report was first presented to John Major during Easter 1996, and, after further redrafts, was approved in January 1997.

In an interview in December 1995, a Central Office director had looked forward to income tax cuts, continued economic recovery and greater discipline among MPs as the election neared. He added:

> But it is vital that we are in the race by next spring. If the politics come right, if the government is seen to have been successful, then all will be well. Without these developments any election strategy would be an exercise in damage limitation.

Another Conservative strategist in July 1996 likened his party's position to an aeroplane taxiing on the runway. 'All the instruments are working but we can't get take off.' In the remaining months morale failed to recover in the constituencies, in parliament and among Cabinet ministers.

Ministers, officials and campaign strategists complained about the extent to which their focus on the election was disrupted by events and the work of government. Compared to the frequency with which Labour's inner core of campaign strategists met, such Conservative gatherings were rare. Representative of the mood were such remarks as 'Labour have 24 hours a day to create propaganda. We only have ministers in government', and: 'In order to think strategically you have to break free of the limits of government.' In January 1997 one of the 'three musketeers', who recalled hearing Michael Heseltine claim six months earlier that there would soon come a time when the Conservative Party would turn its attention to the election and that 'this would be a sight to behold', complained. 'I can only say that I have yet to see it and time is running short.' Frustration was evident throughout the party – among activists, MPs, campaign strategists and even Cabinet ministers. One hope was that a near-term campaign, starting in January 1997, might alert the electorate to the threats posed by Labour. Could the party finally do a better job of staying on message and focusing on Labour?

On 1 January John Major announced that he would be holding presidential-style press conferences every three weeks or so. These conferences addressed various themes, such as education, the economy and pensions, but evaded the Achilles' heels – health and Europe. His prime ministerial routine was revised to make allowances for campaigning and he delegated some meetings with foreign visitors to other ministers. For several months he had conducted regional tours on Fridays, but in the New Year he started to make visits on Wednesdays also, with the aim of attracting regional television coverage. A prime ministerial visit to India on 7 January provided an opportunity to demonstrate Conservative support for the Asian community in Britain. Manifesto meetings were held and ministers made regular announcements of future 'goodies', including privatisation of the London Underground, help for the elderly with the costs of long-term residential care, and plans for private pensions for the younger generation.

In the first three months of 1997, Conservatives found it as difficult as ever to concentrate on the coming election. They failed in their attempts to turn their fire on Labour and to educate the electorate into appreciation of their own achievements. In January the Health Minister, Stephen Dorrell, until then regarded as a pro-European Cabinet minister, voiced his doubts about further European integration; this was immediately interpreted as a bid for support among Euro-sceptics in a post-election leadership contest. There soon followed newspaper allegations about a Conservative MP's illegal (under-age) homosexual relationship with a political researcher. The announcement of government support for rebuilding the royal yacht and privatising the London Underground were both unpopular, according to the opinion polls. Replying to a journalist's question, Mr Dorrell stated that a future Conservative government would abolish a Scottish parliament if Labour established one, but he was at once disowned by Michael Forsyth, the Scottish Minister, and publicly rebuked by Mr Major. Members of EDCP were aghast at how their attempt to focus public attention on inward investment had been thrown off the front pages of the press.

Two figures from the past made unhelpful interventions: the press seized on remarks by a former party chairman, Norman Tebbit, in a *Spectator* review (1 March) of a biography of Michael Heseltine, and Sir Edward Heath attacked the government for its opposition to the European Social Chapter and a proposed Scottish parliament. In addition, Kenneth Clarke and Malcolm Rifkind made divergent statements about government hostilities to establishing the single currency in 1999, and the Secretary of State for Agriculture, Douglas Hogg, continued to be excoriated over the beef issue – he survived a censure motion in the Commons by 18 votes on 18 February.

As a near-term campaign on the 1992 pattern, the Conservative effort was a damp squib. It was difficult to believe that the strategy had been to focus on the dangers and risks which a Labour government would present. In one vigorous House of Commons exchange, Mr Major accused the Labour leader of being a jackdaw – stealing Conservative policies. His aides objected that this was 'off-message'. The Prime Minister's reply was: 'I am the message.' There was consternation at Number 10 and in Central Office. When strategists were taxed about the damaging activities of leading Conservatives they replied:

'One does one's best.'
'What can we do?'
'Politics gets in the way of the campaign.'
'For much of the parliament it has been backbenchers who made the headlines and let us down, but now it is Cabinet ministers who have their own agendas.'

John Major was popular among grassroots supporters. But he himself was less enamoured of his parliamentary colleagues, the 'bastards' in Cabinet and the habitual deserters. One of his staff complained of a new generation of Tory MPs – 'ill-disciplined, greedy, self-indulgent, and with no sense of loyalty to the leadership of the party'. But some complained that John Major's lack of a clear sense of direction allowed dissent to flourish. Instead of strategic thinking at the centre, there was too much crisis-management, dealing with press headlines and parliamentary squabbles.

In January, Brian Mawhinney tried to interest ministers in the line to be taken when, in the general election, many Conservative candidates would inevitably dissent from the government position on the single currency. He received no clear guidance. One senior Cabinet minister had in the past compared John Major's conciliatory, middle-of-the-road style to that of Stanley Baldwin. Near the end of the parliament he thought that the more appropriate comparison was with Arthur Balfour, trying and failing from 1903–1906 to balance the opposing wings of the Conservative Party over tariff reform. Kenneth Clarke thought that 'The issue now is whether the Conservative party is still electable.'

Election manifestos impose deadlines and attention to the coming battle. Conservative study groups had made their recommendations by the summer of 1995 to Norman Blackwell at Number 10 and the first outline of the manifesto was written at this time. In early conversations John Major and Norman Blackwell found that they shared an interest in the themes of enterprise, opportunity, law and order, improving public services and protecting the nation. The Prime Minister regarded these as the core of Majorism, although he did not use the term. Norman Blackwell saw the task of the Policy Unit to develop these into workable policies, and in many respects they shaped the final election manifesto. Mr Major gave a series of speeches on the themes during 1996, and they were published in book form by the Conservative Political Centre in January 1997, under the title *Our Nation's Future*. A little-reported initiative by Norman Blackwell was the holding of a dozen seminars of Cabinet groups on the themes between the spring of 1995 and the end of 1996. The groups were designed to prise Cabinet ministers away from their civil servants and make them think ahead to the election. A brief Policy Unit paper, including analysis, diagnosis and options, was distributed to participants two days in advance of the meeting – 'so that the civil servants could not get at the ministers', said one adviser. The sessions were usually chaired by Michael Heseltine or Tony Newton, although a session on the constitution was chaired by John Major.

Conservative manifesto-making has always been an elite process, and further work was done by groups of Cabinet ministers. Mr Clarke used his position as Chancellor to oppose what he regarded as foolish spending pledges or proposals for tax breaks, such as the complete abolition of capital gains and inheritance taxes, or indeed exempting family homes from inheritance tax. A draft manifesto was produced in December 1996 by Norman Blackwell and Danny Finkelstein. It was subsequently edited by David Willetts (who was appointed Chairman of the Research Department in January following his resignation as Paymaster-General) and George Bridges (the Prime Minister's assistant political secretary).

In contrast to 1992, John Major decided against having an 'A' team of senior Cabinet ministers, on the grounds that it was not worth the jealousies it provoked among those excluded. But he relied on the recognisable core of Heseltine, Mawhinney and Clarke who met with him regularly at Number10. At the end of January, when a March election was still a possibility, a meeting of senior ministers considered the draft manifesto at Chequers. Proposals to reform the state pension and social security, which were launched in early March, would have been included in a manifesto for a March election. The decision to hold on until 1 May meant that all of the new initiatives, except that for transferring tax allowances between married couples, were released before the election. On 25 February, Mr Clarke, Mr Heseltine, Mr Howard, Mr Waldegrave, Mr Rifkind, Dr Mawhinney, Mr Lang, Lord Cranborne and the Prime Minister met again to consider the manifesto at Chequers. The full Cabinet saw the complete manifesto for the first time on 20 March. A number of earlier proposals were omitted, including privatising the Post Office and Channel 4, and reforming the quarantine law.

It was no surprise that, as the polls failed to register any improvement in Conservative standing, stronger criticism was expressed about the party's advertising. Hostility to it was reported particularly among those who had abandoned the party since 1992. There were complaints that the advertisements were submitted to Central Office at such short notice that they could not be properly appraised, let alone pre-tested, and that Maurice Saatchi, having failed to persuade Central Office, would go directly to Number 10. A large poster campaign was launched in early January and provoked much criticism, not least from Conservative MPs. Posters of a red-eyed weeping lion appeared on hoardings across the country with the slogan '£2300 TAX RISK UNDER LABOUR'. In February, Norman Blackwell

Heseltine   Clarke   Major

The Weeping Lion poster was the latest in a series of much-derided Conservative advertisements

Nicholas Garland, *Daily Telegraph*, 7 January 1997

and the Party Chairman pressed for future pre-testing of Saatchi advertisements. This was a sensitive subject. A number of agencies claim that it is not possible to test the effectiveness of advertisements, particularly negative ones, and Maurice Saatchi was no exception. He could recall those who had criticised the agency's anti-Labour tax advertisements in 1992, but who accepted that they had worked, once the result was known. His view was that the only effective test was not whether people said they liked it or not, but what they put on the ballot paper.

The agency had its defence. It could argue that its advertising had exposed the weaknesses of Labour but that Central Office and Number 10 had failed to mount a political campaign to exploit it. Ministers, including John Major, rarely used the message, 'New Labour, New Danger', and warnings had not struck home. But this much had been admitted in the previous October when the agency tried and failed to campaign on the 'danger' of Europe. Ministers played so safe that many initiatives were blocked. Mr Major also vetoed an anti-Blair advertisement which featured the slogan, 'What Lies Behind The Smile?' He preferred, 'What Policy Lies Behind The Smile?', but requests, even instructions, to the agency to make the change were rebuffed and the advertisement was aborted.

The tensions over testing had one ironic outcome. The Party Chairman insisted on testing a hard-hitting anti-Blair advertisement, expecting that it would be found wanting – in fact, it tested well, but Brian Mawhinney, trying to anticipate the reaction of John Major, still vetoed it. It was replaced with the 'Tony and Bill' poster which found few supporters but was run as a substitute because the sites had been booked. In February, the Party Chairman instructed Maurice Saatchi to abandon the phrase 'New Labour, New Danger'. It appeared to lock the agency into a restrictive and failed format for posters. The Chairman did not want to see or hear it again.

Like most prime ministers, John Major was keen to promote his positive policies and his doubts about the advertisements were reinforced by complaints from MPs and the constituencies and by press criticism. One adviser complained: 'All this mood and image stuff works up to a point, but it is better for corporate positioning rather than politics. We need to attack Labour on its policies.' Although press reports of the internal clashes were exaggerated, pressure on the agency increased. In February Dr Mawhinney actually authorised retrospective testing of the 'weeping lion' advertisement and the most recent election broadcast – without the agency's knowledge.

The party's research seemed to suggest that the Conservatives had to point out the contrasts – stability versus risk; keeping Britain on the right track versus turning back; staying the course versus taking a leap in the dark. Tim Bell's proposed 'Better the devil you know than the devil you don't know' was dismissed by the Prime Minister as 'ridiculous'. Privately, however, Conservative strategists admitted that their campaign message was essentially just that. 'You can only be sure with the Conservatives' – a variation on 'Better the devil you know' – was the message launched at the Central Council gathering at Bath on the weekend of 15–16 March. The Saatchi campaign advertisements were presented to the Prime Minister on 17 March. The campaign poster of 'Britain Is Booming, Don't Let Labour Blow It' was only a slight variant on the 1959 Tory appeal ('Life's Better with the Conservatives. Don't let Labour Ruin it'). Mr Clarke backed the sentiment, but doubted the wisdom of using the word 'booming' – the British economy was doing well, but voters did not think that it was booming; besides, the word was, unfortunately, associated with the word 'bust'. He also objected strongly to being consulted about the slogan when it was already with the printer. He was told by Mr Heseltine: 'I'm sorry Ken, you are just going to have to accept this.'

Central Office was determined not to repeat the experiences of 1987 and 1992, when it had exceeded its planned expenditure. Indeed, after 1992, the party owed Saatchi money for the press advertisements. A budget of £15m was agreed early in the spring of 1996 to cover the costs of the summer campaign and the general election. During 1996 the Conservatives slightly outspent Labour (£981,000 to £664,000 on press advertisements and £2.5m to £1.6m on posters). The Royal Bank of Scotland also ruled that no payment from Saatchi to a newspaper could be made without its prior approval. Moreover, the agency wanted to protect itself from a repeat of the 1992 experience, when the party could not pay the bill for its press advertisements. The arrangements would limit the party's ability to mount a major press advertisements campaign unless John Major or Brian Mawhinney could be persuaded to raid the party coffers.

As the party strategists moved towards a firm decision on the election date they could look back on four frustrating years when events and the grim message from the opinion polls had depressed or nullified their efforts. Could the Conservatives rediscover their traditional campaign magic in the final months? The biggest problems for the party centred on Europe. Could the party get through a general election without a spectacular outbreak of disunity. In the 1992 parliament a major change had occurred within British politics. The Conservative Party, traditionally the pro-European party, was now clearly the home for sceptics. The Labour Party, traditionally resistant, was now a pro-European party. The problems for the Conservative Party were increased because it was not sceptical enough for the Conservative press, while it was not sufficiently pro-European for its traditional allies in business and finance. By January 1997 there was little time left to sort such things out.

NOTES

1. P. Whiteley et al., *True Blues* (1994).
2. On Mr Major and the tabloids, see Kelvin McKenzie's article 'Hair Yesterday and Gone Today' in the *Spectator*, 19 July 1997.
3. The regular members of the committee were Michael Heseltine, Roger Freeman (Chancellor of the Duchy of Lancaster), Alistair Goodlad (Chief Whip), Anthony Newton (Leader of the House of Commons), Lord Cranborne (Leader of the House of Lords), Brian Mawhinney, Central Office Directors Charles Lewington and Danny Finkelstein, and from Number 10, Howell James and Norman Blackwell, Alex Allen (the Number 10 Private Secretary) and John Ward (John Major's PPS).
4. The regular members, apart from Michael Trend, were Charles Lewington, Danny Finkelstein, Tony Garrett, Andrew Cooper, Michael Dobbs, Michael Simmonds (Secretary, and after whose initials the committee was named) and Shirley Stotter, as well as Howell James and Norman Blackwell from Number 10.

3 The Road to New Labour

Labour's 1992 election defeat proved to be a watershed in the party's history. Each of the three previous election defeats, starting with 1979, was followed by a reappraisal of strategy and significant shifts in policy, but 1992 was a particularly bitter blow, because many factors had favoured Labour. The result appeared to underline Conservative hegemony and Labour's minority status. In general elections between 1922 and 1974 Labour had trailed the Conservatives by an average of 4 per cent of the vote, but over the four general elections from 1979 to 1992 the average deficit had grown to 10 per cent. Whether the party shifted to the left in 1983 or to the centre in 1987 and 1992, defeat was the result. According to Anthony King, the election might be a signal that the long historical era in which the two major parties in Britain alternated reasonably frequently in office had finally come to an end.[1]

The shock of a fourth successive loss and the hunger for office explains much of the party's history after 1994 – the dominance of the leader, the shifts in policy and the changes in party structure and ethos. If, as Peter Jenkins wrote, Labour lost the 1992 election because it was Labour, then the answer was to create what was, in effect, a new party. The changes to the party and its return to electability within months of the 1992 defeat were remarkable. The defeat was an essential precondition for the reformers to go further and transform the Labour party when Tony Blair was elected leader in 1994.

Labour leaders offered various analyses for – and responses to – the 1992 election.[2] The left claimed that what colleagues called 'the Kinnock project' had failed to make Labour electable. Rather than compete on ground chosen by the Conservatives, the party should now provide a different agenda and move to the left. Although few in the party heeded this analysis, some critics of the campaign, notably John Prescott, complained about the lack of political control over the Shadow Communications Agency and the reliance on public relations and opinion polling, particularly among uncommitted Labour voters.

Optimists argued that Labour had made up so much ground, regaining over 3 per cent of the vote from 1987, that it only required 'one more heave' for victory. The party had modernised sufficiently. With marginal changes to policy and the replacement of Neil Kinnock as party leader, it could wait for the Conservatives to make mistakes and for the swing of the electoral pendulum. To some extent this consolidationist strategy represented the thinking of John Smith in his two-year period of leadership.

The so-called 'modernisers' argued that the party had not changed enough, that it was still too much 'old Labour'. They were impatient and wanted fundamental change. Their ranks included Gordon Brown and Tony Blair.[3] They complained that Labour was too dependent on the working class, on trade unions and on council estates – and each of these was in decline. Policies, party structure and ethos must all be transformed to take account of shifts in society and values, as well as the impact of Thatcherism. Society had become more middle class and individualistic. Psephologists calculated that the Labour party's 'normal' vote had slumped to 33 per cent of the electorate in 1992, compared to 40 per cent for the Conservatives.[4] Surveys conducted for the party during and immediately after the election were damning. Working-class Conservatives in the South, the party's target voters, associated Labour with holding people back and with levelling down. Aspirational members of the working class had come to identify their interests with the Conservatives. They often liked Labour's social policies but would not trust it to run the economy; they regarded it as a 'tax and spend party', a party for the poor and the disadvantaged. Giles Radice, the Labour MP for Chester-le-Street, reported these findings in his study *Southern Discomfort*, and called for the party to assume a new identity.[5]

Within days of the election defeat Philip Gould, a key figure in the Shadow Communication Agency in the 1987 and 1992 elections, set out a formidable list of reasons which he thought had caused the party's long-term decline. The modernisers' critique of Labour in the 1990s included:

- The voters' diminishing affinity with the party, a consequence of an electorate that was becoming more upmarket and more aspirational.
- The voters' more open statement of self-interest, to explain their votes.
- The price of voting Labour, in terms of more tax and higher interest rates.
- Mistrust of Labour, encompassing fear of strife, fear of unions and fear of change.
- The failure before 1992 to erode the party's deficits on leadership and economic management.
- The clarity of the centre-right message of less government and fewer taxes; by contrast, the left lacked a clear message.
- The question of organisational homogeneity; Labour had modernised at the top but not at the bottom.
- The effect of the partisan tabloid press, which added to the negative image of the party, put Labour politicians on a backward footing and helped to set an anti-Labour agenda.

A leader wishing to act on this analysis would radically reform the party structure and ethos, change policies to accommodate a more socially and economically conservative electorate, and take steps to win over a hostile media. Hardly anybody was confident that Labour could make such a fundamental change in time for the next election. Some modernisers were so pessimistic about the prospects of Labour alone gaining office that they argued for proportional representation and an electoral pact or some other cooperation with the Liberal Democrats to unseat the Conservatives. They were reinforced in their thinking by the conclusion of the main voting study of the 1992 election, *Labour's Last Chance*? that a hung parliament was probably the party's best chance of averting a fifth successive Conservative victory.[6]

Within days of the election, Neil Kinnock announced that he was resigning the leadership. He was aware of the evidence, both anecdotal and survey-based, that he was an electoral liability, and he recognised the doubts which senior colleagues expressed about his competence. He had done much to modernise the party, including the use of modern communications for campaigning and the policy review. Labour was a more formidable electoral force, but he knew that the task had required so much of his energy and time that he had failed to project himself as a credible national leader. Having rescued the party from the abyss of 1983 Kinnock himself was a barrier to the election of a Labour government.

John Smith's election as party leader in June was a formality. For some time he had been widely regarded as Neil Kinnock's inevitable successor and he had made it known that he would stand in the event of a Labour defeat. In the leadership contest he was opposed by Bryan Gould, who offered a Keynesian package to tackle mass unemployment and who criticised membership of the ERM. John Smith won by a 9 to 1 majority and Margaret Beckett. his junior at the Shadow Treasury team, was elected as deputy; the two provided something of a politically balanced right–left ticket. Some modernisers regretted that the party had missed an opportunity to skip a generation and choose Tony Blair or Gordon Brown, neither of whom was prepared to stand. Other experienced front-bench figures like Roy Hattersley and Gerald Kaufman returned to the back benches.

As leader, John Smith took few policy initiatives, but he encouraged the setting up of the Institute for Public Policy Research (IPPR) commission on social justice and the welfare state under Sir Gordon Borrie. Its sponsors hoped that this body would suggest ideas for reforming welfare but without the need to raise taxes. In spite of his support for redistribution and full employment, Mr Smith accepted that Labour's policies should be proof against Conservative accusations that the party would put up taxes. Labour modernisers had identified his redistributive Shadow Budget in the 1992 campaign and the Tory onslaught on it as a liability; they were not convinced by the academic research in *Labour's Last Chance*? showing that the party's tax and spending plans had not lost votes. As far as they were concerned, Labour had lost too many elections through promising to spend more on services and to put up taxes to pay for them. This view was to culminate by 1997 in Gordon Brown's acceptance of Conservative public spending levels and income tax rates (see p. 78). As early as August 1993 Mr Brown, as Shadow Chancellor, had repudiated the party's tax and spending commitments of 1992. A sympathetic commentator stated that Labour leaders were 'obsessed' with avoiding the charge that they were a tax and spend party.[7]

The Shadow Communications Agency was disbanded; key members like Philip Gould and Peter Mandelson had little contact with the Smith leadership and control of campaigning was left in the hands of Margaret Beckett. During John Smith's leadership Labour profited from Conservative misfortunes. It enjoyed a large lead in the polls and made sweeping gains in the 1994 local and Euro-elections, despite the death of John Smith during the latter. However, few Labour leaders believed that the opinion poll leads for the party would guarantee an election victory in 1996 or 1997 – they had seen previous mid-term leads fade away by polling day.

Although John Smith had been elected to the leadership with strong trade union support, he helped to reduce union influence over the party. The 1993 Labour Conference narrowly accepted a version of one member, one vote which eroded the unions' block vote at the annual party conference as well as in the electoral college for the leader and in the constituency party ballots to select parliamentary candidates. Members of unions who paid the political levy and declared themselves to be Labour supporters were allowed to vote. The union role in the electoral college to elect the party leader and deputy leader was reduced from 40 per cent to roughly a third, the same share as MPs and constituency parties. The Conference also agreed to cut back the union vote to 50 per cent when the party's individual membership reached 300,000. These steps effectively broke the power of the unions in the party. As leader, Tony Blair was to go further. He made clear that the unions could expect no special favours from a Labour government and that most of the Conservative industrial relations legislation would stay. In a daring theft from the Conservatives he claimed that Labour was a 'one-nation' party. In 1996 the party, against the wishes of most unions, revealed plans for binding arbitration to settle disputes involving public sector workers.

John Smith died suddenly on 12 May. Only two years earlier Gordon Brown, his protégé, was regarded as his successor and took over his brief as Shadow Chancellor. Tony Blair, however, had made an impact with the

Home Office brief and became the front-runner. Over dinner Mr Brown agreed to back Mr Blair; after that, there was little doubt about the outcome. On 21 July 1994 Tony Blair was elected decisively as party leader, with 58 per cent of the total votes, and John Prescott, a spokesman for the political left and supporter of the union connection, was elected deputy leader.

Tony Blair energetically built on the policy and organisational changes of Neil Kinnock. He made no effort to present himself as a man of the left or as one who would try to balance the party factions. Mr Blair rose to the party leadership without a background in the trade unions or the public sector and was not a member of the factions of the 1970s and early 1980s. Indeed, he was educated at a public school and his father was a Conservative. In social background and political style he personified what he termed 'New Labour' in a way that Neil Kinnock or John Smith could not. Like Labour leaders over the previous two decades, he operated against the background of the party's electoral decline, but more than any of them he was impatient with much of the party, convinced that it urgently needed to modernise and redefine its message. He dismissed warnings to go slow on his plans for reform – unless the party changed it would wither, and deservedly so. Both Mr Blair and Mr Brown had become dissatisfied with the slow pace of change under John Smith.

Like Mrs Thatcher in 1979, Tony Blair said he was committed to changing Britain, but first, he had to change Labour. Indeed, creating 'new' Labour was a means to the former and provided the only opportunity for him to prove his leadership credentials. A priority was to remove the reasons which people gave for not supporting the party and so deny the targets which Conservative could exploit in a general election. They included fears that a Labour government would result in greater union power and increases in taxes, inflation and crime.

Tony Blair selected the famous Clause Four of the party's 1918 constitution as a test of the party's willingness to change; he saw the blanket commitment to public ownership as a key symbol of old Labour. He made the decision in principle during his August vacation (although it was only finally confirmed a few days before the speech) and only confided in a handful of his senior colleagues. Not until the end of his 1994 conference speech, on the twin themes of New Britain and New Labour, did he show his hand to a surprised audience and media. Although the party had no intention of taking more industries and firms into public ownership, the existence of Clause Four allowed critics to say that it did. It remained because of sentiment, but it was electorally damaging and prevented the party from recognising the needs of a modern global economy and the role of markets. The party should say what it means and mean what it says. He called for debate on a new statement of party aims and values and he was accorded a respectful hearing, in contrast to the stormy reception given to Hugh Gaitskell's similar message to the 1959 conference. It was important that John Prescott gave his consent, after initial resistance. The left looked in vain to David Blunkett and Robin Cook to defend the old Clause Four.

By the turn of the year it was apparent that the campaign faced resistance, particularly among some of the major trade unions. Tony Blair therefore decided to link his leadership to the issue and, going over the heads of activists and trade union leaders, he appealed directly to party members at meetings. He was prepared to resign if he failed, since it would signal that the party was not serious about change. At a special conference in April 1995 the new clause was carried by a 3 to 1 majority. Virtually all of the constituency parties balloted their members (nearly a third of whom had joined over the previous year) and they voted 9 to 1 for change. The new clause pledged that the party would work for 'a dynamic economy ... enterprise of the market ... the rigour of competition ... in a just society ... an open democracy'. There was little protest: Mr Blair had succeeded where Hugh Gaitskell and Neil Kinnock had failed. The modernisers noted that resistance to his proposal was concentrated among trade unions which had not consulted their members. The change and the manner of its achievement were presented as symbols of a new Labour Party. [8]

The reform of Clause Four was not the end of the modernising project. Tony Blair believed that centre-left parties in the West were facing common problems. Increasingly, voters were resistant to paying more taxes, disliked strikes by trade unions, demanded more responsive public services and greater opportunity to exercise choice, and did not identify with the state-owned enterprises. Labour supporters were more aspirational, and the party had to respond. Mr Blair had a clear idea of what such a party would look like. A new Labour Party would have a mass membership, and no trade union block vote; it would accept the market economy, and be centralised in its structure but also responsive to party members. The leader thought that politics at the end of the twentieth century could move beyond the battle between socialism and capitalism: Labour had to reoccupy the centre ground.

Tony Blair worked closely with Gordon Brown and with Donald Dewar, whom he brought in as the Chief Whip in 1995. The fact that Mr Blair appointed a Chief Whip rather than leaving the post to be decided by MPs attracted little media attention, but he regarded it as a significant step in reforming the party. He exercised strong control over policy and strategy. Most Labour MPs were hungry for electoral success and the sceptics and critics of the Blair project kept their doubts to themselves. A large block of Labour MPs were convinced of the merits of modernisation and knew that the lurch to the left after 1979 had alienated supporters. Many also acknowledged the need for greater discipline and for Labour leaders to speak with one voice. They left the initiative with the leader and his team. None of this meant, however, that they did not resent some of the heavy-handed methods of the leadership.

A key figure on policy was the Shadow Chancellor, Gordon Brown. He imposed an iron grip on the spending plans of Shadow Cabinet colleagues who advocated better funded public services. Protests in the Shadow Cabinet were muted because of Tony Blair's strong support for Gordon Brown. His far-reaching remit as Treasury spokesman certainly impinged on the role of colleagues, notably that of John Prescott. In November 1995 Shadow ministers complained about Mr Brown's failure to consult them when he suggested cutting back on universal entitlement to child benefit among 16–18-year-olds. Gordon Brown was determined above all to kill off Labour's image as a profligate party. He ruled out any increase in public borrowing in a speech on 18 May 1995 (echoed in Tony Blair's Mais Lecture four days later); he offered more independence to the Bank of England and promised to bear down on inflation. The party made few explicit spending pledges (being determined to deny the Conservatives opportunities to translate these into taxes) and any new outlays were to be funded by switching spending from elsewhere. If the assisted places scheme were ended it would release money to fund lower class sizes in primary schools; if taxes were earmarked it would be possible to use a windfall tax on the profits of the privatised utilities to finance an attack on youth unemployment. During 1996 there was still debate about raising the top rate of income tax from 40 per cent to 50 per cent on incomes over £100,000, but by October, agreement had been reached on leaving the rates unchanged and delaying a decision until Kenneth Clarke's final Budget in November.

Across the fields of social and economy policy the party shifted towards acceptance of much that the government was doing. The 'welfare to work' scheme aimed to shift the long-term young unemployed into work and make receipt of benefits conditional on seeking work or receiving training. The 1992 election promises to upgrade child benefit and pensions, and to link future pension increases to rises in prices or earnings – whichever was higher – were abandoned. The party accepted grammar schools, leaving their future to be decided by ballots of parents, and it agreed to allow streaming in comprehensive schools. It would not abolish grant-maintained schools but would permit schools that had opted out to convert to foundation schools, although local authorities would be represented on the school's governing body and would control admissions. On health, Labour would abolish the internal market but preserve the split between providers and purchasers and

"SPARE A POLICY, GUV?"

        Prescott   Blair   Major
Beggars with dogs had become a familiar sight in London streets.

Nicholas Garland, *Daily Telegraph*, 8 January 1997

replace GP fund-holding with collective commissioning. Conservative legislation on industrial relations would remain largely intact but the unions were offered a statutory minimum wage and signing up to the Social Chapter; there would be a guarantee of union recognition where this was favoured by a majority of workers. Labour restated its longstanding commitment to a Scottish parliament and to abolishing the voting rights of hereditary peers in the House of Lords. The party's position was virtually identical to the government's on the European single currency – to 'wait and see' and hold a referendum before entry.

The draft manifesto covering these proposals, *The Road to the Manifesto*, easily won National Executive Committee (NEC) approval on 2 July 1996. In a replay of the successful campaign to rewrite Clause Four, Tony Blair decided that the draft would be voted on by party members following the 1996 Conference. Initially, the NEC had objected that the ballot would undermine the authority of Conference, but Mr Blair went ahead. The exercise certainly devalued the policy role of Conference and was presented to members on a take-it-or-leave-it basis. Binding the party membership to the programme could be used to refute later charges of betrayals by a Labour government. It had echoes of the Republican Newt Gingrich's 'Contract with America' in the 1994 mid-term elections, as did the list of Five Pledges also officially unveiled at the draft manifesto launch on 4 July, committing a future Labour government to:

1. cut class sizes to 30 or under for 5-, 6- and 7-year-olds by using money from the assisted places scheme;
2. fast-track punishment for persistent young offenders by halving the time from arrest to sentencing;
3. cut NHS waiting lists by treating an extra 100,000 patients as a first step by releasing £100m saved from NHS red tape;
4. remove 250,000 under-25-year-olds from benefit and into work by using money from a windfall levy on the privatised utilities; and
5. no rise in income tax rates; cut VAT on heating to 5 per cent, and keep inflation and interest rates as low as possible.

Party critics tolerated Mr Blair's assertive and personal style of leadership because it was electorally appealing; they knew that any contentious behaviour that threatened the party's election prospects would bring retribution.

Tony Blair's cult of decisive leadership was both a legacy from Margaret Thatcher – he praised her conviction style and sense of purpose – and a reaction to perceptions that Labour had lacked strong leadership. He found congenial a theme which Philip Gould noted from focus groups – that voters wanted bold leadership, a clear sense of direction, even another Thatcher. Strong leadership would reassure voters that 'old' Labour was firmly under control. Mr Blair was obsessive about party discipline. He did not want to provide tabloids with material about Labour 'splits' and Labour could present a sharp contrast to the divided Conservative Party. Shadow ministers were sometimes presented with policy proposals over which they had little say. Dissenters, potential or actual, found themselves deprived of official party slots in the media. Michael Meacher (on taxes), David Blunkett (on the charitable status of private schools), and Clare Short (on rail privatisation, drugs and income tax) were all quickly slapped down. Clare Short's complaint in a *New Statesman* (8 August 1996) interview that some of Mr Blair's advisers were 'people who live in the dark' achieved immortality in the Conservative posters of Blair's demon eyes. The Parliamentary Labour Party (PLP) had traditionally elected the Chief Whip but Tony Blair assumed this power in 1995 with his appointment of Donald Dewar. The NEC increasingly interpreted its role not as the voice of the mass party, as in the 1970s and early 1980s, but as a body which supported the Labour leadership. Only Dennis Skinner and Diane Abbott regularly voted against the agreed line. In January 1997 the NEC approved changes to the conference which would emphasise its role as a 'partner' to a Labour government rather than as an alternative voice for the party.

As party leader Tony Blair took risks, abandoning traditional policies and symbols. In December 1995 he chose an opted-out school for his son and then faced down the fury of back-benchers when Harriet Harman, the Shadow Health Minister, sent her son to a selective school. In September 1996, the Scottish Party found that the promised Scottish parliament was to be subject to two referendum questions over setting it up and giving it tax-raising powers. Much of the resentment for this high-handedness was visited on Peter Mandelson and on the leader's office for seeming to take the PLP for granted. But the symbols were significant. Mr Blair's acceptance of Harriet Harman's choice of school testified to his respect for parental choice, and his action over the Scottish parliament showed that he was serious about not wanting to increase taxes. That the media paid less attention to his critics on the left was a tribute to the way in which he had marginalised them and the acceptance that he, and only he, spoke for the party.

Tony Blair also persuaded the unions to switch sponsorship funds from MPs and candidates to constituency parties. Labour reduced its traditional financial dependence on union affiliation fees, as it raised large sums from other sources. Between 1986 and 1996 the union contributions to party funds declined from three-quarters to a half of the total. According to one insider, private business provided some £15m for the party over a nine-month period from June 1996. The standing-order payments raised over £10m between the end of 1995 and the general election. This diversified funding-base gave the party a larger and more predictable flow of revenue. The insurance tycoon and Chelsea FC supporter, Matthew Harding, gave £1m. Increased contributions came from a larger individual membership and the Thousand Club, which arranged dinner for wealthy supporters. Tony Blair successfully sought public endorsement from leading business people.

Identifying Labour with the aspirations of the majority of voters meant appealing to the middle class and the prosperous working class. Many of the former had been lost in the 1980s to the Social Democratic Party (SDP) and Liberals, and some of the latter to the Conservatives. Mobilising traditional support among the trade unions and the poor was no longer sufficient; it had to find new voters and show that it could provide opportunity and choice. Labour had to show that it could help people to realise their ambitions, but within an improved social framework which promoted a sense of community.

One way to reach beyond the party's declining core was to appeal to the Liberal Democrats and forge a new progressive coalition of voters. Both parties already shared an interest in constitutional reform – and a new pressure group, Charter 88, had mobilised remarkable public support for the subject. Tony Blair went further and paid tribute to the reforming achievements of Liberals like Keynes, Beveridge and Lloyd George. In turn Liberal Democrats formally abandoned the policy of equidistance between Conservative and Labour (see p. 68), and cooperated informally with Labour in parliament. Before the election a joint party commission agreed proposals on constitutional reform. The strategy of broadening Labour's support by cultivating the City and the Conservative press, as well as the Liberal Democrats, inevitably involved some dilution of the traditional appeal to the working class and trade unions. In place of public ownership, equality and redistribution, Tony Blair stressed community, social justice, personal responsibility, fairness and opportunity. The shift disillusioned some in the party who suspected that Mr Blair lacked feeling for the activists.

As Tony Blair resumed the modernisation project, it was not surprising that he recalled two of the figures associated with the 1987 and 1992 election campaigns, Peter Mandelson and Philip Gould. Under Blair, they were probably even more influential than they had been under Mr Kinnock. Philip Gould described himself as a political strategist, not a campaign consultant, and certainly not a spin-doctor. His central task was to help develop New Labour's message. He sent memos, at least weekly, to Tony Blair, Gordon Brown, Peter Mandelson and the journalist Alastair Campbell, Blair's Press Secretary. Mr Mandelson, Mr Campbell and Mr Gould wanted Mr Blair to shift from the consolidation they associated with Mr Smith to renewal and change.

Philip Gould was strongly influenced by his experience with the 1992 Clinton presidential campaign. On his return he drafted papers for John Smith on the lessons for Labour.[9] The Democrats, like Labour, had suffered a run of presidential defeats, were losing support among the prosperous working class, and were tied to declining sections of society. Clinton, however, presented himself as a new Democrat and managed to win votes on the economy and turn around the 'tax and spend' image of his party, and adopted a language which connected with the 'working middle class'. Labour, according to Mr Gould, should develop:

- A rebuttal unit which would allow it to make a rapid response to opposition attacks. To work effectively this would require a good research base, something lacking in 1992.
- A clear, consistent message, as Clinton had with his themes of economic recovery, health care reform and change. Labour had lacked such a message in 1992.
- Flexibility. Clinton's campaign had dispensed with the daily press conferences and the candidate's schedule was decided only a day in advance.
- A campaign structure which would be open, friendly and mutually supportive. Again this was a contrast with the tensions in the Labour team in 1992.

American lessons for Labour on campaign organisation were presented in an internal party paper, 'The American Presidential Election 1992 – What Can Labour Learn?', co-authored by three party workers who helped on the 1992 Clinton campaign.[10] The authors were particularly impressed with the need for a coherent political message, as well as with the need to stay 'on message' and to use regular polling and telephone canvassing to monitor campaign progress. Many of the Clinton messages in 1992 were borrowed by Tony Blair in 1997:

- Time for change
- The failure of Bush (Major)
- Clinton (Blair) is young and dynamic
- We offer a partnership between government and people

Labour's campaign approach should not have come as a surprise to the Conservatives, for this and other documents came early into the possession of Central Office.

President Clinton had created a new Democratic Party; Tony Blair tried to do likewise with the Labour Party. Some commentators have claimed that there was a 'Clintonisation' of Labour; certainly there were many personal links between the parties, and Mr Blair and Mr Brown had been impressed in their talks with Clinton's colleagues in Washington in January 1993. There was also a common emphasis on party 'renewal' and on identifying with the aspirations of the majority of voters rather than with minorities, but it needs to be emphasised that the significant changes in campaign organisation and culture date only from the arrival of Tony Blair. One of the authors of *The American Presidential Election 1992* recalled the reaction of NEC members in 1993 – 'It fell like a lead balloon. People did not want to know.'

The leak of a Gould memo to the *Guardian* in September 1995, on the eve of Tony Blair's speech to the Trades Union Congress (TUC), aroused controversy even though it had been written six months earlier. It admitted that Labour was still not ready to form a government or to win an election with a good parliamentary majority. Perhaps more significant for party critics of the Blair project was its advocacy of a single line of command, leading to Mr Blair: it wanted central control of communications, and an end to different Shadow ministers saying different things to the media. There should be a new campaign structure, located in a new building, and a war room occupied by the key campaign personnel. Links with the trade unions should be further reduced as Labour became a mass, one member, one vote, party. The leader should be encouraged to make a bold statement of a New Labour message in time for the 1996 Conference. Labour had to change and be seen to change.

Many of the recommendations were realised. The party became more centralised and *The Road To The Manifesto* in July 1996 was, effectively, New Labour's message. In September 1995 the NEC voted a sum of £2m to cover the rental and refurbishment costs of a new campaign and media centre at Millbank Tower, close to Westminster. The campaign team was located there. The party headquarters remained in Walworth Road, South London, but as key staff moved to Millbank it was marginalised. Labour was increasingly a leader-driven party. The 250 staff in Millbank worked for the leader as much as for the party. A 30-year decline in individual party membership was reversed and by the end of the parliament, membership had grown to 420,000 and overtaken the Conservative figure. The NEC also agreed to commit the sum of £13m from the party's General Election Fund. This early allocation of funds was unprecedented: in the past the money was released on the eve of the election.

The Millbank centre was under the direction of Peter Mandelson, who had been a driving force in setting up the Shadow Communications Agency in 1985, when he was the party's Director of Communications. From 1995 Mr Mandelson was Chair of the General Election planning group, and in 1996 he was appointed Shadow Minister for Election Planning. He controlled operations in the centre, continued to brief the media, and prepared the party's election campaign arrangements. He was single-minded in keeping party leaders 'on message'. Conservative media specialists watched in admiration as Labour politicians repeated their soundbites on the main evening news programmes. His own modernising policy agenda was set out in *The Blair Revolution*, co-authored with Roger Liddle.[11] Peter Mandelson had constant access to Tony Blair and was strongly supported by him; and he worked closely on political strategy with Alastair Campbell, the leader's Press Secretary. Mr Campbell had served as a political editor on tabloid newspapers as an open Labour supporter. He also wrote the 'New Labour, New Britain' line, and drafted a large part of Blair's key speeches. He was the architect of the tabloid press strategy, particularly the wooing of the *Sun* (he had a crucial meeting with the paper's editor on the day before it endorsed Labour). Tony Blair and Gordon Brown, backed by these two, were in charge of campaign strategy.

The Blair team openly cultivated the tabloids, particularly the *Daily Mail* and the *Sun*, in 1995 and 1996. Alastair Campbell ensured that the Labour leader and his front-bench colleagues supplied these newspapers with scoops about new policy initiatives and responses to articles or editorials that were critical of Labour. In conversation he reassured the editors that Labour could be trusted on Europe, taxes and education. He realised that many of these papers were no longer naturally Conservative and that there was an opportunity for Labour. Tony Blair went to Australia to address executives of News International, telling them, on 17 July 1995, that Labour had changed from the early 1980s 'when it was not electable'. Campbell was not looking for endorsement from traditional Tory newspapers but hoped that the emergence of New Labour would help to tone down the hostility which had been heaped on previous party leaders. The tabloids, in turn, were interested in Blair partly because of their growing disenchantment with the Major government, partly because of their scepticism about the European single currency, and partly because they knew that their readers had shifted in large numbers to Labour.

The centrepiece at Millbank was Excalibur EFS (Electronic Filing Software), a computerised database for the Labour rebuttals, financed by Philip Jeffrey, a former owner of the *New Statesman*. Labour strategists had been impressed with the rapid response unit that the Democrats had used to reply to Republican charges in 1992, always within the same 'news cycle'. High-quality research was a requisite to the success of the unit. The Conservative party's formidable Research Department and reliable press support had long given it an advantage over Labour. Excalibur was a symbol of Labour's new professionalism and enabled it to overtake the Conservative party.[12] 'Would that we had had something like that in 1992 to combat the Conservatives' negative campaign' said one strategist. The operation proved its worth in helping Robin Cook at short notice to reply so impressively in the February 1996 Commons debate on the Scott Report. In November 1996 it provided a detailed rebuttal of Conservative costings of £30bn for Labour promises.

Alongside the Rapid Rebuttal Unit in Millbank was a taskforce on the key seats, led by Margaret McDonagh until the end of 1995. Ms McDonagh was General Election Coordinator from October 1996 overseeing the various strategy committees in Millbank. The party invested heavily in contacting the key voters in the 90 seats which Labour would gain on a swing of 6 per cent or less. 'Soft' Conservatives and those switching to Labour in these seats were identified through canvassing in 1994 and 1995 and then regularly contacted by telephone and insited by candidates. Information about their political views and social characteristics was logged on computer and a typical target voter was contacted four times before the campaign began.[13]

The party's advertising was at first handled by an agency headed by Les Butterfield, who had worked with the Shadow Communications Agency for the 1992 election, but in late May 1995 the account was transferred to the commercial firm BMP. In the past many BMP personnel had also worked for the Shadow Agency; indeed, the relationship between the two was so close that some regarded it as a BMP front. In previous elections BMP had avoided a formal relationship with the party, doubting the commercial quality of the work and fearing to upset other clients. Tony Blair, however, offered a more business-friendly image and Labour signed up on a commercial basis. The agency regarded the key voters as 1992 Conservatives who had become disillusioned with the tax increases. Tax was now Labour's weapon to attack the Conservatives – for breaking election promises and damaging personal prosperity – and John Major's trustworthiness. When presented with the strategy in September 1996, Tony Blair's response was: 'If we can force a draw on tax, we will win.' Its hardest-hitting advertisements tackled the Conservatives on taxes – '22 tax increases since 1992' – and warned of plans to put VAT on food: 'Why not? They broke promises before by putting up VAT on fuel', said one agency member when challenged about the claim. Advertising also attacked Mr Major's 'honest John' image for his broken promises. A more positive poster theme highlighted Labour's pledges.

Labour invested heavily in market research by NOP under Nick Moon, at a time when the Conservative Party was doing little, and an academic, Roger Jowell, presented the data to various party groups until late 1994, he was then succeeded by Greg Cook as the party's polling expert.

The focus groups were an important source of guidance for the Blair team. Throughout 1995 and 1996 a number of themes surfaced regularly. They included:

- the perceived strength of Tony Blair, a man clearly in control of his party compared to John Major, who was reported in May 1996 to be 'weak, weak, weak'.
- the economy was seen to be improving in 1996 but few voters felt that they were becoming better off.
- voters complained that 'Enterprise Britain' was also 'Insecurity Britain'.
- voters intensely disliked much of the Conservative advertising and rejected the claim that 'it hurt but it worked'.
- in spite of a recovery of economic optimism, feelings of insecurity were a dampener on further improvement.
- in spite of reservations about Labour, 'the overwhelming force in British politics is that the Conservatives have been in power too long'.

How much truth was there in the complaint from party critics and Conservatives that policy and strategy under Tony Blair were driven by the opinion polls? Blair's positioning usually commanded public support, and themes, slogans and phrases were pre-tested in focus groups, as were reactions to Labour and Conservative initiatives. But, like Neil Kinnock, Tony Blair had his own realistic idea of the party's negatives, not only among ordinary voters but also among Labour's solid supporters. Had Mr Blair and Mr Brown merely followed the polls they would not have promised to rule out tax

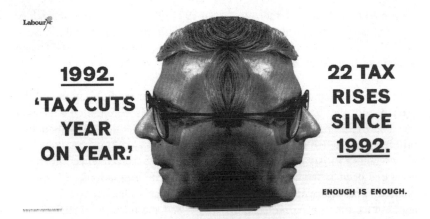

increase to boost spending on public services. The regular feedback from focus groups affected the leader's tone and language. According to Peter Mandelson: 'They also taught us the necessity of humility – people dislike the idea that you are taking them for granted.'

At party headquarters Tom Sawyer succeeded Larry Whitty as General Secretary in July 1992. Like Mr Whitty, Mr Sawyer had a trade union background and believed that the leadership should respect the mood of the party, but he belonged to the camp of the modernisers and played a major role in setting up the Millbank centre and the task forces, including the key seats operation. He also laid the groundwork for longer-term changes to the role of the conference and the NEC. Fraser Kemp acted as General Election Coordinator on Tom Sawyer's behalf and attended key strategy meetings until October 1996, when he was adopted as parliamentary candidate for the safe seat of Houghton & Washington and replaced by Margaret McDonagh. Peter Coleman served for nearly five years as Director of Organisation and Development until early 1997 when he was replaced by David Gardner. Matthew Taylor assumed the post of Policy Director in 1995, having previously served in the Rebuttal Unit. Increasingly, policy making was passing from conference and the NEC to the joint NEC Shadow Cabinet policy groups in which the initiative lay with the party spokesman. Blair was unapologetic about the shift. 'In the mass media age, policy is there to win elections', said one adviser.

There was much turnover at press and publicity. For the first few months after the 1992 election David Hill held the post before switching to become John Smith's press officer in the House of Commons. Sally Morgan took over as Director of Campaigns, Elections and Media at Walworth Road, and then joined Blair's office in the House of Commons, with responsibility for liaison with the NEC and trade unions. In 1994 Joy Johnson, a political editor with the BBC, was recruited to fill the post. This appointment did not work out. From the outset she was marginalised by Mandelson and Campbell when it came to presenting the party line and there were clashes of personality. She left in February 1996 and was not replaced.

In the constituencies, discontent with the pace of modernisation and the breach with many of the left's cherished symbols was muted – largely because of the party's big lead in the polls. Reselection presented few problems and when the party, in response to a legal ruling, abandoned its all-women shortlists, the objective of getting women selected in competitive seats had been achieved – 38 per cent of key seat nominations had gone to women. The rightward shift in the constituencies had been reflected in annual elections to the NEC before 1994, and the influx of 150,000 new members between late 1992 and the end of 1996 only reinforced it. This matched the mood of new Labour supporters. Peter Kellner found that in the 1997 general election new Labour voters were less hostile to private enterprise and less supportive of redistribution compared to 1992 Labour voters.[14]

Tony Blair's office was run by Jonathan Powell, recruited in January 1995 from the British Embassy in Washington. He was more of an administrator than a fixer with union leaders and other Shadow ministers, and he assumed special responsibility for civil service contacts and the arrangements for the transition to government. Induction courses for Shadow ministers were held at Templeton College, Oxford; these were organised by Mr Powell and Patricia Hewitt, formerly Neil Kinnock's Press Secretary but now a research director for Andersen Consulting. The youthful David Miliband came from the Institute for Public Policy Research to be the leader's policy adviser. He had good links with the universities and sympathetic think-tanks like Demos and Charter 88, and was a co-founder of Nexus, a grouping of centre-left intellectuals. He contributed speech drafts for Tony Blair and Gordon Brown.[15]

Like John Major, Tony Blair was impatient with talk of big ideas, although investment in training, stakeholding and communitarianism all had a run. He thought that the party had enough policies and should concentrate on projecting them. He did not want a detailed Labour programme, in part to avoid giving hostages to fortune; promises should be concrete, costed, and deliverable. The reluctance to make ambitious commitments was found across the political spectrum. It took account of the popular distrust of politicians, the breaking of the Conservative 1992 tax pledges and the relentless media chorus of 'Where's the money coming from?' This was another tribute to the Thatcherite influence on the agenda – that spending programmes had to be paid for – and to the scars from the 1992 election defeat.

Tony Blair's essential message was that Britain had to retain the dynamics of the market economy so that it could compete globally, but this had to be combined with social cohesion.[16] New Labour was also helped by stirrings in the intellectual climate – about welfare, constitutional reform, and the economy. The writings of Will Hutton, John Kay and Frank Field were supported by the work of sympathetic think-tanks like Demos and the Institute of Public Policy Research.[17]

Tony Blair was a relentless campaigner. The three years of his party leadership resembled a permanent electioneering operation, with daily meetings of strategists. Gordon Brown chaired a 9 a.m. gathering on Mondays, Wednesdays and Thursdays on daily news management. This was attended by key figures from the party organisation, the leader's office, and Peter Mandelson, Philip Gould and Alastair Campbell. The other regular members were Donald Dewar, Jonathan Powell, David Hill, Joy Johnson (until January 1996), David Miliband and Charlie Whelan (Press Secretary to Brown). Gordon Brown also chaired another weekly meeting at 5 p.m. On Mondays and Thursdays there was a 'general election strategy meeting' at which Mr Campbell, Mr Mandelson and Mr Gould joined the leader. Mr Brown also chaired an additional monthly strategy meeting, which was attended by Tony Blair and John Prescott. For a period there was some overlap and confusion between the roles of Gordon Brown, John Prescott and Peter Mandelson and these were exacerbated by personal rivalries.[18] Eventually, John Prescott was given charge of the key seats exercise and Peter Mandelson took control of the General Election Planning Group. There were also regular launches of policy and press conferences, many convened at short notice to take advantage of government mistakes or to rebut or even pre-rebut Conservative claims. Local elections, by-elections and Euro-elections were approached with the intensity of rehearsals for the general election.

It was possible from the late 1980s to discern two Labour parties. So-called 'old' Labour was the target of Conservative rhetoric and advertising which was designed to warn the voters that underneath the changes the old leftist dangers still lurked. The Kinnock–Blair project accepted that old Labour was no longer electable and that the changes required would be so far-reaching that a virtually 'new' successor party would have to emerge. Although the terms 'old' and 'new' were stereotypes, they did capture the essence of a division in the party and were used in internal party discussions. The 'old' was portrayed as favouring high taxation, high levels of public spending, pursuing full employment by increased public borrowing, granting the trade unions a dominant position in the party and over economic policy, and preferring government action over market forces. Redistribution and state intervention were its key themes.

New Labour, by contrast, accepted the case for low marginal rates of income tax, low inflation, and levels of public spending and borrowing which would reassure financial markets and business. Tony Blair openly accepted the essentials of Thatcherism – regulation of the trade unions, prioritising the fight against inflation, privatisation and the role of the market. Thatcherism was not an accident, or a swing of the pendulum, but a tide of history. The contribution of the state should be to work with and not replace the market, and to help people to achieve things for themselves, as Mandelson and Liddle pointed out. New Labour wished to preserve its ties with the trade unions, but not at the cost of forging a relationship with business. The Labour leader spoke to several gatherings of businessmen at home and abroad and reassured them about the party's economic policies. He also went out of his way to consult and involve business leaders in shaping Labour's thinking. What was crucial was New Labour's acceptance of a new role for the state and different macro-economic priorities from those of the 1970s.[19]

The terms 'old' and 'new' had been used by Neil Kinnock's associates, and some of the leader's reforms were designed to modernise the party, but whereas Neil Kinnock would never use the term 'New Labour', Tony Blair had no such inhibitions. The theme of 'New Labour, New Britain' was launched at the 1994 conference; the lukewarm reaction of party officials in Walworth Road to the slogan only reinforced the views of the leader and his associates that change was urgent. 'New' was a Blair mantra, used 37 times in the Conference speech and 107 times in Labour's *Road to the Manifesto*. 'Change' was another key word, used 36 times in the early manifesto. In party structure and ethos, little remained of the left's triumphs in the party in the early 1980s. The significant shifts included clipping the wings of the trade unions, ending the nationalisation commitment expressed in the old Clause Four, detaching the party from its belief in the virtues of high taxes, and creating the Millbank media centre. Each change built on the work of Neil Kinnock, but the achievements in total did amount to a qualitative difference.

In contrast to many earlier election defeats, those of 1987 and 1992 actually gave the Labour leader more room to make radical changes and, essentially, to accept much of the Conservative agenda. The Kinnock and Blair reforms centralised decision making in the hands of the party leader and his office, and were used to marginalise the party's left wing, to reassure middle-of-the-road voters, and to convince finance and business that Labour was a competent party of government. Talk of socialism, redistributive taxation and nationalisation was downgraded as an electoral liability. Tony Blair's speeches and interviews regularly mentioned the importance of the personal responsibilities that went with rights.

Policies and communication strategies were drawn up with the aim of appealing to non-Labour voters and softening the hostility of the Tory tabloids. One strategist bluntly defended the changed policies on income tax and schools as necessary 'to keep the middle class on board'. The concerns of target voters were studied through opinion polling and focus groups (held with Tory switchers) rather than through resolutions passed by party activists and trade union conferences. The party's links with the trade unions were weakened. Increased reliance was placed on the mass media and public relations. In policy and structure, Labour's modernisation distanced it from the past and brought it into line with West European socialist parties. It was now a non-socialist party of the left, although Tony Blair and some of his associates might have wished to omit even the leftist label. They were impressed also with the 'market socialism' in Australia where Bob Hawke and Paul Keating, the Labour Prime Ministers, had pushed privatisation and deregulation. Indeed some insiders stressed the Australian influence, and Paul Keating was frequently in touch with Tony Blair. Full note was taken not only of lessons from Labour's thirteen years in power from 1983, but also of John Howard's 1996 Liberal victory, based on minimal commitments that might offend 'the middle Australian voter'. Indeed Labour's 'Enough is Enough' was a direct copy from the Australian Liberal slogan.

The Labour leader claimed that his party was now in the political centre and some associates asserted that not only socialism but also the left was dead; that the only two credible positions in politics were the right and the centre. No party would succeed unless it accepted the market and promoted policies which reassured business and finance. It was no surprise that many ex-SDP supporters, including its first leader, Lord Jenkins of Hillhead, welcomed Blair's modernisation of Labour. After all, on Europe, defence, trade unions, the market and party structure, it had adopted many of the SDP's policies.

Labour's electoral recovery was sudden and sustained. The first breakthrough came in the wake of Britain's forced exit from the ERM in September 1992 and the party quickly moved into a 20 per cent opinion poll lead. For some months, however, there were still doubts that the lead was firm or that the party could win the next general election. Disappointment with the outcome of the 1992 election and doubts about the strength of Labour support in the opinion polls had left its mark. Was this any more than the usual mid-term dissatisfaction with the government? Would errant Tories return to the party, as the election neared? There was evidence that some converts to Labour might change again. NOP (October 1996) reported that 75 per cent of defectors to Labour claimed that their support was weak or very weak. With the election of Tony Blair in July 1994, Labour's lead in the opinion polls increased further and the party continued to do well in by-elections and local elections, in spite of the improving economy. There seemed to be a 'Blair effect'. Some of John Smith's admirers claim that the party's breakthrough had been achieved before Tony Blair took over. The British Election Study panel survey reports that the improvements in Labour's image as a moderate, 'good for all classes' party had all been achieved by 1994 – pre-Blair. Private polls found that post-Blair, Labour moved into a lead on economic competence and leadership and showed an increased lead on party identification. Under Blair, Labour captured much of the centre vote. His success cut heavily into Liberal Democrat support. Beyond the public perceptions, the new leader certainly did much to change the policies, culture, vocabulary and machinery of the party – including the acquisition of the Millbank centre. He and those around him injected discipline and sharpened the focus on the coming general election.

By the end of 1996 Labour's campaign plans were virtually complete. The party had a draft manifesto, an agreed strategy, and its lead in the opinion polls was so large that, even assuming a major Conservative comeback, a Labour victory seemed assured. Surveys showed that many voters accepted that Labour, under Blair, had indeed changed for the better. The perception may only have been reinforced by the 'New Labour, New Danger' Conservative slogan.

What puzzled Labour strategists was the ineffectiveness of the Conservative campaign. Their research showed that the Conservative advertisements and broadcasts confirmed the negative views that people already had about the party. As the strategist, Philip Gould, commented:

> Why spend money to do that? Why do the Conservatives complain that Labour has changed, that we've accepted so much of the Conservative agenda? Why do they talk about tax? They should do the three A's: Apologise, Achieve and Attack.

But how much enthusiasm was there for New Labour? One MP contrasted the Wilson slogan of 'Let's Go with Labour' in 1964 with Blair's 'Enough is Enough'.

Public and private surveys showed that on most policies, on perceptions of party unity and on leadership, Labour led the Conservatives. The deficits in 1992 on leadership and economic competence had been reversed. Some polls showed that on tax – so long Labour's Achilles' heel – the electorate was now persuaded that the Conservatives were more likely to put up taxes than a future Labour government. This was testimony not only to Gordon Brown's grip on spending plans, but also to the tax increases imposed by the Conservatives in 1993 and 1994. There was some concern among party strategists in June 1996, when the tracking polls reported that Labour's hitherto large leads on taxation and party identification had fallen to single figures and that it now trailed the Conservatives as 'the best party' on interest rates, inflation and managing the economy. But the Conservative revival tailed off. The focus groups suggested that Labour decisively outscored the Conservatives on trust, on change and on being 'a party for all the people'. The potential weaknesses remained the fear of change and the fear that Labour might mismanage the economy (an umbrella term for taxes, inflation and interest rates). But overriding these fears was the sense of Conservative failure:

> people still believe that the Conservatives do not deserve to be re-elected. Rejection of the Conservatives is so ingrained as to be almost visceral. People believe the country needs change, the Conservatives are tired – stagnating, out of touch, drifting (War Book, p. 5).

Even the more cautious strategists around Tony Blair now admitted to a confidence in victory. In the last quarter of 1996 the Conservatives had had their opportunities at the party conference, in the Queen's Speech and in the November Budget to set the agenda in the final quarter of 1996. They failed to make any breakthrough.

The election still had to be won. Labour did not know for certain when the dissolution would come or whether the Conservatives, seasoned at winning elections, still had tricks up their sleeve. There was tension as the party positioned itself for the final pre-campaign and for the real fight.

NOTES

1. A. King, *Britain at the Polls* (1993).
2. Cf. D. Kavanagh, *The Reordering of British Politics* (1997).
3. See J. Sopel, *Tony Blair: the Moderniser* (1995) and J. Rentoul, *Tony Blair* (1995).
4. On this, see R. Rose, 'Structural Change or Cyclical Fluctuation?', *Parliamentary Affairs*, 1992.
5. Fabian Society, 1992.
6. A. Heath et al., *Labour's Last Chance?* (1994).
7. S. Richards, *New Statesman*, 11 April 1997.
8. *Labour into Power: A Framework for Partnership* (1997).
9. Gould wrote about these experiences in 'The Politics of Victory', *Guardian*, 6 November 1992; 'The American Dream', *New Statesman*, 5 January 1993; 'Class Worriers', *Guardian*, 6 February 1996; and 'Tunes of Glory', *Guardian*, 6 November 1996.
10. J. Braggins, M. McDonagh and A. Barnard.
11. P. Mandelson and R. Liddle, *The Blair Revolution. Can Labour Deliver?* (1996).
12. See J. Carr, 'Excalibur. Democracy's Defender', *New Statesman*, 17 January 1997.
13. See Martin Kettle, 'Zeroing in on the crucial switchers', *Guardian*, 2 April 1997.
14. P. Kellner, 'Why The Tories Were Trounced', *Parliamentary Affairs*, Autumn 1997.
15. See D. Miliband (ed.), *Reinventing the Left* (1994).
16. T. Blair, *New Britain* (1996).
17. See W. Hutton, *The State We're In* (1995); F. Field, *Making Welfare Work* (1995); S. Jenkins, *Accountable to None* (1995); and J. Kay, *The Foundations of Corporate Success* (1995). These and other works are subject to a critical examination by David Willetts in *Blair's Gurus* (1996).
18. These rivalries are fully reported in N. Jones, *Campaign 1997* (1997).
19. Mandelson and Liddle, *The Blair Revolution*.

4 Liberal Democrats and Others

The Liberal Democrats were disappointed to emerge from the 1992 election with only 18 per cent of the vote and 20 seats. They had not made the gains they had hoped for and they had not secured the balance of power that had seemed likely during the campaign. Yet they were also relieved: there had been no wipe-out. The party was united and solvent and content with its leader, Paddy Ashdown. They had a strong and growing base in local government. They continued to flourish as the prime receptacle for those disillusioned with the other parties.

They were, however, quick to change their basic stance. The doctrine of 'equidistance', of an open mind as between the two big parties, which had proved an embarrassment during the 1992 campaign, was abandoned. A month after the election, in a speech at Chard on 9 May, Paddy Ashdown said that the role of the party was to be

> a catalyst, the gathering point for a broader movement dedicated to winning the battle of ideas which will give Britain an electable alternative to Conservative government ... I do not believe that mathematically constructed pacts and alliances are the way forward for Liberal Democrats or for others ... [But we should] work with others to assemble the idea around which a non-socialist alternative to the Conservatives can be constructed.

Des Wilson, who had run the 1992 campaign, withdrew from the scene but there was no major reorganisation in the party headquarters at 4 Cowley Street. Graham Elson continued to supervise the office. Chris Rennard stayed in charge of the organisation in the constituencies. In 1995 Duncan Brack was succeeded as Head of Research by Neil Stockley.

When the major challenge of the 1994 Euro-elections came, Tim Clement-Jones took charge of the campaign. It went well for the Liberal Democrats. For the first time, they elected MEPs (in Cornwall and in Somerset) and they came very near in five other South of England constituencies. They also made great headway in local elections. In 1993 they won at least a share of power in 28 out of the 36 English County Councils and in the next three years they made steady advances in the Districts, so that by 1997 Paddy Ashdown could boast that, across the nation, there were more Liberal Democrat than

Conservative councillors and that the party controlled four times as many authorities as the Conservatives. The party gained greatly from the growing number of members who had real experience of power. It shook off the 'beardy weirdy' image that had sometimes dogged it before the merger with the Social Democrats.

The Liberal Democrats were lucky in the incidence of by-elections during the parliament. The first two, in the summer of 1993, provided Liberal Democrat gains on overwhelming swings at Newbury and Christchurch. Two more by-elections and two floor-crossing MPs had raised strength from 20 to 26 MPs by the dissolution.

Party membership held up at over 100,000 and, with the aid of centralised direct mail, enough money came in to preserve party activities at a respectable level.

As with the other parties, there was an increasingly ruthless concentration on targeting. The 50 most winnable seats were given strong centralised support. By the time of the election there were 30 full-time agents, all but one in target seats.

In the summer of 1994 Lord Holme was appointed to take charge of the election campaign – and, since he was also occupied with business and as a spokesman in the House of Lords, Alison Holmes worked full-time on campaign preparations. Later two other party stalwarts, both businessmen, were added as deputies to Richard Holme – Tim Clement-Jones to deal with the party's internal communications and Richard Newby to deal with the media. In 1996 Jane Bonham-Carter was recruited from television as Director of Communications.

In the public mind, the Liberal Democrats had long been differentiated from the other parties on just two issues – enthusiasm for European integration and for proportional representation. During the parliament, the party, while staying strongly pro-European, drew back from any commitment to Euro-federalism; it was plain during the 1994 Euro-elections that there was nothing to gain from being too zealously European.

However, the general position of the Liberal Democrats was transformed by the arrival of New Labour. The whole *raison d'être* of the SDP element of the party seemed usurped as Tony Blair moved Labour to the right and espoused many of the positions that had led Roy Jenkins and Shirley Williams to the break away in 1981. Some leading Liberal Democrats, such as David Marquand and Roger Liddle, reverted to Labour. Many voters, too, made the switch. There was little that Tony Blair stood for which was objectionable to the average Liberal Democrat. However, as New Labour drifted rightwards, close-marking the Conservatives, a space was created for a party that wanted to differentiate itself from the Tweedledum and Tweedledee of the major contenders for power. After Gordon Brown committed Labour to the Conservatives' spending and tax proposals, Paddy Ashdown was able to appeal for support from the wide band of people who accepted that more money must be spent on education and the social services.

The Liberal Democrats were also able to attract some attention with their demands for constitutional reform. They had worked with Labour and others in the Scottish Convention. Robert Maclennan was especially vigorous in promoting discussions with Labour at Westminster on open government, freedom of information, and electoral and parliamentary reform.

One achievement for a party that sank in the nationwide polls from 25 per cent in 1993 to 12 per cent in 1996 was that it managed to secure a continuation of the 5–5–4 ratio in electoral broadcasting. But it had a hard task in keeping itself in the public eye while Conservative misfortunes and Labour successes were making the headlines.

The Liberal Democrats entered the election with a solid base of active party members and local councillors, with a modest but efficient central machine, and with political space to develop a distinctive message. In January 1997 there were vigorous efforts to inculcate in the party's MPs the key themes that were to be used in television interviews, with special emphasis on the need for public expenditure on schools and the health service, responsibly costed, and on the party's commitment to referendums on Europe and constitutional issues.

Paddy Ashdown was naturally at the forefront of the party campaign. He had built up an image as a lively, energetic campaigner, outspoken on foreign issues – especially the former Yugoslavia – and effective in his allotted twice weekly soundbite during Prime Minister's Questions. He entered the election confident of some breakthrough for his party, not expecting or desiring the balance of power position which had seemed to be the Liberal goal in the previous three elections.

The Scottish National Party (SNP), although founded in 1934, only achieved substantial electoral success in 1974. In 1992 it won 21.5 per cent of the Scottish vote but only 3 of the 72 Scottish seats. In 1994 it gained a second MEP in the Euro-elections when it polled a record 32 per cent of the Scottish vote. Standing as it did for full Scottish independence, the party refused to participate in the Scottish Convention assembled by Liberal Democrats, Labour and others.

The SNP gained a fourth MP in a Perth by-election. Under Alex Salmond the party kept largely clear of the faction fighting which had sometimes bedevilled it in the past. It argued for a full independence option to be added to Labour's Scottish referendum, and mocked Labour's hesitancies over devolution. In 1996 it secured control of three of Scotland's new districts, but its poll rating drifted down to 21 per cent. Although it could boast that it was, without doubt, the second party in Scotland, it never came near to denting Labour's dominance north of the border.

Plaid Cymru, established in 1925, fought every seat in Wales, as it had done in each election since 1970, but, as a party drawing much of its inspiration from the Welsh language, it had difficulty breaking out of the five constituencies where Welsh was widely spoken. It seemed secure in its four seats in West and North Wales, but its only other prospect, Carmarthen, was made much more difficult by boundary revisions. Its leader, Dafydd Wigley, had secured 34 per cent of the vote in North Wales in the 1994 election, coming within 7 per cent of victory. The party won control of the new Caernarfonshire and Merionydd district and took a few council seats in the valleys, but it got little encouragement from the opinion polls. Plaid Cymru was more explicitly on the left than the SNP, yet it shared a similar vision as a prophet of small nations within the European Community.

A record number of parties were to put themselves forward in the 1997 election, many of them happy to lose the £25,000 in deposits required to qualify for the five minutes of television time given to any party putting up 50 candidates.

The Referendum Party, however, was on a grander scale. It was launched on 27 November 1995 by the multi-millionaire Sir James Goldsmith, who offered to spend up to £10m in its support. Its aim was to stand candidates in every seat except where someone was standing who was explicitly committed to a referendum on Britain's future in the European Union. The party promised to dissolve as soon as the referendum took place. Sir James's advertisements drew a lot of publicity and attracted some minor celebrities (Sir Alan Walters, John Aspinall, David Bellamy and Peter de Savary) to the cause. The Referendum Party recruited quite a number of Conservative Party members, especially in the south, as well as a significant group of Old Labour supporters, mainly in the north, but the party never rose above 3 per cent in the opinion polls and the initial anxiety at Conservative Central Office soon subsided.

On 28 November 1996 the Referendum Party advertised the question it wanted put to the British people:

Do you want the UK to be part of a Federal Europe? or Do you want the UK to return to an association of sovereign nations that are part of a common trading market?

The wording was mocked for its unrealistic ambiguity. The party was also challenged for suggesting that Edward Heath had deliberately deceived the British people about the nature of the decision made in 1972. The party had no membership but claimed 230,000 registered supporters. It had a large Westminster headquarters, headed by Tim Williams (with Patrick Robertson in charge of publicity), as well as 10 regional offices, and, at its peak, it employed 60 people. Several million professionally made videos were distributed around the country, and the party was ultimately able to muster 547 candidates. They left alone some constituencies where the sitting MP (Conservative or Labour) had made his hostility to Euro-federalism absolutely clear.

On 9 March the Referendum Party was able triumphantly to announce its first MP; Sir George Gardiner, deselected by his Reigate constituency association for his attacks on John Major, declared his candidacy for the party.

The UK Independence Party was founded in August 1993 as a successor to the Anti-Federalist Party. It set itself up as a middle-of-the-road party, dedicated to the withdrawal of the UK from the European Union. It put up 24 candidates in the 1994 Euro-election and they won on average 3.3 per cent of the vote. From 1994 it fought every parliamentary by-election but never secured more than 2.9 per cent of the vote. At the party's 1996 conference its leader, Dr Alan Sked, appealed to Sir James Goldsmith to put his wealth and influence behind the UK Independence Party (UKIP) but he was rebuffed. Of the party's 194 candidates, 169 fought Referendum Party candidates; only 25 had a clear run. A few disillusioned Referendum recruits switched to UKIP, but the party secured no celebrity support more famous than the actor Leo McKern. The party claimed 15,000 members.

The Natural Law Party was established in Britain on 15 March 1992 and it fielded 310 candidates in that year's election; on average they received 0.4 per cent of the vote. The party, part of a worldwide organisation of devotees of Mahareshi Mahesh Yogi, believes in yogic flying and the solution of national and international ills by the development of cosmic consciousness. Under its leader, Dr Geoffrey Clements, it managed to assemble 195 candidates for the 1997 election.

The Pro-Life Alliance was founded in 1996 by Bruno Quintavalle and initially funded by Mohamed al-Fayed (though he later withdrew support). Its aim was to secure the repeal of the Abortion Act and the Human Fertilisation and Embryology Act. It put up 53 candidates. Its main national publicity was gained with its plans to screen a horror depiction of an abortion, later banned by the broadcasting authorities.

The Liberal Party was a small residue of old Liberals unreconciled to the merger with the SDP in 1988. Its leading figure was the former MP Michael

The question the people must be allowed to answer.

DO YOU WANT THE UK TO BE PART OF A FEDERAL EUROPE?*

OR

DO YOU WANT THE UK TO RETURN TO AN ASSOCIATION OF SOVEREIGN NATIONS THAT ARE PART OF A COMMON TRADING MARKET?†

* By "a Federal Europe" it is meant a European Union with supranational political institutions, including The European Parliament, The European Commission, and The European Court of Justice, and in which every nation must apply European Law, and which would bring about Economic and Monetary Union.

† A common trading market would allow the free movement of goods, services, labour and capital, whilst limiting the power of the Community institutions exclusively to ensuring that that marketplace would be efficient, competitive and fair.

N.B. The precise wording of the question to be put by the electorate and the conditions necessary to obtain a fair debate and vote should be established by Parliament

Referendum Party advertisement in November 1996.

Meadowcroft. It had fought 73 seats in 1992 (averaging 1.7 per cent of the vote); it also fought 20 seats in the 1994 Euro-election, and cost the Liberal Democrats one MEP. It fielded 54 candidates.

The British National Party (BNP), the successor to various right-wing organisations, concentrated its efforts in deprived city centres, putting up 57 candidates. It devoted particular attention to Bethnal Green, where it had briefly scored a local by-election success. The National Democrats, a breakaway from the BNP, also fielded 20 candidates.

The Green Party, the successor to the Environmental Party, fell on hard times after its extraordinary success in the 1989 Euro-elections, when it won 15 per cent of the vote and drove the Liberal Democrats everywhere into fourth place. In 1992 it put up 253 candidates, who only averaged 1.3 per cent. In 1997 it nominated 94 candidates.

Labour's drift to the right under Tony Blair caused dismay among many party supporters. But few were happy when Arthur Scargill, the miners' leader, broke away on 1 May 1996 to form the Socialist Labour Party. He argued that it was necessary to have a new voice 'when all the three political parties support capitalism and support the free market'. Its candidate just saved her deposit in the Hemsworth by-election in February 1996. Mr Scargill decided to stand against Alan Howarth, the former Conservative MP in Newport East. The Socialist Labour Party (SLP) put forward 54 candidates; there were also 16 candidates from the Scottish Socialist League.

The multitude of minor party candidates raised questions about the deposit, now £500 and forfeit by those who get less than 5 per cent of the vote. The £150 originally set in 1918 would be £3000 in 1997 money. The possibility of requiring more nominations or finding some other deterrent to frivolous candidates was widely discussed. The broadcasters denied by law the freedom to cover a constituency contest unless all candidates were involved, were particularly interested. This was one of the many issues which could be dealt with if an Electoral Commission, as promised in the Labour and Liberal Democrat manifestos, is set up with a general remit to review electoral law.

5 The Coming of the Election

Choosing the election date proved as difficult for John Major as it had been five years earlier, when he had found himself deprived of a good opportunity in 1991 and, because of the recession, failed to achieve a coincidence of the economic and political cycles. This time there was a difference: the economy was set fair, with inflation below 3 per cent, unemployment at 6 per cent and falling, and the lowest mortgage and interest rates for many years, but the opinion polls were disastrous. In 1992 it had been the opposite. Mr Major's problem was that whatever date he chose in 1996 or 1997, the opinion polls indicated electoral catastrophe. It was not an enviable choice.

In a *Today* interview broadcast on 29 December 1995 the Prime Minister had made his wishes clear:

> I don't expect to have an election in 1996. I have said repeatedly I would expect an election in 1997. No-one can ever be certain of these matters, not even Prime Ministers, but I would expect an election in 1997.

It was always assumed by the staff in Downing Street and by the Chancellor that the parliament would run until 1997. They saw no point in announcing tax cuts in November 1996 and not getting the credit the following April. John Major always ruled out going after 1 May (22 May was the last legal date), but he was prepared to dissolve some weeks earlier if there was a good political case for doing so.

Michael Heseltine was unmoved by the gloomy polls. To the end he talked of a Conservative majority of 60 seats, regarding it almost as an iron law that a government which delivered steady improvements in real disposable income over 12 months would win the election; however, neither John Major nor Kenneth Clarke accepted such rigid economic determinism. Indeed, a Saatchi presentation at the political cabinet in January 1996 warned that this so-called law would probably break down, because of the damage done by the ERM withdrawal to perceptions of the government's competence, and because of the decline in popular fears about voting Labour.

Thinking about the general election timing was dominated by the 3 February deadline for calling the Wirral South by-election following the death of MP Barry Porter on 3 November 1996. This should have been a safe Conservative seat but the opinion polls said otherwise and the party could not afford to

"ABRACADABR ,,,   ,,,ER!"

Conservative hopes that the Wirral South by-election would mark a turn in their fortunes
seemed certain to be disappointed.

Nicholas Garland, *Daily Telegraph*, 26 February 1997

do badly so near to the end of the parliament. Focus group research conducted
in the seat in November and December had shown that a disastrous result
was in the offing. Most Central Office Directors, particularly Tony Garrett,
therefore pressed for the by-election to be held on 12 December, to coincide
with a by-election in Barnsley, a safe Labour seat. They judged that it was
better to get an inevitable defeat out of the way, when turnout would be low,
and to give space for party morale to recover by the time of a general
election. Brian Mawhinney passed on this view but was unwilling to press
the Prime Minister because of the Chief Whip's claims that the loss of
Wirral would deprive the government of its majority in the House of
Commons; if Labour then tabled a motion of no confidence and the Ulster
Unionists supported it, the party could completely lose control over the date
of dissolution. Indeed, on 17 January the death of another Conservative MP,
Iain Mills, put the government into a minority. This situation lasted for a week
until Labour's Michael Redmond died, but it was renewed in March when
Sir George Gardiner, the Euro-sceptic, already deselected by his Reigate local
party, switched to the Referendum Party.

Ministers rejected the simple option of going beyond the three-month by-
election deadline because of the inevitable row in the House of Commons.
Although feedback from the constituency continued to be depressing, they
called the by-election for 28 February. Voters in the Wirral seemed determined

to punish the government, thinking that it was time for a change and that Labour deserved a chance. Some ministers argued that, by calling a general election for 27 February or 6 March, they could still cancel the Wirral by-election. Alistair Goodlad and Lord Cranborne agreed on the merits of a short campaign and an election on 6 March – it would counter the damaging spectacle of the government hanging on and the party could seize the initiative. John Major was almost convinced and Cabinet ministers were pressed to speed their manifesto submissions to Norman Blackwell. At most, half a dozen people were involved in these discussions.

An election on 6 March almost happened. It was stopped by the evident unpreparedness of MPs who, incidentally, would get a pension increase on 1 April, and by the knowledge that Conservative council candidates badly wanted the contest on 1 May, the statutory date for County Council elections. An increased turnout would at least guarantee some Conservative council victories and give them a base for subsequent recovery. John Major was aware of the criticisms which would be levied against any date he chose: 'To take the opposition by surprise is good. To take the media by surprise is a negative.' He could also anticipate charges that to call an election for 6 March would invite opposition accusations that it was a 'cut and run' election, and that bad economic news was on the way.

The scale of the Wirral South defeat was a shock to the party. Party managers believed that they had fought hard and had a good candidate. But with a voter turnout of over 70 per cent and a swing to Labour of 17 per cent, fully matching that in the national polls, it was difficult to find any comfort. For many at the centre the result presaged not just a Labour general election victory but a landslide. 'If only' arguments about a 12 December by-election surfaced strongly after the Wirral outcome, but a Number 10 aide replied 'If Central Office felt that way they should have made it much clearer.'

Once the 6 March and 20 March options had passed it was widely taken for granted that the election would be on 1 May. A few MPs, usually representing university constituencies, pressed for 10 April when students would still be on vacation. The arguments for 1 May were considerable: the income tax cuts announced in the November budget would have arrived in voters' pockets; mothers would have received their nursery vouchers, and although public opinion had not so far shown any signs of movement in the Conservative direction, it still might do so. Kenneth Clarke was an advocate of holding off until 1 May because 'We have to change the climate.' On a personal note, John Major could recall that prime ministers who had dissolved well before their term of office was due to end had often done badly, as with Edward Heath in February 1974 and Harold Wilson in June 1970. On the other hand, Sir Alec Douglas Home in 1964 and John Major himself in 1992 had gone almost to the end of the parliament and fared much better than expected.

At the beginning of 1997 Labour had a substantial polling lead to defend. Its agreed campaign strategy would focus on three themes: the future, leadership, and appealing to the many, not the few. Each campaign day would offer reassurance, hope and fear, and raise issues that exemplified these themes: taxation (reassurance and fear), business (reassurance), education (hope), and family (one-nation values). The pre-election advertising concentrated ruthlessly on tax – a reminder of 22 tax rises, the threat of VAT on food, and the promise that there would not be any income tax increases under Labour.

The party's focus groups were conveying a mixed picture. According to one memo, there was:

Slowly restoring confidence in the Tories and in Major, gradually creating wider doubts about us. *The solution to this is reassurances on tax; and support from business.*

Fear of Labour was also growing, as voters, particularly women converts to Labour, felt that they had something to lose. They were inclined to think 'Better the devil you know'. Labour, according to a Gould memo, should meet an expected massive Conservative advertising campaign about tax by exploiting fears of a fifth Tory term.

The only way that fear of us can be truly defeated is by voters having a greater fear of them. That is the simple, blunt truth ... Fear of a fifth term makes them the incumbents, not us: the issue becoming not the risk of a Labour government, but of another Tory government. This is an essential part of our strategy.

How was reassurance to be provided? Tony Blair's strong leadership was important in convincing key voters that 'old' Labour would be kept in check and that on the crucial issues, the leaders would not allow any clear blue water to emerge between Labour and the government. Above all, the party feared a repeat of the Conservative tax bombshell campaign of January 1992. In January 1997 Tony Blair and Gordon Brown made their key pledges to rule out introducing a 50p top income tax rate under a Labour government. In a much-publicised announcement on 20 January, Gordon Brown promised to freeze public spending totals for the next two years and pledged not to increase the standard rate of tax. In mid-February the newspapers carried photographs of Tony Blair alongside a Labour poster highlighting the party's

Steve Bell, *Guardian*, 4 March 1997

pledge not to increase income tax rates over the next five years. The Shadow Chancellor wrote to households promising that Labour would not increase income tax. Labour was trying to kill tax as an issue. In speeches and advertising the party hammered at the Conservative record on taxes – indirect as well as direct – since 1992 and pledged that Labour would not increase them. The campaign succeeded. Between August 1996 and March 1997 Gallup conducted studies of the voters' fears of what might happen if Labour was elected. Tax fell from second to fourth in the ranking of concerns. Its rhetoric sought to persuade voters that life would be better under Labour and was backed by specific costed pledges. In February Gordon Brown warned that a Labour government would not provide a blank pay check for the public sector, promised more independence for the Bank of England, and, the next month, guaranteed that Labour would not increase national insurance contributions. Conservatives complained that whatever they did, Labour copied it, equivalent to 'close-marking' in football. If Tony Blair was trying to persuade voters that life would be better under Labour, he was also offering continuity on income tax and total public spending.

There was reassurance elsewhere. The party stressed its support for business and the 'real economy.' Business endorsements were used to neutralise voters' fears about economic management. A by-product of the closer Lib–Lab cooperation was the work of the two-party commission on constitutional reform. Robin Cook for Labour and Robert Maclennan for the

Liberal Democrats announced agreements on a number of measures, including holding a referendum on electoral reform. On Europe the party moved to a more sceptical position, as Mr Brown and Mr Blair expressed doubts that Britain would enter the single currency in 1999 and gave assurances that the priority in Europe would be to protect British national interests. Alastair Campbell arranged for the party leader to produce an article on these lines for the *Sun* and considered the statement important in persuading the paper to endorse Labour. Tony Blair also announced that he would retain the controversial Chris Woodhead as Chief Inspector of schools and David Blunkett reassured selective schools that Labour would not abolish selection or remove charitable status from independents. The Shadow Home Secretary, Jack Straw, supported Michael Howard's tough crime bill. The key announcements were essentially Blair/Brown decisions, with the Shadow Cabinet simply being informed. In March Tony Blair told the Newspaper Society that Labour had changed, and changed for good.

It was difficult for the Conservatives to find encouragement anywhere. Opinion poll findings on voting intentions had been pretty constant for over 12 months, showing Labour with about 50 per cent support and the Conservatives seldom getting above 30 per cent. Of 13 national opinion polls conducted between 1 January and 14–17 March, the unadjusted figures showed the Conservatives scoring 30 per cent or just over in eight and Labour 50 per cent or more in ten. When voters were asked which party they preferred on a wide range of policies, the Conservatives trailed Labour, usually by large margins; only the economy and tax, where the parties were closely matched, provided any comfort. However, voters were not rejecting the Conservative Party or John Major because of particular issues; there was a more generalised negative mood, represented in the parties' focus groups and on the doorstep. Voters were saying that it was time for a change, that the Conservatives had been in office too long, that they were uncaring, and that politicians, particularly Conservative, were out for themselves and did not help ordinary people. The Tory press allies showed little enthusiasm for the party and the leadership feared the worst about the *Sun*. Dissident Conservative MPs still attracted coverage and sleaze allegations would not go away. In surveys, public perceptions of party unity, competence and trustworthiness were all damning for the Conservatives. As Ivor Crewe put it, they were suffering from 'the deepest and longest electoral slump in modern British politics'.[1]

The Conservatives lamented that so many hoped-for developments had not happened. Some months earlier Norman Blankwell and Maurice Saatchi had agreed that the party had to achieve four targets by the end of the parliament to have a chance of victory. First the party had to revive the fear of Labour, but Tony Blair's New Labour had removed many of the targets from which the Conservatives had profited in the past. Second, the party had to be united on Europe. Clearly this was not achieved and a regular feature of current affairs programmes was the claim and counter-claims of the party's Euro-philes and Euro-sceptics. Third, the party had to gain the credit for its achievements on the economy. The economy continued to do well but this was not appreciated by voters. In an analysis of the economic stories on the main ITV and BBC news bulletins over the six months prior to the election, Neil Gavin and David Sanders show that coverage of the economic successes was rivalled by stories of Conservative troubles on Europe and positive coverage of Labour policy initiatives.[2] Many voters believed Tory warnings that Labour would put up taxes, but they would still not vote Conservative. Finally, the party had to show that it had policies for the future. In early March Peter Lilley unveiled proposals for radical changes to the old-age pension. The state pension would be privatised, but there would be a fall-back state guarantee in cases of hardship. However, many voters still did not regard the Conservatives as fit to form the next government. One strategist said: 'We may still be 25 per cent behind in the polls but we are still setting the agenda. The trouble is that the voters do not want to know. They have made their minds up long ago.' A Downing Street aide suggested that one political editor had expressed an uncomfortable truth, when writing:

> The Conservatives have lost the most precious commodity in politics – the trust which persuades voters to give their politicians the benefit of the doubt.[3]

Just as in 1992, John Major used the party's annual Central Council conference at Bath on 15–16 March to build up anticipation of the election announcement. At the conference some Conservatives took little care to hide their gloom in talking to journalists. Morale was not improved by the extensive coverage for the outspoken Edwina Currie's appeal in a radio interview for John Major to stand down immediately if he lost the election. This prompted John Major to comment resignedly to Charles Lewington, 'I sometimes wonder why I bother.'[4]

NOTES

1. I. Crewe, 'Electoral Behaviour', in D. Kavanagh and A. Seldon (eds), *The Major Effect* (1994), p. 419.
2. N. Gavin and D. Sanders, 'The Economy and Voting', *Parliamentary Affairs*, 1997.
3. P. Stephens, 'No Escape from the Past', *Financial Times*, 4 March 1997.
4. C. Lewington, 'Inside the Bunker', *Sunday Telegraph*, 8 June 1997.

6   The National Campaign

On Monday 17 March, John Major returned to Downing Street from a brief visit to Buckingham Palace and, to no one's surprise, announced that the Queen had approved a dissolution. On the steps of Downing Street he acknowledged that:

> People are looking for change. But we are the change and we will carry forward what we have been doing for the last 18 years ... I believe this election is winnable ... I think we are going to win.

The electoral timetable had two unusual elements – the duration and the early prorogation.

Announcement	Monday 17 March
Prorogation	Friday 21 March
Dissolution	Tuesday 8 April
Nominations end	Thursday 17 April
Election Day	Thursday 1 May
Parliament meets	Wednesday 7 May
Queen's Speech	Wednesday 14 May

There were groans about the longest campaign. As Lady Thatcher commented later, 'Three weeks is quite enough.' The time between the announcement and the vote (45 days) was not in fact much longer than in 1945 (42 days) or 1950 (42) or 1955 (41), but the median length since 1959 had been 31 days.

John Major's decision to have a six-week campaign, as opposed to the traditional three- or four-week one, was designed to put Tony Blair under pressure and to expose Labour's policies to more intensive scrutiny. For the first third of the period the gamble obviously backfired, as the press carried stories of sleaze. Later the media had time to focus on Conservative divisions over a single European currency. Conservatives were frustrated that they were unable to launch their messages, but the Labour and Liberal Democrat parties also feared that they too were suffering from the 'plague on all politicians' mood.

The main shock from the announcement came because parliamentary activity was to be wound up in three days, although there was no obvious need for the immediacy of the prorogation. MPs would remain MPs until

8 April (and therefore get the pay and pension rises due on 1 April), but no business could be conducted after 21 March. This produced the first controversy of the election. Sir Gordon Downey's report on various sleaze allegations was due the following week, but the Standards and Privileges Committee would be in suspension, unable to receive or comment upon anything presented to it. A brief report from Sir Gordon was in fact issued on 20 March, exonerating fifteen of the MPs who had allegations pending against them, but ten MPs were left under a cloud of uncertainty. Sir Gordon's views on some of the accused, notably Neil Hamilton and Tim Smith, were not released.

The leaders of the opposition parties united in a letter demanding that prorogation be postponed so that the Committee could deal with the matter. There were dark hints that the unexpectedly swift prorogation was part of a cover-up. The government pointed out that the Committee could not possibly deal fairly with the matter in the few days before Easter, and that the timing of the publication of the full report was not in their hands. It does indeed seem that the muzzling of parliament was more due to a desire to get MPs away to their constituencies (and to avoid the banana-skins that the final few days of sittings might provide) than to any specific plan to suppress Sir Gordon Downey's observations on Mr Hamilton.

In the last three sitting days the Labour Party cooperated with the government in completing some of the pending legislation. Jack Straw agreed to help Michael Howard to 'fast-track' the law and order bill, subject to a vote on certain amendments. David Blunkett assisted Gillian Shephard in getting through the uncontroversial parts of her education bills.

The biggest news at the start of the campaign came with the *Sun*'s decision to switch its support to Labour, saying that the Tories were 'tired, divided and rudderless'. The headline on the day after the 1992 election – 'IT'S THE SUN WOT WON IT' – was widely quoted, and commentators speculated about a possible deal between Rupert Murdoch, the head of News International, and Tony Blair. It was noted that Labour had dropped its plans to block cross-media ownership. On 20 March the Scottish *Sun* also switched its support from the SNP to Labour.

On 24 March Lord Rothermere, of Associated Newspapers, indicated that the once staunch *Daily Mail* would not necessarily back the Conservatives and, at the end of the campaign, Rupert Murdoch's *News of the World* broke with precedent by endorsing Labour. 1997 was to provide the first election where a majority of the press were not anti-Labour. Indeed, Labour enjoyed a lead on press readership of 10 million. Even the pro-Conservative papers were strongly critical of the government on the central issue of Europe, with most demanding outright rejection of a single currency.

At the outset of the campaign the headline opinion polls showed, on average, a 22 per cent lead for Labour. None gave the Conservatives more than 31 per cent of the vote, while the Liberal Democrats languished around 12 per cent. Spread betting in the City suggested a Labour majority of 50, and Ladbrokes quoted Labour at 8 to 1 on. Nobody in the press or the parties believed in the 300-seat majority that the poll figures implied. But the fact that Labour stayed so overwhelmingly ahead and that only three surveys showed the Conservatives above 33 per cent (see p. 123) affected the whole campaign. Until the end there were attempts to portray the possibility of a close finish, but almost all political thinking was based on the assumption that Labour had won.

The campaign was blessed by good weather. The sun shone warmly over most of the country, producing unseasonable warnings about drought. It did not rain in the south of England from 17 March to 20 April – and then only slightly. The mellowness induced by the weather was not much disturbed by major stories from abroad or by domestic disasters. In contrast to 1992 there were no big royal revelations. An intermittent strike by Essex firemen, at odds with a largely Labour County Council, was not much exploited by the media, despite Conservative efforts. Foreign policy, except for the Europe issue, did not enter the campaign.

After announcing the election the Prime Minister went off to his roughest meeting of the campaign in marginal Luton. Standing on a soap-box he declared to *Socialist Worker* hecklers:

I have no intention of being deterred by the ugly chanting of the traditional left. When the demonstrators are pushed to one side and the ordinary people are heard I have no doubt that the Conservative government will have five more years.

Tony Blair's first action was a visit to a South London school to underline his commitment to education; he was then filmed on a train to Gloucester, a marginal seat where success was necessary for a Labour victory. There he set up his stall before 20 floating voters (and as many cameramen). His essential message was that:

The election will be a battle between hope and fear. People will be saying Labour is going to do this to you and to do that to you. We have got to settle and reassure the people.

Paddy Ashdown welcomed the chance for the voters to say what they thought of the government's 'broken promises, incompetence and divisions'.

The Iron Men of Europe...?

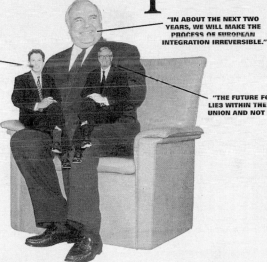

"UNDER MY LEADERSHIP I WILL NEVER ALLOW THIS COUNTRY TO BE ISOLATED OR LEFT BEHIND IN EUROPE."

"IN ABOUT THE NEXT TWO YEARS, WE WILL MAKE THE PROCESS OF EUROPEAN INTEGRATION IRREVERSIBLE."

"THE FUTURE FOR THE UK LIES WITHIN THE EUROPEAN UNION AND NOT BEYOND IT."

Men of unshakeable and deep rooted convictions? As the British people wake up, we witness an almost comical U-turn from our politicians.

What's more, don't be fooled by their promises of a 'referendum.' It's a phoney. It deals only with the side issue of a single currency - not whether Britain should remain a free nation or become a province of Europe.

The people of Britain must have a full referendum on Europe that is legally binding on a future government. Vote Referendum Party.

REFERENDUM PARTY

Stop the betrayal – Let the people decide

This advertisement prepared by Banks Hoggins O'Shea on behalf of the publisher the Referendum Party, 1st Floor, Dean Bradley House, 52 Horseferry Road, London SW1P 2AF.

1. Referendum Party copy of the Conservatives advertisement on 18 April which showed only Tony Blair with Chancellor Helmut Kohl and was headed Labour's Position on Europe.

2. John Major launches the Conservative Party manifesto with Dr Brian Mawhinney.

3. John Major campaigns on his soap box accompanied by Norma Major.

4. John Redwood

5. John Major with Michael Heseltine.

6. Michael Howard.

7. Charles Lewington, director of communication.

8. Lord (Maurice) Saatchi.

9. Kenneth Clarke.

10. Tony Blair at the
Labour media centre.

11. Gordon Brown and
David Blunkett

12. Tony Blair
accompanied by Ch
visit a London sch

13. Peter Mandelson with Philip Gould.

14. Tony Blair, John Prescott and Gordon Brown.

Robin Cook
ressing the European
vement Business
im.

16. Don Foster, Paddy Ashdown and Lord Holme.

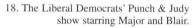

17. Paddy Ashdown launches the manifesto.

18. The Liberal Democrats' Punch & Judy
    show starring Major and Blair.

19. Paddy Ashdown steps out of the Liberal Democrats' battle bus.

20. John Aspinall campaigns for the Referendum Party.

21. David Mellor is heckled by the other candidates, including Sir James Goldsmith, at the Putney declaration.

22. Arthur Scargill launches the Socialist Labour Party manifesto.

23. Dafydd Wigley (Plaid Cymru) and Alex Salmond (SNP) jointly attack New Labour.

24. Martin Bell confro
Neil Hamilt

John Major's statement, on 16 March, of his willingness to participate in a televised leadership debate led to delicate negotiations between the broadcasters and the parties. During 1996 ITN and LWT had made some approaches to Downing Street suggesting a debate, but it was on 19 November 1996, at a meeting of the European Media Forum, that Peter Mandelson brought the issue to the fore; he repeated a challenge to John Major to confront Tony Blair in a face-to-face broadcast debate – 'anytime, anywhere', as John Prescott later emphasised. The idea was spurned by the Conservatives, as it had been by every incumbent prime minister since 1964, except for 1979 when Prime Minister Jim Callaghan, trailing in the polls, challenged and was reluctantly refused by the leader of the opposition, Margaret Thatcher.

Nonetheless, the BBC wrote to the parties on 19 December with proposals for a debate. The Conservatives officially put off any discussions until John Major had accepted the basic idea. However, talks took place with Labour and with the Liberal Democrats in January and informal contacts were made with key figures in Conservative Central Office. John Major did not welcome the idea of a debate: he thought it would distract from the campaign, and that the election might turn on a single incident in the studio confrontations, but he also realised that it offered a lifeline for his party. He despaired of what he regarded as the easy ride that interviewers were giving Tony Blair.

On 13 January, after talks with ITN and LWT, Marcus Plantin, the ITV Network head, wrote to all three parties proposing a 90-minute Sunday evening programme. In February there were signs that the Conservative line was changing, although it was still cautious and as late as 25 February Brian Mawhinney wrote to the Network in a negative tone. However, some ideas were exchanged: ITV suggested two 90-minute, three-part programmes with two Major–Blair 'head-to-head' segments, with questions being put by Jonathan Dimbleby, Sue Lawley and Michael Brunson; there would be a third segment with questions put to Paddy Ashdown.[1] (The BBC proposal was to involve David Dimbleby as presenter.)

Each network was eager to secure the debates for its own channel. ITV knew that if the broadcast occurred simultaneously on both channels, the BBC would secure the lion's share of the audience, as it does on all major national occasions, and Sunday evenings were very important, commercially, to the ITV companies. The BBC offered a clean feed of any programme it might produce to all other broadcasters, but it chose not to join forces with ITV in the dealings with the parties; some people considered that the BBC–ITV rivalry had been unhelpful. Adam Boulton of Sky Television wrote (*Independent*, 3 July 1997), 'In their self-serving attempts to secure the kudos of the debates ... they failed to live up to their public service remit.'

The soundings had not advanced far before Sunday 16 March, when John Major indicated publicly that he would welcome a debate. The next day the election was announced and delicate negotiations began. Michael Dobbs represented the Conservatives, Lord Irvine the Labour party and Lord Holme the Liberal Democrats. Tony Hall, Chief Executive of BBC News, and Anne Sloman, Chief Political Adviser, spoke for the BBC, while Nigel Dacre, Editor of ITN News, and Marion Bowman, Deputy Controller ITV Factual Programmes, put the commercial broadcasters' case in simultaneous but quite separate negotiations. Sir David Frost also made an independent approach to the party leaders.

Some of the discussions turned on whether there should be an audience. Labour and the Liberal Democrats wanted voters putting questions but the Conservatives were initially reluctant. Following a disorganised Carlton TV debate on the monarchy on 5 January, there were Conservative fears of a 'bear-garden'. But the broadcasters were eventually able to reassure all concerned that an orderly and balanced audience could be guaranteed and the Conservatives explicitly withdrew their objections. There were detailed talks over the duration of answers, rebuttals and cross-questioning, but there was no trouble over the suggested presenters. The broadcasters started work on venues and set design.

The Conservatives initially demanded a straightforward Major–Blair 'head-to-head' confrontation without Paddy Ashdown and firmly refused any compromise that would not be predominantly head-to-head. John Major believed that, in an extended confrontation with Tony Blair, he would triumph through his much greater command of detail; Paddy Ashdown would be an anti-Conservative distraction, 'like having the best man in the bridal chamber'. The Liberal Democrats indicated that they would go to court if they were excluded from the main debate or 'confined to a corner' (and indeed the Scottish Nationalists went to law on this issue, prematurely). ITV and the Liberal Democrats sought a ruling from the Independent Television Commission on the interpretation of 'due impartiality' in relation to a debate.

Intense shuttle diplomacy went on for several days. The Conservatives came to accept an Ashdown role. One ITN formula suggested 30 minutes of Major–Blair head-to-head, coupled with 30 minutes of three-way discussion, following an Ashdown rebuttal. Another from the BBC envisaged 12 minutes of three-way discussion, followed by 24 minutes of a Major–Blair head-to-head, then Ashdown alone for 5 minutes, then 24 minutes Major–Blair, then 5 minutes Ashdown, and ending with 12 minutes three-way. The BBC and ITV devised different ways of accommodating the Scottish and Welsh Nationalists; one suggestion involved a follow-up four-way discussion within their own regions.

" RIGHT, LADS, THIS IS HOW WE GET OUT OF IT... "

Prescott   Blair   Cook   Straw   Brown

The media were suggesting that Labour was plotting desperatley to avoid taking part in a leaders TV debate.

Peter Brookes, *The Times*, 25 March 1997

The parties and the broadcasters had taken senior counsel's advice over what might be challenged in the courts and Lord Irvine in particular was adamant about not getting entangled in any scheme that might result in judicial involvement. This gave strength to Lord Holme's efforts to secure the largest possible role for Mr Ashdown. The Conservatives regarded Labour's position as a ploy to prevent anything happening.

ITV was informed on Tuesday 25 March that Labour had set a Thursday deadline on the negotiations. Any debate would involve major modifications of their detailed day-by-day plans for the campaign and for the use of Tony Blair's time. It was widely thought that the Labour Party, being so far ahead, saw no possible advantage in the debate. But some Labour strategists were convinced that the Conservatives were only playing with them in pursuit of distracting headlines and the implication that Tony Blair was frightened. They also felt that reports of the debate discussions were drawing away headlines from their own message and distorting campaign planning.

However, there is no doubt that the Liberal Democrats were convinced that they had agreed a formula with Labour which would have obliged them to participate, if it had not been vetoed by the Conservatives. On 26 March, the BBC thought they were close to achieving this deal, but Michael Dobbs was clear that the proposal did not contain enough head-to-head to be acceptable. Things then fell apart. Michael Dobbs suggested to the press that Labour was making 'bizarre excuses to kill the debate' and, on 27 March, the talks collapsed before Labour's 5.30 p.m. deadline, with both major parties blaming each other for 'pulling out'. After Labour had confirmed the breakdown, the Conservatives publicly accepted both the BBC and ITN proposals as the only realistic basis for an agreement.

The Conservatives complained of Labour's arbitrary deadline while Labour argued that the Conservatives had shown they were 'not serious'. Some broadcasters were convinced that Brian Mawhinney had pulled back on 25 March from positions he had earlier accepted, though the Conservatives deny this. Tony Blair and close colleagues concluded that the elaborate negotiations about the debates were a Tory device to distract from press coverage of sleaze and Labour attacks on their record, but John Major thought Labour never intended to take the risk: 'Once the debates were possible you could physically see Labour moving away from the idea.' The maverick Labour MP, Austin Mitchell, attacked Peter Mandelson, calling 'his weasel words of withdrawal' a 'sad blow to democracy, to viewers who want and deserve this debate and to the Labour Party itself' (*Sunday Times*, 30 March).

The Conservatives, in one of the more publicised but less happy gimmicks of the campaign copied from American practice, hired an actor to dress as a chicken and to haunt Tony Blair's public appearances. The chicken's head was stolen more than once and persons dressed as foxes appeared. On one occasion, the chicken had to be taken into police custody for protection against an attempt to throw him into a harbour. Labour was unworried by what they saw as a puerile stunt.

On 11 April the Editor of *The Times* tried vainly to intervene, offering a debate forum outside the confines of broadcasting regulations, but the parties were only interested in something that the networks would carry in full without incurring a legal challenge.

Those involved in the affair do not agree on what went wrong. Within both of the two main parties there were divided views on whether the debates were desirable and on how toughly to negotiate. Both the Conservatives and Labour suspected the other side of not being serious and, in some cases, felt that those appointed to negotiate did not have the full authority of their leaders. A deal came quite near, but trust was lacking and time was short.

The Conservatives probably scored few points over the issue, although the story had attracted plenty of headlines over the first two weeks of the campaign, and polls showed that the public wanted a debate and thought that Labour was running away. The Liberal Democrats were relieved not to have had to appear as spoilers by going to law, and Labour was relieved not to have the debates at all.

John Major, who had had to be persuaded to switch his position and accept the challenge, seems to have had little enthusiasm for the idea unless it gave him a prolonged, uninterrupted confrontation with Tony Blair. In fact a sustained encounter between two politicians as skilled as John Major and Tony Blair would probably have ended fairly equally – but the event, in anticipation and in retrospect, would almost certainly have dominated the campaign.

It is plain that time was too short to make the arrangements for the debate, and, as the BBC negotiators wrote, 'None of [the parties] wanted it enough to make it happen.' Richard Tait argued this in a lecture to the European Media Forum on 19 May 1997:

> The prospect of a debate threatened to disrupt the careful election planning by the party campaign teams ... I have no doubt that the three main party leaders wanted a debate but none of them had time for the detailed negotiations that would make a deal. The Tories believed Labour was dragging its feet because it did not want a debate. Labour believed the Tories were exploiting the debate negotiations to attack them. Liberal Democrats thought it was not worth doing if their leader was being seen in a significantly inferior role ... The next election is probably the last chance to establish leaders' debates as a key part of British elections before the television audience fragments [into a multiplicity of channels]. For history not to repeat itself there has to be an agreement long before the last few weeks of the present government's term ... There has to be an early agreement between the two broadcasters who can most easily deliver a mass audience – BBC and ITV – to share the debates ...

Other broadcasters take the view that, even with time on their side, the essential ingredient – a genuine desire on all sides to make the debate happen, not for the general good but for their own advantage, would have been missing. As Tony Hall and Anne Sloman wrote in the *Independent* (2 July 1997):

> Elections are the point in the political cycle when politicians are least likely to be high-minded about engaging in debate for debate's sake or making sensible (negotiated) concessions to their opponents.

Hall and Sloman urged the parties to reconsider while there was time for calm reflection. Adam Boulton concluded in a letter to the *Independent* (3 July):

a third party – neither broadcaster nor party political – should take the lead in establishing a format which could then be offered to the politicians and broadcasters on a take-it-or-leave-it public access basis.

High-level debates were, however, broadcast. On 6 April, the BBC's *Money Programme* staged a 'Chancellors' Debate' between Kenneth Clarke and Gordon Brown, with substantial participation from the Liberal Democrats' Treasury spokesman, Malcolm Bruce. The *ITV 500* and BBC's *On the Record* staged similar three-way debates on the economy later in the campaign, while *Channel 4 News* put on a two-way encounter. A week later Michael Howard debated home affairs with Jack Straw and Alex Carlile. There was also a Deputy Leaders' debate on *On the Record* between Michael Heseltine, John Prescott and Alan Beith before a lively audience on the final Sunday, 23 April. One participant in these encounters commented that the Liberal Democrat presence had destroyed the impact; the experience made him feel that he would certainly not recommend them at the prime ministerial level. An ITV view was that 'televisually, three-ways don't work', but, as the law stands, a two-way debate is probably out of the question unless the country somehow reverts to two-party politics.

Campaign reporting focused to an overwhelming degree on the utterances and the carefully orchestrated activities of the three main party leaders. A certain amount of limelight also fell on Michael Heseltine, exuding rumbustious optimism at Central Office, and on John Prescott, doggedly visiting all the key marginals in his 50-seat silver bus, the 'Prescott Express'. The media suggested that he was being kept out of the limelight, but there was plenty of coverage and only one reported slip in his utterances: in a *Sunday Times* interview of 13 April, he was reported as admitting that the legal minimum wage could cost jobs, adding, 'you can't tell the truth all the time'. Conservatives sought to exploit the comments, but Brian Mawhinney clearly exaggerated when he declared them a 'defining moment' of the campaign. Shirley Williams attracted good audiences and some publicity in an exhaustive nationwide tour for the Liberal Democrats, and Sir David Steel, retiring from his constituency obligations, was much in evidence.

From time to time the press commented on the fact that certain front-benchers were seldom seen on television – suggesting that they were regarded as potential embarrassments. Among those named were Douglas Hogg and Virginia Bottomley on one side, and Harriet Harman and Frank Dobson on the other. Left-wing MPs, such as Tony Benn, Dennis Skinner, Diane Abbott, Jeremy Corbyn and Ken Livingstone, were known to be critical of New Labour but, because of discretion on their part and, perhaps, lack of aggression by the media, nothing of substance was reported from them to damage the party's momentum.

The running of a campaign depends upon the party leader, who must be the ultimate campaign director and the central bearer of the party message, but the impact of the leader and the message will depend upon the key strategists. John Major had Brian Mawhinney, together with Michael Trend, Charles Lewington and Danny Finkelstein, not to mention Lord Saatchi and Sir Tim Bell: they supported him in devising and implementing tactical responses as the campaign developed. Except in relation to advertising strategy, it was a harmonious group, but it suffered from the physical and psychological gap between 32 Smith Square and 10 Downing Street (where Lord Cranborne together with Norman Blackwell minded affairs). Brian Mawhinney was the main link between Central Office and the Prime Minister, but some staff at Number 10 disapproved of the speed with which he shared problems with the Prime Minister. One of John Major's staff noted: 'When he phones it always seems to be bad news. We want to be uplifted, not depressed.' If John Major had found the behaviour of his back-benchers a trial during the parliament, the campaign was no different. According to Charles Lewington (*Sunday Telegraph*, 8 June 1997), John Major was 'reconciled to defeat'. At times he seemed to be fighting apart from his own party, as he made personal appeals to the voters to trust him on Europe, on pensions and on health. 'Why not?' commented one aide, 'the party is unelectable'.

Tony Blair had Gordon Brown and Peter Mandelson in charge at the Millbank media centre; they, together with Alastair Campbell and Philip Gould (with Jonathan Powell and David Miliband in the background) constantly monitored events and suggested the best response. Yet none of them regarded Tony Blair as their puppet; like John Major, the leader really did determine day-by-day the party line. Advisers would say that Tony Blair stayed 'on message' more faithfully than the Prime Minister. On his battle bus Tony Blair stayed constantly in touch with the small coherent group at Millbank. In public he appeared as a prime minister designate, but he certainly did not expect Labour to win by more than 50 seats. Philip Gould's nightly memos could not fail to report the many positive signs and the internal difficulties of the Conservative Party, but they also highlighted potential weaknesses. As the campaign advanced, Tony Blair spoke more and more spontaneously and, as his aides put it, 'found himself'.

Election Call Question: "Why do you always wear Tory-blue ties?"
Blair: " Oh, come off it. I just take the first one that comes to hand..."

Mandelson   Blair

Peter Brookes, *The Times*, April 1997

Campaigns are about organisation and style. Each party had a daily routine of meetings to implement their well-prepared war books and to adapt them to changing circumstances. For the Conservatives Brian Mawhinney chaired a press conference preparation meeting at 8.30 a.m. John Major would come in at the end and then adjourn for a few minutes with Howell James. There would be a brief post-mortem on the conference before Mr Major left on his travels. At 8 p.m. there was a strategy meeting with Downing Street advisers and Central Office directors. At 9 p.m. Dr Mawhinney with Danny Finkelstein and Charles Lewington went to Downing Street to brief the Prime Minister.

The Labour team at the Millbank media centre had a 24-hour day. At 1a.m. a 'Daily Brief', anticipating the press conference, was faxed to all candidates. At 7a.m. Gordon Brown chaired the war room group to preview the press conference and confirm the day's agenda before the 8.30 a.m. press conference. At 11 a.m. Gordon Brown's group met again to assess all the parties' press conferences. There were further meetings at 3 p.m. and 7 p.m. to review the findings of focus groups, of public and private polls and of the feedback from key seats.

The Liberal Democrats began with a 6 a.m. meeting between Lord Holme and Alison Holmes, followed by a fuller gathering at 7 a.m. to finalise the press conference release and the day's plans. Following the press conference

Paddy Ashdown would meet briefly with his colleagues – but he was usually on the road by 9 a.m. The campaign team had a full meeting at 10 a.m. and another at 5.30 p.m. Paddy Ashdown usually came back to town for a late-night confabulation with Lord Holme, who played a central role in a smooth-running operation.

After Easter, a routine developed around Westminster. At 8 a.m. the Liberal Democrats held a press conference in Church House, chaired by Lord Holme. A couple of brief prepared statements were followed by 10–15 minutes of questions. But the conference had to end by 8.20 a.m. to allow journalists time to walk to the media centre at Millbank where New Labour's more elaborate affair was due at 8.30 a.m. It began with theme music entitled 'Things Can Only Get Better' and a video clip, before Gordon Brown, a forceful chairman, entered, usually with Tony Blair and another spokesperson beside him. Again two brief prepared statements were read, followed by 20 minutes of questions. The press then marched on to a 9.15 or 9.30 a.m. conference at Conservative Central Office, chaired unobtrusively by Brian Mawhinney and often with John Major making the main statement.

The questioning at each of these conferences assumed a ritual. The leading correspondents from the broadcast media were given the first opportunity, followed by the representatives of the broadsheets. Some of the questions were provoked by the rival press conferences or by private briefings from leading politicians. Relatively few from the provincial or foreign press managed or even tried to get recognised, though one Russian journalist managed to ask why the Conservatives were struggling while the economy was flourishing. The questioning was quite aggressive but, since supplementaries were seldom allowed, it was hard to pin the parties down and very few gaffes were spotted. The most memorable unpremeditated news break came on 17 April when John Major told Elinor Goodman of *Channel 4 News* that he would allow a free vote when EMU came before the Commons. He was surprised at the excited media reaction: 'I am an old Whip and the idea that you could whip the party on this issue is for the birds.'

The Conservatives made more last-minute variations in their press conference programme than Labour. On 25 March a Gillian Shephard statement on education was sidetracked to provide space for a Heseltine broadside on union power. On 16 April John Major pushed aside a plan to boast of falling unemployment to talk about Europe. On 26 April Kenneth Clarke was substituted for Michael Howard, who pulled out on learning that John Major would not be appearing.

The press conferences served to launch each party's theme for the day – and to provide copy for the lunchtime bulletins, but it was notable that, before and after each gathering, officials from the party press offices moved around among the senior journalists, explaining and amplifying any current themes. The efforts at spinning were more systematic and obvious than in previous elections.

After the morning press conferences, the leaders usually rushed off by battle bus or plane to visit key constituencies and give interviews to the local media. Each battle bus was equipped with a space for the leader to work in peace as well as full facilities for electronic communication. Each had a folding rostrum for impromptu speeches. All the leaders set aside time to prepare for their major national television interviews. John Major was regularly accompanied by Howell James, his Political Secretary, together with Shelia Gunn as Press Officer and Shirley Stotter as Organiser. Norma Major came with him most of the time. Tony Blair travelled with Anji Hunter as Secretary and Alastair Campbell as Press Officer; Cherie Blair usually accompanied him. On most evenings Mr Blair returned to his Islington home by 8 p.m. and Mr Major was usually in Downing Street at about the same time.

There were fewer rallies than in previous elections. Labour had embarrassed memories of the 1992 Sheffield gathering, and the Conservatives were not altogether happy with their past stage-managed assemblies at the Wembley Arena. The Conservatives drew 2000 in the Royal Albert Hall meeting on 4 April. John Major had many *ad hoc* stops where he spoke from his battle bus, having early abandoned his portable soap-box. Security considerations, as well as anxiety about organised heckling, meant that the leader's travels were not advertised in advance. Tony Blair delivered four prepared lectures to businessmen, teachers and other selected targets; he also spoke during his travels to a dozen assemblages of supposedly Tory waverers. Mr Blair grew in confidence as the election advanced. When his microphone failed at Edinburgh he gave up his script and walked to the front of the platform to orate to his audience in a spontaneous, old-fashioned style, speaking eloquently of trust and vision. Those who travelled with him paid tribute to the evolution of his campaigning skills.

Paddy Ashdown, campaigning by battle bus or, in the last week, by helicopter, repeatedly visited the 75 seats his party held or had targeted, and spoke regularly to captive audiences of schoolchildren. He boasted that he had travelled 17,300 miles, twice as far as John Major or Tony Blair, visiting 64 constituencies. In fact Mr Major and Mr Blair each travelled about 10,000 miles; Mr Major visiting 56 seats, and Mr Blair 60.

The journeyings were facilitated by friendly tycoons. British Midland provided a plane for John Major. Lord Hanson, Sir Michael Bishop and others lent helicopters and executive jets to the Conservatives. Labour insisted that they pay for all their transport. The Liberal Democrats were proud of having booked a large helicopter for Mr Ashdown the previous October. Only small helicopters were available for Mr Blair, who sometimes travelled in a small whirling flotilla. Jaguar Motors also provided a car for each party leader. The parties managed to offset the substantial costs of the leaders' campaigns by making the media pay. Each newspaper was asked for about £8000 to secure a seat on the plane or battle bus throughout the campaign. There was an outcry on 15 April after Labour had apparently overcharged journalists in a Birmingham hotel to meet the costs of the leader's entourage.

There were large numbers of young apparatchiks in their twenties in all three headquarters. In Central Office it was possible to discern a certain dignified defeatism and gallows humour. At weekends some experienced strategists were surprised at the absence of manpower both in Central Office and in Downing Street. For Labour, security was intense at Millbank Tower. No journalists were allowed access to the second and third floors, where campaign operations were based. Again, perhaps scarred by the 1992 defeat and fears of a late swing, victory was not taken for granted, let alone a landslide. Philip Gould, for instance, continued with his focus group sessions until the Tuesday before polling day.

Margaret Thatcher had been a brooding presence over Conservative politics since the party rejected her in 1990. Would she embarrass the leadership this time with her extreme Euro-scepticism? She was in fact brought smoothly on board, visiting Central Office to join John Major in addressing 300 candidates in a private meeting on 26 March. She also made trips to Dorset and Hampshire (9 April) and Teesside (16 April), saying little to discomfort Mr Major's campaign. On the Labour side, very little was heard from Neil Kinnock and Michael Foot.

The Prime Minister refused to delay the prorogation of parliament or to intervene actively against the readoption of the candidates most involved in the sleaze accusations. Michael Heseltine said repeatedly that 'a man is innocent until proved guilty', but on 21 March the *Guardian* produced further damaging documentation about payments to MPs. Sir Gordon Downey objected to this selective leaking of evidence as 'against the interests of natural justice'. Tim Smith, the Member for Beaconsfield, promised to 'keep on fighting', and Neil Hamilton was endorsed by his Tatton constituency association AGM.

The Conservative leadership was much embarrassed and indignation grew. On 26 March Mr Smith 'did the decent thing' (in the words of Central Office) and withdrew from the fray. Neil Hamilton was more obdurate, despite concerted pressure from the Conservative hierarchy to 'lance the boil' by going.

Sleaze was dominating the campaign, posing serious problems for the Conservatives because it tapped public doubts about the trustworthiness of politicians and about John Major's leadership. Labour and Liberal Democrat campaigners reported that voters were being switched off from the election. However, on 28 March Labour stirred the pot by persuading their candidate in Tatton to offer to stand down if others would cooperate in presenting an 'anti-sleaze' nominee. The Liberal Democrats were unhappy at being bounced without notice into this strategy but, in the end, they joined in a three-day search for a nationally known figure who was above reproach. On 30 March Martin Bell, the veteran BBC war correspondent, emerged and quickly secured endorsement.

There was a much televised encounter between Martin Bell and Neil Hamilton, together with the formidable Mrs Hamilton, when Mr Bell had his first informal press conference on Knutsford Heath; thereafter Mr Bell in his rumpled white suit provided one of the enduring images of the campaign. He had to stand as an 'Independent' after Mr Hamilton threatened legal action if he used an 'Anti-Corruption' label.

Other embarrassments followed. On 25 March Allan Stewart, the Conservative candidate in Eastwood, the party's safest seat in Scotland, had to withdraw following a publicised nervous breakdown. On 29 March, his likely successor, Sir Michael Hirst, the party's Scottish Chairman, suddenly gave up public life because a revelation of some past indiscretion was thought imminent. The press carried tales of internal feuding within the Scottish Conservative Party.

On 27 March, the *Sun* splashed a story, with photographs, of an affair between Piers Merchant, the Conservative MP for Beckenham, and a teenage nightclub hostess. Michael Heseltine, speaking on the BBC, said that 'obviously we are bound to feel let down. I haven't the slightest doubt that Piers Merchant, his family and his association will want to consider very carefully the consequences of what has happened for the party at large.' Nonetheless, many people, including the Beckenham Conservative Association, thought that a private sex scandal, revealed through a nasty newspaper 'sting', was very different from the kinds of financial corruption which Sir Gordon Downey was investigating. After an Easter weekend of awkward headlines, Mr Merchant survived. As one Conservative candidate remarked, 'Voters know the difference between sleaze and sexual indiscretion.'

When the campaign really began the following Tuesday, 1 April, Mr Major decided to tackle the sleaze issue head-on, answering every question about it at the morning press conference. He refused to join a 'witch-hunt', but spoke strongly in support of tough action by the Standards and Privileges Committee. To some extent he satisfied the media, and the sleaze issue, which had so dominated the headlines, gave way to more important themes once Mr Hamilton had been formally readopted as a candidate on 8 April.

There were many who believed that Mr Major should have acted more strongly to disavow Mr Hamilton. His candidacy and his wife's tough style kept the sleaze issue alive, and senior Conservatives spent a lot of time agonising over the best course to take. John Major felt he was damned if he did and damned if he didn't. To intervene would have been controversial and would have dominated the news for several days. In the end he sought to make the best of a bad job, but Tony Blair made the failure to repudiate the Tatton candidate a symbol both of Conservative standards and of Mr Major's weakness.

There was much talk about positive and negative campaigning. All the parties repudiated the charge that they were fighting negatively. The Liberal Democrats were probably the most successful in their claims to righteousness, focusing heavily on their theme of higher income tax to pay for education and health. The Labour Party gave positive themes to Tony Blair, leaving the negative lines to lesser figures and to the press conferences and press releases. The Conservatives, like any party in power, had to concentrate on the dangers presented by a change to the other side. As we show later (p. 239–241), negative themes were most prominent in their literature. Labour spokesmen directed journalists to a speech given by John Major in Plymouth for its hostility to Labour, and complained about the personal nature of the remarks about the Blairs' 'hypocrisy' over their son's schooling.

One of the more successful Conservative thrusts came early in the campaign, following a story in the *Daily Mail* about the return of union power under Labour. At a hastily organised press conference, Michael Heseltine developed the theme, saying that it had been a long battle to curb the unions since 1979:

A Labour government could blow it. The evidence stares one in the face. Today a shocking revelation – a list of 63 British companies that have been targeted as the first victims of Labour's payback to the union bosses.

In a stumbling demonstration of their rapid rebuttal system, Labour produced an instant point-by-point answer to the *Daily Mail* story, but at first there was confusion over whether a judge or a Central Arbitration Committee would decide if a majority of workers actually supported a union. Tony Blair tackled the issue head-on at his press conference:

The unions will get fairness but no favours from us ... This is a party that will govern for all the people, the whole country and no single interest group within it.

Other press conferences were called in response to newspaper stories. Labour picked up a *Mirror* accusation of 26 April concerning political donations made by Michael Heseltine's Charitable Trust, while on 27 April the Conservatives called a press conference to develop a *Sunday Times* story that Gordon Brown was planning an emergency Budget in July.

The campaign proper began with the manifesto launches. Each document was lavishly illustrated in colour and set out like a company brochure rather than the traditional letterpress pamphlet.[2]

The first manifesto to be launched, appearing on 2 April, was the Conservatives' 20,000-word *You Can Only Be Sure With The Conservatives*. Its contents could hardly be new without being a condemnation of what the government had been doing, although Mr Major managed to call it 'a watershed manifesto' and *The Times* referred to it as 'a cautious but coherent package'. Its freshest proposal was a plan for tax benefits to married couples and others with dependants. It also spoke of privatising Parcelforce and the London Underground. It referred to the Conservative goal of a 20p basic rate of income tax, committed the party to get and keep public spending below 40 per cent of GDP, and envisaged the phasing out of State Earnings-Related Pension Schemes. It emphasised opposition to the creation of a European federal state and to any single currency based on fudged criteria. The option to join such a currency was, however, left open.

On 3 April, Labour unveiled its 19,000-word manifesto, *New Labour Because Britain Deserves Better*, in a well-orchestrated presentation in the Institute of Civil Engineers' building off Parliament Square. It focused on Tony Blair's ten-point 'contract with the people':

1. Education will be our number one priority and we will increase the share of national income spent on education as we decrease the bills of economic and social failure.
2. There will be no increase in the basic or top rates of income tax.
3. We will provide stable economic growth with low inflation and promote dynamic and competitive business and industry at home and abroad.
4. We will get 250,000 young people off benefit and into work.
5. We will rebuild the NHS, reducing spending on administration and increasing spending on patient care.
6. We will be tough on crime and tough on the causes of crime, and halve the time it takes persistent juvenile offenders to come to court.

7. We will help build strong families and strong communities, and lay the foundations of a modern welfare state in pensions and community care.
8. We will safeguard our environment and develop an integrated transport policy to fight congestion and pollution.
9. We will clean up politics, decentralise political power throughout the United Kingdom and put the funding of political parties on a proper and accountable basis.
10. We will give the leadership in Europe which Britain and Europe need.

The manifesto reiterated Labour's 'Five Pledges' (see p. 54). Tony Blair spoke of the party's 'opportunity to demonstrate in government that we have changed. If we blow this opportunity we blow our place in history.'

It was noted that some of New Labour's earlier rhetoric had disappeared; 'stakeholding' and 'socialism' were not mentioned, but it was nevertheless a break with the past. As the *Independent* wrote:

> On Tony Blair's young head the cloth cap of Keir Hardie is as invisible as Mr Attlee's [Homburg] ... The man and his document owe nothing at all to Gaitskell [and] Crosland.

Labour's plans for a windfall tax on 'utilities regulated and licensed by the state' provided a recurring theme in the campaign. Would British Telecom and the British Airports Authority be included? How much money would be raised? Would the whole process be invalidated by the obligation of European law? Gordon Brown expressed complete confidence in the viability of the scheme, though he would not say how much money would be raised or specifically which companies would pay. However, speaking on the *World at One* on 3 April Mr Brown conceded that Labour's self-restricted budget might face a £1.5bn deficit, a 'black hole' that could only be filled if the party went along with Conservative plans for the privatisation of the National Air Traffic Control system. He said that Labour did not rule out privatisation on principle, a point stated more clearly by Tony Blair in his Corn Exchange speech four days later. The Conservatives were quick to draw attention to this apparent *volte face*. A damaging clip of Andrew Smith denouncing air traffic privatisation at the previous autumn's party conference was shown, while Mr Heseltine pointed to a letter written in February by Labour's transport spokesman confirming that the party was 'completely opposed' to air traffic privatisation.

The Liberal Democrats came third in launching their manifesto on 4 April. Their 14,000-word text, *Make the Difference*, also put education first. The party renewed its pledge to increase education spending by £2bn a year. It also promised to recruit more doctors and nurses and to restore free eye and dental checks. The Liberal Democrats boasted that every one of their spending commitments had been carefully costed and could be met if 1p was added to income tax and 5p to the cost of each packet of cigarettes.

The Liberal Democrats made much of the similarity of policy between Conservative and Labour, satirising their disagreements as a Punch and Judy show (which was the theme of their television broadcast on 11 April). The big parties' agreement on taxing and spending policy gave Paddy Ashdown space to develop a distinctive and more radical position. Indeed he quoted back to Labour the famous words of Neil Kinnock, who warned voters in 1983 on the eve of Margaret Thatcher's election victory 'not to be ordinary ... not to be young ... not to fall ill ... not to get old'.

The Conservatives' long campaign was based on the hope that Tony Blair and his allies would break under pressure. They began to believe they were justified when Labour did seem to have a 'wobbly week' at the beginning of April. John Major said on the Frost programme on 6 April: 'They had three years to prepare their manifesto and in three days it's falling apart.' Michael Heseltine announced on 9 April that 'Tony Blair is cracking under the strain.'

The Conservatives could point to five Labour embarrassments:

1. The situation over union recognition after the adoption of the Social Chapter. There was the party's uncomfortable response that the marginal decisions would be left to a commission.
2. The black hole that Labour's Budget might face if Gordon Brown did not go along with the Conservative plans for the privatisation of Air Traffic Control.
3. Tony Blair's likening of the Scottish parliament's taxing powers to those of an English parish council.
4. The IRA bomb threats that drew attention to the Labour party's past failure to support the Anti-Terrorism Act.
5. A European fishing dispute, which raised difficult questions about how far Labour would go in using obstructiveness in Brussels to defend Britain's fishing interests.

The confidence of politicians often derives as much from a belief in the validity of their arguments as from their standing in the opinion polls. John Major and his immediate staff felt that they had good arguments and that these were now getting through. He remarked to an aide: 'We can win this', and exemplified what he hoped was happening to Mr Blair in his speech at the Albert Hall on Friday 5 April. His large audience cheered his attack on the Labour leader's performance in Scotland.

> It's a man way out of his depth, struggling and losing his grip on his own policy – this is incompetence pure and simple ... With his words Mr Blair both insults Scotland and breaks the promise he's given for a long time ... What a fall is here, from power-house to parish council in one soft phrase too many.

The *Daily Telegraph* on 24 March and the *Daily Mail* on 25 March both ran front-page stories on Labour's alleged plans to boost union power. On 25 March, the Conservatives cancelled a scheduled press conference on education and substituted it with one on the dangers of revived trade union power. Union leaders were indeed discreetly unobtrusive during the campaign. Although Bill Morris of the TGWU and Rodney Bickerstaffe of Unison explicitly denied that they had been silenced, on 3 April the *Daily Mail* reported that there had been a deal to gag the unions. Tony Blair dismissed this as 'complete nonsense' and, in a BBC broadcast the next day, said:

> I did not spend three years turning the Labour Party into a modern party that is true to the principles of progress and justice, which is why the Labour Party was founded, that is facing the modern world, to go backwards, ... So that everybody who is listening to this is clear whether they are a trade unionist or a member of the public or anybody else, we are not going back to those days. We paid a heavy price for it in the past, we are not paying that price again.

There were anxieties that the annual conference of the Scottish TUC, which began on 20 April, would produce old Labour statements embarrassing to Tony Blair. John Edmunds, head of NUGMW, revealed in his speech that he had been asked not to attend. However, nothing seriously embarrassing was said.

When the election came, the country was already plastered with nationwide hoarding advertisements. On 25 March, the Conservatives launched their main election poster, 'Britain Is Booming, Don't Let Labour Blow It'. On 13 April at Milton Keynes, Labour countered with 'Britain Deserves Better'. Labour also put out a series of posters with reassuringly 'positive' messages drawn from their 'Five Pledges', such as 'Young Offenders Will Be Punished and Income Tax Rates Will Not Rise'. Tony Blair, fearing that the negativism of the campaign was breeding a mood of indifference among voters, was insistent that the party's advertising agency, BMP, should provide positive posters.

The Liberal Democrats could not afford a nationwide campaign, but they did have one permanent poster site, adjacent to the Vauxhall Bridge in London. They secured further publicity by sending a number of trailers carrying their 'Punch and Judy' and other advertisements into target seats. From time to time the parties' election broadcasts made news. The BBC and IBA banned the Pro-Life Alliance from showing a film of aborted foetuses in their allotted five minutes; there were attempts to block the BNP effort on the ground that it excited racial hatred; and the Natural Law Party's belief in yogic flying excited hilarity.

The Conservatives made an impact with John Major's impromptu exposition of his European position (see p. 105). In a break with recent practice, three of their five broadcasts were straight-to-camera appeals by the Prime Minister. The party was also proud of their parable, likening the Labour Party to a group planting a tree without roots. The Labour Party ran into criticism for its image of a sad bulldog, revivified by the arrival of Labour; its biographic presentation of Blair was better received. The Liberal Democrat picture of the main party fight as a Punch and Judy show drew headlines, as did their 'Ashdown, the movie' broadcast. (see pp. 149–154)

On 18 April there was an unexpected announcement of Dissolution Honours. Twenty peerages went to retiring MPs, mainly eminent front-benchers, but a couple of the new Lords had been among the eight Labour MPs who had belatedly announced that they were not standing again. These last-minute vacancies were filled amid some controversy from shortlists provided by the party's national executive and there were some wry comments about finding places for New Labour favourites. Among those who obtained seats in the final scramble for Commons' nominations were Alan Howarth, who had crossed the floor from the Conservatives; Yvette Cooper, a former assistant to Gordon Brown; Rosemary McKenna, previously a leader of Scottish local authorities; and Alan Johnson, head of the Communications Workers Union and a staunch Blairite. Sir Ray Powell, a former Labour whip, standing again in Ogmore, alleged that Ron Davies, the Shadow Welsh Secretary, had offered him a peerage if he would stand down. Mr Davies flatly denied the story.

When the lists closed on 18 April, a record 3724 candidates had been nominated, 825 more than in 1992. The Conservatives, Labour and Liberal Democrats fought every seat in mainland Britain except Speaker Boothroyd's in West Bromwich and Neil Hamilton's in Tatton. The SNP and Plaid Cymru were present throughout their own territories.

The Referendum Party, with 547 candidates, represented the largest-ever minor party intervention. It was followed by the UK Independence Party with 194, and the Natural Law Party with 195. But five further parties put up over fifty candidates each to secure a broadcast, including the Greens (95), Socialist Labour (64), the British National Party (57), the Liberals (54), and the Pro-Life Alliance (53). There were also interventions from the Scottish Socialist Alliance (16) and other left-wing dissidents, as well as from over 200 other more or less independent 'Independents'.

However, apart from Martin Bell in Tatton and Sir James Goldsmith in Putney, none of the lesser candidates attracted any widespread attention. The Referendum Party, with repeated advertisements in the national press, made some mark but, as the results showed, it was usually only by special local effort that deposits were saved.

The Referendum Party did mount the largest meeting of the campaign, a rally of 7000 at Alexandra Palace on 13 April, which heard more xenophobic oratory than Sir James Goldsmith may have intended. Sir James launched his party's manifesto at the Cornish port of Newlyn on 8 April to highlight the local grievance against the EU's Common Fisheries Policy. There was no suggestion during the campaign of the long-standing malady which led to his death on 19 July.

Paul Sykes, a Yorkshire millionaire, paid for nationwide press advertisements and by the end of the campaign had given money to the local Conservative associates of the 317 candidates who had committed themselves to oppose a single currency. It was said that, leaving out government ministers, only 30 candidates in seats won in 1992 had rejected his largesse. In the final week Mr Sykes appealed to Sir James Goldsmith to get his standard-bearers to withdraw in favour of any Conservatives who had made their opposition to a single currency plain. Sir James rebuffed him, saying that the Referendum Party had a wider remit than blocking EMU.

At his only national press conference on 29 April Sir James announced that, whatever happened on 1 May, his party would continue so as to provide a 'conduit for mobilisation against future betrayal'.

Some Conservatives, most notably Kenneth Clarke and Michael Heseltine, believed that the election should be about the economy. Unemployment was falling, inflation and interest rates were low, growth was accelerating; on every index Britain had the best recent record of any major European economy. This was a theme to which John Major and his colleagues returned constantly – yet it made few headlines. Some suggested that the party was somewhat inhibited by Kenneth Clarke's reluctance to emphasise the British achievement by attacking Europe's performance. In fact, the attack on the economy was rarely given priority by Central Office. For example, it took two weeks for the Conservatives to find a press conference slot to launch the Treasury's fully worked-up assault on Labour's July Budget.

LABOUR AND THE LIBERAL DEMOCRATS HAVE PROMISED TO GIVE AWAY MORE POWER TO BRUSSELS AND THE EUROPEAN BANKERS.

●

CONSERVATIVE MPs WILL VOTE AGAINST A SINGLE CURRENCY AND FURTHER INTERFERENCE FROM BRUSSELS.

●

IF YOU DON'T WANT THIS COUNTRY RUN BY BRUSSELS YOU *MUST* VOTE CONSERVATIVE.

●

WITH YOUR SUPPORT WE CAN RETAIN OUR NATION'S SOVEREIGNTY.

Advertisement placed by Paul Sykes, Esplanade, Harrogate. HG2 0LN

Paul Sykes, a Yorkshire millionaire, paid for nationwide press advertisements.

It was, of course, Europe that took most media space, coming to the fore time and again during the campaign. John Major had resisted heavy pressure from Cabinet colleagues, back-benchers, Central Office and the advertising team, as well as from the Conservative-supporting press, to come out squarely against a single currency, but, even if he had been so minded, he could not have done so without losing Kenneth Clarke, as well as risking the loss of Michael Heseltine and others. He insisted on a manifesto that adhered firmly to the 'negotiate and then decide' line agreed in Cabinet the previous autumn.

However, the line was under constant battering from the Conservative press as well as from the Referendum and UK Independence parties and, more seriously, from his own candidates. As their constituency addresses appeared, it became plain that a majority were implacably opposed to any possibility of UK entry into EMU. Over the period 12–16 April, leading back-benchers produced statements to the effect that under no circumstances would they vote to accept the Euro in place of the pound.

Dame Angela Rumbold, a Vice-Chairman of the party, and Angela Browning, a junior Treasury Minister, started the rush, but the issue came to a head when two junior ministers, John Horam and James Paice, issued addresses which said 'never' to EMU. Some people in Central Office urged that Mr Major should sack them for breaching collective Cabinet responsibility, but, after some hesitation, Mr Major refrained, fearing that he would then be forced to sack several more. Instead he apologised for the dissidents, saying that they had been 'very naïve'. Senior Cabinet colleagues also came to the brink of disloyalty: Peter Lilley, asked if he could ever envisage supporting EMU, answered 'I have a very vivid imagination, so I can envisage almost anything', and Michael Howard said on the BBC's *Election Call* on 21 April that 'The Amsterdam Summit ... would indeed put our survival as a nation state in question.'

The pro-Europeans in the Conservative Party were not altogether mute. On 22 March it was reported that more than 50 MPs had written to Mr Major shortly before the election was called demanding that the government stick to the agreed policy on Europe.

The pressure grew. On Tuesday 15 April, John Major returned from a particularly successful question-and-answer session at Westminster Hall sponsored by *The Times*. That evening he had remarked to a colleague: 'You know we are not going to win. What will be my place in history?' No sooner had he entered Downing Street than Brian Mawhinney was on the phone with the bad news that junior ministers had broken the government line on the single currency. Although Central Office strategists agreed among themselves that Mr Major should confront the issue at his next morning press conference, it was an early morning call from Lord Cranborne that spurred him. When his staff visited him at 7.30 a.m. on 16 April he was already rehearsing his arguments, having decided to junk the planned press conference agenda lauding the fall in unemployment and instead to launch into what became the most memorable utterance of the campaign – a passionately ambivalent statement on the pros and cons of considering monetary union.

Whether you agree with me or disagree with me, like me or loathe me, don't bind my hands when I am negotiating on behalf of the British people.

John Major's stand was not activated simply by a wish to keep Kenneth Clarke and Michael Heseltine on board. Over the preceding months he had increasingly come to doubt that the single currency would go ahead as scheduled, and he did not envisage himself signing up. Nevertheless, he could not see any national interest being served by closing the door at this stage; he could do most to stop EMU by staying within the negotiations. He was certainly concerned that foreign investment might be hurt by any negative pronouncement. A 'not yet' decision could easily be seen as 'never' and tantamount to a withdrawal from the European Union. Britain already had an opt-out from EMU, and John Major simply thought it pointless to throw away the option. The argument was coherent, and Major repeated it, slightly less eloquently, in a hastily improvised election broadcast that night, but it did not persuade the Euro-sceptics and it was difficult to sell to the electorate.

The Conservatives were in a dilemma over Europe. There were ministers who claimed – and some actually thought – that a Labour victory might result in Britain's absorption into a federal European state, yet they could not argue this too vigorously because of the pro-European views of Kenneth Clarke and Michael Heseltine. Some ministers, notably Mr Clarke, complained that the intense media interest in Europe was really about Conservative divisions, and that voters were not really bothered by the issue, yet on 16 April, when he upstaged the favourable unemployment figures by his impassioned statement on his EMU stand, John Major said: 'There is no doubt in my mind that [the single currency] is the single most important decision that any government has been asked to make for generations.'

Several months before the campaign, Brian Mawhinney had failed to shift John Major from his 'negotiate and then decide' line. Questions about what would happen when candidates repudiated the government position had not been answered at Number 10. Mr Major hoped that, by confronting the issue head-on, as he had confronted sleaze eight days earlier, he could dampen things down, but the media had the bit between their teeth. *The Times* and the *Daily Telegraph* published daily lists of Conservative candidates who were defying Mr Major's line. The final *Daily Telegraph* tally, based on 385 candidates, found only three pro-European statements – Sir Edward Heath, Hugh Dykes and Ian Taylor stayed loyal to the dream of 1972.

Against any common currency	190
Anti-Europe tone, not specific	26
Anti-Brussels tone, not specific	52
Neutral	2
Support government line	57
No mention of Europe	51
Pro-Europe	3

On 17 April, in a casual answer to Channel 4's Elinor Goodman at the morning press conference, Mr Major said he would allow Conservatives a free vote on EMU. In a BBC interview at lunchtime Kenneth Clarke revealed that he had not been consulted on this development. At 5 p.m. Michael Heseltine added to the confusion by saying that a free vote was only a possibility.

On 18 April, the Conservatives produced the most controversial advertisement of the election, showing Tony Blair as a ventriloquist's dummy on Chancellor Kohl's knee. The original drawing was sketched by Michael Heseltine, who, as the media emphasised, had previously been seen as a pro-European. Edwina Currie immediately denounced the advertisement as 'puerile' and was soon joined by heavier Conservative guns. Ian Taylor, a junior minister, publicly criticised it. Lord Howe described it as 'damaging' and Sir Edward Heath condemned it as 'abhorrent', saying that those responsible should be sacked. Kenneth Clarke made it plain that he had not been consulted and called the xenophobia of the Referendum Party 'paranoid nonsense'. The Referendum Party then produced a drawing of Mr Blair sitting on one of Chancellor Kohl's knees, with an even more diminutive Major sitting on the other (see plate 1).

European controversies were further stoked when Jacques Santer, the President of the European Commission, in an ill-timed speech on 21 April, said that too many people were bashing Europe and overlooking its achievements. He labelled Euro-sceptics as 'doom merchants' – but, at the last minute, he refrained from attacking the Conservatives' Kohl poster.

Jacques Santer's intervention was widely resented and served only to harden attitudes towards Europe. John Major said that President Santer's remarks reinforced the Conservatives' case. Tony Blair, who had also ruled out any British participation in a single currency based on fudged criteria, described them as foolish, while Robin Cook (who on 6 April had gone further than his colleagues in expressing scepticism about an early entry into EMU) said: 'Labour has set firm limits to European integration.' When the question of fishing quotas came up at Brussels on 15 April, Tony Blair indicated that he too would consider using a blocking veto in the Intergovernmental Conference (IGC) negotiations at the June Amsterdam summit.

Repeatedly the Conservatives attacked Labour's competence to negotiate in Europe. In his Albert Hall speech, John Major said: 'If you are not prepared to be isolated in Europe, you have no right to lead your country.' Mr Major drew attention to Tony Blair's inexperience and his advance abandonment of his bargaining position on the Social Chapter. On 18 April he said that sending Mr Blair to meet other European leaders would be like 'sending a fly to a spiders' convention'. Tony Blair visibly moved to a tougher position during the campaign, stating on 20 April that 'you must always be prepared to be isolated if it is in the national interest'.

A final European twist came on 29 April when Yves de Silguy, the Brussels commissioner dealing with monetary union, suggested that if the UK opted out of a European currency the country would be left in the cold – outside a new G3 relationship between the dollar, yen, and Euro. Both John Major and Tony Blair rejected M. de Silguy's remarks, but for John Redwood they showed that the Commission was planning a single European government.

A late initiative by the Conservatives on 24 April was the revelation of Labour's 'War Book', which had been leaked to them some months earlier. However it contained little that would surprise or shock; it showed that Labour had followed its planned strategy.

On 24 April the Labour Party launched an attack on Conservative pensions policy, suggesting that the Lilley initiative of March, echoed in the manifesto, implied the end of the state pension to which everyone was entitled. The Conservatives saw this as Labour's reaction to its sharp drop in the ICM poll the previous day, which had cut their lead to 5 per cent. They were appalled when they studied its impact; their own tracking polls and focus groups suggested an astonishing dip in Conservative support among the over-65s. Other pollsters failed to find any such reaction. At the morning press conference, Major, Mawhinney and Dorrell accused Labour of 'lying' nine times. Peter Lilley described Tony Blair's 'wild accusations' as 'simply bunkum'. Labour sources firmly deny that there was anything reactive about the launch of their pensions challenge, which had long been planned as an element in their final assault on the 'nightmare' of a fifth Conservative term. In any case, their own polls flatly contradicted ICM's findings, as did the rolling Gallup poll in the *Daily Telegraph*.

Michael Heseltine complained of 'playing on the fears of the elderly' and John Major angrily demanded a retraction of Labour's falsehoods, which he said were part of a carefully calculated and prepared campaign to frighten pensioners into believing that their security and state retirement pension was at risk. He expressed genuine surprise at the 'brazen' conduct of Tony Blair when the latter unequivocally reiterated that the purpose of the Tories proposals was to 'replace the basic state pension with a private pension'.

The Labour Party pursued celebrity endorsements to a greater degree than the Conservatives; their particular focus was on business. Anita Roddick (Body Shop), Alan Sugar (Amstrad) and Geoff Robinson (Granada) were among those explicitly endorsing the need for a Labour victory. Richard Branson (Virgin), without saying how he would vote, travelled ostentatiously on Tony Blair's train. This was a photo-opportunity much prized by both men. Mr Branson gained publicity for his privatised Virgin railway company, while Mr Blair gained the endorsement of the most prominent of entrepreneurs. Labour fought shy of being too obviously linked with the 'luvvies' of the entertainment world, but on 22 April they held their daily press conference in a City TV studio to launch, with Lord Attenborough and many other famous faces, their programme for the arts. This included a proposal to divert £1bn of Lottery money to health and education.

On 7 April, Tony Blair made a high-profile visit to the City of London to deliver a speech at the Corn Exchange. In it he called for a 'third way' between state control of the economy and a *laissez-faire* approach, saying: 'What counts is what works'. A Labour government would be committed to tax cuts and flexible labour markets, and its general presumption would be that 'economic activity is best left to the private sector' – the 'post-war Keynesian dream is well and truly buried'. These themes were elaborated on 11 April, when Mr Blair launched Labour's business manifesto, *Equipping Britain for the Future*. He claimed that it demonstrated that New Labour would work in partnership with business, and it committed the party to, amongst other things, an inflation target of 2.5 per cent or less, tough rules on borrowing and spending, public–private co-operation to modernise transport, and a skilled workforce through cutting class sizes and setting literacy targets. To mark the launch, 84 businessmen wrote a letter to *The Times* saying that small businesses could 'look forward with confidence to a profitable future with a Labour government'.

Devolution and constitutional reform intruded intermittently in the campaign. John Major saw his stress on the unity of the United Kingdom as a key element in his 1992 victory and, together with Michael Forsyth and others, spoke repeatedly of the dangers of a tax-raising Scottish parliament. Tony Blair, though committed to devolution, faced his roughest press conference of the campaign in Edinburgh on 4 April. He emphasised that the Labour party was bound in Scotland, as everywhere else, to keep to its pledge not to increase income tax rates. In a *Scotsman* interview he had, unhappily, likened the spending powers of the proposed Edinburgh parliament to those of the smallest English parish council, adding: 'Sovereignty rests with me as an English MP, and that's the way it will stay.' The Conservatives called his remarks 'ludicrous and patronising', and Alex Salmond for the SNP said that they exposed Tony Blair's 'contempt and derision' for Scotland. Jim Wallace for the Liberal Democrats said that the Labour leader had betrayed his lack of 'any gut conviction' that there should be a parliament in Edinburgh.

Northern Ireland takes part simultaneously in United Kingdom elections but it sees a very different kind of battle. In some of its 18 seats the contest was between rival versions of Unionism or between rival versions of Republicanism. In none was there a collision between the main UK parties. Gerry Adams fought to recover the West Belfast seat from which he had been ousted in 1992; that contest, together with Martin McGuinness's attempt to divert to Sinn Fein enough SDLP votes to gain Mid-Ulster from the Democratic Unionists, provided the main focus of interest.

Sinn Fein's refusal to call a cease-fire hung over the election. On two occasions (26 March and 18 April) bomb threats near to motorways and main railway lines caused massive disruption in the Midlands. On 29 March another bomb threat led to the postponement of the most famous horse race in the world, the Grand National. The British parties maintained bipartisanship, despite Michael Howard's innuendo that Labour had been soft over the Prevention of Terrorism Act. On 30 March, Mo Mowlem, the Shadow Secretary for Northern Ireland, indicated on Radio Ulster that Labour would be more flexible in getting a violence-renouncing Sinn Fein to the conference table. Most Unionists accused her of naivety, but others, even David Ervine of the Progressive Unionists, sprang to her defence.

Tony Blair had declared that 'education, education, education' would be his priority. The cry was taken up by other parties: the leaders frequently visited schools for photo-opportunities, and the schoolteachers' conferences over Easter gave prominence to the subject. David Blunkett, Labour's Shadow Education spokesman, warned the unions not to bully him. The Liberal Democrats exploited their moral advantage in being willing to spend more money to bring down class sizes, to add to nursery education and to provide more books. Labour's stress on ending the new nursery voucher scheme and abolishing assisted places at independent schools contrasted with the Conservatives' dream of a grammar school in every town. Although education came second in polls seeking 'the most important issue', and was much mentioned on the doorstep, close argument on the subject was rarely pursued.

Some issues were little heard during the campaign. A tough report on the handling of a serious food-poisoning outbreak in Scotland passed with scant notice. The vexed issue of fox-hunting was not raised at the national level. The parties did not react strongly to a controversial report (8 April) from the Churches on the moral evil of unemployment. More attention was given to the voting intentions of pop music's Spice Girls, and John Major won headlines on 15 April by his inability to give the names of the five singers.

On 25 March, Nicholas Budgen, Enoch Powell's successor in Wolverhampton, was rebuked by John Major for raising the question of immigration controls; he replied with a spirited article defending the right of an MP to discuss problems of concern to the constituents. However, except for the British National Party in London's East End, and some rival ethnic candidates in Bradford West and Glasgow Govan, racial issues played no part in the national campaign. Michael Howard planned to make an outspoken speech on immigration, but Downing Street sat on it and it was not delivered. After a discussion with John Major, Mr Howard settled for a lower-key interview with the *Daily Telegraph*.

On 28 April John Major cancelled his appearance in *ITV 500* and, in a final grand gesture, spanned the nation with the theme '72 hours to save the Union'. In the morning he appeared in Belfast as the first prime minister to visit Ireland during a general election. At lunchtime in Edinburgh he reiterated his anti-devolution message, supporting the beleaguered Michael Forsyth. In the afternoon he stood on the Menai suspension bridge beside William Hague, his non-Welsh Secretary for Wales. He ended the trip with an open-air meeting on St Stephen's Green outside parliament, warning supporters that they had '72 hours to make sure that the system of government that has prevailed in this country for a very long time is protected and enshrined'.

As the campaign drew to its close, it became harder to pretend that the Conservatives had a chance. The *Sunday Telegraph*'s headline on 27 April was: 'It's All Over, Admit Top Tories'. Michael Heseltine made a gallant effort on the final Tuesday to show that if all the 'don't knows' came down on the right side, and if the opinion polls were as wrong as they had been in 1992, the Conservatives would have a majority of 60, but during the last weekend, Tony Garrett, the Director of Campaigning, forecast a Labour victory with a majority of between 60 and 80. Philip Gould told Tony Blair that Labour would end 10 per cent ahead, while the Liberal Democrats were confident of a breakthrough in seats.

The media scented a Conservative defeat and began to launch stories about candidates positioning themselves for the coming leadership struggle and strategy disagreements between Brian Mawhinney and Maurice Saatchi.

Blair   Major
Howard Hague Heseltine Redwood Portillo

As polling day approached speculation developed about a struggle for the Conservative leadership.

Peter Brookes, *The Times*, 29 April 1997

On 28 April the *Daily Telegraph* headline was: 'Tory Squabbling Mars Final Phase'. It was reported that John Major had vetoed a final £5m publicity blitz, not wanting to saddle his successor with debt, but there were full-page advertisements in the broadsheets in the last two days from the Referendum Party, from Paul Sykes, and from the Conservatives. Revealingly, Labour confined its last newspaper advertisements to the tabloids (see p. 182).

On the whole, the Conservatives were resolute in maintaining a common front as disaster loomed. Equally, the Labour Party refrained from triumphalism until it leaked out on 28 April that the party had booked the Royal Festival Hall for an election night celebration.

On election eve, Tony Blair had an ecstatic homecoming to his Sedgefield constituency, urging people to come out and support Labour if they didn't want to wake up on Friday 2 May and be confronted with another five years of the

> most discredited and sleazy government ... It is 24 hours to save our NHS, 24 hours to give our children the education they need, 24 hours to give hope to our young people, security to our elderly ...

For me, Britain is the best country in the world in which to live.

You can be sure I will keep our great United Kingdom as one country.

You can be sure I will not let Britain go into a Federal Europe.

You can be sure I would give Britain a referendum on a single currency.

You can be sure I will keep prices down and the cost of your mortgage low.

You can be sure I will cut your taxes when we safely can, so you have more money to spend as you wish.

You can be sure I will help you to own more, save more, and pass it on to your children.

You can be sure I will give every four year-old a voucher for nursery education.

You can be sure I will demand higher standards from every school and give every parent more choice.

You can be sure I will give every school-leaver the further education or training they need.

You can be sure I will think first of the victims of crime and take repeat offenders off the streets.

You can be sure I will provide the money for more police to keep us safer on the streets.

You can be sure I will improve our National Health Service, freely available to all, with more money year by year.

You can be sure I will always protect the state retirement pension and offer dignity and security to the elderly.

You can be sure I will govern for everyone.

On Thursday, be sure you mark your cross where you know you can place your trust.

You can be sure I will be true to Britain.

Published by Conservative Central Office, 32 Smith Square, London SW1P 3HH.

Conservatives last week advertisement.

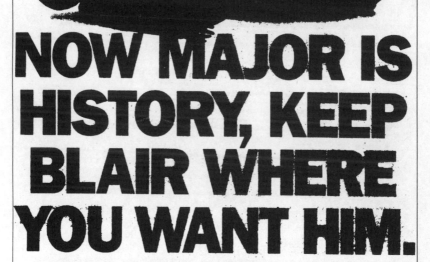

Labour's last week advertisement

Paddy Ashdown, in a final statement, promised that the Liberal Democrats would help to make a 'parliament of historic reform' in the next five years.

John Major, meanwhile, returned to Huntingdon via Stevenage, where he faced one of the few rough meetings of the campaign. He spoke of low inflation, low mortgages and falling unemployment, and appealed to people not, in one careless moment, to 'throw our success away'.

The weather on polling day was good and no significant incidents marred the voting, but reports of a low turnout were to be confirmed: it fell in all but ten mainland seats. 71.2 per cent of the registered UK electorate cast valid votes, in contrast to 77.7 per cent in 1992.

At 10 p.m. on 1 May, the exit polls commissioned by the BBC and ITN confirmed the message which the opinion surveys had so long been giving – there was a massive swing to Labour. Sunderland South at 10.47 p.m. was the first seat to complete its count. Other safe seats followed, and it was not until 12.19 a.m. that Labour could celebrate its first gain: Birmingham Edgbaston was won by Labour for the first time ever on a 10 per cent swing. Gains soon came thick and fast. The Conservatives were eliminated from every seat they held in Scotland, Wales and the provincial cities. It was not only Labour that won: the Scottish Nationalist vote stayed at 22 per cent, but their representation rose from three in 1992 to six; the Liberal Democrats, on a lower vote (17 per cent) won a surprising 46 seats, dominating the south-

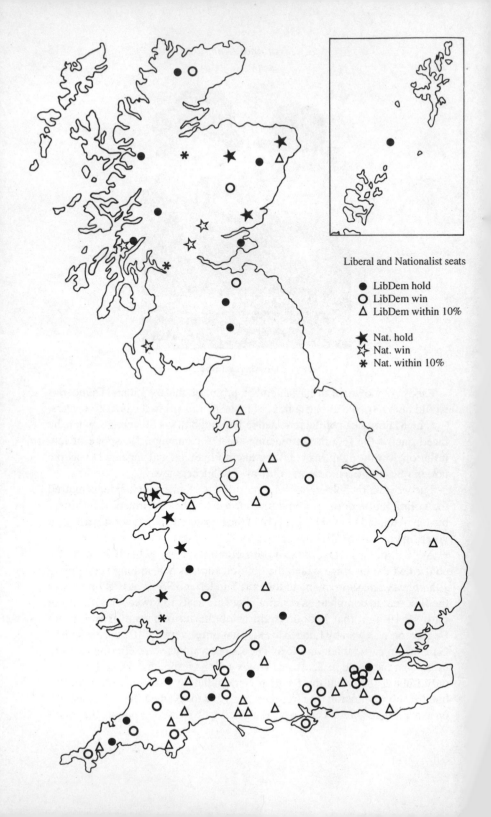

Liberal and Nationalist seats

● LibDem hold
○ LibDem win
△ LibDem within 10%

★ Nat. hold
☆ Nat. win
✳ Nat. within 10%

THE  TIMES 35ᵖ

No. 65,879 FRIDAY MAY 2 1997

Landslide forecast for Labour

Tories facing worst defeat this century, say TV exit polls

Election 97

Results special

Plus 97
The decline of a boxing legend
Review
Mike Newell meets The Mob

45p
Friday
May 2
1997
Published in London and Manchester

The **Guardian**

NEWSPAPER OF THE YEAR

OUT: Portillo – Rifkind – Lang – Forsyth – Mellor – Lamont – Hamilton – Waldegrave

Blair's crushing triumph

The Daily Telegraph

Newspaper of the Year

FINAL No. 44,126   **Britain's biggest-selling quality daily**   Friday, May 2, 1997 45p

Blair wins by a landslide

FINANCIAL TIMES

Landslide victory for Labour

Blair's Britain is born

Big majority breaks 18 years of Tory rule

Anthony Bevins
Police & Editor

west but also having unexpected triumphs in Harrogate, in Sheffield Hallam, in five south-west London suburbs, in Lewes, and finally, by only two votes, in Winchester;[3] in Tatton, Martin Bell triumphed over Neil Hamilton; and in Northern Ireland, the Republican vote went up, with Sinn Fein (+6 per cent) gaining at the expense of the SDLP. Gerry Adams and Martin McGuinness won.

The swing of 10 per cent from Conservative to Labour far exceeded anything seen since the war; it almost matched the 1945 record swing of 12 per cent. The number of Cabinet ministers defeated, seven, was a record. The casualties included four men who might have aspired to the Conservative leadership had they survived; Ian Lang, Malcolm Rifkind, Michael Forsyth and, most surprisingly, Michael Portillo, William Waldegrave, Tony Newton and Roger Freeman also fell.

The 330th Labour victory in seats came at 3.10 a.m. (only 28 constituencies, mainly in Northern Ireland, waited until Friday to count). In the end Labour had won 418 seats – a clear majority of 179, based on a clear lead of 12.5 per cent over the Conservatives – the biggest victory since 1935. The only comfort for the Conservatives lay in recovering control of seven County Councils.

The Blairs flew down to London in the small hours in time to join a dawn victory rally of the Labour faithful at the Royal Festival Hall. Mr Blair had little rest because at 11.30 a.m. on Friday 2 May, John Major went to Buckingham Palace to resign. Tony Blair saw the Queen at 12.30p.m. and became the fifth Labour prime minister, but the one with the greatest support in the House of Commons. He entered Downing Street to a tumultuous welcome. On the doorstep of Number 10 he made his final election speech.

We have secured a mandate to bring the nation together – to unite us – one Britain, one nation in which our ambition for ourselves is matched by our sense of compassion and decency and duty towards others ... Today we are charged with the deep responsibility of government. Today, enough of talking; now is the time to do.

NOTES

1. The whole issue was discussed in S. Coleman, *Television Debates: An Evaluation and a Proposal* (March 1997). An account of the negotiations by Tony Hall and Anne Sloman, the two BBC negotiators, appeared in the *Independent* on 2 July 1997.
2. The full text of the manifestos is available in *The Times Guide to the House of Commons May 1997* (1997).
3. This produced a petition and the first demand for a scrutiny of ballot papers since 1922.

7 Public Polls and Private Polls

The election provided a major challenge to the opinion polls. The accuracy of their voting forecasts offers the most public test of the reliability of their methods as market researchers – and it is as market researchers that they earn their living. Their credibility had been seriously damaged by the 1992 election. The four surveys published on 9 April 1992 had suggested a narrow Labour lead, ranging between 3 per cent and –0.5 per cent. In the actual vote the Conservatives won by 7.6 per cent. The pollsters were much mocked, and broadcasters and newspapers decided to give their surveys less prominence. However, all the main broadsheet newspapers, in some cases after a pause, continued to publish polls on voting intentions and their findings, showing the government far behind, were to overshadow the politics of the next five years and the 1997 election campaign.

Nonetheless, although consciousness of Labour's overwhelming lead permeated the period, the error in 1992 meant that politicians and journalists refused fully to accept their clear message – that Labour was heading for a landslide victory.

The pollsters themselves had, of course, been shaken by what happened and took steps to examine and improve their methods. They knew that another debacle in 1997 would inflict major damage on their profession. A committee set up by the Market Research Society reported, in 1994, that there had been four main sources of error:

1. *Unrepresentative selection of respondents.* All the pollsters were found to have set quotas that resulted in too few interviews with two-car owners, and too many with council tenants.
2. *A late swing.* Plainly there was a small swing in the final hours between the interviews and the vote, partially linked to differential turnout.
3. *A 'spiral of silence'.* There was a refusal by some voters, disproportionately older and more Conservative, to admit to their voting preference or to be interviewed at all.
4. *Selective participation.* There was a small error due to under-registration which mainly affected Labour voters and was partly attributable to the poll tax.

The MRS committee discounted as unimportant some common explanations: they found no significant evidence of lying by respondents or of results being influenced by the order of questions, or by the method of interviewing, or by the size of the sample.[1]

Up to 1992 there had been a consensus on method in the polling industry. There was general agreement on face-to-face interviews, on ignoring 'don't knows' and 'won't says', and on the quota selection of respondents. In the aftermath of 1992 some or all of these were abandoned or modified by each of the pollsters – though in differing ways.

Anxious to restore their reputation, the five companies which regularly published political polls conducted various experiments. ICM, appearing in the *Guardian*, tried using secret ballots to reassure its respondents before turning to telephone polling (94 per cent of the population were approuchable by telephone); they also introduced adjustments, based partly on reports of past voting and partly on answers to other questions, to allow for refusals and don't knows. At some points in 1994 these adjustments reduced the Labour lead by up to 15 percentage points. By 1997, after some changes in procedure, the adjustment was producing a difference of only 4 percentage points or less.

Gallup, in the *Daily Telegraph*, also switched at the end of 1996 to telephone polls, using random digit dialling to reach ex-directory numbers.

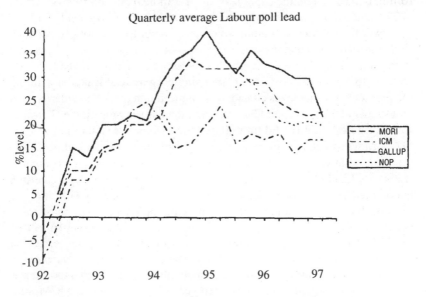

Figure 7.1 Average poll lead 1992–97

Gallup, in addition, made a small adjustment to allow for the bias caused by refusals.

NOP, in the *Sunday Times* from 1995, and Harris, in the *Independent* from late 1996, continued to use face-to-face quota polls, but they too made small adjustments for presumed non-response. MORI in *The Times* was alone in headlining its unadjusted figures; however it used a larger number of smaller sampling points, giving tighter control over the characteristics of the sample.

Figure 7.1 records the contrast between the rival headline figures, but it also underlines the solidity of Labour's lead from 1993 to 1997. The government went into the 1997 election with an average deficit of 22 per cent – compared to 1 per cent in 1992. The worst comparable figures from the past were from 1951 (Labour deficit 11 per cent); 1964 (Conservative deficit 1 per cent); and 1979 (Labour deficit 10 per cent). The largest previous gap at the start of a campaign was Mrs Thatcher's 16 per cent lead over Labour in 1983.

Table 7.1 shows the nationwide polls on voting intentions published during the campaign. ICM's findings appeared every Wednesday in the *Guardian* and on Sundays in the *Observer*; MORI's were in the *The Times* every Thursday. Harris's were in the *Independent* every Friday, while NOP's were reported in the *Sunday Times*. Gallup surveys initially appeared in the *Daily Telegraph* on Fridays but at the beginning of April they moved to a rolling poll, based on the average of the last three days' interviews.

The average Labour lead drifted downwards from 22 per cent to 15 per cent over the six weeks. But only one survey recorded it below 10 per cent. That was in the poll that made most news – the ICM survey which appeared in the *Guardian* on 23 April, eight days before the vote; it showed Labour's lead cut to 5 per cent. As rumours of a single figure lead leaked out during the previous day there was considerable agitation in party headquarters and newspaper offices. Alastair Campbell and then others rang up the *Guardian* for the figures – but the Editor only released the precise data in time to let ITN's *News at Ten* announce them. The poll drew ecstatic headlines in the pro-Conservative papers: '5%: Labour's Lead In Free Fall' (*Express*); and 'Labour's Lead Crashes In The Polls' (*Daily Mail*). The *Daily Telegraph* led on the front page with, 'Labour's Lead Collapses In New Poll', despite the fact that its own Gallup poll was showing the Labour lead rising to 21 per cent on the same page. Over the following days no other survey supported the ICM findings and their failure to do so had a depressing effect on Conservative morale (see p. 108). John Curtice wrote in the *Guardian* on 17 April: 'For an industry hoping to reclaim public confidence after the disaster of 1992, the divergent results published yesterday by Gallup and ICM were a severe embarrassment.'

Table 7.1 Opinion polls on voting intentions, 23 March –1 May

Opinion Polls	Date pub	Sample size	Field dates	Con (%)	Lab (%)	Lib Dem (%)	Con lead over Lab
Gallup/*S. Telegraph*	23.3	985	19/21.3	29	54	10	-25
Harris/*Independent*	28.3	1,096	20/24.3	30	54	11	-24
MORI/*Times*	27.3	1,932	21/24.3	29	50	14	-21
Harris/*Independent*	4.4	1,091	27/31.3	28	52	14	-24
Gallup/*D. Telegraph*	4.4	1,126	26.3/2.4	31	52	11	-21
ICM/*Guardian*	2.4	1,200	29/31.3	32	46	17	-14
MORI/*Times*	3.4	1,118	1.4	28	55	11	-27
Gallup/*C4 News*	9.4	1,035	1/3.4	30	54	11	-24
MORI/*Ind on S./S. Mirror*	6.4	1,069	2/3.4	30	55	9	-25
ICM/*Observer*	6.4	1,793	2/4.4	33	48	14	-15
NOP/*Sunday Times*	6.4	1,575	3.4	28	52	12	-24
NOP/*Reuters*	7.4	1,088	4.4	30	51	11	21
Gallup/*D. Telegraph*	7.4	1,026	4/6.4	32	53	10	-21
Harris/*Independent*	11.4	1,138	4/7.4	28	52	14	-24
ICM/*Guardian*	9.4	1,022	6/7.4	34	46	15	-12
Gallup/*D. Telegraph*	10.4	1,019	7/9.4	30	53	11	-23
MORI/*Times*	10.4	1,114	8.4	34	49	12	-15
ICM/*Observer*	13.4	1,002	9/11.4	32	48	15	-16
Gallup/*S. Telegraph*	13.4	1,043	9/12.4	33	49	12	-16
NOP/*Sunday Times*	13.4	1,595	11.4	28	48	17	-20
MORI/*Eve. Standard*	15.4	1,778	11/14.4	29	50	15	-21
Harris/*Independent*	18.4	1,136	11/14.4	31	49	13	-18
Gallup/*D. Telegraph*	16.4	1,025	12/15.4	30	51	12	-21
ICM/*Guardian*	16.4	1,007	13/14.4	31	45	19	-14
MORI/*Times*	17.4	1,137	15.4	32	49	13	-17
Gallup/*C4 News*	23.4	1,120	18/22.4	31	50	13	-19
Gallup/*D. Telegraph*	19.4	1,018	15/18.4	32	50	13	-18
ICM/*Observer*	20.4	1,000	16/18.4	32	47	16	-15
NOP/*Sunday Times*	20.4	1,595	18.4	31	45	17	-14
Harris/*Independent*	25.4	1,177	17/21.4	30	48	15	-18
Gallup/*D. Telegraph*	22.4	1,294	18/21.4	32	48	12	-16
ICM/*Guardian*	23.4	1,004	20/21.4	37	42	14	-5
MORI/*Times*	24.4	1,133	22.4	27	48	17	-21
Gallup/*D. Telegraph*	24.4	1,069	21/23.4	30	50	12	-20
MORI/*Ind on S./S. Mirror*	27.4	941	23/24.4	29	53	12	-24
Gallup/*D. Telegraph*	26.4	1,012	23/25.4	32	48	14	-16
ICM/*Observer*	27.4	1,000	23/25.4	32	47	16	-15
NOP/*Sunday Times*	27.4	1,588	25.4	29	47	16	-18
Gallup/*C4 News*	29.4	1,466	24/28.4	31	49	14	-18
Gallup/*D. Telegraph*	28.4	1,028	25/27.4	30	49	14	-19
Harris/*Independent*	1.5	1,154	27/29.4	31	48	15	-17
Gallup/*D. Telegraph*	30.4	1,038	28/29.4	31	51	13	-20
NOP/*Reuters*	1.5	1,093	29.4	28	50	14	-22
MORI/*Times*	1.5	2,304	29/30.4	28	48	16	-20
ICM/*Guardian*	1.5	1,555	29/30.4	33	43	18	-10
Gallup/*D. Telegraph*	1.5	1,849	30.4	33	47	14	-14
MORI/*Eve. Standard*	1.5	1,501	30.4	29	47	19	-18

A notable polling enterprise emerged on the final Sunday when the *Observer* commissioned ICM to explore tactical voting. Surveys were conducted in 16 seats where the division of the anti-Conservative vote between Liberal Democrat and Labour might make a vital difference. The survey was sponsored jointly by *Scotland on Sunday*, which was able to report the likely defeat of each of the three Scottish Cabinet members. The findings appeared under the *Observer*'s partisan headline: 'What You Can Do To Secure A Total Tory Defeat'. The surveys spotted the correct winner in 12 of the seats – and, in one or two of the four where Labour jumped from third to first place, these polls may actually have decided the result.

Apart from this *Observer* operation there were fewer constituency polls than in past elections, but local surveys did indicate that there would be no swing back from the Wirral South by-election result (MORI/*Sun* 31 March) and that Neil Hamilton was heading for defeat in Tatton (MORI/*Sun* 9 April, ICM/*Observer* 20 April), while Piers Merchant would survive in Beckenham (ICM/*Observer* 6 April). Other surveys confirmed what the nationwide polls suggested, with comfortable Labour victories in Loughborough (*Mail on Sunday* 23 March), Leeds North-East and Stevenage (ICM/*Guardian* 7 April), and Gloucester (MORI/*Sun* 14 April). There were also polls covering Scotland and Wales which gave warning of the likely end of Conservative representation in these regions.

'Why don't you read us some more of that war book, Brian? We need cheering up'

| Major | Howard | Heseltine | Mawhinney |

Griffin, *Express*, 25 April 1997

Table 7.2 shows the Labour lead in the latest poll by each company published up to the Sunday of each week in the campaign.

Table 7.2   Labour's lead in last published poll of each week

	Sunday 6 April	Sunday 13 April	Sunday 20 April	Sunday 27 April	Final Poll 1 May
	%	%	%	%	%
NOP	24	20	14	18	22
MORI	25	15	17	24	18
Harris	24	24	18	16	17
Gallup	21	16	19	17	14
ICM	15	16	15	15	10
Average	22	18	16	18	16

There were some variations in the trends suggested by individual polls, but the only strong pattern, apart from the initial drop, lay in ICM's consistently lower lead for Labour. However, the majority of surveys seem to have slightly underestimated Conservative support. Some observers concluded that the 'don't knows' and 'won't says' were predominantly Conservatives, affected by a 'spiral of silence' as in 1992. There was an even more consistent overestimation of Labour support: only two of the 47 campaign polls, both ICM, put it below 45 per cent – perhaps a 'spiral of fashionability'. There were complaints from party officials and commentators about the effect on the campaign of polls that reported such a large Labour lead and that showed such little movement.

As Table 7.1 makes plain, all the polls picked up an increase in Liberal Democrat support from 11 per cent in late March to 14 per cent at the end of the campaign – but all the final forecasts, except ICM and MORI's *Evening Standard* poll (though not their *Times* report), underestimated the Liberal Democrats' actual 17 per cent. The ICM interviews deliberately included questions mentioning the Liberal Democrats before coming to the key voting question.

Table 7.3 compares the final surveys. NOP's poll for Reuters was completed on April 29, 24 hours before most of the others. Gallup's forecast, based on a single survey, showed a sharp change change from the 19–20 per cent their rolling polls had been showing in the last few days before. MORI had two bites at the cherry. Their *Times* poll showed a 20 per cent lead, but their later *Evening Standard* poll gave 18 per cent.

The pollsters were pleased. All had forecast a Labour landslide and in the figures for party votes, most had come within the 3 per cent margin of error that the pollsters had been offering as their health warning. The headlines applauded them: 'POLLSTERS RESTORE TARNISHED REPUTATION' (*Guardian*), and 'BULLSEYE POLLS WIN BACK CREDIBILITY' (*Sunday Times*). Bob Worcester of MORI proclaimed (*New Statesman* 8 May):

> Finally, how did the polls do? Just fine, thank you ... The British public are vindicated, along with the pollsters, by the accuracy of the polls on the 1997 general election.

However, not all observers shared 'the self-congratulatory verdict offered by many of the pollsters' (*The Economist* 10 May 1997). In fact, 10 of the 47 campaign polls overestimated Labour's final lead by a larger margin than ICM's 23 April 'rogue' poll underestimated it. Moreover, it must be pointed out that there was a spread of 12 per cent between the highest and lowest party lead.

Table 7.3   Final opinion polls

	Con	Lab	Lib Dem	Other	Lab Lead
	%	%	%	%	%
NOP	28	50	14	8	22
MORI	29	47	19	5	18
Harris	31	48	15	6	17
Gallup	33	47	14	6	14
ICM	33	43	18	6	10
Average	31	47	16	6	16
Actual Result	31	44	17	7	13

In the final polls, five out of the fifteen final estimates of each party's support were actually outside the 3 per cent margin of error. Four polls out of five overestimated Labour's vote. There was a 12 per cent range in the final figures for Labour's lead; therefore, if the election had been close and one poll had suggested a 6 per cent lead for the Conservatives and another a 6 per cent lead for Labour, the media would have reverted to the satirical comments which followed the 1992 fiasco.

Nick Sparrow of ICM observed (*Guardian* 11 June) that there was 'no room for complacency'. Most polls had continued to show a pro-Labour bias. Mr Sparrow saw some improvements: the attention given to 'don't knows' and 'won't says' had improved accuracy; so, possibly, had the switch to telephone interviews. He also defended ICM's weighting by recall of past voting as a procedure which, despite the problem of 'false memory', could usually improve any forecast, but he wondered whether the polls would be able to call a close-fought contest in 2001–2.

John Curtice, in one of the most detailed and considered methodologial assessments of the polls' performance, concluded that the polls 'were nothing like as successful as was suggested in the initial press commentary'.[2]

NOP conducted an exit poll for the BBC and MORI did the same for ITN (though MORI's poll was confined to marginal seats). Both gave a reasonable steer to the broadcasters, launching their election night programmes as the booths closed at 10 p.m. The fact that both seemed to overstate Labour's lead was fortunate since, as is discussed on p. 250, Labour's majority in seats (179) was substantially greater than the 133 that a 13 per cent lead would have produced on a uniform swing. ITN started by deducing a 159-seat lead from its exit poll in marginals. BBC commentators said unofficially 'about 200'; and Sky, without an exit poll, split the difference with 175.

As always, media coverage of the polls focused on the 'How will you vote?' figures, yet some newspaper articles, notably those by Peter Riddell in *The Times*, Anthony King in the *Daily Telegraph*, and Peter Kellner in the *Observer*, included substantial evidence on the division of party support by class, sex and age, and of attitudes on issues and leaders. On 3 April Peter Riddell quoted MORI to show how on almost every aspect of party image Labour had gone up and the Conservatives down in popular estimation since 1992. On 24 April Anthony King pointed to Gallup's evidence showing that the campaign had made no significant difference to voters' fears about either a Conservative or a Labour victory. Throughout April Peter Kellner analysed a panel survey on issues in the *Observer*, showing Labour's enormous, if slightly declining, lead on the key themes. It was reported by MORI on 17 April that, by 36 per cent to 23 per cent, Labour was seen as more likely than the Conservatives to improve the standard of living. Although as many people (40 per cent on each side) favoured getting out of Europe as staying in, 18 per cent were Euro-philic to the extent of wanting to stay in and to have a single currency; 36 per cent were at the other extreme. However, Europe was still only eighth among a list of issues which voters thought important.

Some papers, notably the *Financial Times,* the *Independent* and the *Guardian*, turned to professionally conducted focus groups, on the same lines as the parties' private efforts, in order to catch in more depth the mood on issues. Focus groups are structured discussions with a small number of carefully selected voters. They have been increasingly used by the political parties and the newspapers, partly under the influence of American campaigning practice, and partly in reaction to the poor performance of the British polls in 1992. In 1997 the press reports from focus groups emphasised the Euro-sceptic leanings of floating voters, offering a rare bit of comfort for the Conservatives.

It is possible that the pollsters were too much influenced by the supposed 'lessons' of 1992. Was there really a 'spiral of silence' among Conservatives this time? The fact that it existed in 1992 led many pollsters to doubt the huge leads they were finding. The polls reported that the Conservative vote was softer than Labour's, and on so many of the other determinants, such as leadership and economic competence, Labour still was ahead. Bob Worcester was dismissive of the claims that there was all to play for; he pointed out that the number of late deciders hardly differed from 1992 and that the extent of 'churning' revealed in panel surveys was much the same; Figure 7.2 suggests the extent of volatility during the final six weeks.

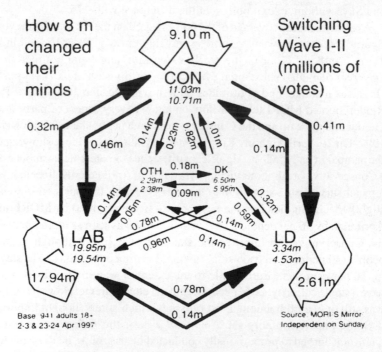

Figure 7.2   Churning among voters during the campaign

No self-respecting party can now campaign without its own private polls. There are, however, problems. Much of the information that private polls can offer is available free from published polls and from the detailed breakdowns of massed samples which pollsters make available. There is also the problem of security: who is to see the private polls? All parties insist on very limited circulation – and not just for fear of leaks; if the findings are depressing they may damage headquarters morale and they may leak to the press. It is relatively seldom that they produce unexpected findings which can lead to an effective change of tactics.

Nonetheless, in 1997 all the parties engaged in private polling. At times, they gave strategic hints of favourable findings. The total amount spent on polls and focus groups was certainly a record for Labour, but the Conservatives cut down on the large sums that Kenneth Baker had authorised back in 1990 on research into voters' values. The Liberal Democrats could only afford limited surveys in target seats.

There were significant differences in the various parties' approach to private polling. Labour retained NOP headed by Nick Moon, which polled throughout the parliament. It began a regular survey (1600 sample) in November 1993, which was revisited quarterly during 1996. The impact of the 1992 election defeat was reflected in the large number of tracking image and issue questions which dealt with the economy, many of them suggested by an academic adviser, Roger Jowell. These included: Which party was the best in managing the economy? Under which party would the economy become stronger or weaker? Which party would improve the voter's standard of living? and Which party would keep taxes at the right level? Voters were also asked to agree or disagree with the propositions that the Conservatives messed up the economy and that Labour would put up taxes for all the people. Labour enjoyed a good lead on all of these questions throughout 1995 but there was a fall in the lead in the summer of 1996. As happens when a party is riding high, Labour had a much more modest advantage on which party the voter identified with.

Philip Gould, guided by the American pollster Stan Greenberg, was an interventionist client. Greenberg suggested questions and provided his own analysis of the responses. His role was kept from the public and he was in London only for the last ten days of the campaign. This was another product of the links forged with the Clinton team in 1992.

During the campaign the party did not repeat the daily polls which it used in 1992. NOP conducted a 1000-sample twice-weekly survey, reporting the findings to Philip Gould initially on Tuesday and Saturday nights. The voting figures provided some reassurance at the critical moment on 22 April when news filtered in of ICM finding that Labour's lead was down to 5 per cent; NOP's private poll found Labour 19 per cent ahead.

Philip Gould had conducted focus groups for the Democrats in the US in 1992 and 1996 and for Labour in 1987 and 1992. From the time that Tony Blair became leader, Gould regularly met focus groups three or four nights a week. By the time the election had come he had conducted a total of 300 groups; he met a further 70 during the campaign. Philip Gould's pre-campaign focus groups always induced a sense of caution. He detected an underlying fear among voters that the old Labour negatives might come to the fore again. On the basis of his focus groups he could not understand why the Conservatives were campaigning on a slogan which implied that Labour was new. Focus groups formed the basis of his constant memos to Tony Blair and other key party figures. The sessions tested reactions to party and Conservative initiatives in policy and in advertising. There were also studies in by-election seats. A member of the BMP advertising agency thought that the research had been overdone: 'the ads were tested to death'. Additional group research was conducted in a number of Pennine constituencies by Deborah Mattinson of Opinion Leader Research.

The Conservative operation reflected the financial restrictions on the party. Apart from a Wirthlin poll in January 1996 (see p. 30) the party did no polling for the first four years of the parliament and only in the late summer of 1996 did it actually appoint an agency, ICM, to succeed Harris (see p. 31). ICM conducted surveys, focus groups and by-election studies. Their first major work was in September on the Liberal Democrats and showed the limited scope for Labour to make inroads on the Liberal Democrat support. In October 1996 ICM began to track opinion movements on key issues with polls which were at first monthly, then weekly from January 1997, and daily for the last month before the election. In sharp contrast to the Labour practice, because of the stubborn resistance of Maurice Saatchi, it was only on the eve of the election that some of the Saatchi advertising copy was pre-tested. Daily campaign polls, discontinued in 1979, were resumed. ICM surveyed 500 voters per day and the samples' design matched ICM's work for the *Guardian*. There was a good deal of secrecy about the ICM findings, which were first reported to Andrew Cooper in Central Office who then conveyed them to Brian Mawhinney and a very small group of advisers – none of whom was allowed to take a copy of the backing tables. It was only three weeks into the campaign that John Major learned that ICM was conducting a rolling poll.

The Conservatives' focus groups told much the same story as Labour's. There was deep disillusion with Conservative politicians and a desire to see a change of government, but voters did not want a change of political direction; rather they sought continuity without risk. One Conservative polling adviser acknowledged Tony Blair's success in providing this reassurance and acknowledged his own party's failure to discover a theme which could exploit latent fears of Labour. 'Tax' no longer worked and the risks to Britain from importing the European social model were both too remote and too complex to sell; indeed, the polls showed that the Social

Brown's promise of no tax or spending increases. During the election the groups revealed that voters did not hold divisions over the single currency against the Conservatives but acknowledged that the party was having a debate on a serious issue. ICM rolling surveys did, however, report a dramatic loss of support among the over-65s when Labour launched its pensions scare on 24 April. The finding caused consternation in Central Office (see p. 108). ICM call-backs on polling day found that many 'don't knows' decided for the Liberal Democrats and the Referendum party and the 'won't says' came down for the Conservative Party. In retrospect, Nick Sparrow calculated from ICM's recall poll after the vote that, in trying to make allowance for the anti-Conservative 'spiral of silence', he had mildly over-adjusted.

Liberal polling was on a more modest scale – a consequence of scarce resources and a need to concentrate on a limited number of seats. Much was done in-house; sympathisers were trained in party headquarters and conducted two sets of telephone surveys in the 30 target seats. Another benchmark survey was conducted by PS Mailing. The results were merged with census data to uncover the salient characteristics of voters in the target seats. This showed that the Liberal Democrats were predominantly middle class, university educated, two-car owners, and elderly.

Pollsters for the Labour and Conservative parties did elaborate regression analysis to find out which issues would decide the vote. ICM in December 1996 reported that the economy and Europe were the decisive issues. A warning for John Major was that the message about economic prosperity had not connected with voters; personally, only 17 per cent felt better off. A week before polling day Nick Sparrow privately advised Brian Mawhinney to base the final Conservative appeal on these two issues. Nick Sparrow's untested theory was that a tougher line on Europe was a 'coat-hanger' for materialists to admit they were voting Conservative.

The Conservative surveys showed that, during the campaign, the party caught up and just overtook Labour as the party having the best policies on the economy, but that it still trailed narrowly on which party was best at keeping its promises or improving personal prosperity. Tony Blair had, at the least, achieved his goal of holding the Conservatives on tax and the economy.

NOP told Labour that the main determinant was the economy, something that strategists always feared might still help the Conservatives, but Philip Gould warned party leaders that three other message contrasts were important; for the people versus for the few, representing change in the future against more of the same, and trust versus betrayal. Gould's 'Message Mantra' in his war book rested on five themes:

1. A New Labour future versus Conservative failure.
2. New Labour for the many, the Conservatives for the few.
3. New Labour is trustworthy, the Conservatives lie.
4. An economy equipped to face the future.
5. Next time it will be worse, enough is enough.

The pre-campaign focus groups warned of Labour's weaknesses. Voters found that the party was untried and it had a hidden left, and that its policies might result in a rise in interest rates and increase in union power. Philip Gould's memos emphasised the need to reassure these voters.

During the campaign, Greg Cook, the party's polling coordinator at Millbank, distributed the findings of NOP's twice-weekly surveys to key figures. He also reported on the polls at a daily meeting at 6.30 p.m. chaired by either Brown or Mandelson. This meeting also received other feedback from the key seats operations – reports from the telephone canvassing and regional borders. Labour polls picked up the growing sense of economic optimism and the improvement in John Major's rating after his European statement on April 16. By the end of the campaign, his standing among Conservatives matched that of Tony Blair among Labour supporters – but Blair scored much higher among Conservatives than Major did among Labour. The focus groups warned the party about the voters' dislike of negative campaigning, not least over the party's pensions claims. They, and the canvassing reports, also warned about Major's potential appeal on Europe. Gould's report warned that Major had moved ' into the right sceptical place in Europe'.

Private polls were as important – or as unimportant – as in any general election in shaping strategy. In no party was the pollster a member of the key groups deciding strategy; the pollsters' research produced material for strategists to digest. Another change lay in the growing importance of focus groups as complementary to the surveys. Strategists appreciated the immediacy of the work and its suggestions for action.

NOTES

1. See Market Research Society, *The Opinion Polls and the 1992 General Election* (July 1994). See also N. Sparrow, 'Improving Polling Techniques Following the 1992 Election', *Journal of the Market Research Society*, 1993, and R. Jowell et al., '1992 British Election: The Failure of the Polls', *Public Opinion Quarterly*, 1994.
2. See J. Curtice, 'So how well did they do? The polls in the 1997 election', *Journal of the Market Research Society*, 1997; see also M. O'Muircheartaigh, 'Election 97: a Triumph for the Pollsters?', *Market Research*, June 1997, and I. Crewe 'The Opinion Polls: Confidence Restored?', *Parliamentary Affairs*, Autumn 1997. The performance of the polls was explored at length at a meeting of the Royal Statistical Society on 17 June 1997.

8 Politics on the Air

Martin Harrison

The thoroughly modern election of 1997 began on radio and television and ended there. It opened with John Major, tracked by helicopter to and from Buckingham Palace in ITN's lunchtime news, then feeding the first soundbites of the campaign into the *One O'Clock News* and BBC Radio's *World at One*. It ended with Tony Blair arriving at Number 10 as excited wellwishers waved their Union flags, declaring that New Labour must now move from words to action. Between those two episodes lay the hundreds of hours of news, analysis, interviews and features, national and local, that now form the core of an election campaign.

This is not to say all that was decisive. Broadcasting's most important contribution to the election arguably lay in its routine coverage during the months and years when the Labour lead opened, and when 'Black Wednesday', sleaze, Europe, Tory divisions and the emergence of New Labour became embedded in public consciousness. By March few politicians or broadcasters expected anything but a Labour victory, yet the firmness of that Labour support fashioned by the daily drizzle of news and commentary had still to be tested in the fire of intensive coverage. There was still much to play for; it was possible that either the tactics of damage limitation or some calamitous gaffe would turn defectors back to the fold. With their press support weakened, hopes of Conservative deliverance lay more than ever before with television and radio. By the same token, Labour had never had less to hope for or more to fear from them.

The broadcasters had made their plans early. ITV's were agreed by the Network Broadcast Board's Election Sub-Group and accepted in principle by the parties in 1995. By coordinating its news, current affairs and results streams, ITV achieved its most coherent coverage to date. The logistics of modern campaigning and coverage make such advanced planning essential. Yet these plans were implemented when the outcome was in little doubt; voters who had been subjected to months of political infighting were faced with a campaign stretching over six weeks rather than the expected four. Some broadcasters gloomily wondered whether they could reach polling day without boring everyone to tears. (Radio 4's *PM* actually featured 'bored' new voters the day after the election was announced.) They brought great professionalism to a task for which many had no great enthusiasm, but the inhibitions and distortions of news values that election coverage entails meant that their efforts met with uneven success.

This was most apparent with the news. The election story rose from nominal levels in early March to over a quarter of BBC1 and ITV main evening news by the time an announcement became imminent.[1] It then took over, with more than half of all news time right through to polling day, apart from weekends and the Easter lull; even then it only once fell below 30 per cent. Every one of 356 bulletins monitored carried some election news. When there was nothing new, Radio 4's breakfast bulletins filled in with crystal-ball gazing – even on Sundays. BBC1's three main bulletins carried 62 per cent, 54 per cent and 67 per cent election news, and ITV's 60 per cent, 48 per cent and 57 per cent. *Channel 4 News* was 78 per cent on the election and even *5 News*, a newcomer targeting a 'popular' market, ran at 46 per cent. BBC1 had election leads on 38 of the 44 evenings after the date was set and ITV had 35. In the early evening the election came first 22 and 24 times in April on BBC1 and ITV, 28 times on Channel 4 and 25 times on Channel 5 – only the IRA, the Israeli political crisis, Zaire and the rescue of the shroud of Turin briefly knocked it off the top spot.

On days when the IRA had not been sowing disruption, BBC1, ITN and Channel 4 normally opened with ten or twelve minutes of 'hard' election news, moving to other matters before returning to 'softer' items – surveys, polls, interviews, analysis and the like.[2] This was especially true of the *Nine O'Clock News*, which doubled its usual 24 or so minutes after Easter. Other national bulletins remained at their normal lengths, though the BBC also ran longer regional news. This was very much in line with 1992, but in 1997 it was less successful. The *Nine O'Clock News* was extended on public service grounds but the public failed to appreciate the compliment. While news ratings are always at risk during elections, few had expected the loss of a quarter of the audience.[3] *News at Ten*, carrying less on the election, lost less ground – as did *Channel 4 News* and BBC2's *Newsnight*, whose audiences are more hardened to intensive politicking. While in several respects the BBC had a better election than in 1992, it had obviously misjudged the public mood. The BBC's Director of News & Current Affairs was remarkably sanguine when he answered listeners' criticisms on Radio 4's *Feedback*, but other broadcasters acknowledged not only that voters were given more than they wanted but also that many found what was on offer boring and unadventurous. Publicly, they blamed the spin-doctors and the constraints of the Representation of the People Act. They were less willing to accept that what passes as 'professional' among broadcasters might also be part of the explanation.[4] Yet it was arguably more remarkable that so many viewers remained switched on than that so many decamped.

Table 8.1   Election leads in main evening news programmes

BBC	ITN

April

1 Major confronts the sleaze issue	Major's rethink in the battle over sleaze
2 Major launches Con. manifesto: the boldest and most far-reaching since 1979	Major's promise: more prosperity, more choice
3 Blair says 'trust me' as he launches Lab. manifesto	Blair's election offer – a bond of trust with Britain
4 Lib. Dems have set out their election promises	Ashdown's election pledge: we'll make a difference
5 (2) Campaign dominated by arguments over which party the voters can trust	(2) The 3 main parties have spent most of the day arguing over who deserves the voters' trust
6 Surprise development: Bell to be anti-sleaze candidate	A surprise challenge tonight for Con. MP Neil Hamilton
7 N. Hamilton says he won't chicken out	(2) The war reporter facing a battle over sleaze
8 Con. activists meet to decide fate of NH	After the confrontation, tonight a decision on Hamilton
9 Election has turned bitter: tax and trust	Election campaign turned nasty with bitter words and insults
10 Politicians fighting for the business vote	Major gets personal with fierce attack on Blair
11 Cons on defensive over EU (Browning)	Con. minister at centre of Euro election row
12 Parties crossed swords over who can make the streets safer from alcohol-related crime	Row broke out between the 3 main parties over negative election campaigning
13 Lab. claims majority of Con. candidates oppose Major on Europe	Blair changes tactics as Cons attack again on trust
14 Blair pushes education to the forefront	A new battle tonight over Britain's place in EU
15 A defeat on cuts in fishing draws threat of defiance from Major, scorn from Blair	Bombshell for Major as minister breaks ranks
16 Major has made an impassioned plea to his candidates to unite behind gvt's line on EU	Major's gamble to contain a Euro-sceptic revolt
17 Major surprised his party and his colleagues by offering Con. back-benchers a free vote	Major's surprise offer – a free vote on a single currency
18 Major said Blair would fly the white flag of surrender in EU. Lab: shows Cons are desperate	(2) Major's new ad draws fire from Lab. – and Germany

Table 8.1   Election leads in main evening news programmes (continued)

BBC	ITN
19 Europe's causing more trouble for the Tories	The Chancellor's warning that describing EU as a threat is paranoid nonsense
20 Lord Archer warns Cons against positioning themselves for a leadership contest	(2) The Opposition says top Cons are at open civil war over EU
21 President of the EU Com. has intervened in the election. Eurosceptics were prophets of doom who didn't know what they were talking about	(2) The Euro President slams sceptics as merchants of doom
22 Main party leaders have been trying to turn the EU issue to their advantage	(2) Parties say EU is now a question of leadership
23 Blair announces plans to channel lottery money into health and education	Election row over Labour's campaign war book
24 Most bitter exchanges of the election after Blair claimed Tories would put VAT on food and abolish the state pension	Blair responds tonight to Con. charges of lying
25 Gvt warns of possible attack on polling day. (2) Major says he'd leave politics rather than scrap state pension, but Lab. repeat the claim	IRA threat sparks security clampdown for election day. (2) Major's fury as the pensions row rumbles on
26 Leaders start last lap with appeals to voters who are still undecided	Major and Blair square up for the last lap
27 Blair warns his party not to be complacent	Major dismisses talk of Lab. landslide even from his own side
28 Into the final round and the speeches take on a new urgency. Major: 72 hours to save UK	Major's plea: you have 72 hours to save the Union. Blair's prediction: there won't be a landslide
29 Cons say Britain's voters are sleep-walking to disaster	New appeals as leaders head for the final push
30 Longest campaign is over; each party leader has rested his case	One last push and the campaigning finally ends. Awaiting the verdict of the last-minute polls

There was actually a wider choice of styles of coverage than ever. The established channels offered their well-proven coverage, branded with election logos – the BBC with a red–yellow–blue rosette that looked fine on studio monitors but was simply garish in the living room; ITN with more discreet tricolour markers. *5 News*, which came on air as the election was getting under way, was still establishing its identity. It featured a chatty young presenter wandering through the newsroom attempting to suffuse urgency and excitement into rather unpromising material. Radio 5 Live, also tackling its first general election with a jaunty, less formal style than Radio 4, offered rolling coverage with extended treatment of events like the morning news conferences (as did *Sky News*). Radio 1's *Newsbeat* made a brave bid to reach a youthful audience, normally oriented to pop. Talk Radio, also a newcomer, targeted a popular audience with round-the-clock news and phone-ins.

Behind this variety of styles there was much less diversity in news agendas. BBC1 and ITV led on essentially the same story on at least 38 evenings out of 44. The evening when BBC1 led on Labour's proposal to divert lottery money to education and health while ITN began with Labour's 'war book' was the rare exception. The same held broadly true elsewhere, though *Channel 4 News* was rather more likely to strike out on its own. Table 8.1 shows just how similar the headlines were both in choice of story and in their negative or boringly bland tone. (*News at Ten* headlines had to be punchier to fit the bongs of Big Ben; the BBC often ran three subheads to give each big party a mention; Channel 4's headlines were so prolix as to constitute a news summary in themselves.) Possibly eight BBC1 top headlines and five on ITN were clearly positive – including the more or less mandatory upbeat opening after each party presented its manifesto. The Conservatives had slightly more positive headlines but also the most negative ones. They lost the battle of the headlines in 1997 as decisively as they won it in 1992.

This consensus over what the election was 'about' held true of coverage generally, day-by-day and over the whole campaign – a tendency that may have been promoted in the BBC by the daily breakfast gathering of all its principal editors to review and plan coverage. From 19 March, when John Major refused to publish the Downey Report, until 8 April the dominant story was 'sleaze'. The Conservatives were furious and frustrated, yet after opting for a long campaign, they had no apparent strategy for generating favourable coverage during that extra fortnight. When Simon Hughes queried the fate of the Downey Report in the House, the bulletins that evening focused more on the Speaker's rebuke than on the underlying issue. However, once it was known that the *Guardian* was splashing the story, pack journalism took over and the next morning *Today* led on Neil Hamilton rather than the 60,000 fall in the jobless figures. 'A scandal', complained Michael Heseltine – but there was no stopping now. Episodes of some importance and none, from the Allan Stewart affair to Piers Merchant, Tim Smith, Sir Michael Hirst and the Hamiltons, became lumped together as 'sleaze', albeit with some pious noseholding. The machinations behind the eviction of Sir Michael Hirst were poorly covered outside Scotland, though they were of greater political consequence for what they revealed about the condition of the Conservative

Party in Scotland. (For that matter, the parlous state of Conservative organisation elsewhere was not adequately reported.)

'Sleaze' obviously had to be reported. However, the volume and placing of coverage and the lumping together of different stories of such varying gravity under one portmanteau heading and with such inadequate perspective was more open to criticism. (A *Newsnight* essay by Gore Vidal setting such matters in a wider context was a notable exception.) Tatton was, of course, a thumping good story, understandably played for all it was worth, and sometimes a little more. Beyond television's preoccupation with one of its own, this was 'news' by any conventional yardstick: an unprecedented situation, raising serious questions about the outgoing government, containing conflict, uncertainty, a clash of cultures, symbols and values, the confrontation between the professional and the raw beginner – above all a human drama everyone could follow and judge. The 'Battle of Knutsford Heath' (see p. 96), while intrinsically of minor importance, captured so many of these elements that it made the most memorable television of the campaign. Eventually Tatton disappeared from lack of fresh fuel and because the opposition of the transvestite candidate prevented further coverage. However, sleaze returned from time to time, even – to his manifest irritation – in one of John Major's final interviews. Labour happily observed the government's discomforture but it was prompt to complain that the BBC's coverage of the allegation by Ray Powell that he had been offered a peerage to stand down was 'completely out of order' (see p. 102).

As sleaze faded, 'Europe' replaced it, dominating the mid-campaign. Thus far it had barely surfaced – EU developments had mostly been reported outside the election package. Then a newspaper was tipped off about Angela Browning's election address and everyone followed. (But why, knowing the Conservatives' disarray over Europe, had journalists not dug out this story themselves?) In terms of hard election news, 'Europe' meant EMU, the Social Chapter and fish – but, more than all these, the divisions in the Conservative Party. This produced some of the most telling moments on the air: John Horam's verbal contortions to show he was loyally 'on message' when manifestly he was not; John Major, in response to a question from Elinor Goodman, making policy on the hoof with his offer of a free vote on EMU; and his passionate plea for his party not to tie his hands on Europe.

For all that was said about spin-doctors, they had relatively little control over the course taken by coverage of sleaze and Europe, where the media had the bit between their teeth; not so with allegations that the Conservatives would put VAT on food and abolish state retirement pensions, timed to unsettle them in the final few days. The first charge had been levelled and denied previously, and rapidly dropped from view in the news. While pensions concern almost everyone, it was unclear why an allegation of such dubious substance was played so hard, albeit for only a couple of days. Whatever the reason, the Conservatives were thrust back on the defensive on pensions specifically, but also on more diffuse questions of truthfulness and trust that recurred under numerous headings throughout the campaign.

Thus, although the Conservatives received more time than Labour on all channels, as Table 8.2 shows, so much of it was on matters where they were weak or divided that they were scarcely favoured. Their good economic figures did not get the attention they looked for, squeezed by 'sexier' material or undermined by sceptical follow-ups.

Table 8.2 Parties' share of news coverage[5]

	Con	Lab	Lib Dem	Others	Total
	%	%	%	%	%
BBC1	34.9	31.1	24.4	9.6	100.0
ITV	34.6	29.7	27.6	8.1	100.0
C4	38.0	34.3	24.3	3.4	100.0
Radio 4	34.1	31.9	24.1	9.9	100.0
All 1997	35.3	31.3	25.0	8.4	100.0
All 1992	36.8	30.8	25.2	7.2	100.0

The Conservatives more than once had Labour floundering, notably over the 'tartan tax' and privatisation, which topped few bulletins but played well while it lasted – not least because of reports featuring a recent clip of their transport spokesman, Andrew Smith, inveighing against privatisation of air traffic control. Conservative allegations of unprincipled Labour U-turns on other matters were also reported, though not often or fully enough to inflict serious damage. Variations on the themes of Labour in thrall to the trade unions, pegged to the Social Chapter or to rumblings at the Scottish Trade Union Congress, hardly came alight. The bid to spoil Labour's initiative on the lottery by releasing the party's campaign 'war book' also failed. ITN led on this non-story at 5.45 p.m. and 10 p.m. but the BBC ran with the lottery, which had substance and greater audience appeal. The 'war book' then disappeared without trace. Another time Labour's attempt to make education the issue of the day was thwarted by the fisheries controversy. Despite such occasional successes the Conservatives' fightback never achieved momentum in the news, while their positive proposals received fairly limited attention; in short, in the battle of the news bulletins they were comprehensively routed.

Sleaze, Europe and pensions came and went; other issues recurred throughout the campaign. Chief of these were the constitution (essentially devolution), education, the NHS, the economy, taxation and expenditure. There was more on the Scottish dimension than ever (hence the improved showing of smaller parties in Table 8.2), though the implications for England received little attention. Arguments and briefings about tax and expenditure were also reported at length, with considerable attention to the difficult choices facing whichever party won. Unlike the poll tax in 1987 and Europe in 1992, no major issue was evaded that would clearly be a major issue for the next parliament. There were, of course, Cinderella issues: the environment, social welfare other than pensions, housing, defence and the world outside Europe, but, even here, if the parties were keeping low profiles, there were news briefings and more detailed explorations of difficult choices in store in current affairs sequences.

Table 8.3   Relative prominence of issues in news coverage

	BBC1	ITV	C4	R4	All 1997	All 1992
Europe	1	1	1	1	1	..
Constitution	2	3	2	3	2	3
Sleaze	3	2	5=	2	3	–
Education	4	4	3	5	4	6
Taxation	6	5	10	4	5	2
NHS	7	9	5=	6	6	4
Pensions	5	6	9	7	7	..
The economy	8	13	7	9=	8=	1
Employment	13=	10	4	9=	8=	9
Law and order	9	8	8	8	10	..
Northern Ireland	12	7	11	14	11	11
Public expenditure	13=	12	6	13	12	10

There was a greater concentration on issues than in recent elections. They took 56 per cent of ITN's coverage, 64 per cent of BBC1's, 72 per cent of Channel 4's, and 74 per cent in Radio 4 bulletins. This was largely because, for obvious reasons, there was less on the election 'horse race'. The polls were demoted, still suspect after their 1992 debacle – and in any case there was little newsworthy variation in them. Channel 4 led once on one of its own polls but usually they were well down the programme and focused on opinion about issues as well as on party fortunes. Commentary repeatedly emphasised margins for error – perhaps to avoid criticism for demoralising Conservatives or demotivating Labour. Peter Snow, for the BBC, as tireless as ever, probed every conceivable gleam of hope for the Conservatives with a greater display of electronic high jinks than ever, but to no avail. Audiences were left in no doubt about Labour's huge lead, but there were so many caveats that it was understandable that 2 May came as such a surprise to so many people. The uneasy feeling that there just might be a rerun of 1992 restrained any tendency to treat the outcome as a foregone conclusion and speculate on what lay beyond polling day.

A further reason why issues got more play was that the proliferation of candidates made it difficult to obtain the consent that the Representation of the People Act requires for constituency features. While this hit regional and local coverage hardest, national news carried fewer of the constituency surveys that customarily provide undemanding local colour and visual variety. Broadcasters complained bitterly, not least at their inability to cover Tatton, but many more possibilities remained open, as items on the youth vote, the ethnic vote, and the grey vote illustrated. A strength of BBC reporting was that it could draw on so many specialist correspondents. Coverage of the Conservative manifesto, which ran for 14 minutes at 9 p.m. on 2 April, included contributions from the Social Affairs and Economics correspondents and the Institute of Fiscal Studies. At other times the Environment, Education and Legal Affairs correspondents were called on. For the notional earnest floating voter, copious additional briefing was available on Ceefax and the WorldWide Web. At the opposite end of the scale, *5 News* each day reckoned to cover the parties' policies on, say, Europe or the environment in 60 seconds flat, backed by an insistent soundtrack. Most viewers could have been little the wiser. ITN's lunchtime forays by helicopter to present ordinary people's experiences as a peg for features on the day's issue were a shade gimmicky and hurried, but clearer. Channel 4 relied on 25-minute discussions of devolution, the economy or Europe as a vehicle for putting the issues across.

As always, the broadcasters came under pressure from the parties demanding that stories be promoted up the running order, or complaining of bias. The Conservatives were thought to have played this game ineptly; 'spin-doctors with nothing to spin' was one leading journalist's most polite description. Labour was 'brutal, single-minded and vicious', said the same insider, yet prepared to back down when robustly resisted. Less experienced journalists and senior management were, for different reasons, not always so tough-minded. It was hardly surprising that so much reporting was bland and unadventurous, and, though there were also signs of greater confidence and incisiveness, one sometimes needed an ear well-tuned to nuances to pick them up. Some items would have been unlikely or unthinkable only a few years ago, such as a report from Brighton on the gay vote or a Channel 4 piece by George Monbiot arguing that environmental protection could not be left to MPs and calling for direct action in preference to electoral politics. The impeccably non-partisan analyses of public finance by the Institute of Fiscal Studies would have provoked fierce exception from the politicians in the recent past. Broadcasters pressing for greater freedom were prone to overlook how much ground had been won since the 1950s when Pinky and Perky were taken off the air in deference to party susceptibilities.

By contrast with the variety lower down the bulletins, top of the bulletin material was often negative, disputatious and repetitive. The snatches from the daily press conferences looked much the same every day, apart from changes in the slogan of the day displayed on screens behind the speakers – 'Britain is Booming', 'You Can't Trust Labour', or the squawking electronic chicken with which the Conservatives taunted Tony Blair. The parties' Rapid Rebuttal units ensured that every proposal or charge was followed by dismissal or counter-charge in a string of mutually cancelling soundbites. Labour ungraciously complained that the resulting tit-for-tattery was crowding out its positive policies, but editors needed no telling of the indignation that omission of the latest riposte would arouse in the Millbank war room. The problem lay less with any one item or day than in seeing the same faces in the same settings trading the same sorts of bite-sized jibes. It was hard to imagine anyone not finding this cumulatively tedious and unappealing. (The chief beneficiaries were the Liberal Democrats, rarely attacking or deemed worthy of attack. They not only looked good in consequence but were compensated with soft coverage later in the campaign for having less than their due previously – *PM* actually interviewed David Steel on Zaire to boost its Liberal Democrat figures.)

A Central TV presenter declared that this campaign would be 'nasty, brutish and long'. It was long, certainly, but not especially nasty or brutish. Attacks were almost all policy-related rather than personal. Kenneth Clarke's characterisation of Labour as 'unmitigated scoundrels' was a rare exception, sounding worse as a five-second soundbite – and soundbites proliferated despite the BBC's Director of News & Current Affairs' promise to do away with them. The two main evening news carried fifty soundbites of under ten seconds and only ten running more than fifty seconds. The average was 16.5 seconds in the *Nine O'Clock News* and 14.7 seconds on *News at Ten*. Longish utterances were liable to be chopped in mid-sentence. Substantial statements were reported salami-style – thin slices of actuality linked in reported speech. Tony Blair was rash to speak of the *seven* pillars of a decent society; what he said received only 13 seconds in an 80-second report mentioning only three. John Major complained, 'I might make a 40-minute speech on the welfare state. I'll get one minute of it on the news if I'm lucky.'[6]

Many soundbites came from the morning news conferences. What subsequent bulletins picked up predominantly were answers to questions from a remarkably small number of radio and television journalists. Sometimes, as with Elinor Goodman's question on a free vote over EMU, these were important, but others appeared motivated by personal or channel promotional purposes, perilously verging on 'celeb' journalism. Yet these exchanges were quite important in crystallising what the election would be deemed to have been 'about' that day. Live, or in Vincent Hanna's amusing reports on Radio 5, the press conferences (like the occasional speech) came across very differently when heard full and direct than when they were covered in later news.

After Easter the other recurring feature was the leaders' tours – three packages in almost every bulletin. Occasionally they provided a morsel of news, but often they did not. Irrespective of whether they had anything new to say, reporters would be called in from car parks, airfields or shopping precincts to answer questions such as, 'What's the word from the PM's camp?', or: 'How are confidence levels among the Liberal Democrats?' It was often hard to tell whether they were offering a professional judgement or replaying a line from the spin-doctors – one reporter, *sancta simplicitas,* actually cited what he termed a spin-doctor's 'honest opinion'.

However, occasional moments were worth seeing – John Major's encounter with an anti-federalist fisherman at Newlyn, which revealed to him the Tories' failure to get their message over on Europe; Paddy Ashdown's encounter with protesters garbed as a cow and a dormouse; Tony Blair's and John Prescott's reception in Stockton market; a scattering of exchanges with hecklers. The reports met editors' craving for different pictures for every bulletin – Tony Blair in the dealing room of BZW, John Major with a Formula 1 car (minus wheels), Paddy Ashdown amid photogenic tots with his unvarying question about computers. 'Why are you visiting this hospital?', one of the leaders was reportedly asked. 'Because that's what leaders do', was the reply. However, the attention paid to these repetitive and deeply inhibited thrice-daily bulletins vastly exceeded any illumination they provided. Parties and broadcasters alike seemed locked into them, each blaming the other for their importance in campaign ritual. Radio covered these same events more efficiently and with far less distraction. The best piece of reportage significantly came from someone who was not one of the regular 'boys on the bus'. Gary Gibbon, for Channel 4, showed John Major at his best, dealing humourously with hecklers in Perth, enjoying being away from Downing Street and relishing 'the power to decide exactly what he does', but he also

Table 8.4   Politicians quoted in radio and television news (number of times)

	BBC1	ITV	C4	R4	Total
Labour					
Blair	117	94	38	79	328
Brown	34	30	7	23	94
Cook	10	4	7	13	34
Straw	11	8	4	11	34
Robertson	6	8	4	9	27
Prescott	7	9	7	—	23
Blunkett	5	6	2	2	15
Mandelson	6	5	1	2	14
A Smith	5	—	1	3	9
Beckett	1	1	3	3	8
38 Others	41	14	23	12	90
Liberal Democrats					
Ashdown	117	99	28	84	328
Beith	10	5	1	10	26
Holme	14	3	1	7	25
Wallace	9	8	1	5	23
Hughes	6	7	3	6	22
Bruce	5	5	2	5	17
Foster	4	5	2	5	16
Carlile	4	2	3	4	13
Taylor	3	4	—	5	12
Kennedy	5	2	2	3	12
27 others	28	30	11	16	85
Conservative					
Major	116	109	37	86	348
Heseltine	31	25	11	19	86
Clarke	17	17	4	11	49
Howard	12	6	4	13	35
Dorrell	10	9	6	8	33
The Hamiltons	8	8	4	8	28
Forsyth	9	5	3	7	24
Mawhinney	9	3	2	7	21
Portillo	6	5	2	7	20
Thatcher	6	5	1	1	13
Shephard	5	4	1	3	13
Currie	1	6	1	4	12
Lang	5	1	1	5	12
Lilley	7	—	1	4	12
Browning	3	3	—	5	11
53 Others	50	26	19	35	130
Other Parties					
Salmond (SNP)	24	22	4	11	61
Bell (Ind)	8	8	3	8	27
Goldsmith (Ref)	6	6	1	4	17
Wigley (PC)	6	6	1	3	16
Adams (SF)	4	4	2	3	13
42 others	38	6	10	10	64

showed the resulting raggedness in the big speech when he threw away the script and failed to deliver a key passage. The most telling moment had Lord Cranborne defending the relaxed atmosphere on the Conservative buses: 'After all, thank God, politics is only a game, isn't it?' Imagine that on Alastair Campbell's lips!

Not content with following the leaders, the news was seized by the urge to be out and about. In addition to ITN's helicopter sorties, the BBC lunchtime news and *Channel 4 News* came from locations like Newlyn, Edinburgh Castle, a factory in Leicester, and Magdalen College, Oxford, while *Today* was presented from a succession of provincial cities. In addition to the attraction of greater picture variety there was a desire to show the news relating to the world away from Westminster (though soundbites introduced from Chester looked remarkably like soundbites presented from the studio). This could be carried to excess. *5 News* picked up a passing reference by John Major to hieroglyphics and reported from the Egyptian gallery of the British Museum and covered his warning about the dangers of a Labour government from The House of Horrors. *5 News* could plead inexperience. The same could not be said of the *Nine O'Clock News*. Its briefing on EMU, concluding that joining would be a gamble, was staged with Peter Jay resplendent in black tie from a casino!

The other recurring element was commentary from the political correspondents – mainly Robin Oakley or John Sergeant for the BBC, Michael Brunson for ITN or Elinor Goodman for Channel 4. They were heard as often and at greater length than the party leaders. The bitiness of soundbite and sightbite reporting made essential their guidance on issues, tactics and prospects, while all were skilled in conveying their assessment of the state of play without rousing the ire of the hawk-eared party monitoring units. They provided a valuable and necessary service. Yet their commentaries, taken with those by specialist correspondents and bodies like the Institute of Fiscal Studies, and the interpretative touches of spin from reporters linking soundbites, cumulatively added up to a style of coverage heavily structured or 'framed' by journalists and experts. Only 17 per cent of election news coverage reported what politicians had said and only about 10 per cent was clips of direct speech. Whatever else the much discussed 'mission to explain' may imply, it presupposes a no lesser mission to report.[7]

Elections are, of course, about individuals as well as issues. As Table 8.4 shows, the dominance of the leaders was as great as ever. Tony Blair took 58 per cent of the time given to reporting what Labour politicians said, with John Major taking 51 per cent for the Conservatives, and Paddy Ashdown taking 58 per cent for the Liberal Democrats. This was much in line with other recent elections: the need for variety probably creates a natural limit.

Outside the reported utterances on which Table 8.4 is based, the leaders were of course seen extensively in non-speaking situations like photo-opportunities and they were also interviewed at length in many programmes outside the news. However, the counter-balance to those forms of 'presidentialisation' was the much greater role of other party spokespersons across the range of current affairs sequences from *GMTV* right through to *The World Tonight*. The number of times people appear in the table combines the nature of the campaign and who the parties wished to promote or sideline. Labour played this customary game highly effectively. Broadcasters spoke with rueful admiration of its ruthless professionalism. Labour's awkward squad was kept silent and invisible by Millbank, as well as by unwonted self-discipline; in a rare sighting of Austin Mitchell on *Newsnight* Robin Cook refused to join issue with him on Europe. Michael Meacher appeared at a morning news conference but was immediately whisked away from the journalists. The one person known to have overridden the party's veto was, as one might have guessed, Clare Short, in BBC2's *Westminster*.

The Conservatives were by no means as well organised or single-minded, and discipline had broken down. They managed to keep the limelight off John Gummer and Douglas Hogg, 'from kindness rather than malice', and Brian Mawhinney featured less than might have been expected for a party chairman. Presumably by accident rather than design, William Hague was not seen in national news, though he appeared in several discussions. The party found it impossible to stifle its Euro-rebels, some of whom received greater play than Cabinet ministers. Women were as ever little in evidence; curiously the Conservatives' smaller band were more prominent than Labour's despite that party's commitment to promoting women, but for different reasons Labour did not often promote Harriet Harman or Margaret Beckett to leading roles. (Women featured more prominently as reporters, with Elinor Goodman nightly; Anne Perkins at BBC1's election desk; Caroline Quinn with the Ashdown campaign; Jackie Ashley, Carole Walker, Margaret Gilmore and others less frequently.) It will be interesting to see what Labour makes of its greatly enlarged cadre of women in 2002.[8]

While the news remained the main means by which most people followed the election, a rich range of other offerings, from *The Breakfast Programme* (Radio 5) through to Channel 4's *Midnight Special*, compensated for its inevitable compressions and omissions – showing that there was more to 'constitutional reform' than Scottish devolution and more to 'Europe' than EMU and quota-hopping. In their customarily differing styles the regular current affairs sequences all covered the issues of the day while also picking up some of the underplayed angles. While *Today* disclaimed any intention of imposing the agenda, with the press more divided and uncertain than in previous elections, its choice of lead each morning had probably never been more influential in shaping the subsequent pattern of the day. At the other end of the day *Newsnight* was as variable as ever. It could offer a totally misconceived discussion of Europe between Frederick Forsyth, Jo Brand and Neil Kinnock, or be wearily cynical with Jeremy Paxman's jibe that manifestos are 'like betting slips: they carry our hopes and dreams, and afterwards are just waste paper'; and it could turn in first-rate journalism in pursuing evasions and half-truths or in tackling Europe before it hit the headlines. Sometimes an irritant, sometimes a bore, it remained a must. Channel 4's *After Midnight,* with an audience of election junkies and insomniacs, was one place where less familiar faces tackled the more unfashionable topics like cultural policy or Britain's place in the world, feeling able to be reasonably unbuttoned because 'nobody' was watching. Regular programmes for the elderly, the young, farmers, people with disabilities, ethnic minorities, even Gaelic speakers, ran election specials. These allowed more detailed and informed exploration of issues than mainstream programmes – for example, Stephen Dorrell, Chris Smith and Emma Nicholson being questioned by a panel of people with disabilities in *From the Edge.*

The range and volume of regional output was greater and more varied than ever. In Scotland, for example, the BBC ran twelve late-evening editions of *Campaign Scotland,* three editions of *Words with Wark* with audience questioning of politicians, four *Election Calls* featuring the Scottish party leaders, and analysis and reports in *Good Morning Scotland, News Afternoon* and *Newsdrive.* Listeners or viewers might at times have imagined they had dropped in on a different election.[9] Wales and Northern Ireland similarly aired a markedly different mix of characters and concerns from the national programming.

Failing the leaders' debate that never was (see p. 85–89), the BBC staged *Debate for a Chancellor* with Kenneth Clarke, Gordon Brown and Malcolm Bruce. Critics dismissed it as a tame affair offering nothing new, yet, despite the awkwardness of conducting a three-way discussion when only two of the participants had any realistic chance of power, it showed that, liberated from the demeaning constraints of the soundbite, politicians were capable of joining issue in a serious and civilised manner. Much the same could be said of several other extended discussions between ministers and their Shadows, which passed almost without comment. However, it was precisely because they were so little remarked on that these encounters shed little light on how a debate between leaders would have affected the campaign.

Peter Jay chaired two BBC2 specials on Britain and Europe and the future of the welfare state, which provided clear analyses and challenging questioning. The *ITV 500* recruited voters from marginal seats, and had them briefed by experts, before they questioned politicians. This was just one of many programmes that brought in ordinary people, whether through phone-ins, studio panels or as 'witnesses' to the impact on them of current or proposed policies. At least one programme dispatched a researcher to scour the land for 'real people'. This increased emphasis on popular participation certainly reflected recognition of a need to persuade a sceptical public that politics was indeed relevant to their everyday lives, and to promote a dialogue between voters and politicians that had to some extent broken down – and, perhaps, a further recognition of the limitations of broadcasters as intermediaries. Again there were styles to suit every taste, from the decorum of *Question Time* to the shouting match conducted by Andrew Neil on *Central Weekend*, where an elderly lady forthrightly concluded a session on pensions: 'I don't really believe any of you!' Fortunately the days when elections on the air were utterly humourless have long since gone, and there also were occasions for laughter with three programmes of election sketches by John Bird and John Fortune on Channel 4, send-ups of the party broadcasts by Harry Enfield on *Newsnight*, and the more laid-back approach of Vincent Hanna and Andrew Rawnsley on *The Week in Politics*.

As usual, the leaders were interviewed at length on programmes as diverse as *Panorama, Breakfast with Frost, On the Record, The World This Weekend, The Jimmy Young Programme, Ruscoe on 5* and *The Enormous Election*, in which John Major was faced by Ulrika Johnson in black leather enquiring what he would do if his unmarried daughter told him she was pregnant. None of these encounters was memorable, not even the last, and commentators concentrated on Tony Blair's nervousness during a tough opening salvo on *Panorama*, or Paddy Ashdown's annoyance over questions querying his prospects of forming a government, rather than the substance of what they had to say. Yet, although questioning was often repetitive and sometimes eccentric, collectively these sessions, with their variation between softer and tougher styles, broader and more specific emphases, were as testing of the leaders' qualities as viewers and listeners could reasonably expect. However intensive the prior briefings, here at least they appeared without the spin-doctors' contrivances.

The closest that broadcasting could come to a debate between the leaders was to have been the *ITV 500* on the last Monday, with the three leaders in turn answering questions from an audience drawn from four marginal constituencies.[10] Tony Blair and Paddy Ashdown were well received, though their sessions had boisterous moments. Michael Heseltine, however, was hissed, accused of conning the public and talking rubbish; he complained that the audience was slanted against him. In fact, his rough reception was largely due to frustration at the non-appearance of the Prime Minister, who had instead embarked on a whirlwind tour of the four countries of the United Kingdom. He pleaded a diary clash, but the booking had been made a year previously and he had resisted all attempts to accommodate his schedule. It seems in retrospect that he had chosen to follow his own preferences with a final, symbolic affirmation of commitment to the Union, even though that meant skipping ITV's most watched political programme of the entire campaign – outside the news. In consequence, Tony Blair was given the programme's closing 'prime ministerial' slot where, ironically, he went out head-to-head with John Major in *Panorama*.

John Major did appear in the traditional *Election Call* phone-ins on BBC1 and Radio 4, along with many other front-benchers. Such programmes hold few terrors for experienced politicians nowadays – though there remains a whiff of danger. There were no disasters, but there were awkward moments. John Major faced a man who, having done everything by the Thatcherite book of self-reliance and enterprise, was ruined, and a Conservative activist who told him roundly that the party was going down to defeat. Another questioner wondered whether he was 'too kind a person to be Prime Minister'. Tony Blair was assailed by an old Labourite who charged him with being 'a plastic Tory. Why have a dummy when you can have the real thing? ... You make [the Vicar of Bray] look like a man who would die for his principles.'

THE PARTY BROADCASTS

The long decline of the party broadcasts continued. ITV had considered dropping the interelection series; the Conservatives had failed to use some of their peacetime slots; and there had been talk of reducing them to one-minute spots. The minor parties at least took them seriously. For all practical purposes news coverage would ignore them but if they mustered fifty candidates they received five minutes on television and radio. To reach an audience of several million people at the cost of fifty lost deposits was a bargain. Sir James Goldsmith contended that, with candidates in over 500 constituencies, 200,000 supporters, and £20m in the bank, he should have three broadcasts. The broadcasters demurred, arguing that the allocation did not rest on candidates alone, but took into account the fact that the Referendum Party was a single-issue party whose goal was to bring about a referendum rather than to govern, it had only one MP (Sir George Gardiner), no electoral record and tiny support in the polls. The party petitioned the High Court for judicial review but was unsuccessful.[11]

The party's single broadcast was delivered by Sir James, glowering from behind a vast desk as if he would have liked to bludgeon viewers into submission, speaking darkly of treachery and cowardice and claiming success by forcing Europe onto the agenda – this when the issue was topping the news agenda nightly. There was neither controversy nor menace about Alan Sked's broadcast for the UK Independence Party. This was a low-key, sober but clear presentation of the party's case against British membership of the European Union, though it strained credulity with its claim that there would be 'no cost – just benefit'. It was marred by over-ripe interpolations from Leo McKern – a familiar face, unlike Sked, but manifestly more talented as Rumpole of the Bailey than as a political broadcaster.

The Pro-Life Alliance was another single-issue party, concerned more with opposing abortion than winning seats. Its programme traced the development of a foetus, culminating in a very late abortion. BBC and ITV officials who previewed the tape and were shocked by this sequence ruled that it broke their guidelines on taste and decency. The Alliance argued that television shows horrific scenes from Bosnia and Rwanda – though in fact it sanitises them to something less than the Alliance proposed to show. They, too, went to court, also without success. The programme was transmitted with the offending material replaced by a caption maintaining that if abortion was indeed too extreme to broadcast, it was too extreme to be legal.

There was a minor problem too with Sinn Fein's broadcast in Northern Ireland, where the BBC required that two shots, which had already been transmitted by Ulster TV, must be cut out as potentially libellous. This was nothing beside the row over the British National Party broadcast. There were protests over its being allowed time, and studios were picketed in the hope that technicians would stop it going out, but the broadcasters were clear they were bound to transmit it as long as it kept within the law. After a preview the BBC and ITV required deletion of shots of an identifiable woman with three children which might imply that she supported the BNP. Channel 5 required deletion of footage of black faces in a street scene and of a school with Urdu signs. Channel 4 then demanded further cuts of street scenes on the ground that clearance had not been obtained from those shown. The BNP could not do this before transmission time and the programme did not go out on Channel 4. This breaking of ranks caused irritation among other broadcasters, who felt Channel 4 had been determined all along to block the programme and win a halo of political correctness. The contention that stock street-scenes required consent had awkward implications – BBC news used an almost identical shot without consent in its piece on the ethnic vote. The broadcast featured John Tyndall, backed by the white cliffs of Dover, then outside parliament, pronouncing his customary commination against the politicians who had betrayed a great nation by throwing away an empire, bowing to Europe and allowing immigration. It was within the law – and actually less anti-immigrant in tone than the BNP's radio broadcast, which passed without comment.

The other minor party broadcasts caused no stir. Socialist Labour featured students, carers, pensioners, and unemployed people with a brief conclusion from a sedately soft-spoken Arthur Scargill. Apart from the way he lumped Conservatives, Liberal Democrats and Labour in common dismissal, this was very much Old Labour at any previous election. The Greens offered graphic visuals of society in ecological crisis. 'It doesn't have to be like this' – but the way ahead lay through lobbying, demonstrations and activism rather than MPs. The Natural Law Party offered a vision of a world beyond politics living in harmony.

There was contention over the SNP broadcasts. Channels 4 and 5 resisted carrying them on technical grounds until the SNP successfully appealed to the Independent Television Commission. Both nationalist parties presented self-government as a solution to every discontent, but, while Plaid Cymru came across as old Labour with a Welsh accent and a Green coat, the SNP was more venturesome. Its star production, by David Hayman (a defector from Labour), was high on atmospherics and overtones of *Braveheart*, but low on party propaganda, with its swirling mists and soft focus battle between two kilted swordsmen whose blades crossed to form the Saltire, its upbeat ceilidh music, twirling Highland dancers and its call to 'unite in a spirit of love ... to embrace our inherent goodness and find purpose in who we are ... the courage to say yes to a parliament of our own in an independent Scotland'. 'Corny', said the critics, but its evocative imagery was skilfully crafted to appeal to non-political viewers – and where else in this election did anyone dare speak of love?

Such flights of fancy were not for the bigger parties. Labour and the Conservatives had recently run utterly negative broadcasts and that vein was by no means exhausted. The Conservatives opened by targeting potential switchers with warnings of what life would be like five years on. As always when parties take the low road, it used actors as 'real people', with not a politician in sight to show what would lie ahead 'if the polls were right': unemployment, inflation, strikes, higher taxes, dearer mortgages. Had it not been so over the top it could well have got under the skin. Saatchi wanted to follow up with a broadcast using the red-eye imagery to sow mistrust of Labour. Although it was said to be 'brilliant' it was made against Brian Mawhinney's instructions and John Major refused to look at it. The next broadcast on 16 April was a change of plan – a piece to camera putting his case on Europe, hastily assembled after his press conference plea to his party. However, where he had conveyed passion and conviction at the press conference, this was the more grey, low-key John Major. Recorded in three takes, it was minimally edited by momentary cuts to black, creating a mildly disconcerting impression as the Prime Minister disappeared, then returned looking slightly less immaculate at each appearance.

Back, then, to negative campaigning. New Labour was a tree without roots, depicted literally as such. It had ditched everything it stood for and would promise anything to win power, but whatever attempts could be made to shore it up would be to no avail. The sole positive note was the closing caption, 'You can only be sure with the Conservatives'. Once more, no politicians. John Major took the fourth and fifth programmes, again solo to camera. The first contrasted Labour and Conservative policies on Europe and devolution, the second argued that Labour had been wrong on every big decision and warned that the unions were still lurking, once more emphasising the threat to the United Kingdom from devolution and a federal Europe', and promising prosperity, with pledges on crime, pensions and schools.

Party broadcasts habitually poach from other genres in the hope of making the medicine go down a bit better. Labour's first was a 'glossy' with prominent business people like Terence Conran, Gerry Robinson and Anita Roddick endorsing New Labour as 'a party that business can do business with'. The second played the patriotic card with 'the most talked about politician of his generation' – Tony Blair. In a chinzy set, he expounded his political ideas and aspirations, interspersed with shots of him meeting world leaders and clips of Fitz. This was Labour's great publicity coup – the only feature of the party broadcasts to gain much attention in the press and in TV news. Fitz was a bulldog of particularly unprepossessing mien – but chiefly, of course, a symbol of patriotism, now being appropriated by New Labour. Sunk initially in apathetic gloom, he roused and then trotted away contentedly as the Blair magic did its work. 'Give Tony Blair your mandate', ran the caption. (Whatever happened to Labour?) Few shots of Blair ran longer than ten seconds before a jump cut to a different camera angle, looking now at the viewer, now over one's right shoulder, now over the left, once at his left ear. Quentin Tarantino without the violence. This was more about conveying impressions of newness, change and youth to Generation X voters than about communicating its formal content.

Back to the fear factor. Labour's dark vision of a Conservative future ran parallel to the Tories' film: over the NHS, crime, the elderly, education, tax and Europe they would cast off all constraints, spreading misery and further decline. It was no less exaggerated but more cunningly executed: sequences illustrating the coming Apocalypse intercut with sightbites doctored to depict prominent Tories as self-satisfied, remote and uncaring fat cats, with 'Land of Hope and Glory' swelling mockingly in the background. (Irony always backfires: Bernie Grant complained that this use of 'colonialist' music was offensive to black voters.)

'Tony: the home video' purported to show the man behind the spin-doctors' image. This was a fly-on-the-wall-style film by Molly Dineen, but based on far less filming and in a much smaller compass than true fly-on-the-wall. Tony Blair was seen with his family, playing tennis, fooling about with kids on a soccer pitch and talking about his background, why he was in politics, his hopes and ideals. One slightly daring sequence had him saying that, in politics, to do what you want you sometimes had to do 'rubbish', over a shot of a vacuous photo-opportunity. Again, the aim was chiefly to convey an impression of Tony Blair as Mr Nice Guy – a youngish, well-intentioned family man, who had known difficult times, had come through and would make a good neighbour. It was skilful and utterly unmemorable.

Finally, there was a bedtime story directed by Stephen (*My Beautiful Laundrette*) Frears. Father and daughter with a broken arm emerge from Casualty after six hours. The polls have closed. They take a taxi. The driver disconcertingly knows all about them and talks about what 'Becky's' life will be under the Conservatives. Eventually he sets them down, saying it is not too late after all. The clock turns back, the polls are still open and, as the taxi drives off, there is a glimpse of the driver's angel's wings. This may have touched a chord with older viewers with its echoes of the James Stewart film, *It's a Wonderful Life*, or of audiences for the more recent *Gabriel* – though Pete Postlethwaite's driver was no John Travolta. It was negative in the nicest possible way and, like the best bedtime stories, it had a happy ending. Its political effectiveness is anyone's guess.

The only politician in the Liberal Democrat series was again their leader. After a conventional tilt at the bigger parties, shown as Punch and Judy battling, they stressed their strength and record in local government, with Paddy Ashdown reiterating their commitment to spend more on education and the NHS. The second broadcast, with echoes of 'Kinnock: The Movie', presented Ashdown the Man, cutting between tributes from 'ordinary' people who had known him at various stages of his life and shots of him jogging through a forest looking craggy and purposeful, in a golden glow. The third alternated between 'blue' and 'red' footballers kicking balls labelled 'education' or 'NHS' and Ashdown the listening politician learning first-hand from teachers and health service professionals, emphasising yet again the theme of 'penny-on-tax-for-education-and-health'. The final programme was again Ashdown, to camera, summarising the party's main proposals and contrasting Tory broken promises and Labour vagueness with the firm pledge to 'put people first'.

Critics are invariably unkind about the party broadcasts. In this election their greatest contempt was directed at talks to camera, seen as wilful neglect of modern communication techniques. None of the to-camera pieces in this election was memorable; some were dire. Yet the suggestion that it is in principle misconceived for a leading politician to address voters directly without interruption and with relatively little artifice, is surely misplaced. Was it really to Labour's credit that Tony Blair did not do so? Viewers could have gained a reasonable grasp of Liberal Democrat and Conservative proposals from their broadcasts, but it is doubtful whether many would have been much wiser about Labour's precise intentions at the end than at the beginning. There were no hostages to fortune, no promises to break – which was doubtless the intention.

As to the future, the litigation and the controversial editorial decisions giving rise to allegations of censorship surrounding the 1997 series, and the uncomfortable awareness of the danger of well-heeled special interests effectively buying normally prohibited airtime, doubtless fostered the broadcasters' readiness to see the end of the party broadcasts. They are under no compulsion to offer time; a public 'save the party broadcasts' campaign is barely conceivable – but will there ever come a time when the nettle can be grasped without a disproportionate fuss from the parties?

And so to the grand finale, with the two television networks locked in costly challenge, each with its Dimbleby, its pundits, its vast Mission Control studio, computer graphics pyrotechnics and more outside broadcasts than ever. And each with its exit poll flashing news of a landslide within minutes of the polls closing. Within an hour it was clear that, this time, the polls had got it right. Here was an event on a scale few had seen previously, the like of which one might never experience again. While radio conveyed and analysed the results with its customary quiet efficiency, this was really television's night with a peak BBC1–ITV audience of more than 13 million. What lingers in the memory is the slow dawning of the magnitude of their victory on Labour faces; Gillian Shephard as pale as death; Michael Portillo, hope shattered yet speaking so graciously in defeat; the furious exchanges between David Mellor and Sir James Goldsmith after the declaration, and Martin Bell stricken with the full realisation that his would-be 48-hour political career would now last five years. And so through to the morning of Labour celebration, with John Major's dignified departure, and shellshocked Conservatives, barely articulate at the extent of the disaster, groping towards a leadership contest. This was compelling television, covered by both networks with sureness and panache right through to Tony Blair's triumph in Downing Street. Here was a Labour leader not only taking power but doing so amid a sea of Union flags, so reasserting New Labour's claim to the most basic image of patriotism that Old Labour had so long allowed to be the monopoly of the right. This was surely also a sign that the thoughtful hand supplying those flags was, even in the moment of victory, looking forward to the campaign of 2002.

NOTES

1. Unless otherwise stated, 'election news' is defined as all material verbally or visually referring to the general election or including statements by party representatives in BBC1 and ITV main evening news, 6 March–30 April, and BBC1/ITV lunch and early evening news, *Channel 4 News, 5 News* and Radio 4 at 0800, 1300, 1800 and midnight, 4–30 April 1997.
   Political coverage not explicitly about the campaign constituted over a quarter of the main evening news in early March but fell to very low levels once the election was under way. The major exception was the IRA bomb attacks and scares – these were covered at length. Apart from a sharp exchange when Michael Howard tried to tar Labour with being soft on terrorism, Northern Ireland reaction to these happenings, and Home Office advice to returning officers about attacks on polling day, coverage of these events was not explicitly keyed into the election – which is not to suggest it therefore had no impact on the campaign.
2. Independent Television News supplies news for ITV, Channel 4 and Channel 5. However, here and subsequently, 'ITN' is used in respect of ITV news only.
3. An ITC research paper put the fall over the six weeks at 20 per cent, but it was greater in the four weeks of the main campaign. J. Sancho-Aldridge, *Election '97: Viewers' Responses to the Television Coverage* (1997). The majority of viewers in the ITC's survey paid 'at least some' attention to the coverage, but four in ten actively avoided it. 57 per cent thought there was too much coverage on BBC1, 46 per cent for ITV, 40 per cent for BBC2, and 28 per cent for Channel 4. The only aspect of coverage receiving 'too little' coverage was 'party policies'. Substantial minorities also thought that the minor parties, including the SNP and Plaid Cymru, received too little coverage. After the election 56 per cent said that coverage had given them what they wanted, with 27 per cent disagreeing and 17 per cent not replying. Many of those who disagreed blamed the parties rather than the broadcasters.
4. See, for example, 'Anatomy of a Turn-off' by Richard Tait, Editor-in-Chief of ITN, *Guardian*, 20 May 1997. Tait described coverage as 'dull and incomplete' but apparently saw no part of the blame as falling on the broadcasters.
5. Time when the party was quoted or its policies or activities otherwise reported, all channels, 2–30 April, excluding 'governmental' stories not reported in an election context – that is, featured within the election package or including partisan statements. (The conventions relating to government announcements during elections meant that there was little of this.)
6. *The Times*, 1 May 1997.
7. See commentaries by Michael Billig and others, *Guardian*, 11, 14, 28 April and 5 May 1997.
8. The ITC survey noted that women felt the news was dominated by men and that issues of concern to them were neglected. They also disliked negative campaigning.
9. However, this did not satisfy the SNP. It contended that in the 80 per cent of coverage seen in Scotland made by the network companies, it featured in only 14 per cent of items, compared with 68 per cent for the Conservatives, 60 per cent for Labour, and 64 per cent for the Liberal Democrats. It was particularly critical of ITN coverage (*Scotsman*, 22 April 1997).
10. There was also a separate *Scottish ITV 500*.
11. This episode laid to rest the Committee on Party Political Broadcasting, at one time deeply involved in the allocation of broadcasts. This had effectively been decided by the broadcasters for many years, and the Committee had not actually met since 1983. Under the Broadcasting Act responsibility now lies with the broadcasters.

9 The Press[1]

Margaret Scammell and Martin Harrop

The 1997 election was a landmark in the political history of Britain's press. It was the first campaign in which Labour secured the support of most national daily newspapers. Six of the ten backed Labour: the *Sun*, the *Daily Star*, the *Financial Times* just about, the *Guardian*, the *Independent* and the *Mirror*, the last three combining their preference for Labour with an appeal for anti-Conservative tactical voting. Conservative support was confined to the *Express*, the *Daily Mail* and the *Daily Telegraph*, with *The Times* advocating a vote for Euro-sceptic candidates of varied hue. At 7.9 million, the combined circulation of Labour newspapers was well ahead of the 4.5 million for the Conservatives (see Table 9.1). By readership rather than circulation, Labour's triumph was even more striking. The Labour papers had 21.6 million readers, double the 10.6 million figure for the Conservative press. True, Labour's lead was smaller than that achieved by Margaret Thatcher; in 1983, after all, the *Mirror* had been Labour's sole voice on Fleet Street. Yet, given the traditional dominance of the Conservative press, Labour's triumph in 1997 was remarkable. In whatever way we interpret Labour's performance in the 'real' election, there is no doubt that in press coverage, 1997 was the party's finest hour.

By contrast, 1997 saw a disastrous press campaign for the Conservatives. The *Sun* and *The Times* abandoned ship. The *Express*, in 1992 virtually the propaganda mouthpiece of Conservative Central Office, was at best lukewarm. Moreover, the *Daily Mail*, together with the most committed Tory adherent, the *Daily Telegraph*, ran stridently Euro-sceptic campaigns rallying the party's rebels into open opposition to the government's single currency policy. With friends like these, John Major had no need of enemies.

How did this striking transformation of press fortunes come about? The omens foretold gloom for Major nearly two years earlier when he sought and won re-election to the leadership of his own party. All the traditional Tory daily press, bar the *Express* group, sought his defeat. Several, prophetically as it turned out, predicted that Major's triumph meant inevitable ruin at the general election. 'Chickens Hand It To Blair' proclaimed the *Sun*, summarising the views of many in Fleet Street. *The Times* warned that Conservative MPs had thrown away their best opportunity, while the *Daily Mail* foresaw the possibility of 'meltdown' at the forthcoming general election.

Table 9.1   Partisanship and circulation of national daily newspapers

Name of paper Ownership group (Chairman) Editor Preferred result	Circulation[1] (1992 in brackets) (000s)	Readership[2] (1992 in brackets) (000s)	% of readers in social grade[3] (1992 in brackets)			
			AB	C1	C2	DE
Mirror Mirror Group PLC (Sir Robert Clark) Ed. P. Morgan Labour victory[4]	2390 (2903)	6389 (8035)	10 (6)	23 (18)	31 (36)	36 (40)
Express United News & Media PLC (Lord Stevens) Ed. R. Addis Conservative victory	1208 (1525)	2878 (3643)	24 (20)	34 (34)	23 (26)	19 (20)
Sun News Corp Ltd. (Australia) (Rupert Murdoch) Ed. S. Higgins Labour victory	3935 (3571)	10211 (9857)	8 (5)	22 (17)	30 (35)	40 (43)
Daily Mail Daily Mail & General Trust PLC (Lord Rothermere) Ed. P. Dacre Conservative victory	2127 (1675)	5159 (4303)	28 (24)	38 (32)	18 (25)	16 (19)
Daily Star United News & Media PLC (Lord Stevens) Ed. P. Walker Labour victory	660 (806)	2089 (2628)	7 (4)	19 (14)	34 (38)	40 (44)
Daily Telegraph Hollinger Inc. (Conrad Black) Ed. C. Moore Conservative victory	1126 (1038)	2542 (2492)	56 (49)	28 (32)	9 (11)	7 (7)
Guardian Scott Trust (Hugo Young) Ed. A. Rusbridger Labour victory[5]	402 (429)	1274 (1214)	57 (52)	29 (27)	5 (11)	8 (11)
The Times News Corp Ltd. (Australia) (Rupert Murdoch) Ed. P. Stothard Vote for Euro-sceptics[6]	772 (386)	1904 (1035)	57 (61)	27 (26)	8 (8)	8 (6)

Table 9.1   continued

Name of paper Ownership group (Chairman) Editor Preferred result	Circulation[1] (1992 in brackets) (000s)	Readership[2] (1992 in brackets) (000s)	% of readers in social grade[3] (1992 in brackets)			
			AB	C1	C2	DE
Independent Newspaper Publishing PLC (Liam Healy) Ed. A. Marr Labour victory[7]	256 (390)	867 (1083)	52 (52)	31 (29)	8 (11)	9 (7)
Financial Times Pearson PLC (Lord Blakenham) Ed. R. Lambert Labour victory	304 (290)	717 (668)	63 (57)	26 (30)	5 (8)	6 (5)

Notes:
1. ABC figures, April 1997.
2. National Readership Survey (NRS), January 1996–December 1996 average.
3. Calculated from NRS which classifies the population aged 15 or over as follows:
   AB (professional, administrative, managerial) – 21% (1992: 18%)
   C1 (other non-manual) – 28% (1992: 24%)
   C2 (skilled manual) – 22% (1992: 27%)
   DE (semi-skilled or unskilled, residual) – 29% (1992: 31%)
   Some of the increase in ABC1s (for individual papers as well as for the whole population) is due to a change in measurement. Social grade is now based on the Chief Income Earner within the household, rather than the 'Head of Household' used previously.
4. To 'gang up on every Tory', also advised Labour supporters to vote tactically for Liberal Democrat candidates in 22 seats; and Liberal Democrats to vote Labour in 95 seats.
5. Also suggested anti-Conservative tactical voting to ensure strong Liberal Democrat representation.
6. Mainly Conservative and Labour Euro-sceptics but also including some Liberal Democrats, two Referendum Party candidates and candidates from a range of parties in Northern Ireland.
7. Also suggested tactical voting to ensure strong Liberal Democrat representation; to preserve pro-Europe one-nation Conservatives; and to help some Scottish Nationalists in Conservative-held seats.

Europe lay at the heart of Major's troubles with the Tory press. All, again, excepting the *Express* and the *Daily Star*, had been critical of him for nearly three years prior to the leadership contest. The pivotal moment was Britain's ejection from the European Exchange Rate Mechanism on 'Black

Wednesday', September 1992, generally welcomed by the Tory press, but with no thanks to John Major. The long-term Euro-sceptics, *The Times* and the *Daily Mail,* were reinforced in 1995 by the addition of the *Daily Telegraph* when arch anti-federalist Charles Moore took over the editorship from Max Hastings.

Changes in press ownership did not aid the Conservative cause. The MAI media empire, headed by Labour peer Lord Hollick, merged with United News in February 1996, and almost immediately the group's stable of papers (*Daily Express, Sunday Express* and *Daily Star*) began to display new-found editorial independence from Conservative Central Office. The once unthinkable did eventually happen, when, after the general election, the editor Richard Addis announced that the *Daily Express* was now supporting Labour.

Fundamentally, though, Labour's circulation lead over the Tories can be accounted for by the *Sun* alone. Rupert Murdoch's News International had plunged the British press into a three-year price war, cutting the cost of the *Sun* to just 5p and *The Times* to 30p (about the price of most tabloids). Both papers emerged clear winners (see Table 9.1), the *Sun* boosting its sales to almost four million, at some cost to the *Mirror*, while *The Times* doubled its circulation, largely at the expense of the *Independent.* Ironically Murdoch's *Today* (another Tory supporter in 1992), was the one fatality of the circulation war, sacrificed in November 1995. Others, especially the *Daily Star* and the *Independent,* teetered on the brink, but survived, in part due to the backing of new Labour-supporting owners. Lord Hollick's MAI owned the *Daily Star,* while the *Mirror* group bought a 43 per cent stake in the *Independent* in 1995 after a period of turmoil in which the founding editor, Andreas Whittam Smith, and the new editor, Ian Hargreaves, quit.

There were other anxieties for the newspapers, not least the continuing threat of legislation to prevent press invasions of privacy. The government eventually backed off statutory controls and a potentially bruising encounter with the newspaper owners, preferring instead to beef up the powers of the Press Complaints Commission. Despite all this turbulence, the press endured to enter the 1997 campaign much as it was in 1992, in name at least, if not in partisanship nor ownership. There were no new titles on the scene and only one casualty, *Today.* [2]

HOW INDIVIDUAL PAPERS COVERED THE CAMPAIGN

Press coverage overall was a curious mix of the tediously familiar and the startlingly changed. In the main, the same newspapers used the same established columnists and correspondents. In style and tone, the broadsheets largely repeated the formulae of 1992, with massively extended political coverage and never-ending punditry. The shocks were provided by the tabloids. Erstwhile Tory tabloids behaved in such unfamiliar ways as to require suspension of disbelief by anyone who remembered their strident aggression during the 1980s.

The *Sun* as ever led the way. In fact, the *Sun*'s decision to back Tony Blair was not a complete surprise. The paper and its proprietor had long acclaimed his leadership and waxed poetic about his party conference performances. Blair and his Press Secretary Alastair Campbell had worked assiduously to thaw icy relations with the Tory press, and a majority of the *Sun*'s readers now supported Labour (see Table 9.2). However, until the paper declared for Labour, with deadly timing on the day after Major announced the election, it had been careful to distinguish between the admirable Blair and his dubious party. Now, on the instructions of Rupert Murdoch, the *Sun* threw its weight behind Labour, to the obvious discomfort of some correspondents, including its political editor, Trevor Kavanagh.[3] The result was that the *Sun*'s coverage was strangely compromised.

It rivalled the *Mirror*'s ardour for Tony Blair. He was a 'strong, dynamic and purposeful leader'; Britain was 'crying out for him', it told readers the day before polling, under the banner 'Who Blair's Wins'. Mr Blair became virtually a regular *Sun* columnist, so often did the paper give him space for his unedited views. Yet, it could not quite suppress its doubts about Labour links with unions or policies on Europe, the Social Chapter, the single currency and the minimum wage. The trick of smothering doubt with trust in Tony was never entirely convincing. Moreover, its old friends, the Tories, were now 'tired and tarnished' but did not present the unambiguous target once provided by Neil Kinnock and the Labour left.

What might the *Sun* of old have made of Labour's early uncertainty on devolution and privatisation? All the *Sun* of 1997 could offer was a feeble defence of Labour. 'The Tory attacks on U-turns are missing the point', ran its editorial (8 April). 'Tony Blair has now pointed his party in the right way.' Gordon Brown's admission, under pressure, that there was a hole in Labour's spending plans, was cited merely as an example of 'honest politics'. The European issue tested the paper's new loyalties and it performed contortions to combine its Euro-hostility with support for the less Euro-sceptic party. Where once there was sharp brevity there was now long-winded ambivalence: Blair should realise that the single currency was not just an economic issue, its editorial advised (17 April).

Table 9.2   *Party supported by daily newspaper readers*

Newspaper		Party supported by readers		
		Con %	Lab %	Lib Dem %
Daily Telegraph	1997	57	20	17
	1992	72	11	16
Express	1997	49	29	16
	1992	67	15	14
Daily Mail	1997	49	29	14
	1992	65	15	18
Financial Times	1997	48	29	19
	1992	65	17	16
The Times	1997	42	28	25
	1992	64	16	19
Sun	1997	30	52	12
	1992	45	36	14
Daily Star	1997	17	66	12
	1992	31	54	12
Independent	1997	16	47	30
	1992	25	37	34
Mirror	1997	14	72	11
	1992	20	64	14
Guardian	1997	8	67	22
	1992	15	55	24

Note: Whole sample: Con 31%, Lab 44%, Lib Dem 17%. Non-readers (30% of whole sample): Con 29%, Lab 43%, Lib Dem 21%.

Source: MORI Political Aggregate, 21 March–29 April (N=13,544).

Normally, the tabloids' electoral stories are dominated by knocking copy. The *Sun* promised more of the same, opening with the Piers Merchant scandal. Yet, thereafter the *Sun* seemed to lose its stomach for the fight. It did not once lead with an attack on its new 'enemy' during the campaign proper (see Table 9.3). With the Tories' early campaign mired in sleaze, the *Sun* responded, not with lethal savagery, but with a pompous editorial. Tatton Tories should kick out Neil Hamilton 'so that we can start thinking about politics again'. In 1992 the *Sun* gave us: 'Nightmare On Kinnock Street.' In 1997 it was reduced to the cliche of every desperate trainee: 'Christmas

Table 9.3   Front-page lead stories about the general election campaign, 9 April–1 May 1997

Date	Mirror	Express	Sun	Daily Mail	Daily Star	Daily Telegraph	Guardian	The Times	Independent	Financial Times
Apr 1	(Hillsborough tape)	(Buried alive)	(Passer-by attacks Di snapper)	Sleaze – Major acts	(Spice Girls)	Thatcher attacks Blair	Labour warns teachers	Expulsion for sleaze	Major slides into sleaze	(Hostile bid restrictions)
2	(Intruder at Palace)	Major 20p tax target	(Palace raps Di)	Tory tax bonus	(TV girl's fury)	Major trumpets booming Britain	Tories close poll gap	Tory 20p tax target	Candidate needed for Tatton	Tory tax plan
3	Major's 'happy family'	Blair's aide in sex gaffe	(Drunk sues pub)	Unions' conspiracy of silence	(Spice Girls)	Tories pitch for family	Fight for the family	Major's 'best country' offer	Tories promise golden future	Tories stress tax and welfare
4	Mirror's chicken licks PM	IRA won't stop the National	Trust Tony	Tycoon claims legal aid	(Countdown host)	Your taxes safe, says Blair	'Trust me' – Blair	Trust me, says Blair	Blair's pledge to Britain	Blair's 10-point 'covenant'
5	(Grand National)	(Di's richer than Charles)	(Tesco bungle)	(Water leaks)	(Grand National)	Blair's Tartan Tax storm	Major stirs Scots row	Blair 'insults Scotland'	(Pensions scandal)	PM attacks Blair on Scotland
7	(Grand National)	White Knight for Tatton	(Grand National)	Bell to fight sleaze MP	(Grand National)	Reporter to fight Hamilton	Bell to fight Hamilton	Bell stands against Hamilton	(Economy growing, people worse off)	Labour will not join EMU
8	(Grand National)	Sleaze wife at war	(Gallagher-Kensit wedding)	(Grand National)	(Oasis)	Unions warn Blair	Bell to fight 'poison'	Blair does not oppose privatisation	Tatton soap opera	(Pound hits high)
9	Martin Bell Reporting	(escape from death)	(Gallagher-Kensit wedding)	Labour's broken Promise	(Gallagher-Kensit wedding)	Hamilton wins backing	Hamilton beats rebels	Tatton Tories back Hamilton	Just 70,000 voters targeted	Hamilton wins fight over seat
10	(Tracy Shaw)	Now it's a real contest	(Tracy Shaw)	(Bodysnatch case)	(Spice Girls)	(National Trust bans stag hunts)	Tories make it personal	Labour's poll lead slashed	New Labour Wobbles	Labour doubt on windfall tax
11	(Mrs Merton)	IRA shoots mothers	(Cops brawl)	(Rape case)	(Spice Girls)	More EU curbs on work hours	(Iranian terror)	Tories flout party line on EU	(CIA botched Saddam defeat)	(Computer 2000 timebomb)
12	(Rape case)	(Tiggy Legge-Bourke)	(Hamster eats through car)	(Rape case)	(Herbie Hide)	Unions flex their muscles	'Cash for quote' row hits Major	Euro-sceptics off the leash	IRA target London	(US & EU end Cuba trade rift)
14	Mowlam tough as old boots	Prescott in 'lies storm	(Grandad aged 29)	Prescott 'lies' Storm	(Spice Girls)	Blair seeks to revive campaign	Blair's education trump card	Blair injects passion & vision	Schools lured to become grammar	Blair to shake up campaign
15	(Merton marriage split)	(Princess Diana)	(Eastenders)	The battle for Britain	(Merton marriage split)	Labour changes tack on EU	'Hypocrisy' outburst by Major	Blair & Major to disrupt EU	Tories at war over schools	(Building society flotation)
16	Tories admit job figure lies	Come clean on Europe	(Rape case)	Europe – the great revolt	(Ron Atkinson argument)	Minister defies Major	Fake job figures	Tories join Euro-sceptic crush	Dare Major sack ministers?	Tory crisis over EU rebels

Date	Mirror	Express	Sun	Daily Mail	Daily Star	Daily Telegraph	Guardian	The Times	Independent	Financial Times
17	Heroin smoked on Major's jet	(Michael Green)	Drug scandal on PM's jet	Major's EU Pledge	(Gallagher-Kensit wedding)	Major gambles all on Europe	Major at war with his party	Don't bind my hands says Major	Major vs. his Party	Major gambles on EU campaign (Co-op suspends 2 executives)
18	Read this & weep - NHS destroyed	Another minister rebels on EU	(slimming pills)	(Leukaemia victim)	(Schwarzenegger operation)	Blair puppet of EU in Tory ad	Meet Joe Bloggs the Chancellor	Major offers free vote on EU	3rd world debt	(Regan bid for Co-op)
19	(£25 flights)	(Television addict)	(Tiggy Legge-Bourke)	(Rape case)	(Spice girls)	Powell backs Tory on EU	Major's bumper honours list	Howe attacks Tory advert	Strategy working says IRA	Tory divisions on EU widen
21	(£25 flights)	(Prison baby)	(Princess Diana)	(Car driver attempts murder)	(Pamela Anderson)	Euro-sceptics to rule Tory Party	(Israel crisis as PM tainted)	Ministers spoil Tory fightback	It's not over yet	(Building society flotation)
22	(£25 flights)	(Migrant can stay)	(lottery jackpot)	Keep your nose Out	(Snooker)	Santer interferes in election	Santer attacks door merchants	Santer accused of interfering	Sinn Fein to sit in Parliament	CBI poised to back Euro
23	(Spice Girls)	Major: I'll wreck EU summit	(le Tissier split)	Labour lead Crashes	(Eastenders)	Labour lead collapses in poll	Poll bombshell for Labour	(ITV rebuked for diet of scaps)	Fight to the death	Tories use leaked Labour strategy
24	(le Tissier split)	(Prince Andrew)	(le Tissier split)	(murder case)	(Oasis)	Labour's scare tactics exposed	Battle of the war book	BMA & teachers' fury at lottery plan	Major: I'll always play fair	(Regan bid for Co-op)
25	MP tries to get pals off gun rap	(Ayckbourn divorce)	(25 1-night stands)	Business leaders don't trust Labour	(adultery revenge)	Liar liar, election on fire	Major & Blair go for the kill	Tories attack Blair lies	The truth about Health	(Regan bid for Co-op)
26	Heseltine's tax Claim	(Royal corgis)	Branson backs Blair?	(water meters)	(Eastenders)	Blair plays on fears of elderly	Tory apart by Tory infighting (Britain tops child poverty league)	Major leads final push	Terror threat to election day	(Regan bid for Co-op)
28	59 doctors break silence	Major's last bid to avert disaster	Blair kicks out lefties	Water firms' record profits	(Spice Girls)	Tory squabbling mars final push		Portillo & Heseltine would fight	Blair turns screw on EU	Tory rift a threat to last days
29	Dorrell's 66p Slaves	Major: I'll quit as leader	(sperm donor baby)	(kidnap)	(Emmerdale baby)	72 hours to save union says Major	Blair plans a benefit freeze	72 hours to save UK says Major	Tories giving up	Tories seek tidy leadership battle
30	The fat lady's Singing, John	Major's rage at Euro plot	Who Blairs wins	1000 years of history at stake	(model mugged)	Britain could lose seat at summits	Sykes paid 237 Tories	Rivals close ranks v. EU chief	Tories praying for a miracle	Blair to choose own cabinet
May 1	Your country Needs Blair	Now it's up to you	It must be you, Blair	The great don't know factor	Labour win odds are 12-1 on	Don't give up on us says Major	Looking into the future	Blair bound for No. 10 say polls	So today is freedom day	Labour set for victory

comes early this year ... on May 2'. The *Sun* in 1992 was aggressive, outrageous and memorable; in 1997 it was almost moderate, mainly positive and eminently forgettable, save for its switch to Labour. The *Sun*, in a word, was tame.

But at what future cost to Labour, commentators asked? The *Daily Telegraph*'s Stephen Glover speculated on the 'devil's bargain' struck between Blair and Murdoch, possibly more profound sleaze 'than anything the *Guardian* has uncovered within the Tory party' (4 April). The *Independent*'s editor, Andrew Marr, watched Blair's increasingly jingoistic columns in the *Sun* with mounting alarm. Finally, when a Blair piece appeared under the headline, 'We'll see off Euro dragons', Marr exploded. Blair had backed himself into a treacherous corner, he wrote (23 April), where he will be either 'betraying the whole emotional tone of his *Sun* piece or betraying our nation's better future.'

For the *Sun,* and for the press generally, 1997 was a low-intensity news campaign. Judged by front-page lead stories and by editorials, the newspapers reduced the priority they gave to this election (see Table 9.4). Only 47 per cent of all editorials focused on the election, compared to 62 per cent among the same papers in 1992. On the front pages, the drop in interest was particularly marked in the tabloids.

The one exception here was the *Mirror* (which had abandoned the word *Daily* on its masthead). The *Sun*'s great rival had a confident and at times jubilant election as it warmed to the prospect of a Labour landslide. It began the campaign proper with an eye-catching front-page swipe at 'Major's Happy Family' accompanied by mug-shots of sleaze-ridden Conservatives, 'the biggest collection of philanderers, adulterers and love-cheats in political history'. It wound up its campaign with a front-page constructed picture of a gloomy Major peering through the Number 10 window at an opera singer outside. 'The Fat Lady's Singing, John', it boomed, announcing joyfully that 'the *Mirror* backs Major ... to lose by the biggest landslide in political history'. In between, the paper did its best to retrieve the tabloid reputation for assault politics, with lead stories and editorials attacking the Tories over sleaze, 'lies' on tax and the NHS, and disarray on Europe. Unlike the *Sun,* the *Mirror* had no qualms about hitting the enemy. Like the *Sun,* however, it had no doubts about Labour's biggest asset: Tony Blair. The *Mirror* sustained a personal campaign focused on the leader's qualities. Its eve-of-poll editorial summed up the reasons to vote Labour in two simple points: 'One is to get the Tories out. The other is to get Tony Blair in.' Its polling day front page could not have made the point more clearly: 'Your Country Needs Him'. The huge headline, echoing the famous First World War recruitment poster, was laid over a picture of the man himself.

Table 9.4   Profile of press content

	Mirror	Express	Sun	Daily Mail	Daily Star
Mean number of pages					
1997	42	78	46	76	40
(1992)	(39)	(52)	(44)	(55)	(37)
Front pages lead stories on election					
1997, 27 days	13	14	6	14	1
(1992, 25 days)	(13)	(19)	(9)	(18)	(5)
Editorials on election					
Number/out of	31/41	24/65	39/76	34/44	19/52
Per cent	76	37	51	77	37
(1992, per cent)	(100)	(97)	(59)	(79)	(34)

	Daily Telegraph	Guardian	The Times	Financial Times	Independent
Mean number of pages					
1997	52	84	67	61	56
(1992)	(41)	(44)	(47)	(37)	(44)
Front pages lead stories on election					
1997, 27 days	25	23	25	21	17
(1992, 25 days)	(24)	(23)	(25)	(22)	(20)
Editorials on election					
Number/out of	38/78	35/71	32/78	27/49	15/70
Per cent	49	49	41	55	21
(1992, per cent)	(68)	(72)	(51)	(52)	(55)

Note: All tables in this chapter cover the period 1 April–1 May. Page count based on Monday to Friday issues only.

In its presidential tone, the *Mirror* followed Labour's campaign. Moreover, its general coverage was clearly coordinated with Labour's campaign headquarters at Millbank. Inside double-spread features coincided exactly with the Labour's same day press briefings on the key issues of education, health, unemployment and so on. The *Mirror* caught perfectly the mood of Labour's campaign – upbeat and optimistic in outlook, moral and angry at Tory failures. It was prepared to steal cliches from its rivals, as with its regular topless 'Blair babes' who offered endorsements for Tony. There was the occasional innovation, such as the front page (18 April) entirely given over to a quote from a 'sobbing nurse' who had phoned the paper to tell it of a young cancer patient who had just died in her arms: 'Read This And Weep' ran the headline. The nurse later announced that she was voting Liberal Democrat, which did not make the *Mirror* front page. Not all the *Mirror*'s ruses could hit the mark. Generally, however, the *Mirror* fought a more vibrant campaign than in 1992 when the paper's dismal tone seemed out of step with the Labour party.

The *Express* (which, like the *Mirror* had abandoned the *Daily*) provided another tale of the unexpected. This most committed of all Tory tabloids in 1992 turned distinctly cool. It showed significantly less interest in the campaign both in its front page coverage and in its comment pieces. Editorials on the election reduced dramatically from 97 per cent in 1992 to just 37 per cent (see Table 9.4). Both in the selection of stories and in general tone of reporting, the paper was relatively fair and balanced, in itself a remarkable change for an election *Express*. This was the paper that in 1992 recalled from Moscow its human rottweiler, Peter Hitchens, to bite chunks out of Neil Kinnock. Mr Hitchens was still there, but this time grinding his teeth forlornly in his daily column while his paper pursued a far less hostile campaign.

Editorial criticism of Labour was muted to say the least, even when opportunities presented themselves. While Chancellor Ken Clarke branded Labour as 'unprincipled scoundrels' for their U-turns, the *Express* contented itself with an extraordinarily lame comment piece under the headline, 'Honest Tony shrugs off baggage of opposition'. While the other Tory papers accused Labour of shameful dishonesty in its attacks on Conservative pension plans, the *Express* muttered thanks for 'noisy and lively' politics (26 April). Occasionally, schizophrenia broke out, with its news and columns at odds with the editorial. 'Prescott Lies Storm,' thundered the lead story headline over the Labour Deputy Leader's admission that the minimum wage would cost jobs, but inside, the editorial was rather kindly to Prescott, 'this very human man'.

The *Express*'s attitude to the Conservatives was particularly striking. John Major's hitherto loyal supporter adopted a carping tone, condemning the Prime Minister's reluctance to back the zero-tolerance crime policy and berating his single currency stance. Even the Prime Minister's 'impressive' defence of 'wait and see' won only grudging praise from the *Express*. 'If Major now has iron in his soul, it is because he has been sitting on the fence too long', suggested its opinion piece (17 April). The *Express* took a long time to summon up reasons for a Conservative vote but eventually found some in the final days before polling. It was a difficult choice, said the paper, and the *Express* had sympathy with voters' frustrations with the government. However, readers should recall the good things the Tories had done with the economy and that 'means a vote for the Conservatives on Thursday'. If this endorsement sounded restrained, the paper compounded the impression with the following day's opinion: 'Another Tory Achievement Worth Noting', said the headline over a piece offering 'some' credit for Conservative management of the NHS in difficult times.

Alone among the traditional Tory popular press, the *Daily Mail* fought a spirited campaign. However, its support for the Conservatives mainly took the form of a steady bombardment against Labour and its leader. It sought, with some vigour but little originality, to resurrect the old demons. A double-page feature on 'Labour's Rotten Core' exposed Labour's 'town hall sleaze' and financial profligacy (10 April). A front-page 'exclusive' warned that Labour's union 'bully boys' were back to their old tricks, destroying jobs (16 April). In truth this was a paltry story, the case of an obscure confectioner's factory, but for the *Daily Mail* it was evidence enough that a Labour government would let the trade unions back off the leash. The *Daily Mail* stood apart from all the other tabloids by finding nothing to admire in Tony Blair. A series of early unconvincing media performances suggested that Mr Blair was the weak link, the paper claimed (11 April). He was not to be trusted on either the economy or Europe. His attacks on Conservative pension plans were 'shamefully disreputable', according to a succession of editorials. Labour's silence on Europe was damning and Tony Blair's 'all things to all men' campaign gave the *Daily Mail* no answers as to how he would behave in government, except, menacingly, a promise of radicalism and a constant threat of ever more regulation.

More than any other paper, the *Daily Mail* pursued its own anti-Europe agenda. Its intervention here altered the shape of the entire campaign and almost certainly influenced Conservative strategy. On 15 April, the *Daily Mail* announced that Europe was *the* issue of the campaign. It denounced all the party leaders for their deafening silence on the single currency. Under the banner 'The Battle for Britain', a full front-page editorial saluted the Tory

Euro-rebels: 'nothing less is at stake than the freedom of Britain as a self-governing nation'. The *Daily Mail* drummed out the 'Battle for Britain' beat for the rest of the election, establishing a hotline to encourage Euro-sceptic candidates to go public, and publishing the names, pictures and constituencies of the growing list. The paper claimed that the 'great revolt' had at last given voters real choice and put clear blue water between the parties (17 April). By eve-of-poll, the *Daily Mail* was able to list 308 Tory candidates (out of a total of 648) opposed to the single currency. Its front page was plastered with the Union flag, inside which it gave a grim warning to voters: 'There is a terrible danger that the British people, drugged by the seductive mantra "time for a change" are stumbling, eyes glazed into an election that could undo 1000 years of our nation's history.'

Obsessed with Britain's 'survival as an independent sovereign nation', the *Daily Mail* displayed an astonishingly critical attitude towards John Major and, to a lesser extent, the Conservative government. As the campaign wore on, any residual sympathy for the Tory leader wore out. By 30 April, the *Daily Mail* could declare that it 'holds no torch for this Conservative administration. Indeed we have been its sternest critic ... Major's incompetence has really marred his administration. To be blunt, he has been an ineffectual leader. Too often he has talked tough and acted weak.' The *Daily Mail,* it appeared, was now more conservative than Conservative: 'this newspaper passionately believes in real conservative values. That is why we have been so critical of much of Mr Major's governance.'

Given that Europe was 'the defining issue of this election', for whom should the paper's readers actually vote? For the 'weak, ineffectual' John Major or for Mr Blair's 'chameleon attractions'? The logic of the *Daily Mail*'s position implied that it should follow *The Times* in inviting its readers to support Euro-sceptic candidates from any party. Indeed, on election eve, when the *Daily Mail* published its final list of candidates opposed to 'abolishing the pound', it did suggest that 'your candidate's position on Europe might help you decide how to vote'. But logic, it seems, is not everything. In its key editorial, the *Daily Mail* drew back from making a historic break with the Conservatives. Its leader writers concluded that 'the great majority of the Tories are more sceptical about a Federal Europe than their Labour counterparts ... It is, therefore, the Conservatives, we believe, who will more vigorously defend Britain's interests against Brussels ... If you believe that this country should retain its independence you must, however reluctantly, vote Conservative.' This was a suitably contorted conclusion to the *Daily Mail*'s campaign. The final twist came later when Lord Rothermere, the proprietor, declared his personal support for Tony Blair.

While the *Daily Mail* worked itself into a Euro-lather, the *Daily Star* could scarcely have cared less about the election. Politics pushed the celebrity stories off the front page just once during the campaign, May 1, and even then a model with suitably positioned red, blue and yellow rosettes posed over the *Daily Star*'s encouragement for its readers to vote. The *Daily Star* found little to choose between the parties but finally it plumped for Labour: 'Blair offers a new team, a new dream. All John Major can offer is extra time'. However the *Daily Star*'s main appeal was for people to vote, come what may: 'marking that X in secret is one of the next best things to sex'.

The contrast between the *Daily Star* and the broadsheets could hardly have been greater. All the qualities, bar the *Financial Times*, devoted several pages each day to election coverage, with the *Guardian*'s daunting eight-page section taking the prize for quantity. The *Financial Times* confined itself to a modest two pages, which it felt was enough to report the news that mattered. The others filled their extra acres with some useful issue analysis, personality and constituency profiles and much unremarkable commentary, often discussing the performance of other media. The battle of the pundits was fought in an overcrowded field; few offered any original insight.

The *Daily Telegraph*, however, had a fine partisan campaign. It was no less Euro-sceptic than the *Daily Mail* and the *Express* but still managed to offer John Major the most committed support of the Tory press. A Conservative vote was the only serious choice, it told readers the day before polling. 'Why buy the imitation when you can have the original?', it asked, echoing Margaret Thatcher's dismissal of New Labour. When, in the last week, others thought all was lost for the Tories, the *Daily Telegraph* urged the party 'to fight the good fight' with all its might. The election was about the integrity and independence of the UK and on this issue, 'right, after all, is on their side'.

Throughout the campaign, *Daily Telegraph* editorials were powerful, distinct and sometimes extreme in their condemnation of New Labour. Tony Blair, sardonically titled the 'Sun King', displayed dangerous enthusiasm for 'what the Germans call the "Fuhrerprinzip"'. Of Blair's manifesto claim that Labour was the political arm of the whole British people, the *Daily Telegraph* responded with venom: 'only a party as unversed in history as New Labour could make a statement so reminiscent of fascism or communism'. It returned to the theme of Labour's potentially sinister rhetoric, contrasting Major's readiness to argue his case with Blair who 'retreats under fire' and relies on assertion. Blairism, it concluded, was a kind of Orwellian doublethink.

The *Daily Telegraph* columnists offered some of the sharpest and widest range of opinions in the press. In addition, Pat Dessoy, John Major's older sister, added some unmissable personal insight: growing exasperated with her brother's undisciplined party, she finally concluded that the Conservatives did not deserve to win. The left-wing playwright David Hare also lent an original perspective: charmingly located opposite the editorials, his column noted that he would be more sympathetic to the Tories if only he could find one genuinely interested in freedom.

The *Guardian*, under its new editor Alan Rusbridger, was clearly more at home with New Labour than it had been with Neil Kinnock. It offered criticism, of course, but there was little of the tortured ambivalence which dogged its 1992 campaign. Its editorials displayed welcome clarity. The paper's number one objective was to get rid of the Tories. 'Change is imperative', it told readers (28 April), not just for reasons of policy but for the health of our culture and institutions. Together with the *Mirror* and the *Independent*, the *Guardian* published a tactical voting guide and urged readers to mark their X where it would do most damage to the Tories. However, this goal was coupled with authentic enthusiasm for the 'radical anger' articulated by Blair in some of his later campaign speeches. The *Guardian*'s optimism was evident in its eve-of-poll editorial. 'May Day and Great Expectations' ran the headline. 'Don't underestimate the possibilities' of a Labour government, it told readers. Victory would bring the best chance for the progressive movement in Britain for a generation. The *Guardian* conveniently arranged its election special coverage in a centre pull-out section. Every day featured a 'Big Issue' profile and, following the *Boston Globe*, it presented regular focus group analysis of two marginal constituencies. It presented the fullest coverage of any daily paper, although its many columnists, with the exception of Hugo Young, were rarely the most enticing.

For the first time since 1966, *The Times* did not endorse any party. 'Principle not party' was its theme. It advised readers to vote for Euro-sceptic candidates, supplying an election day guide to Euro-sceptical voting at constituency level. Most of these candidates, of course, were Conservative although a few were Labour and Liberal Democrat dissidents, and two Referendum Party candidates were named in the list. The paper's editorials were consistent in adopting a cross-party view, running a series in praise of dissidents such as Tam Dalyell, Frank Field and Denzil Davies (all Labour) and Liz Lynne (Liberal Democrat). However, the editorials were out of tune with the opinions of the paper's most respected columnists. Matthew Parris all but forgot his humour in scathing attacks on Blair and the new 'robotic' army of clean-cut, soulless Blairite candidates. Peter Riddell, in trenchant form, suggested that Tony Blair, after effectively changing the party's name from Labour to New Labour, should go further and drop the word 'Labour' altogether. There was ample internal logic to keep *The Times* in the

Conservative camp, yet its 'principle not party' line forced it into some remarkable endorsements. These included, for example, the far-left Jeremy Corbyn in Islington North. However, under reported pressure from its proprietor, *The Times* also abandoned the Conservatives, leaving the *Sunday Times* as the only News International title to remain loyal.

For the first time in its young history, the *Independent* wasn't independent. In the final week, it teased with editorial zest for Ashdown but ultimately it espoused Labour, though this was combined with advocating a tactical vote to ensure a strong Liberal Democrat presence in parliament. On the issues that really mattered, constitutional and electoral reform and Europe, 'a Blair government offers hope – hope in varying degrees, but hope at least'. A Tory party 'corrupted' by being so long in power and so clearly hostile to the European Union was the main reason why the paper chose to break its own convention of offering no partisan endorsement.

In all other respects, however, the *Independent* remained steadfast to 'tradition'. It balanced criticism and praise of all the major parties and its leader columns offered refreshing and original perspectives on the campaign. Despite its preference for Labour, Tony Blair felt the sting of its editorials more often than John Major. The *Independent* mocked Labour's much-reported adoption of passionate purple as a campaign colour – 'a passion for what?' – and disparaged Blair's claim that this would be the last election fought on ideology. Politics is a 'grown-up art' precisely because it recognises that society involves conflict, it chided the Labour leader. Politics is not reducible to a series of managerial decisions.

The *Financial Times* offered the most succinct news coverage and analysis of all the papers, yet its editorials betrayed a weary air. Neither of the two main contenders inspired much optimism in the *Financial Times*; nor did this most 'dispiriting' campaign. In fact, the election rarely moved its leader writers to action. Just 21 per cent of its editorials concerned the election, less than half the proportion in 1992 (see Table 9.4). Eventually the *Financial Times* decided somewhat ambiguously in favour of Labour, and with little enthusiasm for Blair: the closer he got to power, 'the less impressive he has appeared'. However, the deciding issue was Europe and on this the Conservative Party had reached such a pass that it was now impossible for its leaders to behave rationally. The *Financial Times* was a 'natural supporter' of the Conservative Party but there were exceptions, and '1997 is one of them'.

SUNDAYS AND WEEKLIES

Labour has traditionally fared better among the Sundays, attracting the support of two papers with large if declining readerships: the *Sunday Mirror* and the *People*. In 1997, it added another Murdoch scalp: the best-selling *News of the World*, reportedly against the inclinations of its editor, Phil Hall.[4] This conversion gave Labour the lead among the Sundays, as among the dailies. The total circulation of pro-Labour Sunday papers in 1997 was 9.7 million, compared to 5.6 million for Conservative titles – as Table 9.5 shows.

Table 9.5   Partisanship and circulation of national Sunday newspapers

	Preferred winner		Readership (Jan–Dec 96) (000s)	Circulation (Feb 97) (000s)
	1997	(1992)		
News of the World	Lab	(Con)	11864	4655
Sunday Mirror	Lab	(Lab)	7207	2328
People	Lab	(Lab)	5286	2001
Mail on Sunday	Con	(Con)	6294	2172
Express on Sunday	Con	(Con)	3365	1178
Sunday Times	Con	(Con)	3873	1360
Observer	Lab[1]	(Lab)	1295	455
Sunday Telegraph	Con	(Con)	2007	890
Independent on Sunday	Lab	(Not Con)	941	282

Notes:
1.   Labour win plus strong Liberal Democrat presence in parliament.

Sources: Circulation: ABC. Readership: NRS.

The three most popular Sunday papers, the *News of the World*, *Sunday Mirror* and the *People*, offered little politics throughout the campaign; even on the last Sunday before polling. The *Mirror* group pair were predictably solid for Labour but the *News of the World* was less certain. Blair had offered few clues but asked the electorate to trust him, it opined mid-way through the campaign, adding: 'It now looks as though for better or worse, we have decided to do just that.' It raised the tempo slightly for its final campaign edition, under the heading: 'We Back Blair': 'The Labour party [has] never been more worthy of our vote ... The Tories have never been less deserving.'

The *Sunday Express*, Tory in nature, nonetheless found Tony Blair a 'formidable battler' and its last election front page featured Conservative MP Edwina Currie predicting a Labour landslide. The other Tory tabloid, the *Mail on Sunday* was scarcely more robust, finding 'on balance' a better case for Mr Major than Mr Blair. Its top columnist, Stewart Steven, denounced both leaders for their 'trust me' appeals to voters, 'the cry of the confidence trickster throughout the ages'.

The Sunday broadsheets all offered substantial coverage, commentary, analysis, profiles and interviews often spilling over into the ever-thickening supplements. The *Sunday Times* and *Sunday Telegraph*, both under new editors since 1992, were more surely partisan this time. The *Sunday Telegraph*, led by Dominic Lawson, found the policy case for the Conservatives strong to 'overwhelming'. The *Sunday Times* declared for the 'Tories, warts and all', preferring to avoid the risks of a Labour government lacking an 'ideological rudder' and apt to be swept off course by the tide of events.

Labour's only Sunday broadsheet supporter in 1992 was the *Observer*. It stayed loyal, encouraged by the prospect of electoral reform under Labour, but also highly motivated by the 'ghastly vision' of another Conservative victory. Such a nightmare should put the discontent of the 'Groucho classes' into perspective, it editorialised. In fact, the Groucho classes got a fair airing in the *Observer* columns with Martin Jacques and Stuart Hall arguing that Blair represents an 'historic defeat for the Left': 'Is he the greatest Tory since Thatcher?' Another *Observer* writer, Will Self, made national news by being found with a hard drug in the toilet of Major's campaign aeroplane, an act far more memorable than any of his columns. The *Observer*'s series of constituency opinion polls on the final Sunday played a more constructive role. These spelt out to readers (no doubt including worried Cabinet ministers) the consequences in specific seats of Labour's massive lead in the national polls. These seat-by-seat surveys were designed to offer useful information to tactical voters.

The *Independent on Sunday* presented its final election editorial under the Labour slogan, 'Enough Is Enough'. It urged tactical voting to get rid of the Tories and ensure that Labour could govern effectively. Its warmth for New Labour – a picture of 'freshness' and 'moderation' compared to the Tories – was not overwhelming but sufficient to nudge it into the Labour camp, a change from 1992 when its line was more squarely 'not the Tories'.

The political weeklies stayed true to type, the *New Statesman* for Labour, *The Economist* and the *Spectator* for the Conservatives. *The Economist* was the least sure of the three. 'The Tories Deserve To Lose. Labour Doesn't Deserve To Win', announced the front cover of its final election issue. Inside it explained more fully why 'disappointing' Labour did not deserve victory and why the Tories, despite drawbacks on Europe and constitutional reform, remained, on 'fine balance', the better bet. The *Spectator* went wholeheartedly

'For Major', accurately describing itself as the only Conservative publication to make the recommendation enthusiastically. 'Mr Major has proved the best prime minister since the war, after Margaret Thatcher.' The rejuvenated *New Statesman*, solidly pro-Labour, celebrated victory with a 'historic landslide collector's edition' within days of the result.

SCOTLAND AND WALES

The surprise in Scotland was the reluctant conversion of the Scottish *Sun* (circulation 371,495) from SNP to Labour, doubtless under pressure from Murdoch. Its editorials continued to champion independence, and the SNP's star turn, Sean Connery, featured strongly throughout the campaign. 'Bravehearts must wait ... it's time for brave heads', ran its front-page justification for its switch to Labour. With the Scottish *News of the World* also Labour, this meant that all the Murdoch tabloids now declared for Blair. The *Mirror*'s Scottish stable-mate, the top-selling *Daily Record* (circulation 729,391) remained firmly Labour. Elsewhere, the quality broadsheet, the Glasgow *Herald* (111,542), shifted from Liberal Democrat to no party, the *Scotsman* (77,633) from Liberal Democrat to Labour, and its sister paper *Scotland on Sunday* (92,938) also came out for Labour.

Only the Thomson press (*Sunday Post* and *Dundee Courier*) and the *Express* continued to back the Tories. The *Sunday Post*, the most popular Scottish Sunday (874,116), stayed Tory only by strong implication since its editorial line was merely an exhortation to vote. Even the *Scottish Daily Mail* (96,754) was neutral. The *Sunday Mail* (845,776) went further, offering '18 Reasons Why We Need A Breath Of Fresh Blair'. The Aberdeen *Press and Journal* (108,027), normally non-committal, was more evasive than usual. Predictably the news agenda in Scotland was dominated by the issues of devolution and nationalism.

Devolution and home rule were also key issues in Welsh newspapers. Wales generally receives a meagre showing in the British national press, nor are there any Welsh equivalents of the Scottish editions of some London-based papers. The main Wales daily, the *Western Mail* (60,251), was critical of Labour's devolution proposals and generally sceptical of all parties, offering no endorsement. The *Daily Post* (51,000), which primarily covers north Wales, was hostile to Labour but did not support any other party. The only Sunday paper, *Wales on Sunday* (57,400) took a limited interest in the election and also declined to offer any endorsement. The Welsh language weekly *Y Cymro* (4500) sought a Labour majority with a strong presence for Plaid Cymru.

THE CAMPAIGN IN PROGRESS

On both the front pages and in the editorials, the press was dominated by just three main topics: the European Union, party campaigns and prospects, and sleaze (see Table 9.6). These three alone accounted for 52 per cent of all front page leads. This agenda was strikingly different from 1992 when the economy, opinion polls and health had been far more prominent. Health, and tax and spending, generated just 4 per cent of lead stories (17 per cent in 1992), while opinion polls (top of the 1992 agenda) provided the main story on just three days. The polls, of course, were much less newsworthy this time: only two suggested a serious dent in Labour's huge lead, and just one, a rogue ICM poll for the *Guardian* (23 April), hinted at a close result.

Table 9.6   Front-page lead stories and editorials about the election, by topic

| | Front-page lead stories | | | Editorials | | |
| | 1997 | | (1992) | 1997 | | (1992) |
	Number	%	(%)	Number	%	(%)
European Union	37[1]	22	-	54[2]	16	(2)
Party strategies/prospects	31	19	(15)	30	9	(5)
Tatton/sleaze	18	11	(-)	20	6	(-)
Manifestos	12	7	(-)	25	8	(5)
Opinion polls	9	5	(18)	26	8	(-)
Northern Ireland	5	3	(-)	13	4	(-)
Taxation/public spending	4	2	(16)	12	4	(10)
Exhortations to vote/advice						
on voting	4	2	(4)	26	8	(6)
Health	3	2	(3)	8	2	(5)
Other	43	26	(44)	114	35	(67)
Total	166	99	(100)	328	100	(100)

Notes:
1. Of which: Con divisions 17; General 10; EMU 9; Fisheries policy 1.
2. Of which: General 19; EMU 18; Con divisions 10; Fisheries policy 5; Other 2.

Overall, the agenda was more narrowly focused than in 1992, with just nine main subject areas compared to 16 last time. It would have been more limited still had not a series of disruptive IRA bomb scares forced Northern Ireland into the limelight. Remarkably, education, proclaimed by all the major parties as their top priority, did not feature sufficiently to be included in our list. To some extent the narrow agenda may reflect the papers' generally lower interest in this election. Certainly, the efforts of the Conservative press and *The Times* to concentrate readers' minds on Europe played a part in focusing press coverage. More contentiously, the limited range of issues covered may also have been due to the success of the parties in restricting debate to a few favourable issues.

Viewed from a distance, the press seemed to move monolithically, starting out on sleaze, shifting to the manifestos, then Labour wobbles and U-turns, Europe and Tory divisions, and concluding with the conduct of the campaign and the likely turmoil in the Conservative Party following its inevitable defeat. With the exception of the manifestos and Labour vacillation, Conservative tribulations were the major focus of press interest. Almost twice as many front-page lead stories covered the Conservatives as Labour (see Table 9.7), with Tatton and divisions over EMU to the fore. Thus 1997 reversed the pattern of the previous three elections, at which the Labour Party – its divisions, 'extremism' and weak leadership – had provided copious material for the then Tory press.

Table 9.7 Coverage of major political parties in front-page lead stories and editorials about the election

	1997 Number	1997 %	(1992) (%)
Front-page lead stories			
Conservative	65	41	(33)
Labour	34	22	(30)
Liberal Democrat	2	1	(4)
More than one party	56	36	(33)
Total	157	100	(100)
Editorials			
Conservative	76	26	(37)
Labour	94	32	(38)
Liberal Democrat	4	1	(9)
More than one party	118	40	(16)
Total	292	99	(100)

Sleaze dominated the early running. The *Guardian*, printing extracts from Sir Gordon Downey's report into the 'cash for questions' affair, effectively forced the resignation of one Conservative MP, Tim Smith. Neil Hamilton's decision to stand again in Tatton all but united the press in condemnation. The *Daily Telegraph* alone mounted an editorial attack on Martin Bell's decision to oppose Hamilton as an independent 'anti-sleaze' candidate. 'The Bell putsch', it said, was an example of the media, in cahoots with the opposition, 'hi-jacking' the election to foist the false notion that sleaze was more important than all other issues. In fact, after a series of Conservative sex scandals, even the tabloids demanded a return to the 'real' issues – 'We're all cheazed off with sleaze', as the *Daily Star* put it.

The sleaze saga was punctuated by the parties' manifestos. This at least brought some respite if not much cheer for the Conservatives. The *Daily Telegraph* alone was well-disposed. The party had come a long way since Major's early days, it wrote, and the manifesto provided good ground and 'true' on which to stand and fight. The *Daily Mail* and the *Express* stayed on board, but only just. 'Have the Tories run out of steam?', asked the *Mail*; its answer was a guarded – not quite. The *Express*'s uncertain attitude was summed up under its opinion headline: 'Poor record may undermine promising Tory manifesto'. The best of the rest for the Conservatives was *The Times* which found the manifesto cautious but more coherent than in 1992. For the *Independent*, the Tory programme was 'refreshing' in its clarity, but wrong on the key subjects of Europe and constitutional reform. The *Financial Times* was dismayed that the prudence of the previous year's Budget was now replaced by imprudent promises, while the proposed tax allowance for married families was 'a retrograde step' of social engineering. The *Guardian* and the *Sun* were, most unusually, of one mind: the manifesto offered simply more of the same – 'The same old Tory', as the *Sun* put it. The *Guardian*'s chief political commentator, Hugo Young, however, was impressed: the manifesto was energetic, relevant and the pensions proposals contained 'visionary radicalism'. The Tory problem was not policies, but trust, he said.

Labour's spin-doctors must have rejoiced at the Fleet Street reception for their manifesto. They managed two days' headlines for the price of one by releasing Blair's handwritten ten-point 'contract with Britain' a day early. Some papers helpfully subjected it to handwriting analysis, to discover, as the *Daily Telegraph* reported, that the Labour leader was strong, confident and energetic. The manifesto itself played well. The *Sun* and the *Mirror* were gung-ho. 'Tony's Trust What We All Need', said the *Sun*, welcoming the priority of education and the 'cast-iron pledge' not to increase income tax. The *Guardian* was eager: 'it is indisputably a progressive, reformist and inclusive manifesto ... also angry, proud and disciplined'. The *Independent* was keen: 'Daringly modest, and right for the times'. The *Financial Times* called the programme: 'A ticket to Downing Street'. The *Express* was mild: tough questions remained on spending, unions and tax but Labour had come a long way since 1992. *The Times* perceived a 'modest manifesto' and urged Blair to be bolder. Acid commentary was restricted to the *Daily Mail* ('vague, not to say vacuous'), the *Daily Telegraph* ('Britain does deserve better – better than this'), and a few columnists, including Matthew Parris who dismissed it as 'an army of phrases ... in search of an idea'.

The Liberal Democrats won the most unstinting praise but also the slightest coverage. Of the tabloids, only the *Daily Star* favoured it with an editorial: 'Good on yer, Paddy'. The *Independent* called it the most challenging of all the manifestos, saying that politics without the Liberal Democrats would be 'intolerable'. The *Guardian* found it packed with policy and refreshingly free from the dictates of marketing. The *Daily Telegraph* also described it as 'refreshing', more honest than Labour, but unfortunately wrong-headed. *The Times* and the *Financial Times* did not trouble their leader writers, but *The Times* columnist, Peter Riddell, was another to enjoy its 'refreshing candour' and to admire Paddy Ashdown's willingness to leap where Tony Blair feared to tread.

For a short while thereafter, all the press, bar the *Sun* and the *Mirror*, agreed that Labour had gone 'wobbly' under pressure, apparently embracing previously rejected privatisations, admitting a funding gap in its spending plans, and backtracking over devolution for Scotland. Not so much a U-turn, more 'Labour for sale', said the *Daily Telegraph*. The *Independent* thought Blair had crumbled 'rather easily' in a *Panorama* interview. The *Guardian* accused Labour of being 'a bit too uptight', sustaining a succession of punches but failing to land one itself. 'It's beginning to look as though Labour might win the election but lose the campaign', suggested the *Independent* leader.

However, just as the papers began to detect some hope for the Conservatives, Europe erupted. It began in low-key fashion with the Conservative press plus the *Sun* applauding junior minister Angela Browning's opposition to the single currency, in apparent contravention of the government's 'negotiate and then decide' policy. Four days later (15 April) the *Daily Mail* forced the issue under its 'Battle For Britain' banner, listing 76 Conservatives publicly opposed to Britain joining the single currency. The following day the *Express* and the *Daily Telegraph* joined in. 'It's Time To Come Clean On Europe,' the *Express*'s front page told the Prime Minister; 'wait and see' was falling apart. Europe *is* the issue now, the *Daily Telegraph*'s leader said, and with the single currency we would not be one nation, 'we would be No Nation'.

John Major's response, an impromptu press conference speech in which he implored his party 'not to bind my hands', impressed much of Fleet Street – a 'bravura performance', said the *Daily Mail*; he spoke with 'terrifying

Tabloid front pages on 1 May 1997

authority' (*Guardian*); he was 'determined' (*Daily Telegraph*). Most agreed that this was the defining moment of the campaign, but they disputed its consequences. 'Now it's Major versus his party', was the *Independent*'s verdict, its leader pointing out the 'absurd contradiction' that voters who agreed with Major's policy could not now sensibly vote for his party, sentiments echoed by the *Guardian* and the *Financial Times*. For *The Times*, Conservative divisions simply left voters confused; it urged the government to confirm that it would not join EMU in the first wave, but for the *Daily Mail*, the rebellion had at last put clear blue water between the parties, while the *Daily Telegraph* argued that, despite appearances, the Conservative Party was not split; in fact, it was now clearly overwhelmingly opposed to the single currency. The *Mirror* alone made light of this story, tucking it away on page five under the headline, 'P.S. Oh yes, and the Tories were still banging on about Europe yesterday'.

Europe, and the Tory rebellion, continued to dominate the headlines, given added spice by the party's newspaper advertisement depicting Mr Blair as Helmut Kohl's dummy and by the intervention of Jacques Santer, President of the European Commission. By the last week, however, despite a ferocious exchange between Tony Blair and John Major about pensions, most of the papers sensed that the battle was already over. With 11 days still to go, papers began to write stories of the Conservatives preparing for opposition, jockeying for leadership, and apportioning blame for failure. On 20 April, the Sunday broadsheets all focused on the Tory 'civil war' and the bitter fight for succession. The next day's *Express* predicted disaster if the Conservatives continued to 'squander their energies in fruitless squabbling amongst themselves'. The *Sun* said the Tories had achieved the impossible – they had made themselves unelectable. It was all sport to the *Mirror*, which ran a donkey derby of John Major's likely successor.

Nearly all the press complained that the campaign was too long, tedious, negative and sour. Both major parties were at fault. The *Guardian* found the 'totally professionalised' campaign disappointing, and columnist Hugo Young could not recall an election when so many questions were so shamelessly evaded. In similar vein, the *Daily Mail* had rarely seen so much obfuscation, evasion and dishonesty. According to the *Financial Times*'s Philip Stephens, 'this has been the most dispiriting of election campaigns' with the Tories relentlessly negative and Labour remorselessly defensive. The *Sun* thought that 'many people were sick to the back teeth' of politics and that an Apathy Party would win hands down. The rigid discipline of Labour's campaign was clearly disliked by many commentators, culminating in Tory press attacks on Labour's leaked strategy document, the 'war book'. 'Has there ever been so managed and packaged a campaign?', lamented the

Daily Mail, adding that Labour candidates all sounded like programmed Daleks, mechanically intoning platitudes. The *Guardian* offered some defence for this 'necessary' discipline. However, only the *Express* found much joy in the campaign, thankful that it generated heat as well as light.

Table 9.8   Photographs of leading party politicians in national daily newspapers

Politician	Number of photos	
	1997	*(1992)*
Conservative		
Assorted Euro-sceptics	208	(-)
John Major	195	(334)
Neil Hamilton	39	(-)
Margaret Thatcher	38	(98)
Kenneth Clarke	30	(20)
Norma Major	26	(82)
Labour		
Tony Blair	263	(-)
Cherie Blair	52	(-)
John Prescott	31	(-)
Gordon Brown	27	(-)
Liberal Democrat		
Paddy Ashdown	59	(158)
Other		
Martin Bell	45	(-)
James Goldsmith	16	(-)

Labour's discipline and the presidential style of the contest was reflected in the press pictures. It is useful, and not wholly unrealistic, to ask what impression readers would have formed of the parties had they relied not on the text, but just on the photographs, in the press (see Table 9.8). In the Conservative case, the image would be of a party divided on Europe (over 200 mugshots of Euro-sceptics for which the *Daily Mail* was largely responsible), embroiled in sleaze (39 images of Neil Hamilton) and generally backward-looking (38 photos of Margaret Thatcher). The contrast with Labour could hardly be more stark. Tony and Cherie Blair dominated the Labour photographs. Wittingly or unwittingly, the press reflected the campaign Labour wanted – of a youthful, dynamic party recreated in the leader's image.

ADVERTISING

Surprisingly for such a marketed campaign, the amount of paid advertising plummeted. The main parties managed only 40 pages between them, continuing a decline which began after a Saatchi-inspired peak of 336 pages

Table 9.9   *Political advertising in national daily and Sunday newspapers*

	1997		1992
	Number of insertions	*Number of pages*	*(Number of pages)*
Pro-Conservative			
Conservative Party	26	27	(48)
Paul Sykes[1]	12	17	(-)
Entrepreneurs for a Booming Britain	2	2	(-)
Monday Club	3	0.3	(-)
Patrick Evershed	2	0.3	(-)
Pro-Labour			
Unison	16	16	(-)
Labour Party	18	12.5	(65)
National Union of Teachers	1	1	(4)
Other			
Referendum Party	13	13	(-)
Amnesty International	4	4	(-)
People's Trust[2]	3	3	(-)
Bus Employees Superannuation Trust Action Group[3]	4	1.5	(-)
Public Services, Tax and Commerce Union[3]	1	1	(-)
Race for the Election	1	0.3	(-)
Democratic Left[3]	2	0.2	(-)
Liberal Democrats	1	0.2	(6.5)
Society for the Promotion of a European Referendum	1	0.1	(-)
Total	110	99.4	(288.3)

Notes:
1. Pro-Conservative businessman against a single currency.
2. Political and constitutional reform.
3. Anti-Conservative.

in 1987 (see Table 9.9). The advertising battle has moved away from the newspapers and towards poster sites. Unlike 1992, when (unusually) Labour placed the most press advertising, the ratio this time returned to a more customary two to one in favour of the Conservatives. As normal, pro-Labour advertising by trade unions, principally the public service union Unison, helped to even up the balance. However, the situation in 1997 was complicated by Paul Sykes, the Yorkshire businessman who bought 17 pages to press the case for a Conservative vote as a defence against Britain's participation in a single currency. Conceivably, this helped Labour by drawing attention to Conservative divisions; more likely, it had no impact at all. In less direct ways, however, advertising did feature prominently in the election, with press and poster advertisements often reported in the news columns and Party Election Broadcasts (PEBs) always reviewed and sometimes previewed in the papers. The Conservative advertisement portraying Blair as Kohl's dummy and Labour's 'Fitz, the bulldog' election broadcast became news stories with a life of their own. Thus, the campaign confirms that the function of party political advertising is to impinge on the news agenda rather than to influence the voters directly.

CONCLUSION

Labour has never had such a favourable press at a general election, nor has it ever achieved such a stunning majority in terms of seats. It is tempting to imagine that these two facts must be linked somehow. Martin Linton has shown a historic correlation, although not causation, between Labour's press share (that is, the proportion of national dailies supporting Labour) and its share of the vote.[5] Until 1997, the Conservatives had always held a press 'surplus' over Labour, averaging 15 per cent in the pre-Thatcher period (and the last Labour victory) and rising to an average of 45 per cent thereafter. Until 1997, Labour's press share had always been smaller than its vote share, but both have tended to rise and fall along a similar pattern. The question is: who is leading whom? Are editors following their readers' preferences or influencing them? Or are both editors and readers responding in a similar but independent way to the overall flow of politics?

The *Sun* famously declared in 1992, 'It's The Sun Wot Won It'. In 1997 it was at it again, claiming it 'swung it' for Labour, and the editor, Stuart Higgins, made public a handwritten Tony Blair note in which the new Prime Minister thanked the paper 'for its magnificent support' which 'really did make the difference'.[6] However, Table 9.2 shows that since 1992, Labour strengthened its position among readers of every newspaper. It increased its majority among *Mirror* and *Guardian* readers, but it almost doubled its base among readers of the remaining Conservative dailies: the *Daily Telegraph*, *Daily Mail* and *Express*. Even the most Tory newspapers found they could not protect their readers from the Labour tide. In fact the *Telegraph* was the only daily which continued to deliver a majority of its readers to the Conservatives. It is certainly true that for the first time in several elections, most *Sun* readers supported Labour. Further, between 1992 and 1997 Labour support increased fractionally more among *Sun* readers than among readers of any other daily. This finding raises the possibility of a small impact for the *Sun*'s endorsement of Tony Blair, announced just before the start of fieldwork for the surveys reported in Table 9.2. Yet even if the *Sun*'s switch did impinge on its readers to a small extent, this effect was trivial in the overall context of the forces shaping Labour's election victory. The *Sun*'s endorsement of Tony Blair was certainly remarkable evidence of the success of his political project, but like the rest of the press, the *Sun* was following opinion more than creating it. In 1997, for sure, it was not 'The Sun Wot Won It'.

What, then, will be the long-term significance of Labour's press triumph in this election? What is the land which is marked out by this 'landmark' election? The danger here is of reading too much into the campaign. Certainly, it would be naïve to regard the 1997 election as instituting a long-term 'realignment' of Britain's newspapers, at least if that term implies that Labour has now secured a stable hegemony of support in the press. In the papers, as in the electorate, Labour's finest hour owed much to Conservative weakness. Tory newspapers value party unity and strong leadership above all else; in 1997, John Major delivered neither. Conversions to the Labour cause were far from unconditional. The *Sun*, in particular, found more to applaud in Tony Blair than in his party. Thus the key variables in 1997 were short-term and contingent: hardly the stuff of press realignment.

It is more tempting, and certainly more plausible, to treat the 1997 contest as de-aligning, rather than realigning, for the press. Old relationships between parties and papers came under stress and in some cases ended. In all likelihood, the 1997 election will initiate a new period of quieter and weaker partisanship as newspapers respond to the changed character of party politics. From the perspective of 1997, we can now see that the previous election, in 1992, had ended the era of 'partisanship rediscovered' which had characterised the press for nearly twenty years after February 1974. The 1970s and 1980s were decades of full-blooded newspaper partisanship. Union power, the Winter of Discontent, the Falklands, Margaret Thatcher, Michael Foot, Neil Kinnock, nuclear disarmament – these were issues and personalities which carried the papers to a high pitch of excitement, but the election of 1997 played in a lower key – the big issues were no longer there. Press coverage of the election declined in priority and intensity not because the newspapers had changed, but because politics itself had evolved. Only Europe could vitalise, and even here many observers felt the *Daily Mail* and *The Times* were speaking in voices from another time. Europe aside, the press in 1997 was already adopting the hushed tones of a new, and less strident, political era.

NOTES

1. The authors thank Professor James G. Kellas for contributing the section on Scotland, Dylan Griffiths for the section on Wales and Paul Gliddon for preparing the tables in this chapter.
2. Some useful work on the press has been published since 1992 and includes: M. Linton, *Was it the Sun Wot Won It?* (1995); B. McNair, *News and Journalism in the UK* (1994); J. Tunstall, *Newspaper Power: The National Press in Britain* (1996).
3. See R. Greenslade, 'Nice one Sun, says Tony', *Guardian* (Media Section), 19 May, 1997.
4. See S. Glover 'If there were more London fox-hunters, Mr Major would have had Max's support as well as his vote', *Spectator*, 3 May, 1997.
5. Linton, *op cit.*
6. Greenslade, *op cit.*

10 MPs and Candidates
Byron Criddle

The election saw 3724 candidates contest the 659 constituencies; 5.6 per constituency (compared with 2946 in 651 – or 4.5 candidates per seat – in 1992). The ranks were swelled by single-issue parties exploiting the division in the Conservative Party over European integration – Sir James Goldsmith's Referendum Party (547 candidates) and the UK Independence Party (194 candidates). The Green Party (95) and the bizarre Natural Law Party (196) also contributed to candidate profusion.

Of the three main parties, Labour and the Liberal Democrats contested all mainland seats except the Speaker's at West Bromwich West, and the Tatton constituency of the beleaguered Conservative MP, Neil Hamilton, where both parties withdrew their candidates in favour of the independent 'anti-sleaze' candidate, Martin Bell. The Conservatives fought all mainland seats, except the Speaker's, and ventured eight candidates into Northern Ireland. The SNP and Plaid Cymru contested all the seats in Scotland and Wales respectively.

The new intake of 260 MPs (183 Labour, 41 Conservative, 29 Liberal Democrat, 2 SNP, 2 Ulster Unionists, 2 Sinn Fein, and 1 independent) was a post-war record, comprising 40 per cent of the House of Commons. Labour's new MPs accounted for 44 per cent of the Parliamentary Labour Party (PLP); the Conservative intake comprised 25 per cent of the party's halved ranks; and the 29 new Liberal Democrats comprised a majority (63 per cent) of that party's doubled representation. In no parliament since 1945 had there been so wholesale a renewal of parliamentary personnel.

Twenty-five former MPs tried to return to the House at the election: 5 Labour, 13 Conservative, 5 Liberal Democrat, 1 Sinn Fein and 1 Socialist. Seventeen were successful: 5 Labour, 8 Conservative, 3 Liberal Democrat and the Sinn Feiner, Gerry Adams.[1] Of the returning MPs, the Liberal Democrat, Ronnie Fearn, had established a post-war record for candidate persistence in one constituency having contested Southport at seven elections since 1970 (missing only the election of 1983), losing five times and winning twice (1987 and 1997).[2]

The large new intake of MPs was explained not only by the Labour landslide but also by an exceptional number of retirements, 117 in all (compared with 79 in 1992): 72 Conservatives, 38 Labour, 6 Liberal Democrat (of whom two were ex-Conservative MPs) and one Ulster Unionist. Most of the retiring Conservatives were conventionally people at the end of political careers, such as the former Cabinet ministers Kenneth Baker, John Biffen, Paul Channon, David Howell, Douglas Hurd, Michael Jopling, Sir Patrick Mayhew and John Patten – though Mr Patten was quitting at the very early age of 52. In fact as many as 11 Tory MPs were leaving the House without having reached the age of 55 – an indication of low Conservative morale and expectation of defeat, and of the desire to seek financial security in a post-Nolan environment of constraints on the outside earnings of MPs. Richard Needham, Steven Norris, Tony Nelson and Tim Eggar, whose ages ranged from 46 to 55, were all heading back to business careers. Some other early retirements appeared to reflect disillusion: the 50-year-old Dudley Fishburn left his disappearing Kensington seat claiming there was not enough work for an MP to do; George Walden (Buckingham) expressed his distaste for adversarial politics and the need for the electorate to be flattered rather than told the truth.

A good number of retiring Conservative MPs were also involuntary victims of the boundary revision. Hartley Booth, Winston Churchill, Dame Janet Fookes, Michael Stephen, Cyril Townsend and Sir John Wheeler all failed to find new berths following in most cases radical boundary changes. Additionally, David Harris and Terry Dicks retired from their highly marginal seats, only to re-emerge as unsuccessful would-be candidates elsewhere, for which behaviour they were dubbed by Labour spokesmen as part of the 'chicken run'. As at the previous redistribution in 1983, a number of Conservative MPs migrated from vulnerable seats to wholly different constituencies containing no part of their previous seat. Nine Conservatives effected this manoeuvre in 1997,[3] successfully in all but two cases: Norman Lamont and John Watts both lost in their new seats. Notwithstanding the 'chicken run' jibe, however, fewer Conservative MPs migrated to entirely different seats in 1997 (9; 7 successfully) than had done in 1983 (13; 11 successfully). Much media exposure was given to the movements of the Cabinet ministers Brian Mawhinney and Stephen Dorrell but they were in fact only moving to new seats which did contain parts of their old ones.

The boundary revision also contributed to some of Labour's 38 retirements. Bob Hughes lost out by a single vote in the selection for the new Aberdeen Central seat; John Fraser was ousted by Tessa Jowell in the contest for the newly merged Dulwich & West Norwood seat; Jimmy Dunnachie and Mike Watson both lost in Glasgow where the redistribution was radical and the total number of constituencies reduced; Mildred Gordon and Nigel Spearing both failed to gain selection for the new Poplar and Canning Town seat, and Bryan Davies – the only front-bench casualty – suffered a fruitless trawl around the country after being squeezed out of the newly merged Oldham

West & Royton seat by Michael Meacher. In addition to these seven, David Young (Bolton South East) was the only Labour MP deselected in a seat whose boundaries were unchanged.

For the most part Labour's departing MPs were the usual collection of old ex-Cabinet ministers such as Peter Shore, Stan Orme and Roy Hattersley, and fairly obscure back-benchers. This time, unusually, a distinct nudge was given to the process of renewal by the retirement of eight MPs in the immediate run-up to the election – seven after the election had been called. In most cases the retirements were accompanied by life peerages.[4] These sudden last-minute 'retirements' enabled the NEC of the Labour Party to impose shortlists of candidates on the local parties and so facilitate the selection of favoured 'New Labour' people such as the journalist Yvette Cooper (Pontefract & Castleford), union leader Alan Johnson (Hull West & Hessle) and the ex-Conservative MP, Alan Howarth (Newport East). The last-minute retirements in safe seats and the parachuting-in of favoured Blairite candidates, in some cases without a vote of the local membership, inevitably raised hackles, as in Dudley North where the suddenly departing Dr John Gilbert's literature had been printed, and in Pontefract & Castleford where leading local aspirants were excluded from the shortlist.

The smaller parties saw the retirement of former Liberal leader Sir David Steel and the most senior (since 1964) Liberal Democrat MP, Sir Russell Johnston. David Alton – a socially conservative Liberal Democrat long detached from his party's leadership – had had his Liverpool seat abolished in the boundary revision and went, with Sir David and Sir Russell, to the Lords, at the young age of 46. Sir James Molyneux, the Ulster Unionists' lugubrious ex-leader, also retired.

If it was a mix of the big anti-Conservative swing, Conservative MPs' disenchantment, the impact of boundary changes and variously prompted retirements, which combined to produce so large a turnover in the membership of the Commons, it was the Labour Party which contributed the other significant feature of the 1997 election, namely the feminisation of the PLP. Labour had made all the headlines in the matter of candidate selection from the early 1980s, but in the 1990s it was now doing so in a way more conducive to the party's electoral success. The 1993 party conference adopted three innovations: the selection of candidates by one member, one vote (OMOV), without any weighting mechanism – through an electoral college – to privilege affiliated bodies, such as the unions; the strengthening of MPs' security of tenure by unopposed reselection where the MP received at least two-thirds of all nominations; and the institution of women-only shortlists in designated key marginal and Labour-held seats. The first of these changes – OMOV – was intended to complete the process of change from an activist-based system of selection to one in which the wider membership alone determined the choice of candidates. Although affiliated bodies, such as unions, retained influence over the nomination of candidates and over shorlisting (through their delegates on the constituency General Committee), they could not easily determine the outcome of the vote of the wider membership, other than by encouraging their local union members to join the party and gain voting rights themselves. By 1997 about one-fifth of the membership was derived from the unions in this way.

The main impact of OMOV would appear to be the localisation of candidate choice – the selection of people locally known rather than nationally celebrated. A very liberal interpretation of the right to vote postally encouraged this tendency, with members voting from home without seeing or hearing the candidates at the selection meeting, and accordingly voting for known local figures rather than unknown outsiders. There was a Walworth Road view that the new intake of 183 MPs lacked 'stars': overwhelmingly (two-thirds) they were councillors; 80 of them local councillors in the area of their constituencies. But if they were not stars these municipal footsoldiers were presumably – or so it was hoped – practical politicians who had experience of group discipline and tough spending decisions, that would ensure their reliability at Westminster.

Labour's more important innovation was that of designating half of all vacant winnable seats for women candidates; the stark result of this was that from May 1997 until the next election, the viewing public would be presented with the contrast between Labour parliamentary benches containing 101 women, and the Conservative opposition with 13. Two organisations had done much to promote the change: Labour Women's Network (LWN), set up in 1988, and Emily's List, which dated from 1993. LWN, created by four women disappointed by the low number of Labour women MPs elected at the 1987 election (21), produced a series of booklets entitled 'Uphill All the Way', instructing aspirants on the selection process; organised training courses; circulated lists of LWN subscribers interested in being selected to constituency parties; and generally promoted 'networking'. The somewhat oddly named Emily's List (based on an acronym for 'Early Money is Like Yeast', but also honouring the suffragette Emily Davison who threw herself beneath the hooves of the King's horse at the Derby in 1913) was set up by Barbara Follett (herself to become an MP in 1997 but without the aid of a women-only shortlist) to sponsor women applicants by covering some of their costs (of travel, printing and child care). The first batch of eleven sponsored aspirants included three – Joan Ryan, Jacqui Smith and Helen Southworth – who went on to win selection for seats which fell to Labour in 1997. But if the result of this organised pressure for change was ultimately a major propaganda victory for Labour, the process of getting there was messy.

Inevitably there had been resistance to quotas for women candidates, and especially to a more radical suggestion that all candidacies should be given to women until parity between the sexes was achieved in the PLP. Clare Short – the NEC's leading proponent of the change – saw this advanced position as excluding of good men and likely to upset local parties and offend public opinion, but there was a claim that women candidates had scored higher swings in marginal seats in 1992, and that they would also help close the generation gap among middle-aged women in Labour's favour. Equally, Roy Hattersley, a former Deputy Leader, saw the proposal as likely to cause chaos and wondered why there should not equally be 'all black/Asian shortlists' too; Ian Gibson, candidate in Norwich North, predicted a press backlash alleging that Labour would be offering 'second-best candidates', and Anne Carlton, wife of Denzil Davies MP, dismissed the whole proposal as 'wimminist pottyness'. Nevertheless, at the 1993 conference (and again – reaffirmed – in 1994), the party opted for women-only shortlists in 50 per cent of all the marginals winnable on a 6 per cent swing, and in 50 per cent of all vacant Labour-held seats. The identification of the seats for such designation would be determined by regional 'consensus' meetings between national officials and local parties, with the right of the NEC to impose designation where no consensus was reached.

Inevitably there were problems in designating the women-only seats, especially in Labour's northern heartlands; key marginal seats resisted in the north-west and safe Labour seats baulked in Yorkshire and the north-east. Even in the first (agreed) seat to adopt a woman from an all-women shortlist – Falmouth and Camborne – the selection of Candy Atherton prompted the resignation of local male councillors and the eventual rebel candidacy of one of them – John Geach – against Ms Atherton in the election (when he polled 1691 votes).

Some northern male MPs were said to be delaying their retirements in order to thwart the process of allocation of their seats to women; in Manchester Blackley the local agent saw 'imposition from the centre as quite wrong', and in other places such as Jarrow the MPs' resistance reflected the presence of a favourite son candidate waiting to take over. Resistance came to a head at Slough where the local party wanted to reselect Eddie Lopez who had narrowly missed taking the seat in 1992 but where the NEC imposed an all-women list in May 1995, by which time 17 women had been selected from all-women lists. The Slough party vociferously opposed the imposition; the GC voted 370 to 5 against and a hostile petition recruited nearly 80 per cent of the local membership. A factor in this case was Mr Lopez's left-wing affiliation, with one national official opining that 'we are never going to win this seat with Eddie Lopez'. The all-women shortlist was imposed, with Brenda Lopez (wife of Eddie) on it, but Fiona MacTaggart, a Cheltenham Ladies' College-educated millionaire baronet's daughter, won the day.

Unease over the shortlisting practice was reflected in the leadership; in July 1995 Tony Blair intimated that the policy would be dropped after the election – 'it has given us a number of strong and able candidates but the process has not been ideal'. Matters came to a head with the initiation of legal proceedings by two 'excluded' male candidates, Peter Jepson and Roger Dyas Elliott, who had sought selection in the all-women designated seats of Brentford & Isleworth and Regent's Park & Kensington North in the former case, and Keighley in the latter. They claimed the shortlists were in breach of the 1975 Sex Discrimination Act and a 1976 European Union directive on equal treatment. In January 1996 an industrial tribunal duly ruled in their favour and declared all-women shortlists illegal. In order not to delay the process of candidate selection in the last year or so before the election the Labour leadership decided not to appeal and the practice then lapsed.

At that point 38 women had been selected from women-only shortlists. 34 were in winnable seats (either key marginals or vacant Labour-held seats), and 4 in supposedly unwinnable ones, though one of these – Colne Valley – was duly captured on 1 May. Seats where women-only shortlists had been decided but where selections had not been completed at the time of the tribunal's judgment had the process suspended and restarted with open shortlists, but in all but two (Gravesham and Great Yarmouth, where there had been resistance to women-only shortlists) women were still selected. In all, 19 women were chosen in key marginal or Labour-held seats from open shortlists, 15 of them after the suspension of women-only lists in January 1996.[5] That as many as 19 of Labour's key-seat women candidates were chosen in open competition suggests a certain cultural shift was being prompted by the 34 selections in winnable seats. To these totals the unexpected scale of the swing to Labour on 1 May added a further 11 women MPs, selected from open shortlists in seats presumed unwinnable. Certainly there were few echoes of the first disputatious women-only shortlist (at Falmouth & Camborne in January 1995) when all but 5 of Labour's 101 women MPs assembled for the photograph with Tony Blair on the steps of Church House, Westminster, on 8 May. Women now comprised a quarter of the PLP; a rubicon had been crossed.

Labour's preoccupation with feminising the PLP undoubtedly obscured the fact of under-representation of black and Asian voters, even if Roy Hattersley, who was retiring from his predominantly Asian seat in Birmingham, now sought to encourage an Asian successor. A good number of Labour's selection disputes occurred in inner-city seats with large minority ethnic populations in Manchester, Glasgow, Bradford, Birmingham and London. OMOV inevitably encouraged the signing-up of new members to influence selection votes and disputes arose over large infusions of Asian names onto membership lists. In September 1994 in Manchester Gorton three Pakistanis took the party to court under the Race Relations Act claiming that 600 Asian membership applications were being blocked to stop Gerald Kaufman's deselection in favour of Ahmed Shahzad, a Brent councillor. In the same month the NEC set up an inquiry into allegations of similar mass recruitment of Asian members in Birmingham constituencies, and in February 1995 four Birmingham Constituency Labour Parties (CLPs) were duly suspended, including the Small Heath seat of Roger Godsiff (whose disputed selection against Asian competition had involved protracted NEC intervention before 1992), in order to investigate a claim that advice about obtaining housing improvement grants was being used as an inducement to join the Labour Party and enlist support in the selection battle for the new merged Sparkbrook & Small Heath seat. The chairman of Sparkbrook CLP, Kevin Scally, who favoured an Asian replacement for the retiring Roy Hattersley, saw NEC intervention as a ruse to block Asian aspirations; however an NEC report in June 1996 claimed that of the 4000 total party membership in the four suspended CLPs, 800 were not on the electoral register. Eventually, early in 1997, Roger Godsiff was reselected from a long shortlist containing five ethnic candidates.

In Bradford West the replacement of the retiring MP Max Madden was also fractious. Although one of the first Labour MPs to announce his intention to retire, Mr Madden later reversed his decision ostensibly because of conflict between rival ethnic minority candidates and because he feared the seat would fall to an ex-Labour councillor, Mohammed Riaz, who had been selected by the Conservatives. However he failed to find a single ward nomination, allegedly because of an 'Islamic pact' to veto non-Muslim candidates. With the NEC controlling the shortlisting procedure he reached the shortlist, but the vote saw him trounced as the selection went to the Sikh Marsha Singh, whose closest rival was the Muslim Mohammed Taj. This was a case of the overwhelmingly predominant Pakistani Muslim minority losing out to a member of a far smaller ethnic group.

A similar outcome was that in Bethnal Green and Bow where Peter Shore was retiring. This seat was originally designated by the NEC for a women-only shortlist, a decision which ignored the political aspirations of men within the large Bengali community. In 1993 a local Bengali councillor, an ally of the leading would-be candidate from that community, Councillor Rajan Uddin, delivered 217 membership applications to Labour's Walworth Road headquarters accompanied by a single cheque drawn on the personal bank account of one of his associates. Following a two-year investigation by the NEC only nine of the 217 names were accepted as members, the rest being found either not to exist or not to wish to join the party. Five local Bengali councillors threatened to take legal action if the party persisted in its intention to select a woman candidate, but that is what it did in February 1997 with the selection of the half African-American, half Anglo-Jewish woman, Oona King from an NEC-determined shortlist which excluded Councillor Uddin. Both here and in Bradford West the party suffered adverse swings on 1 May, probably on account of the selecting of candidates who, though from ethnic minority backgrounds, were not from the dominant local ethnic group, but where in both cases the Conservative candidate was.

The worst selection conflict with a racial component was at Glasgow Govan where Mike Watson (MP for the disappearing Glasgow Central seat) was seeking to win the nomination against the local cash-and-carry millionaire Pakistani businessman, Mohammed Sarwar, in a very dirty fight. In December 1995 Mr Watson led by one vote (237 to 236) on the first count at the selection conference, tied with Mr Sarwar (245 each) on the allocation of a third candidate's second preference votes, but was declared the winner by virtue of his greater number of first preference votes. But 51 postal votes – mostly of Asians voting for Mr Sarwar – were disallowed, causing Mr Sarwar to appeal to the NEC amid allegations of whole Asian households having been signed up to vote in the selection. The ballot was re-run in June 1996 after Mike Watson had legally challenged 25 names (23 of them Asian) on the Govan CLP's 510 membership list, but Mohammed Sarwar won with 279 to 197 votes. Following his election as Britain's first Muslim MP, Mr Sarwar faced an allegation of paying a bribe of £5000 to a rival candidate after the election and in the wake of a Labour Party inquiry he was criticised for conduct 'unbecoming and totally inappropriate for a Labour MP'. Any further action, such as whip-withdrawal or expulsion, was to be put off pending the outcome of a police investigation into the allegation against him.

Apart from these race-tinged selection conflicts Labour experienced other disputes in three seats: Leeds North East, Swindon North, and Exeter. The Leeds North East trouble was the only obviously ideological one, in which the NEC deselected a left-wing candidate with Trotskyist affiliations, Islington councillor Liz Davies. To add to the trouble, however, she was picked – in July 1995 – from a women-only shortlist. She was refused endorsement by the NEC; it was alleged she had a civil conviction for non-payment of the poll tax, and had been disloyal to the whip on Islington council, but was mainly damned for her links – with her partner Mike Marqusee – with the Trotskyist paper *Labour Briefing*, which had published a scathing attack on Tony

Blair's leadership a mere two months after his election in 1994. Her appeal against NEC rejection was summarily dispatched in a brief and undebated speech from Clare Short at the 1995 party conference when, describing *Labour Briefing* as a 'nasty, vicious publication', she wondered 'how anyone who supports the *Briefing* line would possibly want, with integrity, to be a Labour MP, unless it is just to cause trouble and conflict within the party' A year later, in September 1996, in a selection made open by the collapse of women-only shortlisting, Fabian Hamilton, a Blairite Leeds councillor and businessman who had fought the seat for Labour in 1992, was selected. But there followed a good deal of local left-wing activist resistance to him ostensibly on grounds of his controversial business record. Labour won the seat on 1 May.

At Exeter, Labour's reselected 1992 candidate, a South African-born barrister John Lloyd, was exposed in October 1995 as having testified against a fellow white South African anti-apartheid activist in a bomb trial in the 1960s, the consequence of which was the man's execution. In March 1996 he was deselected by the NEC for alleged 'lack of openness' about his South African past, and considered, but did not take, legal action against his deselection. In September 1996 he was replaced as candidate by the openly homosexual BBC Radio reporter Ben Bradshaw, who duly faced a campaign against him by a stridently homophobic Conservative candidate, Dr Adrian Rogers. The campaign failed to stop the key seat falling to Labour.

The dispute at Swindon North was superficially one of 'old' versus 'New Labour, even if both candidates claimed – inevitably – to support Tony Blair The local favourite son – Swindon councillor and local AEEU Rover factory shop steward, Jim D'Avila, who had fought the key seat in 1992 (and probably would have been reselected by the weight of his union backing under the old electoral college system) was pitted against the metropolitan TV producer, occasional adviser to Gordon Brown, and former associate of Peter Mandelson, public school and Cambridge-educated Michael Wills. Mr Wills won the selection contest by 114 to 84 votes in September 1995, but the result was challenged by Mr D'Avila who claimed postal vote irregularities and with AEEU backing won a High Court recommendation that the ballot be re-run. However, Labour's NEC, contending that dissension in the Swindon North CLP made a re-run undesirable, decided in May 1996 to impose Michael Wills's candidacy, an example of the centre prevailing confidently over the periphery.

Among the difficult cases left until the weeks before the dissolution of parliament, by which time the NEC controlled all shortlisting, was that at Newport East, where a late retirement (of Roy Hughes) gave the chance for Walworth Road to find a seat for the ex-Tory defector to Labour, Alan

Howarth. His symbolic importance, as the first Tory MP to have crossed the floor to Labour, was such that his earlier rejection by hostile party workers in the safe northern seats of Wentworth and Wythenshawe & Sale East – in neither of which did he reach the shortlist – could not be allowed to prevent his being found a secure berth. So it was that with the NEC ensuring his shortlisting, he duly saw off supposedly strong local opposition to win the nomination at Newport East in March 1997. He was pursued to the constituency by Arthur Scargill as candidate for his own rebel Socialist Labour Party, but whose vote on 1 May was the meagre and perhaps chronologically significant one of 1951.

David Young's deselection in 1994 as MP for Bolton North East was the only case of a Labour MP being ousted without involvement of the boundary commissioners. His successful opponent, a local councillor and chemistry lecturer, Dr Brian Iddon, campaigned in the selection contest for an MP with a more active profile, and on a left-sounding agenda notably calling for the renationalisation of the public utilities, but Mr Young's demise was probably due as much to the fact that he was a quiet 65-year-old MP who had served over 20 years since his first election in 1974.

Conservative selection procedures involved no innovation, beyond a slight change in the way in which would-be candidates seeking access to the Central Office list of approved candidates would be screened by a three-person panel, consisting of an MP, a lay party worker and a businessman, before being seen by the Party Deputy Chairman responsible for candidates who would then decide if the person could proceed to one of the periodic weekend parliamentary selection boards at which the final decision as to their fitness would be taken. However, the future of these boards themselves – originally introduced in the early 1980s – was put in doubt in 1995 when Dame Angela Rumbold MP, responsible for candidates from 1993, expressed the view that the boards were producing 'clones' – professional politicians who had worked as special advisers to ministers, party apparatchiks or lobbyists and consultants, but had no experience outside politics. Dame Angela appeared to wish to encourage the selection of older people with a broader range of experience and with the financial independence to be able to serve 20 years in the House – avoiding the problem of relatively impecunious MPs relying on the sort of consultancies on which limitations were now in any event to be placed in the wake of the Nolan report. Dame Angela's ideal candidate would presumably be Archie Norman, the chairman of the Asda supermarket chain, who was selected at Tunbridge Wells in 1996, but very soon was making the somewhat politically unprofessional claim that 'being a backbench MP is not a full-time occupation' and that he accordingly planned to remain a part-time chairman of Asda after his election. Moreover, notwithstanding Dame Angela's resistance to the selection of party apparatchiks, it was from the ranks of such people that many of the new Conservative intake of 41 were drawn in 1997, such as the ex-Central Office staffers Dr Julian Lewis (New Forest East), Andrew Lansley (Cambridgeshire South), Shaun Woodward (Witney) and Tim Collins (Westmorland and Lonsdale).

In the matter of women candidates the Conservatives had no answer to Labour's dramatic innovation. Dame Angela Rumbold sought to place more women on the candidates' list (that is, the list of available candidates), but with only some 100 women on a list of about 600, the imbalance, as she acknowledged, was such that women had no hope of parity in selection outcomes. As ever the blame was laid at the door of local associations who simply would not select women. The former MP Maureen Hicks indeed blamed the 'blue rinse mafia' for her exclusion from the shortlist at Stratford on Avon. Opposition to quotas was extensive throughout the party, with Margaret Daly – one of six women selected for supposedly winnable seats (and the only one of the six who was in fact defeated, at Weston-super-Mare) – claiming that any 'form of positive discrimination would not work in the party ... I just don't see them accepting it.' Nor were Conservative women MPs as cohesive a group pressing for change as Labour's women MPs. Edwina Currie claimed that in 'thirteen years at Westminster I've only once been to a gathering of all Conservative women MPs when we gave a dinner for Mrs Thatcher in 1983 ... Some of us have tried – how we've tried – to form a group which could sit down, talk and hammer out a few issues on which we could cooperate.' Symptomatic of the conservative attitudes of Tory women MPs was Anne Widdecombe's decision to leave the Church of England for the Roman Catholic Church over the question of female ordination in 1995, and the failure of any Conservative women MPs, other than Angela Rumbold, to back Edwina Currie's amendment proposing reduction of the homosexual age of consent to 16 in 1994. But sisterly solidarity was equally lacking in Dame Angela's tetchy response to Emma Nicholson's book *Secret Society*, published following her defection to the Liberal Democrats in 1995, describing Ms Nicholson as 'probably a bit menopausal' and 'a very bitter woman'.

The Conservatives managed to select no more women in vacant seats likely to be held than they did in 1992, namely six. The five actually elected were Theresa May, from the City, at Maidenhead; Eleanor Laing, a lawyer, at Epping Forest; Ann McIntosh, an MEP, at Vale of York; the journalist Julie Kirkbride at Bromsgrove; and Caroline Spelman, a businesswoman and a very last-minute selection, at Meriden. They joined at Westminster a mere eight continuing women MPs, survivors of the landslide.

Three Conservative MPs were deselected: David Ashby (Leicestershire North West), Sir Nicholas Scott (Kensington & Chelsea) and Sir George Gardiner (Reigate). Two others retired before facing proposed reselection ballots: Robert Banks (Harrogate) and Roy Thomason (Bromsgrove). David Ashby's demise was a consequence of press exposure of his private life and a subsequent libel case in which he sued the *Sunday Times* over allegations that he was homosexual, and lost. Ousted in March 1996, he 'blamed homophobia for my defeat: people are frightened of it'. Of his deselectors he observed: 'they are behaving like Smithfield meat-porters – love the Queen Mum and bash the queers'. The seat was a key marginal which fell easily to Labour at the election.

Sir Nicholas Scott's defeat by his local party at Kensington & Chelsea in December 1996 came at the end of a long chapter of accidents involving Sir Nicholas's difficulties with drink, though his reputation had also been damaged by being branded by his lobbyist daughter Victoria as 'underhund' in the way he helped, as Minister for the Disabled, to scupper, on grounds of cost, a private member's bill on the disabled in 1994, an incident which prompted the ending of his long career as an unpromoted former Heathite junior minister marginalised by the Thatcherite ethos of the party. He sought, however, to retain his Chelsea parliamentary seat, merged now to form the new Kensington & Chelsea constituency. His passage should have been facilitated by the retirement of his political rival, Dudley Fishburn, MP for Kensington, but in June 1995 he was accused of leaving the scene of an accident and in September the new Kensington & Chelsea Association executive voted to 'open the selection' (a phrase implying a desire to replace the sitting MP). Although in November 1995 he was reselected (in a final ballot against the ex-MP Michael Fallon), following the long-delayed court case in March 1996 relating to the accident, and in which he was fined and banned for drunk driving, and a further incident during the Conservative Party conference in October 1996 when he was found face down on a pavement, the constituency reopened his selection and in December he was duly dropped. He sought to politicise his demise: 'They wanted somebody who was anti-European and on the right of the party – this is nothing to do at all with the drinking incidents.' His deselection provided an opportunity for Alan Clark, who had retired from the House in 1992 but wished to return, and had sought selection at Sevenoaks, North Dorset and Tunbridge Wells and, against Sir Nicholas, in the Kensington & Chelsea selection in 1995. He reapplied for the seat and won, in January 1997, thus ensuring the resurrection of a parliamentary career at the age of 69 and notwithstanding the revelations of his notorious diaries published in 1993.

Sir George Gardiner's deselection at Reigate was surprising given his record as a staunch right-wing Thatcherite. But he had in fact taken his Euroscepticism too far following his support for John Redwood's failed leadership challenge in 1995. There was also some feeling in the Reigate association – which was affected by the boundary changes – about Sir George's lugubrious manner and even unphotogenic appearance. The association's executive voted in May 1996 to reject Sir George, to which he responded by threatening a by-election if ousted, but in a vote of local membership in June 1996 he survived by a margin of 311 to 206. However, his opponents would not let matters rest, and following an article he wrote in the *Sunday Express* in which he dubbed John Major as 'Kenneth Clarke's ventriloquist's dummy' because of his refusal to rule out joining a single European currency (and which crucially cost him Central Office support), he was ousted by 272 to 213 in a vote of no confidence in January 1997. He talked of a 'packed meeting' and of taking legal action, but opted instead to stand for the Referendum Party in Reigate, polling one of that party's better results of 3352 (7 per cent).

Of the two 'virtual' deselections, Robert Banks, a quiet back-bencher since his appearance in 1974, withdrew after his association executive voted to open the selection to other candidates in the new Harrogate & Knaresborough seat. The move made way for the luckless Norman Lamont, whose passage was to be blocked by the Liberal Democrats on 1 May. Roy Thomason equally faced an executive decision at Bromsgrove to 'open the procedure for the selection of a prospective parliamentary candidate', following revelations about his failed property and nursing home companies, and the need for his creditors to be met following his inability to sustain monthly debt repayments in order to avert bankruptcy proceedings. He avoided the likelihood of losing a contested selection vote by retiring on the eve of a meeting in November 1996, though assuring his party officers there was no danger of his going bankrupt. His withdrawal made the occasion for the selection of one of the party's younger high-profile political journalists – Julie Kirkbride, a right-wing, Cambridge-educated lorry driver's daughter from Halifax.

A good number of Conservative MPs suffered unwelcome tabloid press exposure for private indiscretions: David Mellor (Putney), Tim Yeo (Suffolk South), Gary Waller (Keighley), Michael Brown (Cleethorpes), Hartley Booth (Finchley), Richard Spring (Suffolk West), Jerry Hayes (Harlow), Piers Merchant (Beckenham), Steve Norris (Epping Forest) and Rod Richards (Clwyd North-West) all had their sexual predelictions revealed. Mr Yeo and Mr Mellor survived votes calling on them to stand down, and, like most of the others, they went on to contest, but only Mr Yeo, Mr Merchant and Mr Spring survived the election. Steve Norris retired, Hartley Booth failed to win selection after boundary changes, and the rest were beaten on 1 May.

More serious were the cases of MPs exposed for 'cash for questions' activity. This led to the resignation, first as a minister and finally as an MP, of Tim Smith (Beaconsfield) – for taking money for work with the lobbyist Ian Greer in support of Mohamed al-Fayed's bid to control Harrods – but not of his colleague Neil Hamilton, who, faced with similar accusations, had to be sacked as a minister in November 1994, and who defiantly fought the election – despite calls from local party officials for his deselection – protesting his innocence, but lost by a landslide to the independent anti-corruption candidate Martin Bell in his Tatton constituency.

The number of women MPs elected exactly doubled from 60 in 1992 to 120 in 1997 (18 per cent of the House): 101 Labour, 13 Conservative, 3 Liberal Democrat, 2 SNP, and the Speaker, Betty Boothroyd. The number of women candidates for the three main parties at 360 (Labour 155 [24 per cent], Conservative 66 [10 per cent], Liberal Democrat 139 [21 per cent]) was not much higher than 1992 (341: Labour 138, Conservative 59, Liberal Democrat 144), but what was different in 1997 was the strategic placing of Labour's women candidates, only 54 of whom found themselves in unwinnable seats on the day. The Liberal Democrats, whose candidate selection procedures involved no innovations but who continued mandatorily to shortlist one woman (where available) in any shortlist of 3, fielded 139 women, but with only 4 in winnable seats (Argyll & Bute, Richmond Park, Rochdale and Taunton). The problem, as seen from Cowley Street, was that unlike Labour, whose women were located in urban seats the party could win, the Liberal Democrats' target seats were mostly in rural areas and not in the urban areas where most of the party's aspiring women are based. The SNP fielded 15 women candidates (including 2 sitting MPs) out of 72 (20 per cent), and Plaid Cymru 7 out of 40 (17 per cent).

Black and Asian representation increased with the election of four new Labour MPs to add to the existing five: Ashok Kumar (Middlesbrough South & East Cleveland) – the only black or Asian candidate selected in a key marginal seat (which he had held in 1991–92); Marsha Singh (Bradford West); Oona King (Bethnal Green & Bow) and Mohammed Sarwar (Glasgow Govan). Labour fielded a total of 13 black or Asian candidates, only four of whom contested in unwinnable or non-Labour-held seats. The sole Conservative Asian MP, Nirj Deva, was buried under a Labour majority of 14,000 at Brentford & Isleworth, but the half-Indian former MP Jonathan Sayeed (who did not identify as an ethnic minority candidate) was returned for Mid Bedfordshire. The Conservatives fielded ten candidates from black or Asian backgrounds; all except Mr Deva in unwinnable seats, though two were drawn from the dominant ethnic minority group in two Labour-held seats (Bradford West and Bethnal Green & Bow) where that party riskily selected a non-white candidate from outside the dominant Asian group and suffered its only adverse swings to the Conservatives in Labour seats. Two black Conservative candidates, Hugh Neil (Hyndburn) and Derek Laud (Tottenham), withdrew from their candidacies under personal clouds, though both complained of racist attitudes in the party. The Liberal Democrats claimed the largest number, 19, of ethnic minority candidates, including two of Chinese origin and one from the Middle East, but none of these were fielded in remotely winnable seats.

The total of 42 major party candidates from ethnic minority backgrounds compared with 23 in 1992, with the Liberal Democrats accounting for most of the difference. Given that Labour was the only party with support in strength in black and Asian communities, it was clearly that party's responsibility to augment the number of non-white MPs. That the gains made – from 5 to 9 non-white Labour MPs – though proportionately large were in fact slight, is almost certainly due to the party's far stronger commitment to feminisation, to the divisions between various ethnic minority groups, and to the obvious tenacity of certain white incumbent MPs, unwilling to concede to local non-white challengers in their heavily black or Asian constituencies.

The *Jewish Chronicle* listed 20 MPs as Jewish, based on their self-identification: 13 Labour, 6 Conservative and 1 Liberal Democrat.[6] The total, the same as in 1992, masked a change in the political balance in favour of Labour; six of the Jewish MPs being in the new intake (two of them unexpected beneficiaries of the landslide), whilst three Conservative newcomers failed to compensate for eight defeated MPs, including the former Foreign Secretary, Malcolm Rifkind. The dissolution had seen the retirement of the most prominent Jewish MP, Greville Janner, who vacated the Leicester seat he had represented for Labour for 27 years, and for which his father, Sir Barnett Janner, who had been equally prominent in the ranks of Anglo-Jewry, had sat for the previous 25 years.

The continuing presence on the first bench below the gangway of Sir Edward Heath, long after the rest of his generation had departed for the House of Lords or more ethereal locations, ensured that the status of being the oldest MP remained with him as the sole octogenarian (b. 1916) (see Table 10.1). Sir Geoffrey Johnson-Smith (b. 1924) and Sir Peter Emery (b. 1926) were the only other Conservative MPs over 70. Labour elected three septuagenarians: Robert Sheldon (b. 1923), Piara Khabra (b. 1924) and Tony Benn (b. 1925). The only other MPs in their seventies were the Democratic Unionist Party leader, the Revd Ian Paisley (b. 1926) and the Ulster Unionist, Cecil Walker (b. 1924). The Labour landslide saw the election of some relatively old new MPs: Nigel Beard (b. 1936), Ian Gibson (b. 1938), and Harold Best, Ann Cryer and Desmond Turner (all born in 1939). The oldest

Conservative member of the new intake was the returning MP Alan Clark (b. 1928); the oldest Liberal Democrats the returning MP Ronnie Fearn (b. 1931) and Donald Gorrie (b. 1933).

Table 10.1   Age of candidates (as at 1 January 1997)

Age on 1.1.97	Labour elected	Labour defeated	Conservative elected	Conservative defeated	Liberal Democrat elected	Liberal Democrat defeated
20–29	10	32	1	60	–	64
30–39	55	70	21	164	17	135
40–49	178	83	61	135	9	188
50–59	140	34	61	82	15	156
60–69	32	2	18	30	5	48
70–79	3	–	2	4	–	2
80–89	–	–	1	–	–	–
Median Age						
1997	48	41	50	41	46	45
1992	51	38	48	39	45	43

The landslide delivered ten – all new – Labour MPs under the age of 30 (as at 1 January 1997) – five men and five women, and five of them unanticipated victors. The youngest – the new 'Baby of the House' – was Christopher Leslie (b. July 1972), the surprise winner over Sir Marcus Fox in Shipley. The other nine were: Claire Ward (b. June 1972), Yvette Cooper (b. 1969), Ruth Kelly and Paul Marsden (both b. 1968), and Oona King, Ivan Lewis, Jim Murphy, Gareth Thomas (Harrow West) and Lorna Fitzsimmons (all b. in 1967). The youngest Conservative MP was the newcomer, Graham Brady (b. 1967). The Liberal Democrats elected no candidate under 30, but their youngest candidate was Richard Allan (b. 1966), with five other new Liberal Democrat MPs all born in 1965: Edward Davey, Evan Harris, Michael Moore, Lembit Opik and Steven Webb. With 17 of their 46 MPs in their thirties, the Liberal Democrat benches had the youngest age profile. The Labour and Conservative parties, despite the great disparity in size, had broadly similar age profiles – with three-quarters of their MPs in their forties and fifties.

Despite the imminence of the Millennium, the 1997 House retained a few members first elected in the 1950s (see Table 10.2), seven in all: Sir Edward Heath (1950, entering his second term as 'Father of the House'), Tony Benn (Labour, 1950), Sir Richard Body (Conservative, 1955), John Morris (Labour, 1959) and the Conservative trio who comprised the remnants of Harold

Macmillan's 71-strong 'You've Never Had it So Good' intake of 1959 – Sir Peter Emery, Sir Geoffrey Johnson-Smith and Sir Peter Tapsell. Of the seven, only Sir Edward Heath and John Morris had served continuously. The large, mostly Labour, intakes of the 1960s had also virtually disappeared: eleven MPs elected for Labour in that decade remained, one of whom (Robert Maclennan) was now a Liberal Democrat.[7] Three Conservatives remained from the 1960s parliaments: Sir Teddy Taylor, elected in 1964 (but with subsequently interrupted service), Michael Heseltine (1966) and Tom King (elected at a by-election in 1970, close to the end of the 1966–70 parliament). Of Labour's 418 MPs only 43 (those elected before 1979) had previous experience of Labour in government; and of the Conservatives' 165, only 36 of that party in opposition. Only 30 of the Conservative MPs had parliamentary memories extending further back than the Thatcher and Major leaderships, to the era of 'one nation' Conservatism, making the failure of Kenneth Clarke's leadership bid in June 1997 all the more explicable.

Table 10.2   *Parliamentary experience of MPs*

First entered parliament	Labour	Conservative	Liberal Democrat
1950–59	2	5	–
1960–69	10	2	1
1970–74	27	23	2
1975–79	20	17	–
1980–83	29	32	6
1984–87	62	25	6
1988–92	78	28	3
1993–97	190	33	28
Total	418	165	46

The modest dynastic affiliations of late-twentieth-century MPs were made still more modest by the retirement of Greville Janner, who, with his father, had held a Leicester seat continuously for 52 years, and the unequalled record of the departing Paul Channon, who, with two previous generations of his family, had sat for Southend for all but 15 years of the entire century (1912–97). One dynastic Liberal Democrat appeared in the shape of Sir Robert Smith, third baronet, whose grandfather had sat as a Conservative for part of his Aberdeenshire seat. He joined four other grandsons, 3 Conservative and 1 Labour. Eighteen sons or daughters of MPs were returned – 9 Labour (4 in the new intake), and 9 Conservative (3 newcomers). John Cryer, son of the late Bob Cryer, was accompanied by his mother Ann, making them the first mother and son pair since the Conservative Oppenheims in the 1983–87 House. Five pairs of husbands and wives were elected, two of whom (both Labour), the Morgans and the Keens, involved wives joining their husbands in the House.[8] Ann Keen with Sylvia Heal was also one of a pair of sisters, the others being the twins Angela and Maria Eagle.

Table 10.3   Education of candidates

	Labour		Conservative		Liberal Democrat	
	elected	defeated	elected	defeated	elected	defeated
Type of Education						
Elementary	–	–	–	–	–	–
Elementary +	2	–	–	–	–	–
Secondary	48	19	5	48	5	66
Secondary + Poly/College	86	54	9	74	6	162
Secondary + University	215	120	42	154	16	253
Public School	2	–	9	17	1	8
Pub Sch + Poly/College	5	4	9	28	2	10
Public Sch + University	60	24	91	154	16	94
TOTAL	418	221	165	475	46	593
Oxford	41	11	46	59	11	38
Cambridge	20	16	38	45	4	25
Other Univs	214	117	49	204	17	284
All Universities	275	144	133	308	32	347
	(66%)	(65%)	(81%)	(65%)	(70%)	(59%)
Eton	2	–	15	20	1	–
Harrow	–	–	–	5	–	–
Winchester	1	–	1	3	–	–
Other Public Sch	64	28	93	169	18	102
All public schs	67	28	109	197	19	102
	(16%)	(13%)	(66%)	(42%)	(41%)	(17%)

Ever-rising proportions of MPs had attended university, more still in Labour's case are graduates of the (pre-1992) polytechnics (see Table 10.3). More (66 per cent) Labour MPs had attended university than ever before; when the party last (barely) won a Commons majority in 1974 the figure was 57 per cent. The percentage of Conservative MPs educated at university – at 81 per cent – had also never been higher. The public schools also continued to shape the parties in contrasting ways. They provide two-thirds of Conservative MPs; two-fifths of the Liberal Democrats and about one-sixth of the PLP. This latter figure has fluctuated little over the past six elections, and no appreciable difference was made by the scale of Labour's victory, the proportion of public school products in the new intake being the same as in the PLP as a whole, and most of the new public school-educated MPs clustered in the more winnable seats. A roll-call of the public schools attended by some of the new intake – Cheltenham Ladies' College (2 MPs), North London Collegiate, the Perse Girls', Westminster, Highgate, Haberdashers' Aske's, Christ's Hospital, Tonbridge, Sherborne, Haileybury, Abingdon and Mill Hill – perhaps symbolises Labour's renewed rapport with the home counties.

On the other hand, the lowest ever number of Old Etonians were returned at the election, 18, of whom 15 are Conservative, 2 are Labour and 1 is Liberal Democrat.[9] Thirty-four Etonians had been elected to the Conservative benches in 1992, of whom 12 retired in 1997 and 10 more were defeated. The new intake of 41 Conservative MPs contained only three Etonians. The 15 Etonian Conservative MPs represent only 9 per cent of all Conservative MPs compared with proportions of 10 per cent in 1992, 11 per cent in 1987, 12 per cent in 1983, 15 per cent in 1979, 18 per cent in 1974 and 20 per cent in 1959. The year with which 1997 invites comparison is 1945, when the Conservatives also suffered a landslide defeat which pushed them back into their safest seats. On that occasion 29 per cent of all Conservative MPs were Etonians. It says much for the transformed social background of the party that even when reduced to its safest seats in 1997, the Etonian rump continued to erode. All traces of Harrow School were lost to the House; 5 of the 7 Harrovians elected in 1992 retired, the remaining 2 were defeated. Of the 25 unelected Etonian and Harrovian Conservative candidates only 8 were young men on their way up as distinct from older men or defeated MPs on their way out.

The occupational characteristics of the MPs elected in 1997 are summarised in Table 10.4. Broadly familiar patterns emerge: Labour still relies heavily on the (public sector) professions, mostly teaching and local government administration, but also shows growing reliance on the miscellaneous white-collar category. The 69 Labour MPs included under this heading comprise

Table 10.4   Occupation of candidates

	Labour		Conservative		Liberal Democrat	
	elected	defeated	elected	defeated	elected	defeated
Professions						
Barrister	12	7	20	47	4	6
Solicitor	17	11	9	41	2	27
Doctor/dentist/optician	3	2	2	4	4	11
Architect/surveyor	–	–	2	9	–	7
Civil/chartered Engineer	3	2	–	4	1	10
Accountant	2	2	3	24	1	26
Civil Service/local govt	30	19	5	7	2	28
Armed services	–	–	9	10	1	11
Teachers:						
University	22	4	1	3	2	19
Polytech/coll:	35	17	–	2	1	19
School	54	37	7	19	4	85
other consultancies	3	4	2	1	1	10
Scientific/research	7	2	1	2	–	7
TOTAL	188	107	61	173	23	266
	(45%)	(48%)	(37%)	(36%)	(50%)	(45%)
Business						
Company Director	7	3	17	51	2	25
Company executive	9	13	36	90	7	66
Commerce/insurance	2	9	7	33	1	39
Management/clerical	15	8	1	15	1	30
General business	4	7	4	22	–	41
TOTAL	37	40	65	211	11	201
	(9%)	(18%)	(39%)	(44%)	(24%)	(34%)
Miscellaneous						
Miscellaneous						
white collar	69	29	2	16	1	57
Politician/pol.						
organiser	40	9	15	20	5	13
Publisher/journalist	29	10	14	27	4	18
Farmer	1	2	5	13	1	7
Housewife	–	–	2	4	–	9
Student	–	4	–	2	–	8
TOTAL	139	54	38	82	11	112
	(33%)	(24%)	(23%)	(17%)	(24%)	(19%)
Manual workers						
Miner	12	–	1	–	–	–
Skilled worker	40	20	–	9	1	14
Semi/unskilled	2	–	–	–	–	–
TOTAL	54	20	1	9	1	14
	(13%)	(9%)	(1%)	(2%)	(2%)	(2%)
GRAND TOTAL	418	221	165	475	46	593

31 union officials, 14 social workers, 15 voluntary sector employees and 9 others. The Conservatives continue to lean towards business and the law, but with Dame Angela Rumbold's 'political clones' also in evidence. The still small Liberal Democrat group of MPs is drawn from a wide spread of occupations, but the Liberal Democrat range of candidates resembles both the Conservatives in their background in business, and Labour in their occupation as teachers.

One downward trend that has taken a precipitous turn is the percentage of Labour MPs drawn from manual working backgrounds. At 13 per cent, this is the lowest percentage ever. When Labour last won an election (with 319 MPs in October 1974), 28 per cent of the PLP came from manual occupations, and even if allowance is made for the fact that some former manual workers are hidden elsewhere in the table – notably among the ranks of the trade union officials – the figure is still very low. A PLP comprising 12 miners in a total of 418 MPs is indeed some years on from the legendary 'committee of checkweighmen'. Apart from all the public sector professionals flooding onto the Labour benches, the second largest category (after teachers) has become the political staffers, 18 of whom are in the new intake.

Trade union sponsorship of Labour MPs was discontinued in 1995 and replaced by 'constituency plan agreements' between unions and selected constituency Labour parties, involving some union money going to support constituency activities in return for which the union was to have some representation on the CLP's general committee. The objective of the change was to detach – in the post-Nolan era – individual MPs from union-derived money. Some hundred 'constituency plan agreements' were in place in the early months of the new parliament, concentrated in marginal rather than safe seats, as had been the pattern under union sponsorship; the intention was to build up Labour's organisational strength in the key marginals. Co-operative Party sponsorship had also lapsed; twenty-six 'Labour and Co-operative' candidates fought the election and all were elected, but with the Co-operative Party now running as a 'sister' party and not as a sponsoring organisation. Although fewer union officials were elected in the new intake of MPs than in 1992, virtually all 418 Labour MPs belonged to unions. Unions with the largest membership (excluding MPs with dual or multiple affiliations) were the TGWU (68), GMB (63), MSF (56) and UNISON (44). The once-great AEEU numbered 15 and the NUM 10 (with two other MPs carrying dual NUM/AEEU membership). The bulk of the remaining MPs belonged to one or other of the various teaching unions (NUT, EIS, NATFHE, AUT).

The political orientation of the PLP was a matter for some speculation, particularly given the surprising election of many of the new intake. Some new MPs clearly came with left-wing histories, but many orthodox parliamentary careers have been built on a background of earlier radicalism.[10]

Perhaps significantly only 6 of the 183 new MPs joined the hard-left Campaign Group, taking its membership up to 31. (The Tribune Group had not reconstituted itself by the time the House rose for the summer recess.) Whilst most Labour MPs came from backgrounds in the public sector, they had learned habits of loyalty and discipline as local councillors. Despite the infusion of young blood, the average age of the new MPs – 43 – made them middle-aged parliamentarians who had in many cases striven for years to get to Westminster. Most of the women MPs – despite inflated majorities – were in marginal seats they would have to nurture if they were to effect the long-term cultural change they desired. Caution in sustaining what was only the third Labour government ever with a secure majority was likely to be the watchword.

For the future, the parties could be expected to remain preoccupied with candidate selection procedures. The Conservatives had most to do: the centre proposed, but the local associations seemingly disposed. Central Office purported to dislike the selection of inexperienced political apparatchiks – many from Central Office itself – yet it could find few Archie Normans from the business world prepared to sacrifice high earnings for a parliamentary seat, especially during the powerlessness of opposition. The absence of any will to impose mechanisms to promote women candidates was palpable. Hand-wringing exhortation seemed also to cover the highly embarrassing matter of black and Asian representation. For Labour, whose centralised command of selection processes had become the envy of Central Office, the flaws of OMOV were nonetheless evident. The block signing-up of new members to pack selection conferences was a problem, especially in Asian seats. Postal voting regulations – already tightened up in the later stages of the selection round in 1996 to reduce postal vote proportions from as high as 50 per cent of the turnout to some 30 per cent – needed greater stringency. All-day polling station-type balloting (again in use in some cases in 1996) with the facility for checking credentials was also desirable.

Finally, the 418 Labour MPs would need to look to their own security of tenure. The process of mandatory reselection of MPs – a left-wing imposition of the early 1980s – had never yet been carried out during the period of a Labour government, but the next reselection round at the turn of the century would be.[11] Labour activists could well by then be disaffected and seek to threaten their sitting MP who would need to spend some two months of a selection process drumming up the two-thirds of nominations needed for an uncontested vote: there were some MPs, even ironically from the left of the party, who began to argue for the introduction of a 'trigger' mechanism to prompt a reselection vote, a proposal advocated by Ian Mikardo back in the early 1980s in an attempt to deflect the left-wing activists' successful push for mandatory reselection. *Plus ça change ...*

NOTES

1. The Labour returnees were Huw Edwards (Monmouth), Sylvia Heal (Halesowen and Rowley Regis), Ashok Kumar (Middlesbrough South & East Cleveland) and John Smith (Vale of Glamorgan), all by-election entrants defeated in 1992, and Frank Doran (Aberdeen Central) who had been the only Labour MP elected in 1987 to lose his seat in 1992.

   The Conservatives were Christopher Chope (Christchurch), Alan Clark (Kensington & Chelsea), Michael Fallon (Sevenoaks), Gerald Howarth (Aldershot), Humfrey Malins (Woking), John Maples (Stratford on Avon), Francis Maude (Horsham) and Jonathan Sayeed (Mid Bedfordshire). All but Alan Clark had been beaten in 1992; he had retired then, but later decided to stage a comeback.

   The Liberal Democrat MPs returning were Ronnie Fearn (Southport), Mike Hancock (Portsmouth South) and Richard Livsey (Brecon & Radnorshire) – in seats they lost at earlier elections.

2. Donald Gorrie, newly elected Liberal Democrat MP for Edinburgh West, had shown similar doggedness in fighting his seat on five occasions.

3. David Amess (moved from Basildon to Southend West), James Arbuthnot (Wanstead & Woodford to Hampshire North-East), Sir Paul Beresford (Croydon Central to Mole Valley), Peter Bottomley (Eltham to Worthing West), Eric Forth (Mid Worcestershire to Bromley & Chislehurst), Nick Hawkins (Blackpool South to Surrey Heath), Norman Lamont (Kingston-on-Thames to Harrogate & Knaresborough), Sir George Young (Ealing Acton to Hampshire North-West), John Watts (Slough to Reading East).

   Peter Thurnham (Bolton North-East) announced his intention to retire from his highly marginal seat early in the parliament, then unsuccessfully sought selection in the safe Westmorland & Lonsdale constituency, and finally crossed the floor to join another ex-Conservative MP, Emma Nicholson, on the Liberal Democrat bench in 1996.

4. The late-retiring MPs were: John Evans (St Helens North), Dr John Gilbert (Dudley North), Norman Hogg (Cumbernauld & Kilsyth), Doug Hoyle (Warrington North), Roy Hughes (Newport East), Sir Geoffrey Lofthouse (Pontefract & Castleford), Willie McKelvey (Kilmarnock & Loudon) and Stuart Randall (Hull West and Hessle). All, except Mr McKelvey, were raised to the peerage.

5. New women Labour MPs chosen from open shortlists in key marginals or Labour-held seats were:

   *Charlotte Atkins (Staffordshire Moorlands)
   Hazel Blears (Salford)
   Linda Clark (Edinburgh Pentlands)
   Yvette Cooper (Pontefract & Castleford)
   Lorna Fitzsimmons (Rochdale)
   Caroline Flint (Don Valley)
   *Barbara Follett (Stevenage)
   *Sylvia Heal (Halesowen & Rowley Regis)
   Patricia Hewitt (Leicester W)
   Beverley Hughes (Stretford)
   Joan Humble (Blackpool North & Fleetwood)
   Helen Jones (Warrington North)
   Ruth Kelly (Bolton West)
   Oona King (Bethnal Green & Bow)
   *Tess Kingham (Gloucester)
   Rosemary McKenna (Cumbernauld & Kilsyth)
   Christine Russell (City of Chester)
   Helen Southworth (Warrington South)
   Rosalie Winterton (Doncaster Central)
   (* chosen before the suspension of women-only shortlists)

This list excludes the additional 12 new women MPs elected in seats originally thought to be Conservative – all but one of whom were chosen from open shortlists.

6. 9 May 1997.
7. Labour's surviving 1960s entrants were: Tam Dalyell (1962), Robert Sheldon and Alan Williams (1964), Kevin McNamara (the Hull North by-election victor whose election triggered the 1966 election), Donald Anderson, Donald Dewar, Gwyneth Dunwoody, Ted Rowlands and David Winnick (all elected in 1966, but whose service had been interrupted), and Joe Ashton (1968).
8. MPs' grandsons (* denotes new MP): *Sir Robert Smith (Liberal Democrat), David Faber, Oliver Heald, Geoffrey Clifton-Brown (Conservative), Peter Mandelson (Labour).

   MPs' sons/daughters: Hilary Armstrong, *Charlotte Atkins, Tony Benn, *John Cryer, Mark Fisher, *Lindsay Hoyle, Ian McCartney, Estelle Morris, *Daria Taylor (all Labour); James Arbuthnot, Peter Brooke, *Dominic Grieve, Douglas Hogg, Bernard Jenkin, *Francis Maude, *Charles Prior, Nicholas Soames, Peter Temple-Morris (all Conservative).

   Husbands and wives: Gordon and Bridget Prentice (separated), Rhodri and *Julie Morgan, Alan and *Ann Keen (Labour); Peter and Virginia Bottomley, Nicholas and Ann Winterton (Conservative). In August 1997 Andrew McKay (Conservative) married his new parliamentary colleague, Julie Kirkbride.
9. The re-elected Conservative Etonian MPs were: James Arbuthnot, Geoffrey Clifton-Brown, Michael Colvin, David Faber, Sir Archie Hamilton, David Heathcoat-Amory, Douglas Hogg, Andrew Rowe, Nicholas Soames, David Tredinnick, John Wilkinson and Sir George Young; the newcomers were the returning MP Alan Clark, Oliver Letwin and Nicholas St Aubyn. Labour's Etonians were Tam Dalyell and Mark Fisher; the Liberal Democrats', David Rendel.
10. One of the more interesting to note in the new Labour intake was Charlotte Atkins, daughter of the former left-wing MP Ron Atkins (1966–70 and 1974–79). She had co-written with Chris Mullin in 1981 the left-wing activists' guide to deselecting moderate Labour MPs, at the height of the Bennite surge, but was later imposed by the NEC as candidate in the Eastbourne by-election of 1990, and subsequently became active in the relatively apolitical quest to promote women candidates.
11. Very few Labour MPs had faced contested reselection ballots between 1994 and 1997. Apart from the seven casualties of contests prompted by boundary changes (listed on p. 187–8), four others faced contests: Roger Godsiff (successfully), David Young (unsuccessfully), Max Madden (unsuccessfully) and Roy Hughes (successfully, though he later retired).

11 Constituency Campaigning

British election law remains almost entirely based on the Victorian idea that what is involved is a whole set of separate contests between independent gentlemen fighting individual campaigns in each of 600 or so constituencies. In 1997, 3724 candidates (825 more than the 1992 record of 2899) battled to become MPs in the 659 seats in the new parliament. They were supported by some hundreds of professional agents and some hundred thousands of party workers. Yet a growing body of studies point to the importance of the local campaign, not only in affecting some results but also in recruiting party members and improving the local organisation.[1] Reactions to the activities of leaders and parties at Westminster would largely swamp any local endeavours. In trying to assess what they did, we have been largely influenced by the responses of more than a hundred candidates to a long questionnaire and by our interviews with candidates and agents.

The length of the campaign was widely considered to have taken its toll – on voters as well as activists. It was a general view among candidates of all parties that the majority of the electorate had already resolved to change the government when the election was called; consequently they found the subsequent campaign uninteresting, tedious – even irritating. One senior Labour politician observed that people 'had clearly made up their minds and just switched off. On the other hand, it exhausted us.' A defeated Conservative put the point vividly: 'my result would have been exactly the same if I had spent six weeks in the South of France (provided this was not public knowledge of course). I think the majority of the electorate had decided they wanted a change of government and that was it.' Certainly the campaign's length, far from assisting the Conservatives, stretched the party's weakened resources and probably reinforced the feeling amongst the electorate that it was 'time for a change'.

The 1997 contest was remarkable for a greater degree of targeting on particular constituencies and particular voters than ever before. Conservative and Labour headquarters focused their efforts on almost identical lists of the 90–100 seats where the election would be decided. The Conservatives focused on 130 seats, 30 of them held by the opposition; however, their main concentration was defensive – the 100 seats most vulnerable to Labour. The Liberal Democrats, too, concentrated far more ruthlessly on the 50 seats where they had a chance of breaking through, as well as on the 20 they were defending, but they had many county councillors fighting to survive in seats where there was no parliamentary hope, and this limited the focusing of effort.

As a result the parties often put up only a token presence in the seats they considered unwinnable, sending activists to nearby marginals. One Labour candidate in a safe seat believed that his Liberal Democrat opponent was nothing but 'a paper candidate', while the Conservatives' candidate in Scotland reported that his local party had been asked 'not to canvass but to send people to key seats'; the opposition parties did likewise and were 'almost nowhere to be seen'.

On Labour's target list every seat except one (Brecon & Radnor) was gained – and they took 66 more besides. Every seat on the Conservatives' list was lost except one (Christchurch) which they recovered from a record by-election defeat. The Liberal Democrats gained over half their targets and one, Kingston, which they had thought was out of range. But, as Curtice and Steed explain (see Appendix 2, p. 312) this targeting was largely ineffective or mutually cancelling. The movement in constituencies that had received no special attention was very similar to that in targeted seats. The reward for these special efforts was that turnout fell slightly less.

Targeting moved beyond a focus on particular seats to a focus on particular people. The Conservatives used a PIKE programme (Programme for Identifying Key Electors) in conjunction with direct mail surveys to select 40,000 or so voters in each target seat and showered direct mail upon them. For each seat the party collected a range of political and social information, covering lifestyle, age, ethnicity, housing tenure, employment, council tax and media exposure so that messages could be suitably tailored. In the months prior to the election all the main parties sought to gather data about the interests and concerns of their electors through extensive use of questionnaires. For example, one Conservative sent a survey to every one of his electors in the second half of 1996 at a cost of £10,000. Of the more than 70,000 surveys dispatched, 16,000 were returned. The information thus gained was used by the parties to generate election material focusing upon the particular preoccupations of individual voters.

Labour chose its 90 target seats ruthlessly and focused enormous effort on them, with some direct mailing as well as intensive telephone canvassing, often from Millbank or the party's regional offices. Conservatives claimed to have ceased long-distance telephone canvassing at the dissolution, but they suspected that Labour had not. There remains some confusion on the legal position on telephone canvassing. Computers played a strategic role in these constituency operations. Most constituencies utilised computers for at least routine administrative work, and marginal seats were especially well equipped. Tapes of the new electoral register were supplied in February by council officials. These could be quickly collated with each party's evidence from previous years on canvass contacts, voting patterns, and survey responses (where these existed). Telephone numbers could be added. On the basis of this data set, personalised letters or special leaflets could be quickly directed to sub-groups of the electorate – known waverers, new voters, ethnic groups, doctors, teachers, and the like. A Conservative candidate described how he had used a sophisticated word-processing system to dispatch 2000 personal letters to 'waverers' identified in doorstep canvassing, while a Liberal Democrat in a marginal seat contrasted his single 286 computer in 1992 with the several 486 computers and laser printer he now operated. His biggest asset was an 'in-house Risograph printer which enabled "handwritten letters" and letters from Paddy Ashdown to be widely distributed at minimal cost'.

Canvass cards and knocking-up lists were routinely generated by computer. Much tedious office work was thus avoided. 'Nothing gets hand addressed now', wrote one candidate in a marginal. 'Computers used hugely. Endless target mailings to identified groups of voters. Scores of different sorts. No glue and paste any more.' One Conservative related how the installation of a machine for stuffing envelopes had 'made about 50 of our senior members redundant for a week'.

Telephone canvassing developed, although its costs seldom appeared in expense returns. In the pre-election period both sides used telephone banks from London and from regional offices. Well-trained interviewers engaged in survey canvassing in key marginals and in more general fund-raising. There were suggestions that long-distance canvassing of target seats continued during the campaign, when it would almost certainty have involved breaches of the law on expenses.

There was also an increasing amount of telephone canvassing at constituency level. Party members who were too old to go out in person, or who found council estates or high-rise flats intimidating, were ready to give their time to systematic talking on the telephone. Candidates with dispersed rural constituencies reported that telephone canvassing was vital. In urban areas, too, new private apartments with elaborate security systems meant that the telephone was often the only way to reach voters – though one candidate added that 'obtaining accurate telephone numbers was a nightmare (especially those with Mercury numbers)'. Besides, door-to-door canvassing frequently drew a blank as more and more houses were unoccupied during working hours: 'telephone canvassing was used to follow up people who were out'.

Yet again, like other aspects of the campaign, the constituency experience was far from uniform. If some candidates reported heavy use of telephone canvassing – one Conservative noted that 'some wards used telephone canvassing entirely' – in many other constituencies, considered very safe or unwinnable, or where party workers remained wedded to traditional techniques, telephone canvassing was unimportant, or conducted on behalf of neighbouring marginals. The Liberal Democrats generally eschewed telephone canvassing on grounds of cost, but a Labour candidate in a safe seat was frustrated to find her local party workers 'completely old-fashioned in their approach ... We did no telephone canvassing at all.' Her experience was not uncommon.

If some modern communication forms had entrenched their position within the campaign process, the influence of e-mail and the Internet was clearly at a transitional stage. E-mail came into its own for internal party communications, where its speed and flexibility carried obvious advantages, and all parties made electronic contact with their candidates once or twice a day, updating them on the latest party themes and the appropriate reactions to questions. It was reported by Conservatives that Central Office briefings on issues raised at press conferences were available on e-mail by 10.30 or 11.30 a.m.; previously they had not usually arrived until the next day, when they were already out of date. 'E-mail', said a Labour candidate, 'was the main way of keeping in touch with central HQ at Millbank'. By this means they were able to download graphics and campaign material. An SNP organiser calculated that 60 per cent of his messages to candidates went by fax, and 40 per cent by e-mail. The Liberal Democrats made especially active use of the system: the party had a special e-mail network for daily communication with candidates, at least a quarter of whom preferred to receive their morning briefings by e-mail rather than fax. Not only was literature distributed to constituencies, but constituencies themselves could send locally generated material to London for further work or communicate useful ideas to other seats: 'we swapped a lot of ideas and literature drafts'.

However, e-mail had not yet penetrated sufficiently widely amongst the public to be an effective tool of electioneering. A Conservative candidate in a 'high-tech' area received only one e-mail from a constituent; another was sent only three; though both did better than a candidate who offered an e-mail facility 'and had not a single response'.

The election was covered actively by the Internet at national level. All the main political parties (with the exception of Socialist Labour) established web sites accessible to the general public. They used these sites to publish party and policy information, electronic versions of their manifestos, campaign news, and pictures of posters and advertisements.

Labour had operated a web site since 1994, and on 20 March 1997 Tony Blair launched the party's election site (labourwin97.org.uk), at a press conference. The theme of what he claimed was 'the most developed web site of any party anywhere in the world' was 'All roads lead to Labour'.

Everyone with internet access will be able to find out about our policies, their constituency, and party personalities; they will be able to volunteer for the party; they will be able to find out the latest campaign news; and there is a special part of the web site devoted to school elections, for voters of tomorrow.

On 25 April Labour boasted that its election site had proven a 'huge vote-winner with cyber-surfers', attracting a total of 1.5 million 'hits' – though many of these were from 72 countries overseas, including 250,000 from the US. The Conservative site (Conservative-party.org.uk) claimed to have 16,000 visitors per week, of whom 80 per cent were from the UK; while the Liberal Democrats said their site (Libdems.org.uk) attracted 4000 visitors daily, 70 per cent of whom were from the UK. For the Liberal Democrats, the Internet was peculiarly *their* medium:

> The internet is the best example in the world today of a community which is democratic, open, and in which power is as decentralised as possible. That is what the Liberal Democrats want for Britain.

Yet, notwithstanding the claims of the parties, it cannot be said that the Internet exerted a significant impact on the campaign. Much of the information carried on each site in fact consisted of previous press releases and statements by party spokesmen. Besides being frequently of limited contemporary interest, it reflected the general preoccupation with propaganda and soundbites. As the *Independent*'s Science Editor Charles Arthur observed, a quick tour through the network

> suggests that, rather than offering a means for voters to bypass the media in the search for facts, the main parties see the web as a low-cost extension of their advertising hoardings.

The reach of the medium was also limited. Measures of 'hits' are a rather misleading statistic, as one person's requests to view individual files within a site will generate tens of 'hits'. Charles Arthur estimated, for instance, that Labour's 1.25 million 'hits' could be attributed to at most 125,000 visitors – of whom only around 100,000 would have been UK electors.

More informative were the political and election sites conducted by independent organisations. There were around a dozen such sites, including those operated by the *Guardian*, BBC, ITN, *The Times*, the *Daily Telegraph*, the Press Association, the Microsoft Network, and Keele University, as well as sites operated by the major polling companies. These carried a wealth of material, such as candidate and constituency profiles, maps, party manifestos, voter registration information, news updates and archives, poll and betting information, and expert analysis from political commentators. The BBC provided through the system audio-versions of the Dimbleby interviews with the party leaders, the *On the Record* programme, and the morning election call.

There were also attempts to use the Internet on an interactive basis. UK Citizens Online Democracy, established in 1996, initiated a 'Politician's Forum', with representatives of the major parties meeting on the Internet to discuss a series of issues and responding to questions sent in by the public. It was during another 'interactive chat' session on Microsoft Network's election site that Clare Short admitted to having smoked cannabis – a story later taken up by the press. However, major politicians made few appearances in computer-generated discussions, with most parties preferring to dispatch their technology spokesmen – Ian Taylor for the Conservatives, Geoff Hoon for Labour, and Nigel Jones for the Liberal Democrats.

It has been estimated that these independent web publishers were visited a total of 30 million times between their launch (usually in February) and shortly after the election. The BBC claimed 10 million visits, the *Guardian* 7 million, GE'97 7 million, and ITN 2 million. This overall figure of 30 million was attributed to around 150,000 different people, each accessing an average of 200 pages. Since half of these accesses were from abroad (principally from the US, Australia, Canada and Belgium) it again appears that less than 100,000 UK electors utilised the medium for election information. However, the scale of Internet activity during the 1997 election was far in advance of that in 1992, and it seems reasonable to suppose that its impact in future elections will be substantial. As Paddy Ashdown remarked, 'e-mail had proven in this election incredibly useful in contacting the party machine; in the next election it would contact the voters'.

Some participants noted a tendency for computers to affect more than simply the style and speed of production of constituency literature, believing they promoted the centralisation of campaign work. A Conservative compared 1997 with 1979, the last time general and local elections had been held in his constituency on the same day. Then, 'much of the clerical work was "farmed out" to branches and party workers in their own homes'. In 1997, 'my agent had to cope with 15 county council candidates as well as my own campaign'. Another remarked more cynically: 'the technology helps to give people excuses not to do proper canvassing in my view'.

Certainly the new technologies did have important labour-saving properties, and the Conservatives, in particular, appeared to find this a valuable feature. They were, said one, 'a convenience in compensating for the universally lower numbers of party workers'; another felt there was 'a possibility that new technology and computers, etc., may have disguised the fact that we were short of volunteers'. But in the end, he continued, no amount of technology could replace face-to-face campaigning.

All parties suffered from the fact they had lost workers, but the Conservatives had been hit particularly hard. It has been estimated that their 1997 membership was 400,000, a fall of 350,000 since 1992 and a fifth of the number in the 1950s.[2] The decline in the number and enthusiasm of activists was a frequent complaint. There were, said one Conservative, far fewer volunteers: 'Nothing like the enthusiasm in 1992 or any previous election.' After the 1970 election, recalled one defeated candidate, he had written 800 'thank you' letters to supporters. This time, though his constituency had grown from 52,000 to 78,000, he had written only 170.

The declining Conservative presence in local government was a further weakness. Local councillors had traditionally provided a willing body of active canvassers, and this, and the experience they gained, was often missing. More than 10 per cent of the 3250 council seats up for election on 1 May were not contested by Conservatives, and Conservatives stood in only 84 per cent of the seats in the 21 new unitary authorities. 'Once a party loses its local government base', said one party official, 'it is very hard to rebuild it'. But it was not merely the number of Conservative volunteers that was a problem: it was also their age. It was calculated in 1992 that the average age of Conservative Party members was 62.[3] 'We fielded', commented one Conservative, 'a very elderly army'. The real problem, argued a candidate in London, was the lack of preparatory work during the 'long campaign' owing to 'the age and infirmity of the activists'. The same party workers, said another, 'were always there – but they had got older and more tired'.

Labour membership, 275,000 in September 1992, had risen to 420,000 by early 1997 under the impetus of Tony Blair and New Labour, but it was noted sadly that the new recruits seemed reluctant to attend meetings or go on the doorstep. 'The New Labour men in suits', complained one veteran Labour candidate, 'never dirtied their hands with campaigning'. The Liberal Democrats had 100,000 members, and candidates reported a generally high level of activist enthusiasm.

All parties had some energetic branches, and there were notable instances of teams from safe or hopeless seats moving en masse to help targeted neighbours. Yet, on the nationwide evidence, active campaigning and comprehensive canvassing was far more limited in most constituencies than a generation ago, whatever may have happened in the targeted few. Gallup found in its post-election survey that 2 per cent of voters claimed to have canvassed or done some other work in the campaign.

Table 11.1 Campaign activities

During the campaign did you ... ?

	All (%)	Con (%)	Lab (%)	Lib D (%)
See party election broadcast	52	66	53	47
Listen to a party election broadcast	24	19	27	27
Attend an indoor meeting	4	4	3	5
Attend an outdoor meeting	7	7	4	10
Canvass or work for your party	3	2	3	3
Receive a party visit on 1 May	10	9	11	7

Source: Gallup.

In the run-up to the election the Labour party had about 60 people employed full-time outside London, about 20 as constituency agents and 40 operating from regional offices. The Conservatives had 287 full-time agents outside party headquarters, including one in every one of their 100 target seats.

One Labour candidate seeking to win a marginal seat noted that his party had contacted 40,000 electors (out of 70,000) in person or by phone and that he had physically met 10,000. He blitzed low-turnout areas that were predominantly Labour and he tried to make personal contact with 'switchers' (Tories deserting to Labour) and with 'squeezers' (potential Liberal Democrats who needed educating on how to vote in a Con–Lab marginal). Over his 18 months as candidate he had been supported by two sitting MPs, one from nearby and one a front-bencher. During the campaign he had taken part in weekly telephone conference calls of an hour or more, when candidates in marginal seats could talk with Tony Blair or Peter Mandelson or some other leading figure. Like other candidates in key seats he received briefings from the Millbank media centre twice a day, two pages or so arriving by e-mail at one of the three computers in his constituency office. He was under instructions not to give a media interview without clearing it with his regional press office. He had a full-time volunteer as a personal assistant and his constituency was getting significant union help from Unison.

The new electoral register, coming into force on 15 February 1997 but based on residence on 10 October 1996, contained 43,846,643 names by 1 May 1997, an increase of 500,000 over 1992. The 1997 figure represented about 96 per cent of the official estimate of the population over 18. There is no reason to suppose that duplications and omissions were any less than the 8 per cent found by the OPCS study in 1991, which meticulously compared the register with the census.[4] Changes in local administrative procedures certainly explain some of the variations in turnout; three Brent constituencies and Camberwell & Peckham were the only ones in London to record increases in turnout, and this could only be explained by a cleaning out of dead names. Boundaries had changed significantly in 418 constituencies (over 5 per cent) and, in many cases, resulted in new constituency names, but these had been settled two years earlier and, in contrast to 1983, local party organisations had time to regroup. There were few complaints about administrative confusions or of sitting MPs being accepted in new territories.

There was more recourse to law in 1997. In at least eleven cases candidates took action against rivals whose name or self-designation was misleading. Sir Nicholas Lyell secured an injunction against an independent who had changed his name by deed poll to Sir Nicholas Lyell. Mr Huggett, famous for dislocating the 1994 Devon Euro-election by his 'Literal Democrat' label, was taken to law in Winchester. Labour managed to block the claims of three independents to the label 'New Labour'.

The Labour Party headquarters had to cope with 600 legal enquiries (compared to 200 in 1992); most concerned the law on allowable expenses, but there were also a number querying the rules on meetings. The Conservative Central Office received 1900 legal questions, mostly of a trivial character. However, it was, generally, an orderly and law-abiding election. There were no visible reports of personation, although the rows in Govan raised suspicions about bogus registration and there was a prosecution in the critical Winchester contest. Opportunities for heckling were few – and anyway it appears to be a dying art.

Public meetings organised by the parties locally seemed almost to have died out; it was generally accepted that they absorbed too much time and effort and were usually attended by the party faithful who would be more usefully employed canvassing, but in most constituencies candidates accepted invitations to appear at joint forums arranged by local churches or other bodies. On 22 April Charter 88 organised a Democracy Day which involved 145 local meetings. It was noted that the presence of Referendum or UKIP candidates meant that the European issue became disproportionately prominent at cross-party meetings.

Target seats were, of course, all visited by the party leaders. Often they made only token appearances for the benefit of the media, speaking briefly from the back of the battle bus or the steps of a helicopter. However, there were stories of large crowds assembling for rallies. Sir James Goldsmith drew over a thousand in the main street of Reigate. Paddy Ashdown addressed 500 in the heart of Hereford, and even more at a meeting at Oxford Town Hall, which overflowed into the street outside. Tony Blair had successful street meetings, with several thousand in the street in Chester and huge crowds in Basildon and Crawley. John Major was swamped by crowds in Luton, Stevenage, and London's Brick Lane. He reflected that the people were 'too friendly': they must have decided that the Conservatives had already lost. Tony Blair was increasingly treated as the prime minister designate and at times was received like a pop star.

The national poster campaign meant that the election was slightly more visible than before, at least to those who travelled on the main arteries where the national network of poster sites was concentrated. In the last two weeks of the contest there were 3700 Conservative posters on 48 sheet hoardings as against 2600 Labour ones. The Liberal Democrats sent vans with mobile posters to make a brief splash in target seats. A MORI poll on 23/24 April found 70 per cent claiming to have seen party posters (53 per cent Conservative, 55 per cent Labour, and 16 per cent Liberal Democrat).

In contrast, there were fewer local window bills or roadside slogans than in the past, except where a concerted effort produced a display – usually on streets where commuter traffic had to crawl by, but Gallup found that 13 per cent of Labour voters, as against 2 per cent of Conservatives and 11 per cent of Liberal Democrats, claimed to have put up a window bill.

One innovation of 1996–97 was the distribution of free videos. Labour sent a carefully crafted, only obliquely political, effort to 18-year-olds – MORI found 2 per cent of households claiming to have received a Labour video – but that was nothing to the efforts of the Referendum Party, whose anti-European video was received by 22 per cent; at least 5 million must have been distributed.

Table 11.2 provides a rough summary of the frequency with which national issues were raised with candidates in the course of doorstep canvassing according to the candidates who answered our questionnaire. As is apparent, the issues of Europe, health and education came through particularly strongly. Britain's relationship with Europe (including the single currency) was the issue most frequently raised. This was most noticeably true amongst Conservatives, but amongst Labour candidates also Europe was ranked first alongside health and education, and for Liberal Democrats it came a narrow third to both these issues.

However, the impression made by Europe was clearly strongest in the case of Conservatives: of those citing Europe, 55 per cent placed it at the head of their list of issues, compared to only 4 per cent of Labour candidates and none at all amongst Liberal Democrats. Europe, according to one Conservative, was raised on 'every other doorstep'. Another believed it was raised 60 per cent of the time – while a third put the figure at 70 per cent. Europe, said one successful candidate, was 'by far the most common – all against in various ways'. A Euro-sceptic Conservative claimed to have won more votes on the European issue 'than on all else put together'. Still, there was a suspicion amongst some that Europe had far stronger resonance amongst disaffected Conservatives than among the electorate as a whole. The single currency, it was said by one candidate, was an important issue 'for Tory voters, but not generally'. Another found that Europe was raised 'by a distinctive golf club, gin and tonic, set'. Nevertheless, as the figures suggest, Europe was not raised only with Conservative candidates. Indeed, one Liberal Democrat admitted that he had changed his strategy 'because Europe came up so much'.

Table 11.2   Relative frequency of issues raised with candidates

Issue	Total frequency	Conservative candidates	Labour candidates	Liberal Democrat candidates
	%	%	%	%
Europe	25	30	18	18
Health	20	21	18	20
Education	18	17	18	20
Pensions	9	12	5	4
Time for Change	9	8	13	6
Economy	4	1	9	6
Sleaze	4	4	4	2
Law and Order	3	1	4	6
Leadership	2	2	4	0
Others	2	1	4	4
Taxation	2	2	2	4
Social Services	1	1	2	2

Health and education were widely cited as important issues for the electorate, though here the concerns of constituents often focused upon developments affecting schools and health provision within the local area. Hospital closures were a recurring theme which appeared to damage the Conservatives: one Conservative declared himself convinced that the closure of the accident and emergency facilities at his local hospital cost him more than 1000 votes. Education cutbacks and school closures figured comparably, as did problems associated with the introduction of nursery school vouchers. Pensions were in fourth place amongst issues raised – though here their differential impact upon Conservatives is notable.

Pressure groups exerted a smaller impact upon the campaign than in recent elections; those most frequently cited by candidates being the pro-hunting lobby and anti-abortionists, represented by the Pro-Life Alliance. Amongst the minor parties, the Referendum Party, and to a lesser extent the UKIP, were by a wide margin the most important. Candidates of all parties acknowledged that the presence of the Referendum Party served to raise the profile of European issues at local levels – especially at all-party public meetings. Besides its extensive video distribution, the party also took full-page advertisements in the local press referring to the personal position on Europe of the various candidates. These formed a particular grievance amongst Conservatives, many of whom believed that their attitude towards Europe had been characterised unfairly, with several threatening to sue over the issue.

It was, indeed, Conservative candidates who attached greatest weight to the presence of anti-European parties. Of Conservatives returning the questionnaire, 66 per cent stated that they had lost votes to the Referendum and UK Independence parties, and the great majority believed they had done so disproportionately. Although some put the share of the Referendum vote coming from ex-Tories as high as 80–95 per cent, 66–75 per cent was a more typical estimate: 'about two-thirds of their total vote (1500) was from us'; 'I suspect the Referendum Party candidate probably took votes from me on a basis of three to two'; 'the Referendum Party did matter as they were taking significantly more votes from me than from the other parties. As far as I can tell this was in a ratio of at least three to one.'

Candidates from the Labour and Liberal parties also perceived this differential impact: the 'Referendum Party worried a few people and took mainly Tory votes'; 'The Referendum Party and UKIP (together about 3000 votes) clearly reduced the Tory vote and in a rural constituency pushed a pro-European Tory candidate onto the defensive on Europe generally'; the 'Referendum Party probably took twice as many votes from the Tories as from Liberal Democrats'; the 'Referendum Party scared the Conservative campaign – and took substantial Conservative votes.'

A number of Conservatives were not unnaturally tempted to ascribe their defeat to the presence of the Referendum and UK Independence parties. 'The Referendum party', said one, 'probably lost me the seat; 1000 votes plus another 1000 encouraged to stay at home'. 'The UKIP', said another, 'polled nearly 2000 votes. The Liberal Democrats won the seat by 12 votes. The figures speak for themselves.' Perhaps the general Conservative attitude to the Referendum Party was best expressed by a candidate in Wales, who wrote: 'The Referendum party was a pain in the neck. Everyone had Goldsmith's video and they took more than 1000 votes.' In fact this seems to be a myth, as Appendix 2 demonstrates.

In over 300 English constituencies, County Councils and some unitary authorities were also to be elected on 1 May. This caused many problems for returning officers, not least when it came to separating white from grey ballot papers at the count. Almost nothing about the contests appeared in the media. Battered Conservatives hoped, with some reason, that the higher turnout in a general election might help them back to local power.

Table 11.3   Time of vote

Time	Total	Con	Lab	Lib Dem
7 a.m.–11 a.m.	22	22	24	22
11 a.m.–3 p.m.	20	19	20	20
3 p.m.–7 p.m.	33	33	32	34
7 p.m.–10 p.m.	25	26	24	24

Source: BBC Exit Poll.

People voted later than in 1992. Only 54 per cent of ballots had been cast by 5 p.m., as against 62 per cent five years earlier. But, for the first time, there was no significant difference between the parties. The median Labour vote was cast between 4 p.m. and 5 p.m. and so was the median Conservative vote – perhaps a few minutes later. The old Conservative advantage that came from voting earlier had certainly disappeared.

An election on 1 May might have been expected to provoke an increase in the number of postal votes. So too might the six week election period which added substantially to the opportunities for last minute claims for unforeseen sickness or holidays. In the end there were about 950,000 postal electors of whom about 750,000 cast valid votes – only about 30,000 more than in 1992. But because of the overall decline in turnout, postal votes represented 2.4 per cent of the grand total cast.

	Postal Vote	Conservative Majority	Majority as % of postal vote
Dorset South	1369	77	6%
Bedfordshire S.W.	1275	132	10%
Teignbridge	1836	281	15%
Lichfield	902	238	26%
Hexham	1106	222	20%

Labour was widely recognised to have made a special effort to organise postal votes, especially in marginals and the traditional Conservative advantage among postal electors seems largely to have disappeared. But it is possible that the postal vote may have saved the Conservative incumbent in these constituencies.

Elections are not cheap. The 1997 contest cost the public purse about £52m. in Returning Officers' Expenses, in addition to the £50m annual cost of compiling the electoral register.

The national outlays of the parties are reported on p. 240. They were unrestricted – a very different situation from the constituency level, where the narrow constraints imposed by the Corrupt Practices Act of 1883 are still largely observed. One limitation to the long campaign of 1997 lay in the law on expenses. MPs were free to go off to their constituencies on 21 March but, quite apart from the dangers of boring the electorate and exhausting the party workers, any activities which cost money could be liable to fall under the financial ceiling against which most serious candidates knew they would be liable to bump. Candidates spent nearer to the limit than in 1992, especially in target seats. Table 11.4 offers rough estimates, based on an incomplete list of returns.

Table 11.4   Candidates election expenses by party, 1997

	Average £ per candidate	Per cent of maximu Victorious candidates	All candidates	1992 All candidates
Conservative	5600	89%	71%	80%
Labour	5600	77%	71%	71%
Lib. Dem.	3200	94%	42%	43%
SNP	4100	94%	45%	40%
Plaid Cymru	3400	91%	43%	38%
Referendum	3300	–	38%	–

The grand total of all candidates' declared expenses was between £12m. and £13m. But there were suspicions that there was quite a lot of evasion. The cost of telephone calls were often not recorded, especially when they came from regional bases or from London; there also seems to have been some central distribution of direct mail well after the dissolution had made this chargeable to expenses. What is plain from these figures is that it was the first election in which the Conservatives did not outspend Labour at the constituency level.

NOTES

1. See D. Denver and G. Hands, *Modern Constituency Electioneering* (1997)
2. P. Whiteley et al. *True Blues* (1994)
3. *Ibid.*
4. S. Smith, *The Electoral Register* (1993)

12   The Campaign in Retrospect

The 1997 election campaign did not get a good press. Commentators and candidates complained of its length and of the protracted pre-election build-up. Throughout the parliament, surveys had shown high levels of voter cynicism about politicians of all parties and a declining confidence in political institutions. It was perhaps appropriate that the opening days of the campaign were dominated by sleaze. During the campaign it was widely held that the main parties were pretty similar in their policies, that politicians too often evaded questions posed by voters or interviewers, and that the party arguments were too negative – such complaints are not new but they were stated with more vigour than hitherto. The opinion polls, with only one exception, showed large Labour leads and the foregone conclusion may have contributed to boredom and a low turnout. Conservatives complained of the 'flattening effect' of the polls and Labour feared that they might induce complacency among their supporters. There were also the usual complaints of excessive media election coverage. As reported in Chapter 8, the television news and current affairs programmes lost viewers, and the newspapers lost readers.

In the *New Statesman* Steve Richards observed that the ample space and time which newspapers and broadcasters gave to the election meant that new or even slightly modified party statements received more attention than would be the case when there was no campaign. There was intense media coverage of Tony Blair's comparison of the financial powers of the Scottish parliament to an English parish council: this only repeated what he had said in public the previous autumn, and had then attracted little attention. There was an imbalance between the lavish expenditure of media resources and the amount of news that was newsworthy; the parties had little to say that was fresh. Loughborough University researchers reported that during the campaign, election material accounted for 34 per cent of news space and over 90 per cent of lead stories in the broadsheets and news broadcasts. In four cases the press played an important part in shaping the agenda; the *Guardian* on sleaze and Neil Hamilton's candidacy in Tatton; the *Sun*'s endorsement of Tony Blair and compromising photos of Piers Merchant; the *Daily Mail*'s campaign on the single currency; and *The Times*'s chronicling of the Conservative candidates election addresses dissenting from the government line on the single currency. All placed the Conservative Party on the defensive.

For the first ten days John Major's decision to have a long campaign backfired, as much of the media carried stories on sleaze and, in mid-campaign, on Conservative divisions over a single European currency. As Chapter 9 showed, two of the top three front-page lead stories dealt with Europe and sleaze/Neil Hamilton. Conservatives were frustrated that they were unable to launch their messages – although the troubles were largely self-inflicted. The Labour and Liberal parties also feared that they were suffering from the 'plague on all politicians' mood. The length of the campaign and the politicians' repetition of key soundbites meant that, after a while, Tony Blair, Gordon Brown, Kenneth Clarke and John Major sounded like robots, as they spouted rehearsed messages.

Yet the 1997 campaign, presented as the last general election of the century, raised significant political questions. Regardless of the outcome, Scotland's constitutional position was at a turning point. Was the election Labour's last chance to save itself? Could the Conservatives win an unprecedented fifth successive victory? Would the opinion polls be further discredited if the electorate again confounded their predictions, this time of a Labour landslide?

The campaign had its original features. The investment in modern technology and in lessons learnt from the US meant that Labour and Conservative charges and counter-charges went beyond the usual adversarial campaigning. The two parties' rebuttal units worked flat out to refute the claims of the other party and to put forward rival propositions which would be reported within the same few hours of a media cycle. To be speedy off the mark was regarded by some journalists as an indication of a party's professionalism. Each side could expect its reply to be carried by the broadcasting authorities because of their commitment to political balance. Yet did these contradictory statements contribute much to public enlightenment or simply confuse and irritate voters? Commentators and voters complained about the lack of vision from the two main political parties and there seemed little sense of optimism that any party in office would be able to produce fundamental change. Was such scepticism and lack of optimism a reflection of the voters' political maturity or of their cynicism?

Also notable was the level of abuse, particularly in the penultimate week, as Labour warned of VAT on food and the end of the state pension if the Conservatives won. Conservative and Labour leaders accused each other of lying over pensions, a term not allowed in parliamentary exchanges. Conservative warnings of the break-up of the United Kingdom and the absorption of Britain into a federal Europe under Labour were matched by Labour warnings that a Conservative government would destroy the National Health Service. Such rhetoric fired the sense of moral crusading in both parties

– 'Labour really will say anything to get elected', cried one Conservative strategist. The Liberal Democrats boasted that they occupied the moral high ground, shunning the 'Punch and Judy' attacks of the larger parties.

As usual, each party used statistics selectively, relying on different time-periods and different indicators for the performances of the economy, of schools or of health, to suit their arguments. Some of the media carried their own corrective commentaries and drew on specialist correspondents or independent bodies to provide an independent verdict. For example, the Institute of Fiscal Studies bluntly stated that the spending and tax figures of each of the political parties did not add up. Only the Liberal Democrats admitted what experts claimed was inevitable, that taxes would have to increase substantially to fund even existing spending programmes.

Each party relied heavily on its leader to carry the message, or rather each party leader assumed such a role for himself. Paddy Ashdown was the only nationally known Liberal Democrat standing again: he fought a well-organised, kindly reported campaign, but he sometimes seemed like a lone voice. Tony Blair's speeches and interviews often drew on his personal experiences and he claimed that he had demonstrated his leadership credentials by the way in which he had sorted out his party. On Europe John Major could not speak for his disunited and unpopular party and asked the voters to trust him. He dominated his party's election broadcasts, and at the press conference on sleaze and Europe effectively distanced himself from some members of his party.

It is a cliche to say that election campaigns are not a great national teach-in on the major issues. Each party sought to stay 'on message', to score a 'hit' on the other side and to ensure that leading figures were 'on grid'. The emphasis was on discipline, repetition and getting across key messages rather than on answering questions from the media or challenges from other parties. The jockeying for advantage in abortive negotiations over a leaders' television debate epitomised the approach. The parties gave only qualified answers to the electorate's concerns about how better funding for health and education could be financed within existing income tax and spending figures and whether or not Britain would enter the single currency.

The scale of the Conservative Party's defeat came as a great shock in party headquarters – few were prepared for a defeat by more than 50 seats; none expected a landslide. At the start of the campaign impartial observers, including many pollsters, believed that a significant number of Conservative defectors would return to the fold by polling day and the deficit in the opinion polls would narrow. These notions were sustained by Central Office reports of strong support 'on the doorstep'. The gap did indeed narrow, but the Tory vote did not rise. A lead of 22 per cent in the March polls was reduced to 13 per cent by 1 May, but it was the rise in Liberal Democrat support that largely cut the Labour vote from 51 per cent to 44 per cent.

The Conservative campaign appeared to be more improvised than Labour's and there were many last-minute decisions about party election broadcasts and advertising. John Major's press conferences on sleaze on 1 April and the single currency on 16 April were effectively decided by himself at short notice; he judged that he had to respond to the concerns of the media. His confidence in his own judgement had been greatly reinforced by the experience of winning against the odds in 1992 and his belief that he was the acceptable face of his unpopular party. It was his campaign, and he frequently rejected the suggestion from advisers to fight more aggressively on Europe. Labour campaign managers were surprised – and Kenneth Clarke shared the surprise – that more was not made of the economic recovery.

Many commentators wrote off the Conservative campaign because of the conventional wisdom that voters dislike a divided party. Europe was redolent of Conservative humiliations and leadership indecisiveness over the previous four years. However reasonable the government's 'wait and see' message on the single currency, it was repudiated by much of the party and, given Labour's similar stance, would not win many votes. Plans to link the government's successful economic record with the danger of Labour's approach (combining the party's 'instinct' to intervene and the 'failed' Social Chapter model of the EU) hardly resonated in the constituencies. John Major's refusal to dismiss ministers who departed from the government line of 'wait and see' about the European currency, and his statement, under questioning at a party press conference on April 17, that he would grant his MPs a free vote on the issue, appeared as weakness. In fact, the party's standing in the polls did not obviously suffer and party strategists sought consolation on the grounds that their private polls showed that the rebels may have sharpened perceptions of Conservative as the Euro-sceptical party, which would defend British interests in Brussels.

The Conservative party failed to reap electoral benefit from economic prosperity. In spite of favourable economic trends, polls showed that many voters claimed that prosperity had passed them by. There were areas of the country where, quite patently, 'Britain is Booming' did not sound convincing. The earlier recession, and its toll in job losses, negative equity, tax increases and sense of economic insecurity, had left its mark. Whatever 'feel-good factor' existed was offset by a 'time for a change' mood and a refusal to give the Conservatives credit for economic recovery. It was hard to detect a positive message about why another term of Conservative government would make things better: there was no counterpart to Labour's specific pledges about creating jobs and cutting class sizes and hospital waiting lists. 'Where was the offer in the last week?', asked Labour's Philip Gould.

The economy is a global term, referring variously to such macro-indicators as unemployment, growth, inflation, or the balance of payments, but for voters it may refer to the money in their pockets or to their sense of security. One reason why the improving economy did not work to the party's advantage was suggested by the BBC/NOP exit poll on 1 May. Of those questioned, 35 per cent agreed that the economy had grown stronger over the previous five years but 31 per cent thought the opposite and, strikingly, only 25 per cent thought that their own standard of living had improved over the same period while 38 per cent actually thought it had worsened. The 'gap' between the last two figures represents two million voters who clearly felt that prosperity was passing them by. Some 80 per cent of this group voted Labour or Liberal Democrat. The claim that 'Britain is Booming' may only have made them feel hard done by. Maurice Saatchi was cautious about promoting the 'economic success' story on the grounds that a strong economy would make it more difficult to argue that Labour was a danger. Statistical modelling by Professor David Sanders of Essex University showed a strong correlation in previous general elections between Conservative support, the party's perceived economic competence, and expectations of likely prosperity over the next twelve months. Economic optimism grew over the twelve months to polling day, and the Conservatives should have profited from this. It may be a tribute to the Labour campaign on the economy that throughout this period it maintained a strong lead over the Conservatives as the party most likely to improve living standards. A third reason why the Conservatives did not benefit as much as might have been expected was that their divisions over Europe provided an alternative agenda for the media, before and during the campaign. In other words, the 'good news' story was not effectively communicated.

One consequence of the intense press interest in the conduct of the campaign was the full coverage accorded to rows about advertising – perhaps inevitably, given the role of the Saatchi agency in Conservative campaigns since 1977. No other party had strategists with the experience and track records of Maurice Saatchi and Tim Bell, who had been involved in general election successes as far back as Margaret Thatcher's first victory in 1979. For all the talk of the 'three musketeers' (including Lord Chadlington), they were not a homogeneous group. Tim Bell and Maurice Saatchi were not always at one from the outset of the campaign – but this does not mean that genuine differences of opinion were rightly written up as 'crisis' or 'split'.

As Chapters 2 and 6 recorded, Brian Mawhinney and John Major vetoed many suggestions from the agency, most significantly on the 'danger' of

Europe in October 1996. Anti-EU advertisements were blocked by Kenneth Clarke and Michael Heseltine, as were the 'demon eyes' advertisements, (featuring a close-up of Blair's grinning mouth, with the slogan 'What lies behind the smile?'), the posters of Mr Major and Mr Blair above the respective slogans 'For Britain' and 'For Nothing', and the hard-hitting broadcast in which Tony Blair was portrayed as a Faust-like figure selling out his principles to win the election. Out of deference to his Chairman, John Major refused to look at the film. John Major and Brian Mawhinney were motivated by calculations about party unity, assumptions about the voters' tolerance, and a sense of political etiquette. Mr Major wanted positive advertisements from an agency that had built its political successes on negative ones. For many in Central Office and many Conservative candidates, the lion symbol (see p. 43) was a millstone around the agency's neck, and in the last week, Central Office discreetly liaised with Paul Sykes and an independent group, who ran their own pro-Conservative press advertisements. Maurice Saatchi also failed in his attempts to persuade John Major to fund anything more than a modest last-week press advertising campaign. The money was not available, or was not made available.

In turn, John Major was perceived by many party strategists as reconciled to defeat and perhaps looking to his place in history. 'If he loses, he wants to do so with dignity', said one. Charles Lewington reports that John Major confessed to a friend on 14 April that his party would lose.[1] 'He turns down negative ads because he does not see the Labour ads around the country which are quite tough about him', said another. He rejected the more forceful Euro-sceptic line which most Central Office strategists urged on him because of his views about the national interest and the appropriate behaviour for a British prime minister.

Some Central Office strategists were annoyed by the self-confident ('know it all', was the usual term) demeanour of the advertising men, and reports of these tensions surfaced in the press. Some also complained of a confusion of the client–agency relationship. Maurice Saatchi's feeling that his experience and expertise were not shown enough respect was matched by the Party Chairman's suspicion that media advisers were leaking hostile stories about him. Dr Mawhinney regarded himself as the authoritative spokesman for Central Office to the Prime Minister and resented attempts by Maurice Saatchi (or anybody else) to open his own lines of communication with Number 10. The Chairman was delighted to read in the *Daily Telegraph* on the final Monday a report that he would recommend to his successor that the Saatchi agency should not be retained in a future general election. 'An election too many', was one Central Office verdict on the agency's contribution. Apologists for the agency claimed that their advertising in

1996 had tapped into popular unease about new Labour and that it was up to the party to deliver a campaign to take advantage of this. They felt frustrated that many of their advertising and broadcasting suggestions were vetoed and that the 'New Labour, New Danger' message was aborted (see p. 43). Much of the tension was the product of the frustration and disappointment that defeat was imminent and nothing seemed to offer a way out. Some of the criticisms echoed comments about the 1987 and 1992 winning election campaigns, notably over advertising, the performance of Central Office, and negative campaigning. Such complaints now appear almost inseparable from a modern Conservative campaign.

All these claims and counter-claims provide a sharp contrast with the Labour operation. Few people were aware of the name of the BMP agency, let alone the fact that it was working for Labour. It maintained a low profile, and no stories of conflict appeared (particularly of its advocacy of using more negative advertisements than Tony Blair wished); there was no doubt of its subordinate status in Millbank Tower. This was a different client–agent relationship.

Yet it is doubtful if the Conservatives could have done much in the campaign to alter the final result. The ICM survey on election day found that over half of those who voted Conservative did so because they thought that the party had the best economic policies. Just over a third mentioned the Conservatives' greater experience and just under a third preferred the party's position on Europe. The party played its best cards, but they were not sufficient to stem the mood for change. A significant realignment of party support had taken place early in the parliament and it was still in place on 1 May 1997. The party never recovered its reputation for competence after the ERM fiasco, or for tax-cutting after the 1993 budget. It was widely seen as having discarded the prospectus on which it won the 1992 election. In the European elections of June 1994 Labour gained 44 per cent and the Conservatives 28 per cent – not far from the vote shares in May 1997. Conservative chances of recovery deteriorated sharply when Tony Blair became leader of the Labour Party in July 1994 and set about creating a New Labour Party. A six-week campaign could not undo the memories of the previous five years. The result was, as a Central Office director said, that 'The voters no longer listened to us.'

The BBC/NOP exit poll underlines the weaknesses of the Conservative image and the scale of decline since 1992. Table 12.1 shows how far it had forfeited trust on key economic and social issues. When asked whether the Conservative and Labour parties were good for one class, or good for all classes, a third saw the Conservatives as 'appealing to all classes,' compared with two-thirds who saw them as 'good for only one class', while over two-thirds saw Labour as the party 'for all classes'. Labour had succeeded in capturing the 'one nation' label. A massive 84 per cent regarded the Conservatives as divided, compared to 34 per cent for Labour.

Table 12.1   Party rating on key issues

	Conservative		Labour		Lib Democrat	
	1997	Change since 1992	1997	Change since 1992	1997	Change since 1992
	(%)	(%)	(%)	(%)	(%)	(%)
Q. Which party do you trust most to make the right decisions about ...						
The economy	42	−11	44	+11	13	0
Income tax	36	−19	44	+13	20	+6
Schools/ education	6	−14	48	+ 9	26	+5
Dealing with sleaze	23	n/a	49	n/a	29	n/a

Source: BBC/NOP exit poll.

By contrast, the Labour campaign was more controlled and more disciplined. It stayed on course, apart from the 'wobbly' week when Tony Blair made remarks about the Scottish parliament and there was confusion over the privatisation of Air Traffic Control. The activities and themes used by spokesmen at press conferences and on broadcasts were effectively orchestrated from the media centre. Familiar left-wing figures like Tony Benn, Ken Livingstone and Diane Abbott, as well as trade union leaders – all assiduously covered by the Conservative tabloids in previous elections – were well-behaved and kept off-stage. Labour negotiators frustrated any Conservative hopes for a leaders' debate on television, which might have cut into its commanding opinion poll lead. Media surveys of candidates' views on issues were often met with outright refusals to cooperate or with references to the party manifesto – in accordance with instructions from Millbank Tower. Labour was not in the business of providing 'interesting' copy for the media. Conservative supporting papers did not seem to try as hard to expose Labour's 'hidden face' as in previous campaigns, and Conservative Central Office was less successful than in 1992 in planting stories embarrassing to Labour. This new context reflected the perceived changes in Labour as well as in the national press. During and after the campaign,

Conservatives from John Major down expressed disappointment at what they saw as the absence of tough questioning of Labour. 'We thought that Labour's policies lacked detail, but the media allowed it to bluff its way out of trouble', said an official. For the first time in many years Labour was not faced with a hostile press; rather the opposite – it was treated as a government in waiting.

In many respects, Labour's significant work had been done before the election was called, the old weaknesses on tax, trade unions, spending and law and order had been tackled. The 'squaring' of the press had started three years earlier. As Peter Mandelson said:

> There was no reason left not to trust Labour. All the old 'ifs', 'buts' and 'maybes' had gone. We removed the target. Without New Labour the Conservatives could have won again.

For the previous two years Gordon Brown had convened a campaign group almost every morning to manage the media. Peter Mandelson had planned the details: a grid of 'who does what' in the campaign; lists of themes and 'messages'; research and rebuttal routines; key seats targeting; and central control mechanisms. Authority lay clearly with a mix of politicians and spin-doctors – Tony Blair, Gordon Brown, Peter Mandelson and Alastair Campbell. The party succeeded in avoiding incidents which hostile tabloids could exploit. Some of the elements of this discipline had been present in 1987 and 1992 and lessons from those defeats learned, but 1997 represented a new height of organisational efficiency.

'Time for a change' is the classic appeal of the opposition party, just as the fear of change is exploited by the government. In 1983, 1987 and 1992, Conservatives had countered the theme of change by warning of the risks and dangers of a Labour government. By 1995 party strategists concluded that voters believed that Labour had changed and that therefore they should alter tack. The slogan, 'New Labour, New Danger', sought to advertise the new perils threatened by a new Labour government. Labour replied by offering reassurance; often by matching Conservative policy and ditching its own baggage. The main achievement was to turn around the two key deficits of 1992 on leadership and tax. The Conservative tax rises in 1993 and 1994 substantially eroded that party's advantage on the issue; Labour's advertising had hammered home the impact of the tax rises and linked them to the themes of Conservative 'betrayal', 'failure' and 'incompetence'. Gordon Brown, as Shadow Chancellor, had vetoed most of his colleagues' proposals for spending and so was able in January 1997 to pledge that

Labour would not raise income tax rates. During the campaign Mr Blair confirmed that there would not be tax rises under a Labour-controlled Scottish parliament. The effect was seen in the BBC/NOP exit poll (see Table 12.1), which found that 44 per cent 'trusted' Labour on taxes compared to 36 per cent for the Conservatives. This was better than the 'draw' which Blair had hoped for seven months earlier. In 1992 John Major had led Neil Kinnock by 38 per cent to 27 per cent on the question of who would make the most capable prime minister. In 1997 Tony Blair led Major by 40 per cent to 27 per cent. Two thirds of the respondents to the BBC/NOP poll regarded Mr Major as a weak leader compared to a quarter for Blair and 77 per cent regarded Tony Blair as a strong leader compared to 35 per cent for John Major.

It was also possible to detect a greater focus on winning the election in Labour's camp. If Europe was an obsession for many Conservatives, victory was the obsession for Labour. The key Labour figures were single-minded, aggressive, and intolerant of any shortcomings in campaign structure or strategy although some of the spin-doctoring of the media reflected internal rivalries.[2] All regarded Tony Blair as the key to answering voters' fears about 'old Labour'. 'Have you thought how we would look if Tony died', said one of them, 'and Prescott was interim leader? Think about it!' In the course of an interview with *The Times*, Tony Blair replied to a comment about President Clinton's indifferent first-term performance in the White House: 'But he got re-elected.' When Peter Mandelson was tackled during the election about the caution of the Labour campaign, he replied: 'We have an election to win.' The caution was a reaction to the disappointment of 1992.

Yet Labour's campaign had its critics. Even sympathisers argued that, with such a big polling lead, the party should seek a mandate for a bolder programme of redistribution. The *Guardian* (11 April) complained, 'It's all a bit too uptight ... There is too much calculation and not enough spontaneity.' Peter Riddell, in *The Times* on the same day, warned: 'Leninist style at the top creates party confusion.' The sympathetic *New Statesman* (18 April) bemoaned the party's excessive use of gimmicks and visual symbols and called upon it to 'raise its game': 'Labour's campaign is now so loaded with borrowed symbols and stolen sound bites that the medium appears finally to have become the message.' Philip Stephens, political commentator of the *Financial Times* complained that 'Mr Blair has been suffocated by his image-makers. The Tory phantom of an evasive, unprincipled opportunist has taken on substance.' In turn, Labour campaigners complained that journalists asked them tougher questions at their press conferences because they treated the party as a government in waiting. Some of the criticisms were taken on board, as Tony Blair increasingly spoke without a text, demonstrating, as his press secretary observed, 'passion and commitment'.

The burdens of the past five years meant that the Conservative campaign was handicapped from the outset and rendered it hard for them to put Labour under pressure, but it was too simple for Tim Hames to claim, in *The Times* on 3 May: 'This will go down less as a Labour victory than as the election the Tories lost.' This verdict fails to acknowledge the extent of Labour's internal changes and the way it had overtaken the Conservatives as a campaigning party. It substantially increased its number of members and involved them in key party decisions (electing the leader and deputy leader and voting on policies). It borrowed ideas and techniques from the US Democrats, invested in a state-of-the-art media centre, and out-performed the Conservatives in contacting and encouraging commitment among supporters (see Table 11.1).

The Conservatives' grassroots organisation, by contrast, had been withering for some years, and especially since 1992. At the top the party's leaders were constantly distracted from campaign planning by having to carry on with the responsibilities of government.

A much noticed import from the Clinton campaign in 1992 was the philosophy and practice of rebuttal or rapid response. This required 24-hour monitoring of the mass media and a good research base. Its success depended on a speedy denial or refutation of an opponent, or even the remarks of a colleague who was 'off-message'. But the emphasis on speed could be counter-productive: 'If we have three or four hours to carry a denial, why not make use of the time rather than making an instantaneous rebuttal?', asked David Willetts. It was ironic that Labour complained that television's tit-for-tat reporting failed to do justice to Tony Blair's positive speeches, but, in so far as the broadcasters carried tit-for-tat messages, this was a comment on the effectiveness of the two parties' rebuttal efforts.

Another disadvantage of the emphasis on speed was that some key participants were not always informed of the new line. There were conflicting responses from the Blair and Brown offices on party policy over air traffic privatisation, and Kenneth Clarke told interviewers that he had not been consulted about John Major's decision to hold a free vote on single currency, but compared to earlier elections there was a great improvement in liaison between the centre and the constituencies. The use of mobile phones, fax machines and pagers made this more than ever a high-tech election, although some Tory ministers caused irritation at the centre by switching off their mobiles and pagers. Constituencies received statements of the daily line from party headquarters and these were updated as the hours went by. Key voters in key seats were bombarded with mailshots from the party leaders, telephone canvassing and then personal visits.

As in all good communications, there was an emphasis on repetition and soundbites, although this did not make for interesting listening or reporting.

Before the campaign began, Tony Blair dismissed John Major at the dispatch box as 'weak, weak, weak' and in his 1996 Conference speech claimed that his three priorities in government would be 'Education, Education, education'. The campaign added 'resources, resources, resources' (Paddy Ashdown); 'hypocrisy, hypocrisy, hypocrisy' (Gillian Shephard) and 'positive, positive, positive' (Gordon Brown). In private, one Labour strategist summed up the party's approach as 'reassurance, reassurance, reassurance'. If the politician (usually the leader) could not summarise his argument in 16.5 seconds for the main evening television news bulletins, then he risked being cut. The soundbites were relentlessly repeated:

Two tier health service

Don't throw it all away

Enough is Enough

Britain deserves better

Only the Liberal Democrats can make a difference

Labour will lead us into a federal Europe

Labour appeared to win this battle. In Chapter 8 Martin Harrison judges that 'in the battle of the news bulletins they [the Conservatives] were comprehensively routed'. Good news on the economy was dwarfed by stories of sleaze, while stories of Labour's weaknesses were not strong enough to cause damage. Numbers were popular. Labour variously made five pledges and ten pledges, provided 21 steps for education in the twenty-first century and the Conservatives made five pledges to improve health over five years. Labour's 22 Tory tax rises were countered (rather late in the day and with much less publicity) by the Conservative's 25 tax cuts. Party leaders offered their manifestos as 'contracts', and Paddy Ashdown described the Liberal tax proposals as a tax 'covenant' with voters. The parties offered task forces, programmes and reviews, and they all made play with 'the new millennium' and the opportunities it presented.

Campaigners' morale is often affected by the findings of the opinion polls. In spite of the clear Labour leads, one of Mr Blair's closest aides compared the mood in Millbank Tower to the atmosphere in a girls' school. Conservative morale was never high; when John Major announced his confidence in victory, he was rallying his troops and 'trying to engineer a series of events which would enable us to win'. The series of political and electoral setbacks took their toll and some key figures openly regarded their machine as inferior to Labour's. In fact, morale improved in the second week, due not so much to the polls as to gaffes by Labour spokesmen. It certainly dipped again under the impact of the opinion polls and the European divisions in the third week, but then revived with the ICM/*Guardian* poll on 23 April, reducing the Labour lead to 5 per cent. This caused enough concern in Labour ranks to induce key figures, including Alastair Campbell, to phone the *Guardian* to seek advance information so that they could manage the inevitable reactions.

On the other side Labour hoped that the prospect of a close race would act as a spur to further effort. Labour's private polls were reported within a few hours of the ICM figures and showed the party's lead holding steady at 17 per cent. Labour strategists could always rely on the 'fifth term fear' and warn what could happen if the Conservatives were returned again. The ICM poll reinforced Tony Blair's determination to raise the issue of the state pension. Both Conservative and Liberal Democrat spokesmen refuted the polls by reporting the extent of their support 'on the doorstep' and pointing to the large numbers of undecided voters. In fact, ICM's election-day poll found that few of the latter actually voted Conservative.[3] The election result was complacently claimed as a vindication by some opinion pollsters; certainly it was a blow to those Conservatives who had relied on canvassing reports.

Conservatives were shocked by the impact of Labour charges that they planned to abolish the state old-age pension. Some advisers argued for caution, on the grounds that the party's answer was complex and would only add to the salience of the issue, but the politicians were determined to hit back. Privately, John Major was surprised that Tony Blair would do something so 'dishonourable and dishonest'. Their own rolling polls showed the brief recovery coming to an end, especially among pensioners, as a 14 per cent lead collapsed to a 25 per cent deficit in a week. The effect was short-term – the pensioner vote returned – but Labour's focus groups revealed a hostility to 'scaremongering'. Peter Mandelson and Philip Gould, strong advocates of the last-week pension attack, criticised the high-profile Conservative response: 'I'd have done nothing', Mr Gould said. Danny Finkelstein was a forceful spokesman for a number of Tory staff and advisers who also regarded the response as a major tactical mistake. Philip Gould regarded the episode as 'at best, a messy draw, but it blunted the Conservative message on the economy'.

A recent tendency, observed also in the US, is the growing concentration of media coverage on the conduct of the campaign itself – assessing the performance of the candidates and parties, and dealing with strategies, leadership debates, mood and morale in headquarters as well as opinion poll findings on the personalities, tactics, messages, and on who leads in the election 'horse race'. In advance or instead of the result, the election was analysed almost as a theatrical event. Media researchers at Loughborough University reported that television and press gave only 10 per cent of their coverage to education and health issues (although these were two of the top three issues for voters), a similar proportion to sleaze, but 32 per cent to the conduct of the campaign. They continued: 'The conduct of the election itself was the main item of news during the campaign, with the way it played in the media emerging as a primary focus of interest.'[4]

Two of the most intellectual and policy-orientated figures in the Blair and Major camps were dismissive of such talk. 'It's all so subjective, who is to say?', commented Labour's David Miliband about the criticisms of Labour's lack of vision; at the time the opinion polls were reporting that the party had a 15 per cent lead and was on course to fulfil Tony Blair's ambition of making Labour the natural party of government and mainstream party of the centre left. 'It's the worst form of what I call the British disease', said the Conservative MP David Willetts. 'Brilliant analysis, but so little evidence.' Surveys do not suggest that many voters decide how to vote on the basis of the skill with which a party's campaign is presented. In 1987 and 1992 Labour was widely judged to have fought at least as good a campaign as the Conservatives but lost both elections decisively. This time Labour leaders were prepared to swap the victory for the plaudits of the media about their campaigning.

Also in line with American practice, the broadcasters were given more coverage than the politicians. There was some indignation in all parties at the failure to report what their spokesmen were actually saying. The speeches were covered in soundbites as the commentators introduced, edited and interpreted the statement or films. Commentaries on the leaders' words were given far more space than the words themselves. At the daily press conference there was a pecking order; the prominent broadcast journalists like Jon Snow, Elinor Goodman, John Sergeant, Robin Oakley and Michael Brunson had no difficulty being called, even when they had not raised their hands or prepared a question. Bringing in the star commentator gave the party a good chance of getting television coverage on the questioner's channel.

Party strategists take their campaigns seriously, conducting daily assessments via focus groups, feedback from party activists and target voters, and rolling opinion polls. In the days after 1 May each party conducted its own post-mortem, wondering how it could have done better. Losers inevitably have more 'if onlys' to analyse: for example, what if they had installed more computers in the constituencies, had tried different posters and election broadcasts, or had exploited alternative themes? Such analysis has its place, particularly when the result is close or when one party's support has fallen heavily in the course of the campaign. Both because the result was so overwhelming and the campaign so unsensational, scepticism predominated in all the retrospection. It was more profitable for the Conservatives to look at the events of the previous five years which determined the context in which the election was held. The research of both parties agreed on the state of the public mood – 'we're fed up with the Conservatives'; 'we've been betrayed'; 'Labour deserves a chance'; 'the government has done little for me'. The quality of a campaign may also matter indirectly by contributing to the image of a party's unity, strength of leadership and competence. Even on these criteria, Labour gained and the Conservatives lost – but it is worth noting that in all three respects the campaign confirmed voters' perceptions of the parties' behaviour over much of the parliament.

On selected criteria each of the three parties could claim to have 'won' the campaign. As MORI's Chairman, Bob Worcester, pointed out, Liberal Democrat support rose from 12 per cent at the start to 17 per cent on polling day, and the Conservatives cut the Labour lead from 25 per cent to 13 per cent. However, when voters were asked who had fought the most effective campaign, three times as many mentioned Labour as the other parties (see Table 12.2). Labour outscored the Conservatives on most campaign activities;

Table 12.2   Most effective campaign

	%
Conservative	11
Labour	36
Liberal Democrat	13
Other/none	40

Source: MORI.

for instance, they phoned two million voters, double the Conservative total. In a confirmation of the 'spiral of silence' theory (see p. 120), MORI found that Labour supporters were more confident and proselytising. A quarter of Labour voters reported that they encouraged others to support their party: only one-tenth of Conservative supporters did so, and whereas 12 per cent of Labour supporters actively discouraged people from voting Conservative, only 3 per cent of Conservatives took a similar anti-Labour stance.

Strategists' assessments of the campaign showed a remarkable degree of convergence. One Conservative Director's admission, 'We had no message, or at least not one that the voters listened to, Labour did', was echoed by others. A close adviser of John Major heard his leader's final press conference statement and reflected: 'So that's what the election was about. Why didn't we say this at the start?' Peter Mandelson's verdict that the 'Conservative campaign lacked a strategy, and message and discipline' was one that many Conservatives accepted. Labour strategists thought that a better Conservative campaign could have added some 30 to 40 seats and 4 per cent of the vote. They were contemptuous of much of the advertising – 'too negative'; 'misjudged the mood'; 'offered no hope' – and were not surprised to learn that so much was not pre-tested. They were delighted at the use in Tory advertising of the New Labour slogan – 'doing our work for us'. On the final Monday Blair was seen on television battling for votes in town centres, while Major cancelled his *ITV 500* session and toured Belfast, Scotland and Wales – areas of Britain which he regarded to be more at risk if a Labour government's devolution plan led to the break-up of the United Kingdom. None of these places returned a Conservative MP.

Claims about the Clintonisation of Labour or the Mandelsonisation of campaigning acknowledge the influence of American ideas and practices on electioneering.[5] They refer to the growth, *inter alia*, of targeting, reliance on mass media, professionalisation of communications, as well as the idea of 'image' politics in which the voter is perceived as a consumer of the product – be it a party or candidate. Such trends, most developed in the US, are increasingly common across the globe. Some part of 'Americanisation' is derived from the application of technology, but another part is to do with campaigning skills; for example, concentrating on one simple message and repeating it relentlessly. Labour's war room and the idea of 'New Labour' were both borrowed from Clinton's 1992 campaign. The Conservative's near-term campaign in 1992 was based on Reagan's 1984 campaign. The trends have been reinforced by a growing transatlantic traffic of campaign professionals; Stan Greenberg for Labour in 1997, Dick Wirthlin for the Conservatives in 1990–91, Philip Gould for the Clinton team in 1992 and 1996 and former Central Office officials for the Bush campaign in 1992.

There was also much talk about the American import of negative campaigning and, among politicians and campaign managers, of negative media. The media, as usual, sought to report conflict and hunted for signs of internal splits, rows, falling morale and the impact of opinion polls' findings. In 1997, however, journalists had much less to work with. Attempts to highlight rivalries between Gordon Brown and Peter Mandelson in Millbank Tower or between Michael Heseltine and Brian Mawhinney in

Central Office fizzled out. The only tension reported seriously was between Mawhinney and the Saatchi agency. After the stories of sleaze and Piers Merchant's escapade in the first fortnight, the campaign was remarkably free of scandals.

Negative campaigning – in the sense of pointing to the weaknesses of an opposing party and warning of the dangers of electing it to office – is not new: it has been a persistent feature of British party competition. It was featured in the Labour posters of 22 Tax Rises, VAT on food, and the Conservative poster of Tony Blair on Chancellor Kohl's lap, the Tony and Bill message about the bills for Labour promises, and both parties' election broadcasts (see p. 151). NOP found that 47 per cent of voters thought the Conservative Party had the most negative advertisements compared to 15 per cent for Labour. Politicians are not always comfortable with such messages; indeed, John Major and some Conservatives were offended by the 'demon eyes' poster, and Tony Blair insisted in public and in private on the posters during the campaign being positive. Surveys regularly reported that voters express dislike for negativism (although they may in fact be influenced by it). The *Guardian* noted on 28 April: 'Analysis of stories in all media show that over half reported one or other party attracting the policies and personalities of their opponents.'

Several factors have helped promote negative campaigning in recent years. The Conservatives were thought to have won recent general elections by exploiting Labour weaknesses, although the party presented a ready target. There was also an awareness of the trends in the US and belief that negative campaigning worked. Communication specialists argued that it was much easier to present a 'knocking' message in a sentence or slogan than a positive one.[6] Political managers also believed that the media were more likely to report attacks than positive statements of policy. Television and the press highlight such stories and report the campaign in adversarial terms.

Negativism is more likely to have an effect where it resonates with existing perceptions of a party or candidate. For example, the Conservative tax attacks in 1992 fed on popular memories of the 1974–79 Labour government and concerns about how Labour would pay for its spending programmes. In 1997 Labour's pension charge fed on perceptions that the Conservatives were 'uncaring' and on Peter Lilley's pre-election proposals for long-term changes to the state pensions. It also appears to be more likely to work where it is conveyed in a factual message such as '22 tax rises' rather than in unsubstantiated innuendo or 'slanging'.

Labour spokesmen regularly claimed that they were campaigning positively, and that perceptions to the contrary were a consequence of selective media coverage. Analysis of the Labour and Conservative daily press conferences provides some evidence on the balance between time spent on presenting or defending a party's record or policy proposal (the positive approach) and attacking those of the opposing party (the negative approach). Of the paragraphs in Labour press releases, we judged 60 per cent to be attacking and 40 per cent to be defensive. Of Conservative releases, 65 per cent of the paragraphs were attacking and 35 per cent defensive. The Conservative releases usually began with reports about their achievements in government, followed by attacks on Labour's record in the chosen policy area, pointing in particular to contradictions and shifts in the party's position over time. They claimed that Labour had repeatedly changed what it had said and the presumption was that they were presenting a falsely moderate image. A vote for Labour was a risk; voters could only be sure with the Conservatives. Labour attacks highlighted weaknesses in the Conservative record, the broken tax promises and why the party could not be trusted, as well as its weak leadership. Labour strategists relied on broadcasts and press conferences rather than posters to launch anti-Conservative messages. Labour then usually contrasted two futures – more of the same under the Conservatives versus a series of strong, if rather vague, claims about the future under Labour. A good example was Tony Blair on 15 April: 'The dividing lines are clear on education in this campaign – positive versus negative, the future versus the past, the many versus the few.'

'Spin-doctoring', or the use of press advisers who will coax the media into carrying favourable interpretations of events, is a part of a modern communication systems in many organisations. With Alastair Campbell, Peter Mandelson, David Hill, and Charlie Whelan (press secretary to Gordon Brown) Labour was remarkably successful in gaining a favourable coverage. They were adept at getting their stories on air and in print and in rebutting claims by the Conservative party. A good part of the success was due to Labour's skill and co-operation in meeting the demands of the media, although critics complained of a mixture of bullying and flattery applied to journalists. It accompanied the emphasis on discipline in the party and the need for party figures to adhere to agreed communications strategies. Some dissenters in the party complained that pressure from 'control freaks' in Millbank was stamping out internal party debate.

The 1997 election campaign was expensive. Both parties raised and spent enormous sums of money, greater than in any post-war election. The demands of fund raising placed the party organisations under great strain. One senior Conservative figure reflected uneasily on the scale of the expenditure and wondered if it was now time for parties to do something on the revenue and expenditure side. 'This must be the last of the old song and dance campaigns. It can't go on', he said. It is difficult to be precise about the total spending because of the considerable indirect support provided by the state, not least in the form of broadcast time, and by commercial and business groups. Labour claimed to have spent over £13m from central party funds and the Conservatives £20m in the twelve months up to polling day. The Liberal Democrats spent only £700,000 over the same period. These sums include spending on leaders' tours, help to constituencies, advertising, private polling and research and the salaries of staff recruited for the campaign. Labour spent heavily on surveys – £500,000 on NOP's surveys from 1993 and £180,000 on focus groups for Philip Gould Associates. The Conservatives spent just over £400,000 on private polling over the twelve months to polling day. Conservative spending on tours and rallies, involving the hire of halls (including the Albert Hall and Exhibition Centre of Birmingham) and refurbishment of the battle bus totalled some £4 million. Labour also exceeded planned expenditure on this category and spent a combined £980,000 on the tours of Tony Blair and John Prescott and a further £600,000 on rallies and events for the leader, Gordon Brown and Robin Cook.

As ever, the largest sums of money went on advertising – over £13m for M & C Saatchi and over £7m for BMP (in the summer of 1995 Labour had allocated only £1.8m to advertising but, as funds came in, and together with stories of Saatchi's spending, the sum was progressively increased). Most of this spending was in the first four months of 1997 and went on posters. Table 12.3 shows that the Conservatives were helped, to some degree, by the press advertisements of Paul Sykes and Entrepreneurs for a Booming Britain; and Labour by Unison. The main parties cut back severely on press advertising. The combined number of pages bought by Labour and Conservative during the campaign fell to 39 compared to 113 in 1992 and 319 in 1987. The Referendum Party, bankrolled by Sir James Goldsmith, was easily the biggest spender on press advertising. The Liberal Democrats were easily the most frugal.

Table 12.3   Party spending on advertising

	Press 96/97 inc VAT (£)	Posters 96/97 inc VAT (£)	Grand total 96/97 inc VAT (£)
Conservative Central Office	2,258,000	10,925,000	13,183,000
Referendum Party	6,768,000	440,000	7,208,000
Entrepreneurs For A Booming Britain	868,000		868,000
Paul Sykes	827,000		827,000
Labour	1,481,000	5,905,000	7,386,000
Unison	1,112,000		1,112,000

Sources: All posters: PPL; Lab/Unison press: BMP; other press: Register MEAL.

It is difficult to isolate the effects of advertising spending or indeed of any one campaign appeal. Labour advertising sought to reassure voters about the party, not least that it would not raise taxes. Over the parliament, surveys showed a sharp fall in the number of voters who thought that they would pay more in all forms of tax under Labour; indeed, by February 1997 some opinion polls reported that more voters expected taxes to increase under a Conservative government than a Labour government.

The 1997 campaign will be looked back upon as one that neither changed the outcome of the election nor contained any memorable events, but it will be remembered as one where the techniques of controlled electioneering took a quantum leap forward. Peter Mandelson was credited with many things for which he was not responsible, but the tributes paid by Conservatives to the operations of Labour's Millbank media centre and their determination to learn lessons from it make it possible that 1997 will be seen as a landmark for 'Mandelsonisation'.

NOTES

1. *Sunday Telegraph*, 8 June 1997.
2. See N. Jones, *Sound Bites and Spin Doctors* (1995) and M. Rosenbaum *From Soapbox to Soundbite* (1997).
3. The 1500 respondents in ICM's final sample were offered £1 for any designated charity if they agreed to report on the election day how they had voted. Some 1150 were contacted and reported before the results were known.
4. 'Dominant press backs "on message" winner', *Guardian*, 5 May 1997.
5. D. Butler and A. Ranney *Electioneering* (1992).
6. See: *The New Marketing of Politics* (1995),and D. Kavanagh, *Election Campaigning* (1995).
7. Charles Lewington complained that the Conservatives had too many spin-doctors, providing different messages, and that a party in government is more constrained than a party in opposition. See 'The Art of Spinning', *The Times* 18 August 1997. But see also the reports by N. Jones, *Campaign 1997* (1997) and the review of this book by Joy Johnson, Labour's director of campaigns until late 1996, in the *New Statesman* 8 August 1997. See also N. Jones, *Sound Bites and Spin Doctors* (1995).

13 Landslide

The election outcome was often described in spectacular headlines: 'Triumph' (*Guardian*); 'Massacre' (*Daily Mail*); 'Landslide' (*Express* and *Daily Telegraph*). It was all of these. The total of 419 MPs was a record for Labour; 165 was the lowest Conservative tally since 1906; the Labour majority of 179 seats was the biggest since 1935, and the 10 per cent swing from Conservative to Labour was the largest two-party shift since 1945. The swing was the product of Labour increasing its 1992 share of the vote by a third and the Conservatives losing a quarter. The Conservative vote share, at 30.7 per cent, was their lowest since the coming of mass democracy and only in 1906 had they secured fewer seats. The Liberal Democrats gained a third party's largest number of seats since 1929. The turnout at 71.2 per cent was the lowest since 1935, and a substantial fall from the 77.7 per cent of 1992.

On 1 May Tony Blair and his wife made a triumphalist walk from the gates at the entrance of Downing Street to Number 10, shaking hands with ecstatic supporters. There was a sense of excitement, given the long time Labour had been out of office, coupled with a sense of expectation, now that a government had such a commanding majority. The front pages of the newspapers the next day portrayed the happy couple and their three children on the doorstep. The arrival of a young family at Downing Street seemed to mark a new page in British history. In his remarks before entering Number 10, Mr Blair said that he had run as New Labour and would govern as New Labour. He added: 'This is not a mandate for dogma or for doctrine, but it was a mandate to get those things done in our country that desperately need doing for the future.'

Labour's advance was spread across every region and social group in Britain. Table 13.1 shows that the party made impressive gains among virtually all social groups, particularly so among the C1s or lower middle class. It also made large gains among first-time and young voters, but not among the over-65s. It managed to close the longstanding gender gap: in 1997 women were as likely as men to vote Labour. Its biggest increase in vote share came in Greater London and the rest of the south-east. The party increased its vote the least in its stronger areas – Wales, Scotland and Yorkshire.

The 1997 election marked a reversal of the long-term trend towards the geographical polarisation between a Conservative south and Labour north. Thanks to the outcomes in 1992 and 1997, Labour now had a more even geographical distribution of seats. Perhaps the most remarkable geographical feature of the election was the disappearance of Conservative representation

in Scotland and Wales and further decline in the south-west. The party's decline
in the Celtic regions had been developing for some elections. The Conservatives
now held only 11 of the 74 London seats, and more than ever was a party of
the English suburbs and shires. Liberal Democratic support was evenly
spread across the country, apart from the now established stronghold in the
south-west. It finished third in vote share in every region, again bar the south-
west (where it was second) and Scotland (where it was fourth).

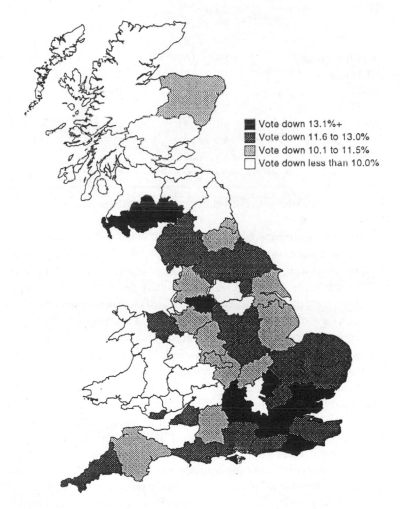

Map 2   Fall in Conservative vote 1992–97, by county

Table 13.1   How Britain voted

| | 1997 vote % (change on 1992 in brackets) | | |
	Conservative	Labour	Lib Dem
All Great Britain voters	31 (–12)	44 (+9)	17 (–1)
Men	31 (–8)	44 (+6)	17 (–1)
Women	32 (–11)	44 (+10)	17 (–1)
AB voters	42 (–11)	31 (+9)	21 (0)
C1	26 (–22)	47 (+19)	19 (–1)
C2	25 (–15)	54 (+15)	14 (–4)
DE	21 (–8)	61 (+9)	13 (0)
First–time voters	19 (–16)	57 (+17)	18 (–3)
All 18–29	22 (–18)	57 (+19)	17 (0)
30–44	26 (–11)	49 (+12)	17 (–3)
45–64	33 (–9)	43 (+9)	18 (–2)
65+	44 (–3)	34 (–2)	16 (+2)
Home–owners	35 (–12)	41 (+11)	17 (–3)
Council tenants	13 (–6)	65 (+1)	15 (+5)
Trade union members	18 (–9)	57 (+7)	20 (+2)

Sources: 1992 data ITN/Harris exit poll; 1997 data BBC/NOP exit poll.

The extent and direction of the turnover of votes and seats was comparable to 1945, which also saw the defeat of a long-established party of government. But, in contrast to 1945, which came as a surprise even to Mr Attlee, the 1997 result seemed preordained for virtually the entire parliament; it also flew in the face of those earlier academic analyses which pointed to the ways in which the embourgeoisement of society was working against Labour. As Britain was becoming more white-collar and home-owning, so the social trends seemed to favour the Conservatives. Other research had suggested that the growing number of safe Conservative and Labour seats and the reduction in the number of marginals meant that there would be a low turnover of seats. The result was all the more striking, considering the many analyses in the immediate aftermath of the 1992 election which argued that Labour faced too high a mountain to climb within the life of one parliament.

The Conservatives lost seats across the board to Labour, Liberal Democrats, Scottish Nationalists, and the independent Martin Bell. Tactical voting by Liberal Democrat and Labour voters lost the party seats, as they cast ballots to maximise the anti-Conservative vote. However, the tactical element can be exaggerated; in some Liberal Democrat target seats the anti-Conservative tide was so strong that Labour captured eight seats from third place and one (Inverness East) from fourth place.

The result was a spectacular rebuff to the normal party of government. By 1997 the Conservative party had lost many of its traditional advantages. Some part of its identity has always been defined by what it was against. With Labour's abandonment of socialism, the old dragons of public ownership, high taxes and public spending, and powerful trade unions were no longer there to frighten the electorate. After 1992, surveys showed that it had lost its lead over Labour as the party of strong leadership and of low taxation. It could no longer rely on the support of the press and business and the City no longer regarded Labour as a threat. The decoupling of these three key interests from the Conservative cause offers impressive testimony to their wooing by Tony Blair. The Conservatives did not lose on the key issues – after all, on taxes, levels of public spending and British membership of a single European currency, there was not much difference between them and Labour – but they lost comprehensively on 'valence' issues (where the parties promote widely shared goals). On such qualities as party unity, competence, newness, trust and integrity, the Conservatives trailed badly.[1]

If ever a party needed a rest from government, it seemed to be the Conservatives in 1997. The ICM recall poll on election day found that of the 1992 Conservatives defecting to Labour and Liberal Democrats, the main reason (given by 54 and 31 per cent respectively) was 'time for a change'. The Conservative Party had been in office for longer than any leading party in the European Union. John Major was heard to reflect that the 1992 victory had 'stretched democracy's elasticity too far'. Tony Blair thought that the electorate had been ready for change in 1992, but that a crucial number of voters drew back because they did not trust Labour enough: 'That the Conservatives did so badly in 1997, was a delayed reaction to 1992.' Conservative and Labour figures agreed wryly that, with the ERM crisis looming and Neil Kinnock as leader, Labour had been lucky to lose the 1992 election.

Surveys found that key groups of traditional Tory voters decisively moved away from the party. These included the middle class as a whole, including the professional and non-manual groups, as well as home-owners and, particularly, those buying their properties on a mortgage. The slump in property prices had made the latter resentful. Table 13.1 shows the relationship between age and vote in the 1997 election. Conservative support, like its grassroots membership, was heavily tilted towards older people, Labour's towards the young. The party would be handicapped because the older voters dying off over the coming years will be disproportionately Conservative, the new voters coming on to the electoral register disproportionately Labour. In 1974 a Conservative official had summarised his party's electoral weaknesses as 'Death, Youth and the Working Class'. The first two remained a cause for concern. Most surveys showed that the Conservatives recovered ground on questions of economic competence from late 1996 onwards and in the campaign had drawn level with the Labour Party, depending on the precise wording of the question, but this recovery of economic competence provided only a modest boost to Conservative electoral support. The long-established link between economic optimism and the government electoral support had broken down.

As John Major made a dignified exit from Downing Street, and colleagues prepared for the battle to succeed him as leader, the Conservative Party faced a major task of rebuilding, comparable to that after 1945. In Smith Square there was a need for a more effective campaign machine and among the constituencies a need for more members and greater levels of activity. Although Mrs Thatcher did much to alter the agenda of British politics after 1979, she had not done much about the party's grassroots. Just as Lord Woolton and R.A. Butler had rebuilt the Conservative Party after 1945, and Kinnock and Blair had transformed Labour, the new Conservative leadership would have to reinvent the party at the end of the century.

The Liberal Democrats recovered from an inauspicious build-up to the campaign. Beset by their poor standing in the opinion polls and loss of a distinctive agenda – as Labour moved to the centre ground and accepted constitutional reform – the party took advantage of its higher media profile

"I assume you vote New Labour?"

JAK, *Evening Standard*, 16 April 1997

and the public hostility to the arguments about sleaze, it could also score with its willingness to raise more money for education. Party strategists could take pride in concentrating votes where they counted and capturing 28 seats (all from Conservatives). Paddy Ashdown's misfortune, however, was that his record number of Liberal seats would count for little in a House of Commons with a 179-seat Labour majority. The party's early campaign appeals for a big national vote were not heeded. The 16.8 per cent share of the vote was a decline on 1992 and a steep fall from the shares gained in 1983 and 1987.

For all its lavish spending, the Referendum Party gained 5 per cent or more of the vote in only 39 seats, doing best in seats with large agricultural or elderly populations. Although its intervention may have directly lost the Conservatives only two seats, it exacerbated tensions within the party and provided a platform for some former Tory Euro-sceptics. Its 3 per cent of the national vote was the largest ever won by a minor party.

Conservative candidates associated with scandals or sleaze allegations suffered above average swings. Tatton, the fifth safest Conservative seat in the country, fell to the independent, Martin Bell. In Scotland, the SNP confirmed their standing as the second party in terms of electoral support and gained three seats, all from the Conservatives, to bring its total to six, but their 23 per cent vote was well below the 30 per cent won in October 1974. In Northern Ireland, no one party spoke for either side of the religious divide. Sinn Fein gained two seats for 17 per cent of the votes, compared to the SDLP's three seats and 24 per cent of the vote. The Ulster Unionists gained ten seats; the Democratic Unionist Party two.

The first-past-the-post electoral system worked even more perversely than usual, helped by anti-government tactical voting and the larger electorates in Conservative seats. Labour gained two-thirds of the seats for less than 44 per cent of the vote and the Conservatives gained a quarter for 31 per cent of the vote. In Scotland the Conservative vote share of 17.5 per cent brought it no seats, while the Liberals, with only 12.5 per cent, gained ten seats. The new line-up did not augur well for the Conservatives; compared to Labour more of their seats were held by narrow majorities. One half of Labour seats were held by majorities of 30 per cent or more. As John Curtice and Michael Steed show in Appendix 2, the electoral system has become heavily biased against the Conservatives.

There was no electoral recovery for the two-party system. In 1997 Labour and the Conservatives shared 75 per cent of the vote (2 per cent less than in 1992). Since 1970 the decline in total vote share and, to a lesser extent, in seats, for the two larger parties has been largely a consequence of Labour's decline. In 1997, however, it was a consequence of the sharp fall in the conservative vote and seats. The total of 75 third-party MPs is the highest since 1923.

The election was perhaps less a swing to the political left than a vindication of New Labour and the work of the party's modernisers. They had learnt the lessons of four successive election defeats and done much to change the party and its image. The appeal to the middle class paid off. Disillusion with the Conservatives' record of increasing tax was ruthlessly exploited in speeches and advertisements, and key voters and business were reassured. For the first general election ever, Labour actually outscored the Conservatives among the middle class and among home-owners (41 to 35 per cent). It was predictable that some commentators on the left had mixed views about the victory of New Labour – it was hardly a mandate to undo the work of Mrs Thatcher.

Table 13.2 reports the flow of the vote from 1992. The salient feature is that the Conservative Party lost nearly 30 per cent of its old voters; Labour only 10 per cent. Fourteen per cent of 1992 Conservatives reported switching to Labour and 10 per cent to the Liberal Democrats. A fifth of 1992 Liberal Democrats claim to have switched to Labour. In every election since 1964, when the British Election Studies began, switchers from the Conservative Party had been more likely to support the Liberal Democrats than Labour. It is almost an iron law of British voting behaviour that direct switching between the Conservative and Labour parties is outnumbered by switchers between these two parties and the Liberal Democrats.[2] It was an achievement of Tony Blair's leadership that Labour won more Conservative defectors than the Liberal Democrats.

Table 13.2   Flow of the vote 1992–97

	Con 1997	Lab 1997	Lib Dem 1997	Other 1997
Con 1992	71.0	14.2	10.2	4.1
Lab 1992	1.1	89.3	7.1	2.0
Lib Dem 1992	5.8	22.2	65.5	5.5
Other 1992	2.0	12.2	2.0	83.6
Too Young	19.8	56.9	18.1	5.2
Abstained	20.0	54.6	19.3	5.3

Source: NOP BBC exit poll, 1 May 1997.

John Curtice and Michael Steed analyse the results in statistical detail in Appendix 2. The main points to emerge from their investigation can be summarised.

1. The geography of the election result supports the view that the electorate's rejection of the Conservatives had little to do with the ongoing economic record of the government. Across the country as a whole, Conservative support fell less heavily in those seats where the party was previously weakest. Once this is taken into consideration, there was little regional variation in Conservative performance. There was a remarkably uniform nationwide swing against the government, regardless of differing economic circumstances.

2. There is little evidence to support the view that voters in predominantly middle-class constituencies were more inclined to swing to New Labour than working-class voters. Equally, there is little evidence that the decision of a number of traditionally pro-Conservative newspapers not to endorse the party in 1997 had any significant impact on the outcome. The similar pattern of Conservative losses regardless of social and political indicators suggests a nationwide disenchantment with the Conservative Party.

3. The lowest ever turnout in a post-war British election does not appear to have been occasioned simply by seats that contained large numbers of Conservative voters. As in 1992, turnout proved to be much lower in traditionally strong Labour areas than in strong Conservative ones. Labour won office with the third lowest share of the electorate of all the post-war British governments.

4. The Referendum Party had only a limited effect on the Conservatives' fortunes. Where a Referendum Party candidate stood and secured the average vote of around 3 per cent, approximately two-thirds of that vote appears to have come from the Conservatives. However, where the Referendum Party vote was above average, the Liberal Democrats appear to have been the main losers, probably because the Referendum Party was an alternative means of casting a protest vote. The net effect of the Referendum Party's and the UK Independence Party's intervention was probably to cost the Conservatives only three seats.

5. There appears to have been more anti-Conservative tactical voting than ever before. Labour's vote rose by more than the national average in those seats where it started off second to the Conservatives, while the Liberal Democrats' support fell by above the average. In contrast, the Liberal Democrat vote usually rose against the national trend in those seats

where they were best placed, while Labour's rose by considerably less than the average.

6. The election outcome provides only limited support for recent claims that intensive local campaigning can win votes. Both Labour and the Liberal Democrats concentrated resources over a long period before the election in a number of 'target' seats. The Liberal Democrats did perform noticeably better in their target seats than in the comparable non-targeted seats, primarily by encouraging voters to switch tactically from Labour, but Labour did not do any better in its target seats than in other seats where it started off second to the Conservatives.

7. Labour's majority of 179 was a third larger than it would have been if the movement in votes since 1992 had been the same in every constituency. The Liberal Democrats won 13 seats more than would have been expected on the same basis. This happened primarily because of, first, the extent of tactical switching between the opposition parties and, second, because Conservative support fell by more than the national average in seats they were defending. The electoral system is now significantly biased against the Conservatives; on a uniform swing from 1997 they would need a ten-point lead in the national vote merely to secure an overall majority of one.

8. Of the two electoral systems that are most widely considered for introduction into Britain, only the Additional Member System could have been relied upon to have produced a reasonably proportional outcome in 1997. Under the Single Transferable Vote, Labour would have benefited significantly from the second preferences of Liberal Democrat supporters, such that the party might still have secured an overall majority.

It is too soon to say whether 1997 will be a realigning election, in which Labour becomes the new majority, and normal party of government. The party's electoral position was a strong one. On the other hand, the powerful anti-Conservative sentiments, based on time for change and reaction against the party's divisions and associations with sleaze, will pass in time. Labour's 43.2 per cent share of the vote is on a par with Harold Wilson's 43.4 per cent in 1964, which produced a Labour majority of only four seats. Labour benefited enormously from the electoral system.

However, the new techniques of campaigning in 1997 are sure to leave a mark. The reliance on television, the use of computers and phones to target key voters, the controlled working of the war room, the practice of rapid rebuttal, the employment of party workers with a background in the communications industries, and the emphasis on discipline and adherence to the message are here to stay. Labour made a breakthrough in its methods of campaigning before and during the election. But the differences between the parties in using these skills and techniques did not decide the election. Over thirty years ago Richard Crossman said that an election 'is the end of a long process'. What happened in 1997 underlines the importance of the perceptions of the five-year record of the Conservative government, with its sustained divisions and setbacks, and, equally, the changes which Labour wrought in its structure, its policy and its image. Tony Blair and his colleagues had achieved major shifts in attitudes towards the Conservative and Labour parties; they had skilfully exploited voters' disillusion with the Conservatives and the acceptance that Labour had become a moderate party. The Conservatives, eighteen years in power, provided the opportunity. Labour seized it.

NOTES

1. R. Rose, 'On the Crest of a Wave', *Parliamentary Affairs*, 1997.
2. A. Heath et al., *Labour's Last Chance?*, (1994) p. 290.

Appendix 1   The Voting Statistics

Table A1.1   Votes and seats, 1945–97 (seats in italics)

	Electorate and turnout	Total votes cast	Conservative[1]	Labour	Liberals[2]	Welsh & Scottish Nationalists	Communist	Others (mainly N. Ireland)
1945[3]	73.3%	100%-640	39.8%-213	48.3%-393	9.1%-12	0.20%	0.4%-2	2.1%-20
	32 836 419	24 082 612	9 577 667	11 632 191	2 197 191	46 612	102 760	525 491
1950	84.0%	100%-625	43.5%-299	46.1%-315	9.1%-9	0.10%	0.30%	0.9%-2
	34 269 770	28 772 671	12 502 567	13 266 592	2 621 548	27 288	91 746	262 930
1951	82.5%	100%-625	48.0%-321	48.8%-295	2.5%-6	0.10%	0.10%	0.5%-3
	34 645 573	28 595 668	13 717 538	13 948 605	730 556	18 219	21 640	159 110
1955	76.8%	100%-630	49.7%-345	46.4%-277	2.7%-6	0.20%	0.10%	0.8%-2
	34 858 263	26 760 493	13 311 936	12 404 970	722 405	57 231	33 144	230 807
1959	78.7%	100%-630	49.4%-365	43.8%-258	5.9%-6	0.40%	0.10%	0.5%-1
	35 397 080	27 859 241	13 749 830	12 215 538	1 638 571	99 309	30 897	145 090
1964	77.1%	100%-630	43.4%-304	44.1%-317	11.2%-9	0.50%	0.20%	0.60%
	35 892 572	27 655 374	12 001 396	12 205 814	3 092 878	133 551	45 932	169 431
1966	75.8%	100%-630	41.9%-253	47.9%-363	8.5%-12	0.70%	0.20%	0.7%-2
	35 964 684	27 263 606	11 418 433	13 064 951	2 327 533	189 545	62 112	201 032
1970	72.0%	100%-630	46.4%-330	43.0%-288	7.5%-6	1.3%-1	0.10%	1.7%-5
	39 342 013	28 344 798	13 145 123	12 178 295	2 117 033	381 818	37 970	486 557
Feb '74	78.1%	100%-635	37.8%-297	37.1%-301	19.3%-14	2.6%-9	0.10%	3.1%-14
	39 770 724	31 340 162	11 872 180	11 646 391	6 058 744	804 554	32 743	958 293

	Electorate and turnout	Total votes cast	Conservative[1]	Labour	Liberals[2]	Welsh & Scottish Nationalists	Communist	Others (mainly N. Ireland)
Oct '74	72.8% 40 072 971	100%-635 29 189 178	35.8%-277 10 464 817	39.2%-319 11 457 079	18.3%-13 5 346 754	3.5%-14 1 005 938	0.10% 17 426	3.1%-12 897 164
1979	76.0% 41 093 264	100%-635 31 221 361	43.9%-339 13 697 923	37.0%-269 11 532 218	13.8%-11 4 313 804	2.0%-4 636 890	0.10% 16 858	3.2%-12 1 043 755
1983	72.7% 42 197 344	100%-650 30 671 136	42.4%-397 13 012 315	27.6%-209 8 456 934	25.4%-23 7 780 949	1.5%-4 457 676	0.04% 11 606	3.1%-17 951 656
1987	75.3% 43 181 321	100%-650 32 536 137	42.3%-376 13 763 066	30.8%-229 10 029 778	22.6%-22 7 341 290	1.7%-6 543 559	0.02% 6 078	2.6%-17 852 368
1992	77.7% 43 249 721	100%-651 33 612 693	41.9%-336 14 092 891	34.4%-271 11 559 735	17.8%-20 5 999 384	2.3%-7 783 991	–	3.5%-17 1 176 692
1997	71.2% 43 846 643	100%-659 31 286 284	30.7%-165 9 600 943	43.2%-418 13 518 167	16.8%-46 5 242 947	2.5%-10 782 580	–	6.8%-20 2 141 647

Notes:

1. Includes Ulster Unionists 1945–70.
2. Liberals 1945–79; Liberal-SDP Alliance 1983–87; Liberal Democrats 1992–
3. The 1945 figures exclude University seats and are adjusted for double counting in the 15 two-member seats.
4. Other results for 1997 include:

Party	Votes	% Share	Av vote %	Candidates	Lost Deposits	Party	Votes	% Share	Av vote %	Candidates	Lost Deposits
Referendum	811 827	2.6%	3.1	547	505	Liberal	44 989	0.1%	1.8	54	52
UK Independence	106 028	0.3%	1.2	194	193	British National	35 833	0.1%	1.3	57	54
Green	63 991	0.2%	1.4	95	95	Natural Law	30 281	0.1%	0.7	196	196
Socialist Labour	52 110	0.2%	1.7	64	61	Pro-Life Alliance	18 545	0.1%	0.7	53	53

For the first time these exceed the N. Ireland element in the 'Others' column.

Table A1.2   Regional results, 1997

UNITED KINGDOM

	Seats won in 1997 (change since 1992)				Share of votes cast 1997 (percent change since 1992)					
	Conservative	Labour	Lib Dem	Nat & Other	Turnout	Conservative	Labour	Lib Dem	Nationalists	Other
England	165 (−159)	329 (+133)	34 (+25)	1 (+1)	71.2 (−6.9)	33.7 (−11.8)	43.6 (+9.7)	17.9 (−1.3)	–	4.7 (+3.4)
South	106 (−86)	108 (+65)	28 (+21)	–	72.0 (−6.5)	37.5 (−12.9)	35.4 (+10.5)	21.8 (−1.3)	–	5.2 (+3.7)
Midlands	42 (−37)	82 (+36)	1 (+1)	–	72.3 (−7.1)	35.1 (−11.5)	46.0 (+9.7)	14.5 (−1.5)	–	4.4 (+3.2)
North	17 (−36)	139 (+32)	5 (+3)	1 (+1)	69.2 (−7.3)	26.3 (−10.6)	54.9 (+8.9)	14.6 (−1.4)	–	4.2 (+3.1)
Wales	– (−8)	34 (+7)	2 (+1)	4	73.4 (−6.3)	19.6 (−9.0)	54.7 (+5.2)	12.4 (−0.1)	9.9 (+1.0)	3.4 (+2.9)
Scotland	– (−11)	56 (+6)	10 (+2)	6 (+3)	71.3 (−4.1)	17.5 (−8.1)	45.6 (+6.6)	13.0 (−0.1)	22.1 (+0.6)	1.9 (+1.1)
Great Britain	165 (−178)	419 (+146)	46 (+28)	11 (+4)	71.4 (−6.5)	31.5 (−11.3)	44.4 (+9.2)	17.2 (−1.2)	2.6 (+0.2)	4.4 (+3.1)
Northern Ireland	–	–	–	18	67.4 (−2.4)	1.5 (−4.2)	–	–	–	98.5 (+4.2)
United Kingdom	165 (−178)	419 (+146)	46 (+28)	29 (+4)	71.2 (−6.5)	30.7 (−11.2)	43.3 (+8.9)	16.8 (−1.2)	2.5 (+0.2)	6.8 (+3.4)

REGIONS

	Seats won in 1997 (change since 1992)				Share of votes cast 1997 (percent change since 1992)					
	Conservative	Labour	Lib Dem	Nat & Other	Turnout	Conservative	Labour	Lib Dem	Nationalists	Other
South East	84 (−69)	93 (+56)	14 (+13)	–	71.1 (−6.7)	37.8 (−13.4)	38.1 (11.5)	19.0 (−1.7)	–	5.1 (3.6)
Greater London	11 (−30)	57 (+25)	6 (+5)	–	67.0 (−6.8)	31.2 (−14.1)	49.5 (12.4)	14.6 (−1.3)	–	4.7 (3.0)
Inner London	2 (−3)	23 (+3)	1	–	60.9 (−8.4)	24.2 (−12.7)	57.1 (10.0)	12.9 (−1.1)	–	5.8 (3.7)
Outer London	9 (−27)	34 (+22)	5 (+5)	–	70.2 (−5.9)	34.5 (−14.8)	45.9 (13.6)	15.4 (−1.4)	–	4.2 (2.7)
Rest of S.E.	73 (−39)	36 (+31)	8 (+8)	–	73.7 (−6.5)	41.4 (−13.2)	31.9 (11.1)	21.4 (−2.0)	–	5.4 (4.0)
Outer Met. Area	41 (−17)	19 (+17)	8 (+8)	–	73.7 (−7.2)	42.7 (−13.1)	32.8 (11.3)	19.3 (−2.0)	–	5.2 (3.8)
Outer S.E.	32 (−22)	17 (+14)	8 (+8)	–	73.6 (−5.9)	40.0 (−13.2)	31.0 (11.0)	23.5 (−2.0)	–	5.6 (4.2)
South West	22 (−17)	15 (+9)	14 (+8)	–	74.9 (−6.2)	36.7 (−10.8)	26.4 (7.2)	31.3 (−0.1)	–	5.5 (3.7)
Devon & Cornwall	5 (−7)	4 (+3)	7 (+4)	–	75.0 (−6.3)	34.8 (−11.2)	23.1 (5.6)	35.3 (1.3)	–	6.9 (4.4)
Rest of S.W.	17 (−10)	11 (+6)	7 (+4)	–	74.9 (−6.1)	37.7 (−10.6)	28.0 (8.0)	29.4 (−0.8)	–	4.9 (3.4)
East Anglia	14 (−5)	8 (+5)	–	–	74.3 (−5.7)	38.7 (−12.4)	38.3 (10.3)	17.9 (−1.6)	–	5.1 (3.6)
East Midlands	14 (−15)	30 (+15)	–	–	73.2 (−7.4)	34.9 (−11.7)	47.8 (10.4)	13.6 (−1.7)	–	3.7 (3.0)
West Midlands	14 (−17)	44 (+16)	1 (+1)	–	70.8 (−7.4)	33.7 (−11.0)	47.8 (9.0)	13.8 (−1.3)	–	4.7 (3.2)
W. Mids. Met. Co.	4 (−6)	25 (+6)	–	–	67.4 (−8.1)	29.8 (−12.3)	53.3 (9.3)	11.3 (−0.7)	–	5.6 (3.7)
Rest of W. Mids.	10 (−10)	18 (+9)	1 (+1)	–	74.0 (−6.8)	37.2 (−10.0)	42.9 (8.8)	16.1 (−1.5)	–	3.8 (2.7)

REGIONS

	Seats won in 1997 (change since 1992)					Share of votes cast 1997 (percent change since 1992)				
	Conservative	Labour	Lib Dem	Nat & Other		Turnout	Conservative	Labour	Lib Dem	Nationalists	Other
Yorks & Humberside	7 (−15)	47 (+13)	2 (+2)	—		68.3 (−7.1)	28.0 (−10.0)	51.9 (7.6)	16.0 (−0.8)	—	4.1 (3.2)
S. Yorks Met. Co.	— (−1)	14	1 (+1)	—		64.1 (−8.1)	16.7 (−9.1)	62.3 (4.4)	16.6 (0.9)	—	4.4 (3.8)
W. Yorks Met. Co.	— (−9)	23 (+9)	—	—		69.2 (−7.0)	28.8 (−9.4)	54.0 (8.5)	12.9 (−2.1)	—	4.2 (3.0)
Rest of Yorks & Humb	7 (−5)	10 (+4)	1 (+1)	—		70.5 (−6.7)	35.0 (−11.9)	41.9 (9.4)	19.3 (−0.7)	—	3.7 (3.1)
North West	2 (−18)	60 (+16)	2 (+1)	1 (+1)		69.9 (−7.4)	27.1 (−10.7)	54.2 (9.3)	14.3 (−1.5)	—	4.4 (2.9)
Gtr. Manchr. Met. Co.	2 (−5)	25 (+5)	1	—		67.9 (−8.0)	24.1 (−11.3)	56.3 (9.0)	16.0 (0.4)	—	3.5 (1.9)
Merseyside Met. Co.	— (−4)	15 (+3)	1	—		67.5 (−6.6)	19.7 (−9.3)	61.9 (10.4)	14.4 (−2.4)	—	3.9 (1.3)
Rest of N.W.	5 (−10)	21 (+9)		1 (+1)		73.4 (−7.2)	33.9 (−11.1)	48.1 (9.4)	12.3 (−3.1)	—	5.6 (4.8)
Northern	3 (−3)	32 (+3)	1	—		69.4 (−6.1)	22.2 (−11.2)	60.9 (10.3)	13.3 (−2.3)	—	3.7 (3.2)
Tyne & Wear Met. Co.	— (−1)	13 (+1)	—	—		65.5 (−7.1)	17.3 (−11.5)	67.1 (10.0)	11.8 (−1.9)	—	3.8 (3.4)
Rest of Northern	3 (−2)	19 (+2)	1	—		71.7 (−7.0)	24.7 (−11.2)	57.7 (10.6)	14.0 (−2.5)	—	3.6 (3.1)
Wales	— (−8)	34 (+7)	2 (+1)	4		73.4 (−6.3)	19.6 (−9.0)	54.7 (5.2)	12.4 (−0.1)	9.9 (1.0)	3.4 (2.9)
Industrial S. Wales	— (−3)	24 (+3)	—	4		72.3 (−6.6)	17.3 (−8.2)	62.9 (3.9)	10.6 (0.6)	5.7 (0.6)	3.6 (3.1)
Rural Wales	— (−5)	10 (+4)	2 (+1)	4		75.3 (−5.6)	23.3 (−10.3)	41.5 (7.7)	15.2 (−1.3)	16.8 (1.5)	3.1 (2.5)
Scotland	— (−11)	56 (+6)	10 (+2)	6 (+3)		71.3 (−4.1)	17.5 (−8.1)	45.6 (6.2)	13.0 (−0.1)	22.1 (0.6)	1.9 (1.1)
Central Clydeside	— (−1)	23 (+1)	—	—		68.6 (−5.8)	11.8 (−6.7)	58.0 (5.9)	7.3 (−1.0)	20.1 (0.2)	2.8 (1.7)
Rest of Ind. Belt	— (−3)	25 (+2)	1 (+1)	—		73.1 (−4.0)	17.6 (−8.0)	51.1 (7.4)	9.8 (−0.2)	20.3 (0.4)	1.2 (0.5)
Highlands	—	2 (+1)	4 (−1)	—		70.6 (−2.0)	13.9 (−8.4)	28.6 (7.6)	31.6 (−2.2)	23.6 (1.6)	2.4 (1.3)
Rest of Scotland	— (−7)	6 (+2)	5 (+2)	6 (+3)		72.2 (−4.7)	25.2 (−10.4)	26.7 (7.1)	19.6 (1.1)	26.8 (1.0)	1.7 (1.3)

Notes: The English Regions are the eight *Standard Regions* as defined by the Office of National Statistics (ONS).

The *Outer Metropolitan Area* comprises those seats wholly or mostly in the Outer Metropolitan Area as defined by the ONS. It includes: the whole of Surrey and Hertfordshire; the whole of Berkshire except Newbury; and the constituencies of Arundel & South Downs; Crawley; Horsham; Mid-Sussex (West Sussex); Aldershot; Hampshire North-East (Hampshire); Chatham & Aylesford; Dartford; Faversham & Mid Kent; Gillingham; Gravesham; Maidstone & The Weald; Medway; Sevenoaks; Tonbridge and Malling; Tunbridge Wells (Kent); Beaconsfield; Chesham & Amersham; Wycombe (Buckinghamshire); Bedfordshire South-West; Luton North; Luton South (Bedfordshire); Basildon; Billericay; Brentwood & Ongar; Castle Point; Chelmsford West; Epping Forest; Harlow; Rayleigh; Rochford & Southend East; Southend West; Thurrock (Essex).

Industrial Wales includes Gwent, the whole of Glamorgan, and the Llanelli constituency in Dyfed.

The *Central Clydeside Conurbation* includes those seats wholly or mostly in the Central Clydeside Conurbation as defined by the Registrar-General (Scotland). It comprises the whole of the Strathclyde region except the following constituencies: Argyll & Bute; Ayr; Carrick; Clydesdale; Cunninghame North; Cunninghame South; Greenock & Inverclyde.

The *Rest of Industrial Belt* comprises the regions of Central; Fife (except Fife North-East); and Lothian.

The *Highlands* comprises the following constituencies: Argyll & Bute; Caithness, Sutherland & Easter Ross; Inverness East, Nairn & Lochaber; Orkney & Shetland; Ross, Skye & Inverness West; the Western Isles.

Table A1.3   Constituency results in Great Britain, 1997

This table lists the votes in each constituency in percentage terms.

The constituencies are listed alphabetically within counties (except that in Greater London the constituencies are listed alphabetically within each borough).

The figure in the 'Other' column is the total percentage received by all the 'Other' candidates – except the Referendum Party, which is listed separately for seats in England (for Scotland and Wales, where all Referendum Party candidates lost their deposit, the Referendum Party has been included amongst the 'Others' so as to make room for the nationalist parties). When there was more than one Other candidate the number is indicated in brackets.

† denotes a seat won by different parties in 1992 and 1997
‡ denotes a seat that changed hands at a by-election between 1992 and 1997

The changes are based on the notional results for the same area as calculated in C. Rallings and M. Thrasher in *Media Guide to the New Constituencies* (BBC, ITN, PA News, Sky, 1995).

In a few cases the difficulties of calculation may make the figures misleading. The likeliest cases of serious error are:

Possible Conservative Overestimate		Possible Conservative Underestimate	
Billericay	Maldon & Chelmsford E.	Basildon	Forest of Dean
Suffolk C. & Ipswich N.	Gordon	Dorset M. & Poole N.	Colchester
Tewkesbury	Hitchin & Harpenden	Newcastle E. & Wallsend	Swindon North
Faversham & Kent Mid		Oldham E. & Saddleworth	

The turnout figures for 1992 were not calculated by Rallings and Thrasher. Here they are based on approximations from the turnout in the old component constituencies.

Redistribution increased the House of Commons from 651 to 659 seats. Only 165 seats were left with unchanged boundaries. In 76 others the change affected less than 5 per cent of the electorate. But in 418 seats there was significant change. Many constituency names were altered and some with the same name took on a quite different party complexion. Because it was possible for a new constituency to be drawn wholly from a single old constituency but not to be identical with it, a summary index provides a guide to the extent of change involved in the creation of a new constituency. This index of change is a measure of the difference between a new seat and the base constituency from which it was formed. The base constituency is simply that constituency which provided the greater or greatest number of electors to the new seat. An old constituency could form the base for more than one new seat. For example, the old seat of Colchester North was the base for both North Essex and Colchester because it supplied the largest number of electors to each of those new seats.

The index of change is calculated by adding all the electors who have been removed from and added to the base constituency in the course of forming the new one, divided by the number of electors in the original, base constituency. Thus

$$\text{Index of change} = \frac{\text{Total deletions from base constituency} + \text{total additions to base} \times 100}{\text{Electorate of the base constituency}}$$

For example, the new constituency of Colchester has the old constituency of Colchester North as its base. 44,963 electors from a total electorate of 86,874 in Colchester North are transferred to Colchester, leaving 41,911 who are not. Colchester also acquires 28,384 electors from the old Colchester South and Maldon to complete its electorate of 73,347.

The index of change for Colchester is thus:

$$\frac{\text{Total deletions from base} (41,911) + \text{Total additions to base} (28,384) \times 100}{\text{Electorate of base constituency} (86,874)} = 31$$

In some cases where the relationship between a new constituency and its base is particularly tenuous, the index of change may exceed 100%. The word 'None' under 'Index of Change' indicates that the new seat is the same as its base; a figure of 0 means that a very small number of electors have been moved from or into the base constituency.

Swing is given in the Conventional (or 'Butler') form – the average of the Conservative % gain and the Labour % loss (measured as % of the total poll). It is only reported for those seats where those parties occupied the top two places in 1992 and 1997. This is the practice followed by all the Nuffield studies since 1955.

Distribution of Economic Indicators by Constituency

On the left of these tables there are listed for the 641 constituencies in Great Britain (but not for the 18 in Northern Ireland) the following information:

% employers and managers: Proportion of economically active persons aged 16+ in Registrar General's socio-economic groups 1, 2, or 13. (Source: 1991 Census)

% good income: Proportion of persons aged 15+ living in households with an annual income above £25,000. (Source: CCN Marketing)

% unemployed: Registered unemployed as a proportion of the electorate, March 1997. (Source: Dept. of Education and Employment)

Population density: Persons per hectare. (Source: ONS New Parliamentary Constituency Monitors)

The following table is designed to show the approximate rank ordering of all the constituencies in terms of these characteristics, as well as the range between the highest and lowest figures for each characteristic. Figures for proportion employers and managers and for household income are not available for Northern Ireland.

Ranking order of decile (%)	Rank order in number	Unemployment (%)	Population Density	Index of Change	Rank order in number	Employers/ Managers (%)	Good Income
0	1	1.0	0.1	0.0	1	5.3	8.4
10	66	1.8	0.9	0.0	64	9.2	16.0
20	132	2.3	1.7	0.0	128	10.6	18.1
30	198	2.7	3.2	0.4	192	11.7	19.7
40	264	3.2	5.3	7.5	256	13.1	21.0
50	330	3.7	9.1	13.4	320	14.1	22.3
60	396	4.2	16.1	19.2	384	15.1	23.8
70	462	4.7	24.6	29.2	448	16.3	25.7
80	528	5.4	33.3	45.6	512	17.9	27.9
90	593	6.6	41.8	68.1	576	20.2	31.0
100	659	13.3	119.0	133.1	641	28.7	39.2

Table A1.3 *Constituency results, Great Britain, 1997*

ENGLAND	% Voting	% Change in voting	% Con.	Con. change 1992-97	% Labour	Lab. change 1992-97	% Lib Dem	Lib Dem change 1992-97	% Referendum	% Other	Swing	Index of change	Population density	Unemployed %	Good income %	Employers/managers %
Avon, Bath	75.5	-7.3	31.2	-12.2	16.4	+8.2	48.5	+1.6	2.2	1.8 (3)	–	11	10.5	4.1	28.4	15.7
Bristol East	69.7	-8.8	23.4	-14.2	56.9	+9.6	14.8	+0.0	3.1	1.9 (2)	-11.9	43	38.4	5.7	18.3	11.3
North-West	73.3	-7.9	29.3	-9.5	49.9	+4.7	13.1	-1.7	2.9	4.7 (4)	-7.1	22	19.0	3.8	21.1	11.0
South	68.7	-7.3	21.2	-12.0	59.9	+12.7	13.4	-4.5	3.0	2.5 (3)	-12.3	16	42.7	5.6	17.7	9.3
West†	72.7	-3.6	32.8	-12.3	35.2	+11.9	28.0	-1.2	2.1	1.8 (3)	–	11	40.5	4.6	34.1	18.0
Kingswood†	77.7	-6.8	29.9	-15.9	53.7	+13.1	12.8	-0.8	2.4	1.1 (3)	-14.5	51	28.1	2.6	22.1	12.6
Northavon†	79.1	-5.7	39.0	-12.8	15.6	+3.5	42.4	+7.9	3.0	–	–	10	2.3	1.9	30.5	18.3
Wansdyke†	79.1	-6.7	35.3	-11.9	44.1	+16.8	16.8	-6.8	2.4	1.4 (3)	-14.4	58	3.0	2.0	27.3	17.2
Weston-Super-Mare†	73.7	-5.8	37.7	-10.3	17.9	+6.5	40.1	+1.6	4.3	–	–	10	6.0	3.6	25.4	17.0
Woodspring	78.5	-2.0	44.5	-8.9	20.7	+8.3	30.4	-1.3	2.9	1.5 (3)	–	33	3.9	1.6	33.6	21.6
Bedfordshire, Bedford†	73.5	-3.0	33.7	-11.8	50.6	+14.2	12.3	-4.1	3.1	0.3	-13.0	47	30.5	4.3	24.9	14.5
Bedfordshire Mid	78.3	-5.0	46.0	-16.4	32.5	+12.7	16.8	+1.0	4.3	0.3	-14.6	99	1.9	1.6	30.2	21.1
North-East	77.6	-6.8	44.3	-15.0	32.6	+12.6	14.2	-4.3	4.9	3.9 (2)	-13.8	78	1.4	1.8	29.1	19.8
South-West	75.2	-6.5	40.7	-15.5	40.5	+14.7	14.3	-2.3	3.3	1.2 (2)	-15.1	13	7.4	2.3	25.4	17.4
Luton North†	73.2	-7.9	34.3	-16.9	54.6	+17.4	9.1	-1.1	–	2.0 (2)	-17.2	35	47.0	3.7	21.7	13.8
South†	70.4	-8.0	31.4	-12.9	54.8	+11.6	9.6	-1.6	2.5	1.7 (3)	-12.3	10	16.2	4.9	19.3	13.1
Berkshire, Bracknell	74.5	-11.1	47.4	-13.0	29.8	+9.5	15.4	-3.9	2.8	4.7 (3)	-11.3	51	10.2	1.5	31.6	20.9
Maidenhead	75.6	-7.9	49.8	-11.8	18.1	+9.5	26.3	-3.6	3.2	2.6 (3)	–	61	5.5	1.6	36.9	25.5
Newbury†	76.7	-6.1	37.8	-18.1	5.5	-0.6	52.9	+15.8	1.8	2.0 (3)	–	12	1.5	1.5	29.8	20.4
Reading East†	70.2	-4.8	35.2	-13.9	42.7	+13.8	18.5	-1.9	2.1	1.5 (3)	-13.9	66	34.6	2.6	28.9	18.0
West†	70.1	-7.3	38.9	-13.4	45.1	+16.5	12.7	-5.1	2.0	1.2 (2)	-15.0	18	18.3	2.5	25.9	16.3
Slough	67.9	-9.1	29.2	-14.8	56.6	+12.5	7.4	+0.2	2.4	4.4 (2)	-13.7	7	36.9	4.0	20.3	13.8
Windsor	73.5	-5.8	48.2	-8.1	18.3	+5.9	28.7	-0.4	3.3	1.5 (3)	–	106	6.2	1.7	33.5	24.2
Wokingham	75.0	-5.0	50.1	-11.7	16.8	+5.5	31.4	+5.7	1.8	–	–	67	6.4	1.0	36.3	24.6

ENGLAND

Constituency	Employers/managers %	Good income %	Unemployed %	Population density	Index of change	% Voting	% Change in voting	% Con.	Con. change 1992–97	% Labour	Lab. change 1992–97	% Lib Dem	Lib Dem change 1992–97	% Referendum	% Other	Swing
Bucks, Aylesbury	17.6	29.3	2.1	4.8	4	72.8	−7.4	44.2	−13.1	22.2	+8.7	29.5	+1.8	3.8	0.3	—
Beaconsfield	26.1	37.3	1.3	4.9	3	70.8	−7.5	49.2	−14.5	20.0	+6.4	21.4	+1.9	4.4	5.0 (5)	—
Buckingham	24.2	32.9	1.3	0.9	5	78.5	−5.2	49.8	−12.5	24.7	+8.7	24.6	+3.8	–	0.9	—
Chesham & Amersham	25.5	38.6	1.1	5.0	4	73.7	−7.3	50.4	−13.0	19.6	+9.3	23.8	−0.7	4.8	1.3 (2)	—
Milton Keynes N.E.†	19.0	28.3	2.6	3.5	0	72.8	−10.4	39.0	−12.6	39.4	+15.7	17.4	−5.6	2.9	1.3 (2)	−14.2
South-West†	14.6	23.7	3.3	14.0	0	71.4	−6.3	33.5	−13.3	53.8	+16.3	11.9	−2.6		0.8	−14.7
Wycombe	19.5	28.7	2.4	6.7	3	71.1	−6.4	39.9	−13.1	35.4	+14.0	18.5	−4.5	4.6	1.6 (2)	—
Cambs, Cambridge	13.6	27.4	3.0	27.2	0	69.2	−4.0	25.9	−12.6	53.4	+13.8	16.1	−3.7	2.5	2.1 (4)	−13.2
Cambridgeshire N.E.	13.9	20.8	3.0	1.1	8	72.8	−7.0	43.0	−10.5	33.8	+20.2	16.4	−14.6	4.8	2.0 (2)	—
North-West	15.5	25.6	2.7	1.5	88	74.2	−4.4	48.1	−14.2	32.2	+6.3	15.1	+6.4	4.0	0.6	−10.3
South	18.9	33.7	1.4	1.5	49	76.1	−5.9	42.0	−16.5	25.1	+9.8	25.8	+1.0	6.1	0.9 (2)	—
South-East	17.9	28.0	1.7	1.2	23	74.8	−5.5	42.9	−14.5	26.5	+7.0	25.1	+3.9	5.0	0.5 (2)	—
Huntingdon	18.1	28.6	1.7	2.2	85	74.9	−4.8	55.3	−4.7	23.5	+9.0	14.7	−6.6	5.5	1.0 (3)	—
Peterborough†	12.2	21.3	5.0	24.7	43	72.8	−1.6	35.2	−14.3	50.3	+12.5	10.7	+1.4	1.9	1.9 (3)	−13.4
Cheshire, C. of Chester†	14.7	26.4	3.1	5.9	7	78.1	−5.5	34.2	−10.5	53.0	+12.4	9.5	−4.1	2.6	0.6 (2)	−11.4
Congleton	18.8	27.4	1.7	4.0	6	77.4	−6.9	41.2	−7.3	27.5	+8.4	29.7	−2.0		1.5	—
Crewe & Nantwich	12.1	21.3	3.1	6.1	21	73.5	−8.4	27.0	−11.9	58.2	+10.6	11.7	−0.8	3.0		−11.3
Eddisbury	19.4	27.5	2.3	1.2	47	75.6	−5.9	42.5	−10.2	40.1	+9.1	13.2	−1.6	4.1		−9.6
Ellesmere P. & Neston	12.8	24.4	3.1	7.7	6	77.6	−6.1	29.1	−13.0	59.6	+11.7	8.9	+0.0	2.5	1.8 (2)	−12.4
Halton	10.1	17.6	5.0	21.0	13	68.4	−8.6	17.7	−12.6	70.9	+11.3	7.3	−1.5	2.3		−11.9
Macclesfield	21.6	29.8	2.0	3.1	8	74.9	−6.6	49.6	−6.4	33.6	+10.8	16.7	−4.0			−8.6
Tatton†	24.0	33.8	1.8	2.4	28	76.5	−4.9	37.5	−24.7		—		—		62.5 (9)	—
Warrington North	13.9	23.2	3.1	10.7	9	70.5	−6.4	24.0	−10.9	62.1	+8.9	10.4	−1.0	3.5		−9.9
South†	16.5	27.0	2.5	10.0	30	76.2	−4.9	32.5	−13.2	52.1	+11.4	13.1	+0.1	2.0	0.3	12.3
Weaver Vale	14.2	23.6	4.0	5.7	121	73.0	−6.1	28.6	−7.2	56.4	+7.7	12.3	−2.2	2.7		−7.4
Cleveland, Hartlepool	8.9	17.1	6.4	9.6	0	65.6	−9.6	21.3	−13.5	60.7	+8.9	14.1	+0.8	3.9		−11.2

ENGLAND

Constituency	% Voting	% Change in voting	% Con.	Con. change 1992–97	% Labour	Lab. change 1992–97	% Lib Dem	Lib Dem change 1992–97	% Referendum	% Other	Swing	Index of change	Population density	Unemployed %	Good income %	Employers/ managers %
Middlesbrough	64.8	–9.2	17.2	–12.8	71.4	+10.3	8.5	–0.4	2.9	—	–11.5	24	34.9	8.2	17.6	8.0
S. & Cleveland E.†	75.9	–4.8	34.9	–10.9	54.7	+11.4	7.5	–3.5	2.9	—	–11.1	12	35.2	5.0	24.1	12.0
Redcar	70.9	–8.1	23.1	–10.9	67.3	+13.8	9.6	–2.9	—	—	–12.3	16	3.9	6.0	18.1	8.7
Stockton North	69.1	–6.7	18.8	–14.1	66.8	+12.8	10.8	–1.1	3.5	—	–13.5	5	9.0	6.6	17.6	8.6
South†	76.1	–3.3	33.0	–12.0	55.2	+19.7	9.1	–10.4	2.7	—	–15.8	23	8.0	4.8	25.8	14.0
Cornwall, North	72.9	–8.7	29.5	–14.8	9.4	+2.9	53.2	+5.8	6.2	1.7 (3)	—	0	0.8	4.6	20.3	14.0
South-East†	75.5	–5.6	35.8	–15.1	12.8	+3.6	47.1	+9.0	—	4.3 (4)	—	0	1.2	3.3	22.6	13.5
Falmouth & Camborne†	75.1	–5.4	23.8	–8.1	33.8	+4.7	25.2	–6.0	6.6	5.5 (5)	—	0	3.8	4.8	20.7	13.0
St. Ives†	75.0	–4.2	31.2	–11.8	15.3	–0.8	44.5	+4.4	6.9	2.3 (4)	—	0	1.5	5.1	19.7	13.3
Truro & St Austell	73.9	–7.7	26.4	–14.1	15.3	+5.5	48.5	–2.0	6.5	3.3 (5)	—	0	1.5	4.7	23.5	14.1
Cumbria, Barrow & F.	72.0	–8.5	27.2	–12.3	57.3	+9.5	8.8	–2.1	2.5	4.1	–11.8	0	5.0	4.5	15.1	9.0
Carlisle	72.7	–5.8	29.0	–14.1	57.4	+12.1	10.5	–2.5	2.8	0.3	–12.2	9	4.6	5.4	18.7	11.3
Copeland	73.6	–6.4	29.2	–11.1	58.1	+9.4	9.2	+1.6	2.5	0.9	–11.8	0	1.0	2.1	17.3	9.6
Penrith & Border	74.3	–5.9	47.6	–14.6	21.6	+10.6	26.7	–2.3	4.1	—	—	25	0.2	1.6	21.5	16.6
Westmorland & L.	75.1	–3.2	42.3	–12.0	20.6	+5.5	33.4	+5.9	3.8	—	—	6	0.5	4.7	22.1	16.5
Workington	76.0	–5.7	24.4	–12.0	64.2	+10.0	8.0	+0.6	2.9	0.4	–11.0	15	0.9	3.0	17.5	11.1
Derbyshire, Amber V.†	71.3	–7.7	35.5	–13.0	54.7	+10.3	7.7	–1.4	4.2	—	–11.7	2	3.0	4.1	18.3	13.2
Bolsover	70.9	–6.8	16.7	–8.5	74.0	+9.5	9.3	–0.9	—	—	–9.0	0	5.7	4.4	16.1	11.3
Chesterfield	73.5	–5.3	9.2	–7.7	50.8	+3.5	39.6	+3.8	0.4	0.3	—	0	26.6	4.2	19.6	11.6
Derby North†	67.6	–6.9	34.3	–14.2	53.2	+12.3	9.0	–0.5	3.2	0.6	–13.2	0	18.8	6.5	20.4	11.4
South	72.6	–8.0	25.2	–15.7	56.3	+8.0	14.4	+3.5	3.6	—	–11.8	0	29.6	3.5	20.3	11.1
Derbyshire N.E.	76.3	–10.5	25.2	–13.0	60.5	+11.6	14.3	+1.4	—	1.0 (4)	–12.3	12	3.8	2.6	24.6	15.9
South†	78.2	–6.6	31.3	–15.9	54.5	+10.5	9.0	+0.7	4.2	2.5	–13.2	0	2.8	1.9	21.4	14.2
West	77.8	–5.9	42.1	–12.1	33.5	+11.2	17.5	–6.0	4.4	0.8	—	10	1.0	3.3	24.3	17.9
Erewash†	78.1	–4.7	36.6	–10.6	51.7	+13.5	8.6	–5.0	2.3	—	–12.1	2	11.8	2.5	19.6	13.1
High Peak†	78.9	–5.2	35.5	–10.5	50.8	+12.9	11.2	–3.6	2.5	—	–11.7	0	1.5	2.9	22.9	15.9

ENGLAND	Employers/ managers %	Good income %	Unemployed %	Population density	Index of change	% Voting	% Change in voting	% Con.	Con. change 1992-97	% Labour	Lab. change 1992-97	% Lib Dem	Lib Dem change 1992-97	% Referendum	% Other	Swing
Devon, East	16.3	20.9	2.0	1.8	14	75.9	-4.9	43.4	-9.2	17.7	+5.5	29.1	+2.0	6.1	3.7 (3)	—
North	14.8	20.4	3.4	0.7	0	77.9	-5.1	39.5	-6.3	9.8	+3.9	50.7	+3.6	—	—	—
South-West	14.4	28.0	2.4	2.1	78	76.1	-5.3	43.0	-14.7	28.9	+13.0	23.7	-1.8	3.2	1.2 (2)	—
West & Torridge†	15.2	20.4	3.3	0.4	3	77.7	-3.5	38.5	-8.6	12.4	+2.9	41.8	+0.1	3.3	4.0 (2)	—
Exeter†	11.6	23.7	3.8	20.5	0	77.6	-4.0	28.6	-12.5	47.5	+11.3	18.0	-1.4	—	5.9 (4)	-11.9
Plymouth Devonport	7.5	18.7	5.2	29.9	15	69.7	-8.7	24.2	-11.4	60.9	+13.8	10.7	-2.5	2.9	1.4 (2)	-12.6
Sutton†	10.3	21.5	7.6	42.5	33	67.0	-12.1	30.3	-11.5	50.1	+10.4	13.9	-2.6	3.5	2.2 (3)	-10.9
Teignbridge	16.5	24.1	2.8	1.6	24	76.9	-5.4	39.2	-11.0	18.0	+5.0	38.8	+3.6	—	4.1 (3)	—
Tiverton & Honiton	16.8	23.1	2.0	0.8	30	77.9	-3.9	41.3	-9.9	12.8	+1.9	38.5	+6.8	5.0	2.3 (3)	—
Torbay†	14.8	21.7	5.2	24.5	0	73.8	-7.3	39.5	-10.3	14.9	+5.3	39.6	-0.2	—	6.0 (3)	—
Totnes	17.8	21.0	3.2	1.3	38	76.0	-7.1	36.5	-14.0	16.4	+4.3	34.9	-0.7	4.7	7.5 (4)	—
Dorset, Bournemouth E.	16.3	27.2	4.0	32.2	16	70.2	-2.5	41.4	-14.0	21.1	+8.3	31.4	+0.4	4.2	1.8	—
West	15.0	23.4	4.8	32.5	50	66.2	-7.7	41.7	-10.8	24.6	+5.1	27.8	+0.3	4.7	1.3 (3)	—
Christchurch‡	19.6	24.6	1.7	7.1	4	78.6	-2.2	46.4	-17.3	6.9	-5.2	42.6	+19.2	3.0	1.1	—
Dorset Mid & Poole N.	15.6	28.8	2.1	4.9	120	75.7	-1.3	40.7	-9.4	15.8	+3.9	39.3	+1.4	4.2	—	—
North	18.0	25.2	1.4	0.9	24	76.3	-5.1	44.3	-12.2	10.2	+4.2	39.1	+1.6	4.9	1.5	—
South	13.3	24.7	3.7	2.3	11	74.0	-2.6	36.1	-14.8	35.9	+15.1	20.2	-6.4	5.7	2.1 (2)	—
West	16.2	22.2	1.8	0.8	0	76.0	-5.2	41.1	-9.7	17.7	+4.8	37.7	+1.5	—	3.4 (2)	—
Poole	15.4	24.4	2.9	24.9	41	70.8	-7.5	42.1	-13.0	21.6	+9.9	30.8	+1.5	4.1	1.3 (2)	—
Durham, Bishop Auckland	11.1	15.8	3.8	0.9	47	68.9	-7.1	20.2	-12.6	66.0	+18.4	9.2	-10.4	4.6	—	-15.5
Darlington	11.3	21.0	5.2	31.6	0	74.0	-8.7	28.3	-14.7	61.6	+13.5	7.2	-1.1	2.9	—	-14.1
Durham North	10.6	18.3	4.1	8.1	9	69.4	-6.9	14.5	-10.3	70.3	+10.4	11.1	-4.2	4.2	—	-10.4
North-West	11.6	17.3	4.2	1.2	10	69.0	-5.9	15.3	-12.0	68.8	+10.7	10.8	-3.9	5.1	0.4	-11.4
Durham, City of	13.0	23.9	3.2	4.3	0	70.9	-3.4	17.5	-6.2	63.3	+10.0	15.3	-6.2	3.5	1.2	-8.1
Easington	7.7	13.5	3.7	8.8	0	67.0	-4.6	8.6	-8.1	80.2	+7.5	7.2	-3.4	2.8	1.0	-7.8
Sedgefield	11.8	18.3	3.1	2.2	56	72.6	-3.7	17.8	-10.3	71.2	+8.9	6.5	-3.2	3.6	1.0	-9.6

ENGLAND	% Voting	% Change in voting	% Con.	Con. change 1992-97	% Labour	Lab. change 1992-97	% Lib Dem	Lib Dem change 1992-97	% Referendum	% Other	Swing	Employers/ managers %	Good income %	Unemployed %	Population density	Index of change
East Sussex, Bexhill & B.	74.3	-4.3	48.1	-12.2	18.1	+8.7	25.5	-3.4	6.7	1.6	–	19.2	23.7	2.2	1.5	0
Brighton Kemptown†	70.8	-6.3	38.9	-13.9	46.6	+14.0	9.7	-4.2	3.3	1.5 (4)	-13.9	14.4	23.1	6.3	20.8	41
Pavilion†	73.7	-2.0	27.7	-17.6	54.6	+14.4	9.5	-2.9	2.7	5.5 (5)	-16.0	17.0	29.2	7.9	28.5	13
Eastbourne	72.8	-8.9	42.1	-10.9	12.5	+7.8	38.3	-2.9	5.2	1.9 (2)	–	15.0	22.3	3.1	12.3	10
Hastings & Rye†	69.7	-3.8	29.2	-18.4	34.4	+18.6	28.0	-7.3	5.1	3.4 (3)	–	15.0	22.0	5.3	7.0	0
Hove†	69.0	-3.3	36.4	-12.6	44.6	+20.1	9.7	-9.7	4.0	5.4 (3)	-16.4	17.4	26.2	5.4	36.0	0
Lewes†	76.4	-5.4	40.6	-10.8	10.6	+2.4	43.2	+4.1	5.0	0.5	–	19.5	26.2	2.3	2.0	32
Wealden	74.3	-7.0	49.8	-12.0	17.2	+8.0	25.7	-1.3	6.0	1.3 (2)	–	21.4	31.3	1.3	1.7	0
Essex, Basildon†	71.6	-7.8	30.8	-14.3	55.8	+15.1	8.7	-5.5	4.6	–	-14.7	11.7	20.1	4.3	9.6	68
Billericay	72.1	-8.6	39.8	-17.9	37.3	+17.3	15.8	-6.5	–	7.1	–	17.7	28.2	3.2	11.5	57
Braintree†	76.1	-7.9	40.1	-10.5	42.7	+15.3	11.5	-9.2	3.9	1.8 (2)	-12.9	16.6	24.4	2.7	2.8	22
Brentwood & Ongar	76.9	-6.8	45.4	-12.2	22.1	+11.2	26.3	-4.2	5.2	0.9 (2)	–	21.6	33.0	1.9	2.7	0
Castle Point†	72.3	-6.7	40.1	-15.5	42.4	+18.4	9.2	-9.9	5.6	2.7	-16.9	16.1	28.1	3.2	18.4	45
Chelmsford West	76.9	-8.1	40.6	-14.2	26.4	+11.2	29.2	+0.2	2.6	1.3	–	17.9	27.8	2.5	4.5	80
Colchester†	69.6	-7.3	31.4	-10.7	30.6	+6.5	34.4	+1.7	3.4	0.3	–	13.1	24.1	3.0	16.4	7
Epping Forest	72.8	-6.3	45.5	-14.3	35.6	+13.0	13.3	-3.4	4.2	1.4 (2)	-13.6	18.6	30.8	2.8	6.8	80
Essex North	75.3	-6.0	43.9	-13.8	33.2	+14.1	19.6	-2.6	–	3.3	–	18.7	28.8	1.8	1.7	6
Harlow†	74.4	-7.9	32.1	-13.9	54.1	+11.3	9.5	-1.8	3.0	1.4 (2)	-12.6	13.6	19.6	3.6	13.0	8
Harwich†	70.5	-5.7	36.5	-15.2	38.8	+14.1	13.1	-10.0	9.2	2.4 (2)	-14.6	14.1	20.2	3.9	7.0	80
Maldon & Chelms E.	76.0	-3.8	48.7	-15.2	28.7	+16.0	19.4	-2.7	–	3.2	–	20.0	30.6	2.5	2.0	18
Rayleigh	74.7	-5.9	49.7	-11.4	28.9	+14.1	19.8	-2.2	–	1.6 (2)	-11.2	19.0	30.7	2.2	5.2	19
Rochford & South'd E.	63.6	-12.3	44.7	-10.3	39.7	+12.2	9.4	-2.4	4.0	2.2	–	15.7	23.8	6.1	9.3	5
Saffron Walden	76.6	-7.1	45.3	-11.2	21.5	+7.2	26.8	-1.8	3.7	2.3 (3)	–	22.0	29.3	1.8	1.0	0
Southend West	69.8	-7.3	38.8	-15.9	22.8	+10.5	33.1	+2.3	–	1.6 (2)	–	17.3	25.6	4.3	44.3	0
Thurrock	65.8	-12.3	26.8	-16.9	63.3	+17.5	8.1	-1.4	2.1	1.8	-17.2	10.8	19.6	4.8	10.9	0
Glos, Cheltenham	74.0	-7.4	56.2	-7.9	10.1	+3.4	49.5	+1.8	–	2.0 (4)	–	15.2	24.7	3.7	24.9	15

ENGLAND	Employers/ managers %	Good income %	Unemployed %	Population density	Index of change	% Voting	% Change in voting	% Con.	Con. change 1992-97	% Labour	Lab. change 1992-97	% Lib Dem	Lib Dem change 1992-97	% Referendum	% Other	Swing
Cotswold	20.0	25.5	1.4	0.7	55	75.9	-6.5	46.4	-8.0	22.7	+11.8	23.0	-10.4	6.6	1.3 (2)	–
Forest of Dean	16.1	24.0	2.6	1.3	22	79.1	-4.0	35.6	-5.5	48.2	+5.8	12.3	-3.8	3.2	0.7 (2)	-5.6
Gloucester†	13.0	22.7	4.1	24.9	6	73.6	-7.6	35.7	-9.8	50.0	+13.2	10.5	-7.2	2.6	1.3 (2)	-11.5
Stroud†	17.5	25.5	2.2	2.2	19	78.8	-4.6	37.9	-8.3	42.7	+13.3	15.5	-6.1	–	3.9 (2)	-10.8
Tewkesbury	16.9	27.1	2.0	2.2	92	76.5	-5.5	45.8	-8.1	26.2	+16.1	28.0	-7.1	–	–	–
Greater London																
Barking & D., Barking	10.0	14.0	5.4	42.7	10	61.4	-7.7	17.6	-16.3	65.8	+13.6	9.5	-4.4	3.9	3.2 (2)	-14.9
Dagenham	9.5	14.9	4.2	42.9	2	61.7	-8.0	18.5	-18.3	65.7	+14.0	7.5	-4.0	3.9	4.4 (4)	-16.2
Barnet, Chipping B.	23.0	35.2	2.8	26.5	19	70.9	-6.4	43.0	-13.6	40.9	+14.7	12.3	-3.7	2.4	1.3 (3)	-14.1
Finchley & Golders Gn†	23.7	35.8	4.0	46.2	73	68.2	-5.4	39.7	-15.0	46.1	+15.2	11.3	-1.5	1.4	1.6 (2)	-15.1
Hendon†	19.3	31.9	4.3	30.9	40	64.6	-9.7	37.0	-16.6	49.3	+15.8	10.8	-0.8	2.0	0.8 (2)	-16.2
Bexley, Bexleyheath & C.†	16.1	26.6	3.2	36.8	74	76.1	-5.0	38.4	-15.8	45.5	+14.2	11.2	-3.2	3.2	1.7 (2)	-15.0
Erith & Thamesmead	11.6	18.4	7.5	33.9	94	66.0	-8.2	20.2	-11.4	62.1	+19.1	12.0	-13.4	3.4	2.4 (2)	-15.3
Old Bexley & Sidcup	18.0	28.5	2.7	33.4	38	75.5	-5.3	42.0	-14.2	35.1	+14.0	16.1	-4.8	4.8	2.0 (3)	-14.1
Brent, East	14.1	25.3	10.1	68.8	0	65.9	+1.5	22.3	-14.3	67.3	+14.5	7.8	-1.1	–	2.6 (4)	-14.4
North†	18.8	31.4	4.6	43.7	16	70.5	+2.5	40.1	-17.3	50.7	+20.4	8.1	-2.5	1.4	1.1 (2)	-18.8
South	10.6	19.4	10.8	53.4	16	64.5	+1.1	15.9	-15.2	73.0	+15.4	7.7	-1.7	3.1	1.9 (3)	-15.3
Bromley, Beckenham	22.0	32.5	3.9	34.5	24	74.0	-3.5	42.5	-17.7	33.4	+12.2	18.1	+1.4	–	3.0 (3)	-15.0
Bromley & C'hurst	22.8	33.9	2.7	23.1	81	73.6	-5.4	46.3	-15.6	25.2	+8.0	23.8	+5.9	–	4.7 (4)	–
Orpington	20.0	31.8	2.5	12.3	41	76.4	-4.7	40.6	-14.7	17.9	+3.1	35.7	+7.4	3.8	2.0 (3)	–
Camden, Hampstead & H.	21.9	32.3	6.4	72.5	7	64.7	-7.7	27.2	-13.5	57.4	+11.2	12.4	+1.4	1.5	1.4 (5)	-12.4
Holborn & St. Pancras	14.3	23.0	8.5	87.4	6	57.2	-4.6	17.9	-10.3	65.0	+10.8	12.5	-1.4	2.1	2.5 (6)	-10.5
Croydon, Central†	17.6	26.4	4.9	38.7	87	69.6	-5.2	38.6	-16.9	45.6	+14.1	10.9	-2.1	3.4	1.6 (2)	-15.5
North†	14.0	23.5	7.0	63.1	45	68.2	-4.1	27.2	-17.5	62.2	+17.8	7.7	-3.2	2.2	0.8 (3)	-17.6
South	23.4	37.9	2.4	23.6	16	73.5	-4.5	47.3	-14.3	25.3	+9.0	21.1	-0.5	4.9	1.4 (3)	–
Ealing, Acton & S.B.	19.0	27.3	7.5	56.2	74	64.0	-8.7	25.8	-13.6	58.4	+12.0	10.7	-1.3	1.3	3.8 (6)	-12.8

ENGLAND

Constituency	Employers/managers %	Good income %	Unemployed %	Population density	Index of change	% Voting	% Change in voting	% Con.	Con. change 1992–97	% Labour	Lab. change 1992–97	% Lib Dem	Lib Dem change 1992–97	% Referendum	% Other	Swing
North†	15.4	25.6	4.3	44.8	16	72.5	-4.2	39.4	-12.0	51.8	+16.0	6.7	-4.0	–	2.1 (2)	-14.0
Southall	15.5	24.6	4.8	57.6	13	65.7	-8.5	20.8	-15.5	60.0	+14.7	10.4	+2.3	1.6	7.2 (4)	-15.1
Enfield, Edmonton†	12.9	20.4	6.3	51.5	0	70.4	-4.3	30.2	-16.0	60.3	+15.2	6.3	-1.9	1.6	1.6 (2)	-15.6
North†	14.3	21.3	4.7	24.1	0	70.4	-6.1	36.3	-16.6	50.7	+15.7	8.9	-2.1	1.8	2.3 (2)	-16.1
Southgate†	22.9	33.4	4.0	30.5	0	70.7	-4.5	41.1	-16.8	44.2	+18.0	10.7	-3.8	2.9	1.1 (2)	-17.4
Greenwich, Eltham†	13.4	23.1	5.1	39.7	25	75.2	-1.3	31.2	-12.8	54.6	+14.5	8.5	-7.0	3.3	2.5 (2)	-13.6
Erith & T. (See Bexley)																
Greenwich & Woolwich	13.9	20.4	8.3	42.4	37	64.9	-6.2	18.6	+0.3	63.4	+18.8	12.5	-22.6	4.1	1.4 (2)	–
Hackney																
N. & Stoke Newington	11.8	19.7	12.6	108.7	0	51.2	-2.2	16.9	-10.0	65.3	+7.4	10.2	-1.3	1.7	5.9 (3)	-8.7
South & Shoreditch	9.3	15.5	13.3	81.9	0	54.0	-0.7	13.3	-15.7	59.4	+6.0	15.0	+0.0	1.8	10.5 (5)	–
Hammersmith																
Ealing Acton & S.B., (See Ealing)																
Hammersmith & Fulham†	21.2	31.0	7.1	100.1	38	68.7	-7.2	39.6	-12.0	46.8	+8.1	8.8	+0.5	1.9	2.9 (5)	-10.1
Haringey																
Hornsey & Wood Green	19.1	32.1	7.6	62.0	0	66.9	-8.2	21.9	-17.2	61.7	+13.3	11.3	+1.3	1.6	3.5 (2)	-15.3
Tottenham	9.3	20.3	12.7	72.5	0	55.0	-8.8	15.7	-14.1	69.3	+12.8	10.8	-0.6	–	4.2 (4)	-13.4
Harrow, East†	18.3	30.4	3.5	38.6	2	70.7	-6.7	35.4	-17.5	52.5	+18.7	8.2	-2.6	2.7	1.1 (2)	-18.1
West†	20.5	32.8	2.8	41.0	0	72.2	-5.2	39.2	-16.0	41.5	+19.0	15.5	-4.7	3.8		-17.5
Havering, Hornchurch†	14.2	24.8	2.7	20.9	0	72.2	-6.3	37.3	-16.2	50.2	+15.7	7.8	-3.3	3.6	1.0 (2)	-16.0
Romford†	14.9	26.6	2.6	27.5	11	70.5	-7.1	41.6	-16.5	43.2	+14.8	7.9	-4.5	3.4	3.9 (2)	-15.6
Upminster†	16.5	26.3	2.9	13.6	9	72.1	-7.1	39.5	-14.7	46.2	+16.1	9.5	-6.3	4.8		-15.4
Hillingdon, Hayes & H.†	12.8	22.3	3.9	21.0	0	72.3	-1.8	27.2	-17.7	62.0	+17.2	7.4	-2.9	1.9	1.6 (2)	-17.4
Ruislip-Northwood	20.4	31.1	2.0	17.2	9	74.2	-3.8	50.2	-12.6	32.9	+13.0	16.2	-0.4	–	0.7	-12.8
Uxbridge	16.4	27.4	2.8	27.6	8	72.3	-3.6	43.6	-12.8	41.8	+12.8	10.9	-1.6	2.8	1.0	-12.8
Hounslow, Brentford & I'worth†	18.8	28.0	4.3	36.6	15	69.5	-4.7	31.8	-13.9	57.4	+14.7	8.2	-1.9	–	2.6 (3)	-14.3

Employers/ managers %	Good income %	Unemployed %	Population density	Index of change	ENGLAND	% Voting	% Change in voting	% Con.	Con. change 1992–97	% Labour	Lab. change 1992–97	% Lib Dem	Lib Dem change 1992–97	% Referendum	% Other	Swing
13.3	21.2	4.4	32.1	11	Feltham & Heston	64.9	−8.0	26.9	−15.9	59.7	+14.2	9.1	−2.4	2.4	1.8 (2)	−15.1
14.2	23.4	11.5	118.8	0	Islington, North	61.4	−6.6	12.9	−10.8	69.3	+11.8	13.6	−1.5	–	4.2	–
12.9	20.1	9.3	103.8	1	South & Finsbury	60.1	−13.0	13.0	−11.7	62.5	+11.3	21.3	−1.9	2.1	1.1 (3)	–
28.7	35.6	4.2	109.7	50	Kensington & Chelsea	49.6	−16.8	53.6	−14.6	28.0	+11.3	15.3	+2.1	–	3.1 (6)	−12.9
					Regent's P. & Ken. N., (See Westminster)											
					Kingston-upon-Thames											
19.7	30.6	2.8	35.6	65	Kingston & Surbiton†	74.4	−5.3	36.6	−16.5	23.0	+3.4	36.7	+10.7	2.6	1.1 (3)	–
					Richmond Park, (See Richmond)											
					Lambeth, Dulwich & W. N., (See Southwark)											
17.1	26.3	9.2	87.0	27	Streatham	59.0	−11.1	21.7	−16.7	62.8	+13.4	13.6	+3.6	1.9	–	−15.0
12.8	20.3	11.1	100.2	12	Vauxhall	53.5	−10.2	15.2	−11.4	63.8	+7.7	16.0	+1.6	–	5.0 (3)	–
10.7	21.6	10.3	73.0	1	Lewisham, Deptford	57.9	−7.5	14.7	−12.9	70.8	+10.2	8.9	−2.8	2.6	3.0	−11.6
15.1	21.0	6.3	60.8	0	East	66.4	−7.8	25.9	−16.9	58.3	+13.0	11.2	−0.2	2.4	2.2 (3)	−14.9
14.2	22.9	7.8	67.9	0	West	64.0	−8.1	23.8	−19.0	62.0	+15.0	9.8	−0.1	2.9	1.5 (2)	−17.0
13.1	20.6	5.2	49.8	0	Merton, Mitcham & Morden†	72.4	−10.7	29.7	−16.8	58.4	+15.3	7.6	−1.6	1.7	2.7 (5)	−16.0
22.5	34.7	2.9	40.3	0	Wimbledon†	73.3	−8.6	36.6	−16.4	42.8	+19.5	16.6	−4.7	2.1	2.0 (4)	−17.9
9.2	17.6	8.1	53.6	19	Newham, East Ham	60.3	−1.3	16.1	−15.9	64.6	+10.7	6.5	−7.5	2.1	10.6 (3)	−13.3
					Poplar & Canning T., (See Tower H.)											
10.1	17.6	10.4	73.4	38	West Ham	58.4	+0.1	15.0	−15.0	72.9	+14.9	7.4	−2.2	–	4.8 (3)	−15.0
					Redbridge, Ching'f'd & W. G., (See Waltham F.)											
18.1	25.3	3.4	44.0	75	Ilford North†	71.6	−2.4	40.8	−17.1	47.4	+17.5	10.3	−1.9	–	1.5	−17.3
15.1	24.3	5.7	56.4	39	South†	69.4	−7.2	30.1	−16.8	58.5	+16.4	6.3	−4.1	2.1	2.9 (2)	−16.6
					Leyton & Wansted,(See Waltham Forest)											
25.0	36.9	2.7	26.7	57	Richmond, Richmond Park†	77.3	−8.2	39.5	−12.4	12.6	+3.8	44.7	+7.0	2.6	0.7 (3)	–
25.4	34.0	2.5	34.0	14	Twickenham†	78.1	−5.2	37.8	−11.8	15.6	+5.2	45.1	+5.8	–	1.5 (3)	–

ENGLAND

Constituency	Employers/managers %	Good income %	Unemployed %	Population density	Index of change	% Voting	% Change in voting	% Con.	Con. change 1992–97	% Labour	Lab. change 1992–97	% Lib Dem	Lib Dem change 1992–97	% Referendum	% Other	Swing
Southwark																
Camberwell & Peckham	8.4	15.7	11.7	103.7	34	55.6	+4.3	11.6	-12.2	69.5	+9.2	11.3	-3.8	2.4	5.2 (4)	-10.7
Dulwich & West Norwood	16.5	27.9	7.9	59.8	73	64.5	-3.2	24.2	-18.6	61.0	+14.6	10.8	+1.0	2.0	2.1 (4)	-16.6
Southwark N. & Bermondsey	11.0	14.6	9.2	71.9	15	60.9	-1.5	6.9	-5.0	40.3	+5.8	48.6	-2.8	1.3	2.8 (4)	–
Sutton, Carshalton & W.†	16.3	27.3	3.4	34.4	0	73.3	-7.5	33.5	-16.2	23.9	+6.2	38.2	+7.3	2.7	1.8 (3)	–
Sutton & Cheam†	20.2	31.2	2.4	45.7	0	75.1	-7.2	37.8	-17.3	15.5	+5.5	42.3	+8.5	3.8	0.6 (2)	–
Tower Hamlets,																
Bethnal Gn & Bow	9.7	14.8	9.5	92.6	25	61.2	-6.9	21.1	+4.7	46.3	-7.2	12.0	-13.8	1.2	19.4 (5)	–
Poplar & Canning Town	8.7	13.6	9.5	46.6	66	58.5	-7.2	15.0	-10.7	63.2	+11.9	10.4	-9.2	2.8	8.7 (2)	-11.3
Waltham Forest																
Chingford & Woodford Green	17.8	28.1	3.3	38.6	42	70.7	-7.8	47.5	-13.9	34.6	+13.7	15.5	+1.2	–	2.4	-13.8
Leyton & Wanstead	14.4	24.4	7.4	58.7	40	63.2	-5.7	22.2	-8.7	60.8	+15.0	15.1	-5.4	–	1.9 (2)	-11.8
Walthamstow	12.4	19.6	7.3	55.8	33	62.8	-8.6	20.3	-16.9	63.1	+18.8	13.7	-2.1	2.8	–	-17.9
Wandsworth, Battersea†	19.4	29.3	6.0	78.4	0	69.0	-8.8	39.4	-11.0	50.7	+9.5	7.3	+0.3	1.7	0.8 (2)	-10.2
Putney†	20.7	29.7	4.3	56.0	0	71.4	-6.6	38.9	-13.3	45.7	+9.0	10.8	+1.2	3.5	1.2 (6)	-11.2
Tooting	16.8	28.7	6.4	82.3	0	67.9	-8.2	27.1	-13.0	59.7	+11.5	9.4	+2.0	1.8	2.0 (5)	-12.3
Westminster																
Cities of Lon. & W.	21.7	28.5	5.2	56.3	19	58.2	-7.4	47.3	-12.0	35.1	+11.0	12.3	-1.8	2.9	2.4 (6)	-11.5
Regent's P. & Kensington N.	17.5	25.7	8.3	115.9	54	64.2	-10.7	29.0	-12.1	59.9	+11.6	8.5	+0.6	1.8	0.8 (2)	-11.8
Greater Manchester																
Altrincham & Sale W.	20.6	33.5	2.3	17.4	52	73.3	-5.1	43.2	-11.3	40.3	+13.8	12.6	-5.8	2.6	1.4 (3)	-12.6
Ashton-under-Lyne	10.3	16.2	4.0	32.0	52	65.4	-7.9	18.9	-9.8	67.5	+10.5	9.7	-2.2	2.8	1.0	-10.2
Bolton North-East	14.0	20.8	3.8	25.0	16	72.4	-7.6	30.4	-11.7	56.1	+8.7	9.9	-0.2	2.2	1.4	-10.2
South-East	9.4	15.3	3.8	27.6	0	65.2	-9.1	19.7	-9.0	68.9	+14.6	8.8	-1.8	2.2	0.4	-11.8
West†	18.8	26.5	2.1	11.3	13	77.4	-5.1	35.1	-12.2	49.5	+10.4	10.8	-2.4	1.8	2.8	-11.3
Bury North†	15.6	24.1	2.2	16.4	0	78.1	-5.8	37.5	-12.1	51.8	+10.2	8.2	-0.3	2.4	–	-11.2

ENGLAND

Constituency	Employers/ managers %	Good income %	Unemployed %	Population density	Index of change	% Voting	% Change in voting	% Con.	Con. change 1992-97	% Labour	Lab. change 1992-97	% Lib Dem	Lib Dem change 1992-97	% Referendum	% Other	Swing
South†	15.5	25.2	2.7	19.8	0	75.6	−6.0	32.2	−13.7	56.9	+12.3	8.4	−0.6	2.4	—	−13.0
Cheadle	22.7	39.2	1.5	23.5	2	77.3	−5.4	43.7	−13.9	15.7	+3.3	37.7	+8.1	2.9	—	—
Denton & Reddish	11.6	18.0	3.4	34.2	24	66.8	−8.3	21.3	−12.5	65.4	+12.4	13.3	+3.3	—	—	−12.5
Eccles	10.9	19.0	3.4	19.4	34	65.6	−8.8	18.7	−12.4	66.7	+9.1	10.7	+1.1	3.9	0.9 (2)	−10.7
Hazel Grove†	17.8	28.3	2.0	14.2	0	77.3	−6.3	30.5	−14.3	11.9	+0.2	54.5	+11.4	2.1	1.5	—
Heywood & Middleton	13.0	21.3	4.2	14.0	29	68.3	−6.2	23.0	−8.6	57.7	+11.2	15.6	−4.3	2.1	—	−9.9
Leigh	11.6	17.6	3.5	16.2	30	65.7	−9.3	15.6	−11.7	68.9	+9.6	11.2	−1.2	4.2	—	−10.7
Makerfield	11.1	19.9	3.7	15.5	26	66.8	−8.7	15.4	−9.0	73.6	+10.2	8.3	−0.9	2.7	—	−9.6
Manchester Blackley	8.8	17.0	6.1	34.7	17	57.3	−9.1	15.3	−10.8	70.0	+7.9	11.0	+0.0	3.7	2.7 (2)	−9.3
Central	8.3	17.2	10.1	32.6	49	52.0	−6.8	11.8	−7.6	71.0	+1.8	12.3	+1.8	2.2	3.3 (2)	—
Gorton	8.1	19.1	7.7	48.8	0	55.8	−4.7	11.7	−7.8	65.3	+2.9	17.5	+3.5	2.2	3.0 (4)	—
Withington	13.3	27.0	6.3	41.4	0	66.0	−4.9	19.4	−11.9	61.6	+8.9	13.6	−0.6	2.5	1.1 (2)	−10.4
Oldham E. & Saddlew'th†‡	14.4	20.5	3.2	8.1	59	73.9	−3.4	19.7	−15.7	41.7	+11.5	35.4	+1.0	2.1	3.4 (2)	—
West & Royton	11.1	16.4	4.1	31.8	88	66.1	−8.9	23.4	−14.7	58.8	+9.7	11.9	+0.4	2.5	1.8 (2)	−12.2
Rochdale†	12.5	17.5	4.7	13.5	46	70.0	−7.2	8.8	−14.4	49.4	+11.7	40.0	+2.0	—	—	—
Salford	9.5	18.5	5.5	38.0	15	56.3	−8.9	17.4	−9.0	69.0	+9.9	10.3	−2.3	2.8	0.5	−9.5
Stalybridge & Hyde	13.5	18.2	3.6	14.2	24	65.7	−7.5	24.5	−11.4	58.9	+7.3	12.0	+3.0	4.6	—	−9.3
Stockport	15.0	23.3	3.6	38.4	13	71.3	−8.8	22.3	−15.5	62.9	+14.8	10.6	−2.2	2.7	1.4 (3)	−15.2
Stretford & Urmston	11.4	22.4	4.0	20.9	98	69.7	−5.2	30.5	−10.3	58.5	+9.5	8.2	−1.1	2.9	—	−9.9
Wigan	12.1	20.1	4.5	15.8	10	67.7	−7.8	16.9	−8.4	68.6	+7.9	10.0	−1.7	3.3	1.2 (2)	−8.2
Worsley	14.1	21.9	3.1	15.2	34	67.8	−8.2	24.2	−7.9	62.2	+8.4	13.6	+0.9	—	—	−8.1
Wythenshawe & Sale E.	11.9	18.8	5.1	26.7	47	63.2	−8.6	25.1	−9.8	58.1	+8.6	12.4	−2.1	2.3	2.1 (3)	−9.2
Hampshire, Aldershot	15.9	28.4	1.7	16.7	8	71.1	−7.2	42.7	−15.4	24.1	+10.3	30.5	+4.1	—	2.7 (3)	—
Basingstoke	16.6	27.7	2.0	1.6	9	73.8	−9.9	43.3	−10.2	39.1	+14.0	17.0	−3.4	—	0.5	−12.1
Eastleigh†	16.0	26.5	1.8	11.8	26	76.6	−6.7	33.7	−17.2	26.8	+7.4	35.1	+5.4	3.6	0.8	—
Fareham	17.6	28.7	1.8	13.3	19	75.9	−5.5	46.8	−13.8	27.0	+12.1	19.6	−3.6	5.6	1.0	—

ENGLAND	Employers/ managers %	Good income %	Unemployed %	Population density	Index of change	% Voting	% Change in Voting	% Con.	Con. change 1992-97	% Labour	Lab. change 1992-97	% Lib Dem	Lib Dem change 1992-97	% Referendum	% Other	Swing
Gosport	11.5	23.2	2.7	24.4	0	70.3	-6.3	43.6	-14.5	30.7	+17.1	19.6	-8.0	5.2	0.9	–
Hampshire East	18.7	30.9	2.0	2.8	109	75.8	-4.6	48.0	-12.6	17.1	+7.7	28.1	+0.6	4.7	2.0 (2)	–
North-East	22.2	35.2	1.3	2.5	42	73.6	-6.5	50.9	-13.1	16.0	+5.9	22.7	-2.4	4.7	5.6 (2)	–
North-West	18.0	28.6	1.2	4.1	25	74.4	-6.1	45.2	-12.8	23.6	+11.0	24.1	-3.9	2.8	4.3 (4)	–
Havant	14.6	22.7	3.5	19.1	49	70.4	-6.8	39.7	-13.1	32.0	+12.3	22.4	-3.7	5.0	0.9	–
New Forest East	15.7	28.6	2.0	2.1	51	74.4	-7.5	42.9	-10.1	24.8	+12.1	32.3	-1.1	–	–	–
West	20.7	25.7	1.9	2.1	15	74.5	-5.3	50.6	-10.2	14.3	+6.1	27.8	-2.8	4.3	3.1	-13.5
Portsmouth North†	11.8	19.5	3.9	33.3	18	70.1	-6.2	37.6	-13.1	47.1	+13.9	10.6	-4.5	3.9	0.8 (2)	–
South†	11.6	19.0	5.3	60.9	104	63.8	-5.6	31.1	-11.4	25.3	+10.7	39.5	-2.5	3.2	0.9 (3)	–
Romsey	20.4	33.5	1.7	2.0		76.4	-6.2	46.0	-17.2	18.6	+5.7	29.4	+6.3	2.5	3.5	–
Southampton Itchen	11.4	19.8	4.5	31.6	28	69.7	-7.8	28.4	-13.8	54.3	+10.8	11.7	-2.2	3.1	2.1 (5)	-12.3
Test	10.6	22.3	5.0	41.2	28	71.2	-3.9	28.1	-12.4	54.1	+8.7	13.7	+0.6	2.7	1.5 (4)	-10.5
Winchester†	20.2	31.7	1.5	1.5	44	78.3	-5.7	42.0	-9.7	10.5	+3.0	42.1	+5.2	2.6	2.8 (4)	–
Hereford & Worcester																
Bromsgrove	19.5	29.3	2.5	4.2	0	77.1	-5.6	47.2	-6.9	37.8	+7.1	11.9	-1.9	2.7	0.5	-7.0
Hereford†	14.1	21.2	3.3	1.0	1	75.2	-5.5	35.3	-11.7	12.6	+2.0	47.9	+6.6	4.2	–	–
Leominster	18.0	22.7	2.3	0.6	19	76.6	-4.4	45.3	-11.1	17.5	+5.2	27.8	+0.7	5.6	3.9 (3)	–
Redditch†	16.7	22.3	3.7	9.9	35	73.5	-7.3	36.1	-11.0	49.8	+9.4	11.0	-0.7	2.6	0.5	-10.2
Worcester†	14.7	24.1	3.1	24.6	15	74.6	-8.3	35.7	-9.8	50.1	+10.2	12.5	-0.6	–	1.7	-10.0
Worcestershire Mid	19.3	26.4	1.9	1.6	107	74.3	-4.5	47.4	-7.5	28.9	+11.3	18.6	-7.5	3.5	1.6 (2)	–
West	19.1	28.6	1.9	1.4	49	76.3	-3.7	45.0	-9.7	15.7	+1.9	37.2	+8.0	–	2.0	–
Wyre Forest†	16.3	23.2	2.7	6.1	2	75.4	-6.8	36.1	-1.3	48.8	+17.5	8.0	-13.3	3.6	3.6 (2)	–
Herts, Broxbourne	17.5	27.4	2.9	16.7	8	70.4	-8.6	48.9	-13.4	34.7	+13.3	11.3	-4.7	3.5	1.7 (2)	-14.4
Hemel Hempstead†	17.9	26.3	2.1	8.5	19	76.7	-5.3	39.1	-10.8	45.7	+13.2	12.3	-3.0	2.4	0.5	-13.4
Hertford & Stortford	21.3	31.1	1.7	5.2	26	75.6	-4.6	44.0	-12.5	31.4	+14.6	17.7	-7.7	3.9	3.0 (3)	-12.0
Hertfordshire N.E.	18.9	28.1	1.9	1.8	62	77.4	-7.5	41.8	-9.9	35.8	+14.5	18.3	-8.2	4.2	–	–

Employers/ managers %	Good income %	Unemployed %	Population density	Index of change	ENGLAND	% Voting	% Change in voting	% Con.	Con. change 1992–97	% Labour	Lab. change 1992–97	% Lib Dem	Lib Dem change 1992–97	% Referendum	% Other	Swing
24.4	35.7	1.6	5.6	38	South-West	76.8	–7.4	46.0	–13.3	27.9	+10.4	22.3	–0.2	3.3	0.5	–
21.3	32.1	2.0	9.1	8	Hertsmere	73.4	–6.2	44.3	–13.5	38.2	+16.4	12.8	–6.9	3.4	1.3 (2)	–15.0
22.8	33.6	1.8	3.5	101	Hitchin & Harpenden	78.0	–3.3	45.9	–15.6	33.1	+15.3	20.1	+0.3	–	1.0 (2)	–
20.5	33.5	1.7	12.9	61	St. Albans†	77.5	–2.3	33.2	–12.4	42.0	+17.0	21.0	–6.9	3.2	0.5 (2)	–13.9
16.7	23.5	3.4	10.0	5	Stevenage†	76.8	–5.0	32.8	–11.1	55.3	+16.8	8.9	–8.2	2.3	0.6 (2)	–13.9
17.3	27.3	2.6	25.7	24	Watford†	74.6	–6.5	34.8	–13.3	45.3	+11.8	16.8	+0.0	2.7	0.4	–12.3
18.1	26.1	1.9	6.9	6	Welwyn Hatfield†	78.6	–4.7	36.5	–11.0	47.1	+11.1	13.5	–2.5	–	2.9 (2)	–11.0
					Humberside											
16.9	26.4	2.9	1.1	89	Beverley & H'ness	72.9	–6.2	41.2	–13.3	38.9	+18.8	18.4	–6.9	1.5	– (2)	–
13.2	22.0	3.7	1.2	86	Brigg & Goole†	73.5	–7.7	36.5	–13.3	50.2	+14.5	10.0	–4.5	3.2	–	–13.9
14.2	21.9	4.5	2.7	17	Cleethorpes†	73.4	–4.6	33.4	–14.5	51.6	+15.7	11.4	–3.3	3.5	–	–15.1
10.0	17.6	7.0	32.4	0	Great Grimsby	66.1	–8.1	22.1	–14.1	59.8	+8.8	18.1	+5.4	–		–11.5
19.2	30.0	2.0	1.7	68	Haltemprice & Howd.	75.4	–3.8	44.0	–15.3	23.6	+8.3	28.8	+3.7	2.8	0.8 (2)	–
7.7	15.0	5.7	34.3	0	Hull East	58.9	–9.8	13.7	–10.1	71.3	+8.4	9.8	–2.9	4.4	0.8 (2)	–9.2
9.2	17.4	6.9	35.1	0	North	57.0	–8.7	15.0	–8.6	65.8	+9.9	14.6	–5.4	4.0	0.6	–9.2
9.9	16.3	6.3	35.0	19	West & Hessle	58.2	–9.0	18.1	–12.2	58.7	+7.1	18.2	+0.8	4.2	0.8	–
9.6	16.5	4.3	5.4	26	Scunthorpe	68.8	–9.2	26.3	–9.6	60.4	+6.1	8.4	+0.7	3.9	1.0	–7.9
15.9	22.3	3.6	0.8	70	Yorkshire East	70.5	–5.3	42.7	–7.9	35.9	+9.4	18.5	–4.3	–	2.9 (2)	–8.7
14.4	22.3	4.9	3.3	0	Isle of Wight†	71.7	–6.5	34.0	–13.9	13.2	+7.2	42.7	–2.9	6.5	3.6 (5)	–
					Kent,											
16.7	24.9	3.2	1.6	0	Ashford	74.2	–4.5	41.4	–13.2	31.7	+11.7	19.7	–4.3	5.8	1.4	–
16.1	25.8	3.3	3.3	4	Canterbury	72.6	–4.6	38.6	–11.8	31.3	+15.9	23.8	–8.8	4.5	1.7 (3)	–15.1
14.6	23.6	3.5	59.2	74	Chatham & Aylesford†	70.8	–7.6	37.4	–13.8	43.1	+16.4	15.0	–6.2	3.1	1.3 (2)	–11.5
15.5	25.1	3.4	9.0	7	Dartford†	74.6	–8.3	40.3	–10.6	48.6	+12.4	9.3	–2.9	–	1.8 (3)	–11.6
14.1	23.7	4.9	4.2	0	Dover†	78.6	–4.2	32.8	–11.3	54.5	+11.9	7.9	–2.9	3.9	–	–13.9
19.0	27.3	2.8	2.2	124	Faversham & Kent Mid	73.3	–8.4	44.4	–14.8	36.0	+13.0	12.4	–4.7	4.2	3.1 (5)	–
16.3	24.0	5.1	2.6	0	Folkestone & Hythe	72.7	–8.7	39.0	–13.3	24.9	+12.8	26.9	–8.5	8.0	1.2 (3)	–

ENGLAND

	Employers/ managers %	Good income %	Unemployed %	Population density	Index of change	% Voting	% Change in Voting	% Con.	Con. change 1992–97	% Labour	Lab. change 1992–97	% Lib Dem	Lib Dem change 1992–97	% Referendum	% Other	Swing
Gillingham†	14.5	24.9	3.5	29.6	2	72.0	−7.1	35.9	−16.0	39.8	+15.0	19.0	−4.4	2.9	2.3 (4)	−16.0
Gravesham†	14.9	23.6	4.4	9.4	0	76.7	−6.3	38.8	−10.8	49.7	+9.3	7.8	−1.1	2.7	1.0 (2)	−10.0
Maidstone & The Weald	19.3	27.4	2.5	3.2	62	73.7	−6.5	44.1	−11.9	26.2	+13.8	22.4	−7.9	3.7	3.6 (4)	–
Medway†	13.3	22.2	4.5	5.7	0	72.2	−7.7	36.9	−15.5	48.9	+14.3	10.2	+0.6	3.2	0.9	−14.9
Sevenoaks	21.0	34.2	2.0	3.6	22	75.4	−4.8	45.4	−12.2	24.6	+8.4	24.1	−0.5	4.3	1.7 (3)	–
Sittingbourne & Shep.†	13.2	20.9	4.7	4.3	26	72.3	−5.3	36.4	−12.4	40.6	+16.6	18.3	−8.5	2.3	2.4 (2)	–
Thanet North	13.9	21.4	5.1	10.2	0	68.8	−6.4	44.1	−13.1	38.4	+15.0	11.4	−6.3	5.2	0.9	−14.0
South†	13.3	20.8	4.9	5.5	0	71.6	−5.3	39.8	−12.0	46.2	+18.0	11.7	−6.6	–	2.3 (2)	−15.0
Tonbridge & Malling	22.3	29.8	2.0	2.4	45	75.6	−5.1	48.0	−12.8	27.2	+10.2	19.2	−1.5	4.1	1.4 (2)	–
Tunbridge Wells	20.2	31.6	2.2	4.2	14	74.1	−3.5	45.2	−9.8	20.4	+5.7	29.7	+0.2	3.8	0.9 (2)	–
Lancashire, Blackburn	10.4	16.4	4.3	19.9	0	65.0	−9.8	24.6	−12.9	55.0	+6.6	10.5	−1.0	4.0	5.9 (5)	−9.7
Blackpool N. & Fleetw'd†	13.1	22.0	3.9	32.7	98	71.6	−8.6	35.5	−14.2	52.2	+14.6	8.6	−3.4	3.2	0.5	−14.4
South†	10.9	20.4	5.5	41.5	35	67.7	−10.8	34.4	−9.7	57.0	+13.6	8.6	−3.6	–	–	−11.6
Burnley	11.5	16.8	2.5	8.2	0	66.9	−7.3	20.2	−10.4	57.9	+4.9	17.4	+1.0	4.4	–	−7.7
Chorley†	17.5	24.8	2.5	4.8	7	77.6	−4.8	35.9	−9.9	53.0	+11.4	8.5	−3.5	2.3	0.2	−10.6
Fylde	18.2	26.0	1.6	3.7	12	72.8	−2.3	48.9	−11.4	31.7	+13.1	14.6	−6.1	4.6	0.3	–
Hyndburn	12.7	15.6	2.6	10.0	12	72.3	−11.0	31.9	−11.3	55.6	+8.7	8.6	−1.0	3.4	0.6	−10.0
Lancashire West	14.5	24.6	3.9	3.7	20	74.8	−7.0	29.1	−13.3	60.3	+10.9	7.2	+0.2	1.9	1.5 (2)	−12.1
Lancaster & Wyre†	14.6	25.8	2.4	2.0	76	74.9	−3.7	40.6	−11.6	42.8	+9.7	11.6	−2.4	2.6	2.5 (2)	−10.6
Morecambe & Lunesdale†	13.5	22.3	4.3	2.4	20	72.3	−5.8	36.7	−12.5	48.9	+19.4	11.4	−7.7	2.7	0.3	−16.0
Pendle	12.6	16.3	2.7	5.1	0	74.5	−7.7	30.3	−10.0	53.3	+9.0	11.6	−3.4	4.8	–	−9.5
Preston	9.8	16.3	5.0	26.1	30	65.7	−10.1	21.9	−10.4	60.8	+7.7	14.7	+0.8	1.9	0.7	−9.0
Ribble South†	15.5	26.4	2.0	5.7	36	77.1	−5.9	37.6	−12.2	46.8	+12.0	10.6	−4.1	2.7	2.3 (2)	−12.1
Valley	19.7	28.1	1.4	1.3	11	78.5	−5.9	46.7	−5.9	15.8	+7.0	35.1	−3.2	2.3	0.3	–
Rossendale & Darwen	15.3	18.1	2.1	4.4	9	73.4	−8.5	32.3	−11.2	53.6	+10.1	10.6	−1.2	2.2	1.3	−10.6
Leicestershire, Blaby	17.9	27.0	1.6	2.9	18	75.9	−7.6	45.8	−11.0	33.8	+12.0	14.9	−5.1	3.8	1.7 (2)	−11.5

Constituency	Employers/ managers %	Good income %	Unemployed %	Population density	Index of change	% Voting	% Change in voting	% Con.	Con. change 1992–97	% Labour	Lab. change 1992–97	% Lib Dem	Lib Dem change 1992–97	% Referendum	% Other	Swing
ENGLAND																
Bosworth	16.8	24.0	1.5	3.1	17	76.6	−7.6	40.6	−11.0	38.7	+12.3	17.8	−2.9	2.9	–	−11.7
Charnwood	17.8	27.9	1.7	5.0	133	77.2	−3.7	46.5	−14.1	36.0	+14.4	12.9	−5.0	3.7	0.9	−14.2
Harborough	18.1	26.8	1.7	4.1	11	75.3	−6.2	41.8	−10.9	25.2	+12.9	29.5	−4.9	3.5	–	
Leicester East	8.1	15.4	4.5	35.8	0	69.1	−8.8	24.0	−9.7	65.5	+9.2	7.0	−1.1	2.3	1.2 (2)	−9.4
South	10.2	19.5	5.6	45.7	0	66.3	−8.1	23.7	−10.9	58.0	+5.7	13.8	+2.1	2.5	2.0 (2)	−8.3
West	9.2	15.6	6.0	31.4	0	63.1	−9.7	23.7	−14.8	55.2	+8.4	14.2	+0.9	2.4	4.5 (5)	−11.6
Leicestershire N.W.†	14.3	21.7	2.4	2.9	13	79.8	−6.7	31.0	−14.5	56.4	+12.5	8.6	−1.7	4.0	–	−13.5
Loughborough†	13.8	24.4	2.5	6.3	34	75.5	−1.3	37.7	−9.1	48.6	+8.8	11.8	+0.6	1.9	–	−8.9
Rutland & Melton	18.1	27.7	1.4	0.8	38	74.9	−7.1	45.8	−15.6	29.0	+13.3	19.2	−1.6	4.4	1.6	
Lincolnshire																
Boston & Skegness	13.6	21.3	3.6	1.3	72	68.9	−8.3	42.4	−8.4	41.0	+12.8	16.6	−4.4	–	–	−10.6
Gainsborough	14.6	23.3	3.0	0.6	13	74.6	−5.8	43.1	−10.3	28.8	+7.9	28.1	+2.4	–	–	
Grantham & Stamford	13.9	23.6	2.4	1.2	91	73.3	−6.9	42.8	−15.1	37.7	+11.6	12.5	−3.6	5.1	1.9 (3)	−13.3
Lincoln	11.2	19.0	6.1	18.1	17	70.9	−8.7	31.0	−13.2	54.9	+8.9	10.8	+2.0	2.9	0.4	−11.0
Louth & Horncastle	15.8	21.4	3.3	0.6	41	72.4	−6.6	43.4	−9.3	29.6	+16.0	24.4	−7.2	–	2.5	
Sleaford & N. Hykeham	15.5	25.5	2.2	0.8	52	74.2	−6.1	43.9	−14.5	34.3	+12.4	15.2	−1.5	5.5	1.1	−13.4
South Holland & Deepings	16.3	24.0	1.6	1.0	83	71.8	−7.4	49.3	−7.8	33.3	+9.2	15.6	−3.3	–	1.8	−8.5
Merseyside, Birkenhead	9.3	18.9	8.6	38.5	13	65.8	−5.8	15.2	−9.9	70.8	+7.1	9.0	−0.6	2.0	3.0	−8.5
Bootle	7.1	15.1	8.2	41.0	51	66.7	−4.6	8.5	−5.6	82.9	+6.3	5.7	−0.7	1.5	1.4 (2)	−6.0
Crosby	16.7	32.9	4.0	17.2	87	77.2	−4.1	34.8	−13.9	51.1	+22.4	11.5	−8.5	1.8	0.8 (2)	−18.2
Knowsley N. & Sefton E.	10.1	21.9	6.0	10.7	14	70.1	−5.1	17.3	−9.5	69.9	+15.5	11.1	−4.5	–	1.7	−12.5
South	8.7	17.6	6.7	19.4	21	67.5	−6.3	12.6	−7.9	77.1	+7.6	8.3	−0.7	2.0	2.1 (3)	−7.8
Liverpool Garston	10.1	21.7	5.8	26.9	44	65.0	−5.8	15.7	−9.3	61.3	+10.2	19.0	−2.7	1.9	5.2 (5)	
Riverside	6.8	16.0	9.7	34.6		51.6	−7.5	9.5	−1.3	70.4	+2.0	13.3	−5.2	1.5	2.6 (3)	
Walton	6.3	13.8	8.4	57.3	0	59.5	−6.9	6.3	−6.2	78.4	+6.0	11.1	−0.9	1.5	2.0 (3)	
Wavertree	9.6	21.3	7.1	55.5	63	62.7	−7.6	10.8	−1.7	64.4	+23.1	21.5	−13.2	1.3		

ENGLAND

Constituency	Employers/ managers %	Good income %	Unemployed %	Population density	Index of change	% Voting	% Change in voting	% Con.	Con. change 1992–97	% Labour	Lab. change 1992–97	% Lib Dem	Lib Dem change 1992–97	% Referendum	% Other	Swing
West Derby	6.9	16.7	8.2	43.8	21	61.3	−8.3	3.7	−5.9	71.2	+6.6	9.0	−6.3	1.6	9.6	–
St. Helens North	11.5	20.1	3.9	12.1	0	69.0	−7.7	17.3	−11.1	64.9	+7.0	12.7	−0.4	2.6	2.4 (2)	−9.1
South	10.4	18.5	4.8	15.3	0	66.5	−6.6	15.0	−9.5	68.6	+7.6	13.4	−0.5	2.6	0.4	−8.5
Southport†	17.3	29.0	3.7	20.4	0	72.1	−4.2	35.9	−11.1	12.1	+1.9	48.1	+6.6	2.7	1.1 (3)	–
Wallasey	9.9	21.3	6.9	37.8	0	73.5	−7.9	23.9	−18.0	64.5	+15.7	8.3	+0.6	3.2	–	−16.8
Wirral South†	14.7	28.2	3.5	12.1	0	81.0	+0.1	36.4	−14.5	50.9	+16.4	10.4	−2.6	1.6	0.7 (2)	−15.4
West†	15.6	28.8	3.7	16.7	0	77.0	−3.4	39.0	−13.7	44.9	+13.9	12.7	−1.9	3.4	–	−13.8
Norfolk, Great Yarmouth†	13.4	20.0	6.6	4.8	9	77.1	−6.8	35.6	−12.3	53.4	+15.4	11.0	−2.6	–	2.6 (2)	−13.9
Norfolk Mid	16.1	26.6	2.4	1.0	0	76.1	−7.5	39.6	−15.0	37.3	+11.2	15.0	−4.0	5.6	–	−13.1
North	14.3	21.5	2.8	0.9	0	76.1	−5.0	36.5	−11.7	25.1	+1.9	34.3	+6.9	4.2	1.4 (2)	–
North-West†	13.5	22.3	3.4	1.1	6	74.6	−5.9	41.5	−10.6	43.8	+10.2	9.6	−4.2	5.1	–	−10.4
South	16.6	26.2	2.3	1.1	1	78.4	−5.7	40.2	−12.2	26.1	+7.7	28.3	+1.4	4.1	2.0 (3)	–
South-West	14.3	21.0	2.7	0.8	12	73.1	−6.0	42.0	−12.7	37.8	+10.8	13.9	−4.3	6.3	3.1 (3)	−11.8
Norwich North†	12.7	22.1	3.6	18.2	8	75.7	−4.9	32.5	−11.7	49.7	+9.4	12.6	−2.0	3.2	1.2 (2)	−10.6
South	11.4	22.3	5.3	24.5	0	72.6	−7.2	23.7	−14.5	51.7	+5.7	18.6	+4.5	2.9	1.0 (2)	−10.1
Northamptonshire, Corby†	12.8	19.3	2.8	1.7	14	77.7	−4.2	33.4	−11.1	55.4	+11.5	7.5	−2.7	2.5	0.3	−11.3
Daventry	20.5	27.8	1.6	1.1	5	76.8	−5.8	46.3	−11.4	34.4	+10.5	15.0	−2.7	3.3	1.2 (2)	−11.0
Kettering†	16.7	23.6	2.3	1.9	4	75.5	−5.4	42.9	−9.8	43.3	+11.4	10.7	−4.7	2.7	3.0 (2)	−10.6
Northampton North†	12.2	19.7	3.6	34.2	11	69.9	−7.4	33.4	−12.4	52.7	+14.1	12.7	−2.5	–	2.6 (2)	−13.3
South†	16.3	26.0	3.0	5.2	0	71.7	−8.7	41.1	−14.6	42.4	+12.2	11.1	−3.1	2.5	–	−13.4
Wellingborough†	14.3	21.1	2.6	4.9	0	74.8	−6.6	43.8	−9.6	44.2	+10.3	9.4	−3.4	–	–	−9.9
Northumberland																
Berwick-upon-Tweed	13.8	19.7	3.8	0.3	0	74.0	−4.5	24.1	−8.7	26.2	+3.4	45.5	+1.1	3.4	0.8	–
Blyth Valley	11.4	19.7	4.6	11.2	0	68.7	−11.5	13.3	−2.3	64.2	+14.3	22.5	−11.1	–	–	–
Hexham	18.3	28.3	2.3	0.3	0	77.5	−4.5	38.8	−13.7	38.3	+14.1	17.4	−4.3	3.0	2.6	−13.9
Wansbeck	10.6	19.4	4.9	5.9	0	71.7	−7.9	13.9	−9.6	65.5	+5.7	15.9	+0.7	2.5	2.1	–

ENGLAND

Employers/ managers %	Good income %	Unemployed %	Population density	Index of change		% Voting	% Change in voting	% Con.	Con. change 1992–97	% Labour	Lab. change 1992–97	% Lib Dem	Lib Dem change 1992–97	% Referendum	% Other	Swing
					North Yorkshire											
17.6	29.9	2.3	16.5	15	Harrogate & Knaresb'h†	72.9	–3.8	38.5	–13.3	8.7	–4.8	51.5	+18.2	—	1.3	—
15.3	25.4	2.2	0.4	22	Richmond (Yorks)	73.4	–4.7	48.9	–11.6	27.8	+16.3	18.4	–8.8	5.0	—	—
14.5	21.7	2.0	0.5	38	Ryedale	74.7	–6.3	43.8	–11.6	18.0	+3.3	33.4	+3.4	3.0	1.9	—
15.2	20.8	4.3	1.3	0	Scarborough & Whitby†	71.6	–5.7	36.2	–13.6	45.6	+15.8	14.1	–4.8	4.0	—	–14.7
17.8	26.4	2.7	1.2	6	Selby†	74.9	–5.6	39.1	–12.1	45.9	+10.2	12.0	–1.0	2.1	1.0	–11.1
19.8	23.4	1.5	0.4	7	Skipton & Ripon	75.4	–5.7	46.5	–11.3	22.4	+7.6	25.2	–2.1	5.9	—	—
19.4	26.7	1.6	0.7	108	Vale of York	76.0	–4.9	44.7	–15.9	26.5	+15.4	23.8	–4.1	4.7	0.4	—
12.1	19.8	4.3	33.7	0	York, City of	73.2	–7.9	24.7	–14.5	59.9	+10.8	11.2	+0.6	1.9	2.3 (3)	–12.6
					Notts,											
10.2	15.7	4.2	9.2	0	Ashfield	70.0	–9.5	20.3	–12.4	65.2	+10.3	9.6	–2.9	3.7	1.2	–11.3
12.2	20.4	4.3		0	Bassetlaw	70.4	–8.1	24.7	–10.3	61.1	+7.8	10.3	–1.3	3.8	—	–9.0
15.9	25.1	2.9	12.9	0	Broxtowe†	78.4	–4.1	37.4	–13.5	47.0	+12.3	11.9	–1.8	3.6	—	–12.9
15.4	26.8	3.4	21.1	0	Gedling†	75.6	–6.4	39.5	–13.7	46.8	+12.3	9.9	–2.2	3.8	—	–13.0
11.6	19.9	4.6	18.3	0	Mansfield	70.6	–10.8	21.2	–11.9	64.4	+10.1	11.1	–1.5	3.3	—	–11.0
14.8	23.2	3.4	1.5	0	Newark†	74.4	–7.1	39.4	–11.0	45.2	+9.4	11.5	–1.5	3.9	—	–10.2
9.8	17.9	9.2	43.6	0	Nottingham East	60.2	–9.3	23.5	–12.9	62.3	+9.7	10.1	+2.3	4.1	1.5	–11.3
7.9	13.7	6.8	40.3	0	North	62.9	–11.3	20.3	–14.8	65.7	+10.0	8.0	–0.6	4.5	0.9	–12.4
11.4	19.9	5.8	26.9	0	South	66.6	–8.0	27.7	–14.1	55.3	+10.6	12.9	+2.9	3.1	0.8 (2)	–10.8
20.6	33.7	2.5	2.4	0	Rushcliffe	78.9	–4.4	44.4	–10.0	36.2	+13.0	14.3	–5.7	4.3	0.8	–11.5
15.6	23.9	3.5	2.8	0	Sherwood	75.5	–9.1	28.8	–14.1	58.5	+11.0	8.6	–1.0	3.3	1.8 (3)	–12.5
					Oxfordshire,											
15.5	24.9	1.8	1.8	3	Banbury	75.1	–5.8	42.9	–11.9	34.8	+7.9	16.7	–1.1	3.8	1.7 (3)	–9.9
21.5	32.8	1.3	1.5	3	Henley	77.6	–2.0	46.4	–13.6	22.7	+7.9	24.7	+0.8	4.5	3.6 (5)	—
11.4	23.7	4.0	30.2	12	Oxford East	69.0	–3.9	22.0	–11.5	56.8	+6.6	14.7	+0.7	2.9	2.2 (5)	–9.1
16.1	31.0	1.4	8.1	24	West & Abingdon†	77.1	+0.4	32.7	–13.6	20.2	+4.1	42.9	+7.1	2.1	2.0 (5)	—
18.3	30.6	1.4	1.5	0	Wantage	78.3	–4.5	39.8	–14.3	29.0	+9.6	26.5	+1.5	2.8	2.0 (2)	—
17.2	27.4	1.3	1.3	18	Witney	76.7	–7.0	43.1	–14.8	30.6	+12.5	19.9	–2.7	4.0	2.5 (2)	—

ENGLAND	Employers/ managers %	Good income %	Unemployed %	Population density	Index of change	% Voting	% Change in voting	% Con.	Con. change 1992–97	% Labour	Lab. change 1992–97	% Lib Dem	Lib Dem change 1992–97	% Referendum	% Other	Swing
Shropshire, Ludlow	19.0	21.5	1.9	0.5	15	75.5	–5.6	42.4	–9.2	25.4	+4.0	29.7	+4.1	–	2.6 (2)	–
Shrewsbury & Atcham†	14.2	25.4	2.2	1.5	0	75.3	–5.6	34.0	–11.8	37.0	+11.0	25.0	–2.0	2.4	1.6 (3)	–
Shropshire North	15.1	21.9	2.3	0.9	16	72.7	–5.5	40.2	–10.6	36.0	+9.8	20.4	–2.6	3.4	–	–10.2
Telford	10.7	18.2	3.4	16.4	37	65.6	–5.5	27.4	–5.9	57.8	+5.1	11.8	–0.6	3.0	–	–5.5
Wrekin, The†	13.7	23.5	2.1	2.2	89	76.5	–7.2	40.2	–7.5	46.9	+15.0	12.8	–6.5	–	–	–11.3
Somerset, Bridgwater	13.2	21.0	3.8	1.2	0	74.6	–5.4	36.9	–9.8	24.8	+3.0	33.6	+4.0	4.7	–	–
Somerton & Frome†	16.4	22.8	2.3	2.6	1	77.4	–4.9	39.3	–8.1	16.3	+5.9	39.5	–0.8	4.3	0.6	–
Taunton†	15.1	23.5	3.1	1.2	0	76.5	–5.8	38.7	–7.3	13.5	+0.8	42.7	+1.9	4.5	0.5	–
Wells	17.3	24.3	2.8	1.5	0	77.8	–4.6	39.4	–10.2	18.1	+7.5	38.5	+0.4	3.9	0.2	–
Yeovil	14.5	19.8	2.4	1.0	1	72.7	–8.7	27.7	–9.3	14.9	+5.3	48.7	–2.9	6.6	2.1 (3)	–
South Yorkshire																
Barnsley Central	8.9	15.1	4.9	19.6	14	59.7	–10.5	9.8	–8.7	77.0	+6.2	9.5	–1.2	3.6	–	–7.5
East & Mexborough	9.7	15.8	4.8	6.1	56	63.9	–8.3	11.4	–6.0	73.1	+0.2	10.4	+0.6	1.8	3.3 (2)	–3.1
West & Penistone	12.9	19.3	3.7	3.6	0	65.0	–10.3	18.4	–9.7	59.3	+1.0	18.0	+6.4	4.3	–	–5.3
Don Valley	13.4	22.7	4.6	3.5	44	66.3	–12.5	24.6	–12.2	58.3	+7.7	9.7	–1.4	3.2	4.2 (3)	–9.9
Doncaster Central	11.2	18.7	6.6	19.1	0	63.8	–10.1	21.0	–12.5	62.1	+7.7	9.4	–2.4	2.9	4.6 (3)	–10.1
North	9.9	15.2	5.7	4.1	15	63.3	–7.8	14.8	–7.5	69.8	+5.4	8.4	–4.8	4.0	3.0	–6.4
Rother Valley	13.1	20.1	4.5	5.5	0	67.2	–7.5	16.7	–10.2	67.6	+7.1	11.6	–1.1	4.2	–	–8.6
Rotherham	9.7	16.9	6.5	21.7	0	62.8	–7.3	14.3	–9.4	71.3	+7.4	10.4	–1.9	3.0	1.0	–8.4
Sheffield Attercliffe	11.0	17.7	4.4	21.2	0	64.7	–6.6	16.1	–10.3	65.3	+7.8	15.7	+1.1	2.9	–	–9.0
Brightside	6.4	12.0	7.3	39.6	0	57.5	–8.2	8.4	–8.4	73.5	+3.1	14.6	+2.1	1.8	1.6 (2)	–
Central	9.2	18.2	8.9	32.4	24	53.0	–6.3	11.9	–6.8	63.6	+4.0	17.2	–1.7	2.4	4.8 (4)	–
Hallam†	21.7	37.2	2.5	10.6	19	72.4	–0.8	33.1	–16.5	13.5	–4.9	51.3	+20.6	1.7	0.3	–
Heeley	10.4	17.0	5.7	37.7	0	65.0	–5.4	15.6	–10.3	60.7	+5.1	21.3	+2.9	2.4	–	–
Hillsborough	12.8	20.3	3.9	4.9	0	71.0	–6.7	14.5	–5.0	56.9	+10.7	25.8	–8.5	2.8	–	–
Wentworth	10.6	17.4	5.1	10.1	0	65.3	–7.8	15.0	–6.8	72.3	+3.3	9.3	–0.4	3.4	–	–5.3

Appendix 1: The Voting Statistics

ENGLAND

Constituency	Employers/ managers %	Good income %	Unemployed %	Population density	Index of change	% Voting	% Change in voting	% Con.	Con. change 1992-97	% Labour	Lab. change 1992-97	% Lib Dem	Lib Dem change 1992-97	% Referendum	% Other	Swing
Staffordshire, Burton†	12.8	20.5	3.6	3.1	4	75.1	-6.6	39.4	-8.8	51.0	+9.8	8.5	-2.1	–	1.1	-9.3
Cannock Chase	12.2	20.5	3.2	11.7	60	72.4	-12.0	27.2	-11.0	54.8	+5.8	8.7	-3.5	3.2	6.2 (3)	-8.4
Lichfield	18.4	28.3	2.0	3.0	103	77.5	-6.2	42.9	-14.1	42.4	+5.8	11.3	+5.5	3.4	–	-10.0
Newcastle-under-Lyme	11.3	19.5	2.8	10.5	0	73.7	-6.3	21.4	-8.1	56.5	+8.5	14.0	-8.0	3.1	5.0 (2)	-8.3
Stafford†	15.7	27.7	2.4	5.4	50	76.6	-6.3	39.2	-8.9	47.5	+12.6	10.6	-5.9	2.2	0.5	-10.7
Staff. Moorlands	14.2	20.2	2.2	1.9	59	77.3	-2.9	32.5	-6.1	52.2	+11.3	12.1	-5.3	3.1	–	-8.7
South	19.8	28.8	2.5	2.1	17	74.2	-6.9	50.0	-9.1	34.7	+8.9	11.3	-3.7	3.9	2.4 (2)	-9.0
Stoke-on-Trent C.	8.8	14.5	4.6	28.8	0	62.5	-5.4	16.7	-11.2	66.2	+8.2	11.9	-1.7	2.7	–	-9.7
North	8.7	15.4	3.1	14.2	32	65.4	-8.2	20.2	-13.5	65.1	+10.4	10.7	+0.2	4.0	3.1 (3)	-11.9
South	9.8	17.1	3.1	26.9	0	66.0	-7.5	22.4	-14.4	62.0	+12.2	10.2	-2.8	2.4	1.5 (2)	-13.3
Stone	19.0	27.8	1.5	1.3	127	77.8	-6.0	46.8	-9.2	39.6	+10.8	12.0	-1.5	–	1.1 (2)	-10.0
Tamworth†	15.7	23.4	2.9	4.9	7	74.2	-7.4	36.7	-12.6	51.8	+12.6	8.1	-1.9	2.3	0.5	-12.6
Suffolk, Bury St. Ed.	15.6	24.7	2.1	1.8	96	75.0	-4.9	38.3	-7.6	37.7	+11.7	18.2	-8.7	5.3	0.7 (2)	–
Ipswich	11.4	21.2	4.6	28.3	0	71.9	-7.1	31.1	-12.2	52.7	+8.8	12.2	+0.8	3.4	0.9	-10.5
Suffolk C. & Ipswich N.	15.3	25.3	2.4	1.1	67	75.2	-4.9	42.6	-13.2	35.9	+15.2	20.6	-1.3	–	1.2 (2)	–
Coastal	14.3	24.5	2.8	1.2	38	75.8	-6.0	38.6	-13.9	32.8	+9.5	21.4	-1.3	6.1	0.4	-11.7
South	18.7	26.5	2.1	1.3	23	77.2	-3.4	37.3	-14.0	29.3	+7.5	27.7	+1.5	5.3	0.3	–
West	12.5	21.6	2.5	1.2	67	71.5	-7.3	40.9	-12.9	37.1	+13.1	14.0	-7.3	7.6	0.6	–
Waveney†	12.2	19.5	5.5	3.7	12	74.6	-6.6	34.5	-12.5	56.0	+16.2	9.0	-3.8	–	2.8 (3)	-13.0
Surrey, Epsom & Ewell	22.3	36.1	1.5	18.7	24	74.0	-6.0	45.6	-15.4	24.3	+9.3	22.8	-0.4	4.3	1.6 (2)	-14.4
Esher & Walton	26.2	38.1	1.5	11.9	64	74.3	-2.2	49.8	-10.9	22.8	+5.4	20.4	-1.6	5.4	1.2 (2)	–
Guildford	20.1	33.2	1.4	5.0	2	75.4	-2.2	42.5	-12.8	17.5	+6.1	34.1	+1.3	4.7	3.5 (3)	–
Mole Valley	24.9	35.3	1.0	2.4	35	78.9	-2.8	48.0	-13.3	14.8	+5.4	29.3	+0.6	4.4	1.5 (2)	–
Reigate	22.8	34.2	1.5	7.4	29	73.8	-5.0	43.8	-13.7	27.8	+10.3	20.0	-4.1	7.0	0.9 (2)	–
Runnymede & Weybridge	23.1	33.1	1.6	9.7	68	71.5	-7.5	48.6	-12.8	29.4	+13.5	16.3	-4.8	4.2	1.5 (2)	–
Spelthorne	18.3	29.5	2.0	15.9	0	73.6	-13.2	44.9	-13.7	38.2	+15.3	13.1	-3.4	2.9	0.9 (2)	-14.5

ENGLAND

Constituency	Employers/ managers %	Good income %	Unemployed %	Population density	Index of change	% Voting	% Change in voting	% Con.	Con. change 1992–97	% Labour	Lab. change 1992–97	% Lib Dem	Lib Dem change 1992–97	% Referendum	% Other	Swing
Surrey East	21.8	34.1	1.6	3.6	26	74.6	−7.0	50.1	−10.9	21.2	+10.7	22.5	−4.4	4.9	1.4 (2)	—
Heath	21.9	35.6	1.2	8.9	47	74.1	−4.3	51.6	−12.1	21.0	+9.8	21.8	−1.3	4.4	1.2	—
South-West	22.8	34.6	1.1	3.7	0	78.0	−4.0	44.6	−13.9	9.4	+3.0	39.8	+6.3	5.0	1.2 (2)	—
Woking	21.1	33.4	1.3	9.5	14	72.7	−7.2	38.4	−20.7	21.0	+7.6	27.3	+0.2	4.3	9.0 (3)	—
Tyne & Wear, Blaydon	11.9	20.6	4.0	7.7	0	71.0	−5.8	13.2	−13.5	60.0	+7.3	23.8	+3.1	—	3.1	—
Gateshead E & Wash. W	10.7	18.2	4.2	31.2	68	67.2	−4.5	14.2	−13.6	72.1	+14.1	10.7	−3.6	3.1	—	−13.8
Houghton & Wash. E	9.0	16.5	4.4	11.0	41	62.1	−7.3	12.9	−8.8	76.4	+9.4	7.7	−3.6	3.1	—	−9.1
Jarrow	10.3	18.1	5.2	16.2	21	68.8	−4.4	14.9	−8.5	64.9	+2.4	11.1	−3.0	2.4	6.8 (2)	−5.4
Newcastle-upon-Tyne C.	12.7	25.5	5.4	36.7	14	65.3	−5.2	23.4	−12.2	59.2	+7.5	15.0	+2.0	2.4	—	−9.8
East & Wallsend	8.1	17.1	6.5	35.3	44	65.5	−4.6	13.9	−8.6	71.2	+14.0	10.6	−8.0	2.3	1.9 (2)	−11.3
North	11.0	20.5	4.3	12.5	0	69.1	−6.4	19.4	−12.4	62.2	+12.8	14.5	−4.2	3.8	—	−12.6
South Shields	9.0	14.7	7.0	42.3	9	62.6	−7.1	14.6	−12.1	71.4	+10.3	8.8	−3.5	4.3	1.0	−11.2
Sunderland North	8.4	15.7	5.4	35.7	11	59.1	−9.3	16.7	−11.1	68.2	+8.6	10.4	−0.6	3.6	1.1	−9.9
South	9.3	18.0	6.5	38.1	25	58.8	−10.9	18.9	−10.4	68.1	+10.6	11.5	−0.3	—	1.5	−10.5
Tyne Bridge	6.8	14.4	8.8	33.9	24	57.1	−6.6	11.1	−11.0	76.8	+10.0	8.0	−3.1	2.6	1.5	−10.5
Tynemouth†	15.3	23.9	4.4	30.1	9	77.0	−4.1	33.3	−15.3	55.4	+13.1	8.8	+0.7	1.6	0.9	−14.2
Tyneside North	8.6	16.8	5.3	17.8	30	67.8	−6.0	13.7	−12.3	72.7	+11.8	10.6	−2.5	3.1	—	−12.1
Warwickshire, Nuneaton	13.6	22.3	2.9	4.8	0	74.2	−8.3	30.9	−12.1	56.2	+10.5	8.8	−2.4	2.9	1.2 (2)	−11.3
Rugby & Kenilworth†	16.4	26.2	2.3	3.6	0	77.1	−5.9	42.3	−10.2	43.1	+11.1	14.3	−1.0	0.4	(2)	−10.6
Stratford-on-Avon	20.3	29.1	1.7	1.1	6	76.3	−5.5	48.3	−10.5	20.5	+7.1	25.5	−0.1	3.3	2.3 (4)	−12.0
Warwick & Leamington†	17.5	27.3	2.3	3.6	7	75.2	−5.2	38.9	−10.7	44.5	+13.3	11.9	−5.3	2.5	2.3 (4)	−12.4
Warwickshire North	13.2	20.7	2.6	3.1	0	74.6	−8.2	31.2	−12.5	58.4	+12.3	7.4	−2.8	1.7	1.3 (2)	—
West Midlands																
Aldridge-Brownhills	15.5	22.9	2.9	16.1	0	74.3	−7.6	47.1	−7.2	41.7	+8.4	11.2	−1.2	—	—	−7.8
Birmingham Edgbaston†	14.3	24.8	5.0	31.9	32	69.0	−2.7	38.5	−10.7	48.6	+9.3	9.7	−0.5	2.2	0.9	−10.0
Erdington	8.5	13.7	6.6	44.5	39	60.9	−7.2	27.5	−9.0	58.8	+5.5	10.2	−0.1	3.5	—	−7.3

ENGLAND

Constituency	Employers/ managers %	Good income %	Unemployed %	Population density	Index of change	% Voting	% Change in voting	% Con.	Con. change 1992-97	% Labour	Lab. change 1992-97	% Lib Dem	Lib Dem change 1992-97	% Referendum	% Other	Swing
Hall Green†	11.7	20.4	4.8	45.4	0	71.2	−6.0	33.4	−12.7	53.5	+15.2	9.6	−6.0	3.5	–	−14.0
Hodge Hill	6.7	13.0	6.8	46.3	0	60.9	−9.1	24.0	−12.3	65.6	+12.0	8.5	−0.7	–	1.9	−12.1
Ladywood	5.9	12.9	11.9	37.3	95	54.2	−4.3	13.3	−7.1	74.1	+2.7	8.0	−0.2	2.9	1.8	−4.9
Northfield	9.5	16.0	4.6	41.2	24	68.3	−6.1	28.0	−14.5	57.4	+11.5	10.5	−1.1	3.2	0.9	−13.0
Perry Barr	9.4	17.2	6.3	40.4	56	64.6	−8.8	21.7	−15.6	63.0	+11.1	9.9	−0.9	1.8	3.6 (3)	−13.4
Selly Oak	12.0	22.5	4.8	38.0	0	70.2	−5.7	27.8	−14.5	55.6	+9.6	12.1	+1.8	3.0	1.5 (3)	−12.1
Sparkbrook & Small H.	6.9	14.9	9.9	61.7	40	57.1	−10.6	17.5	−8.1	64.3	+1.2	9.3	+1.4	1.8	7.1 (5)	−4.6
Yardley	9.4	15.9	5.1	41.8	0	71.2	−5.5	17.8	−16.7	47.0	+12.2	33.0	+2.8	1.7	0.4	–
Coventry North-East	9.2	14.1	5.3	41.6	18	64.4	−8.5	19.3	−8.7	66.2	+16.6	8.0	−2.5	2.3	4.1 (3)	−12.7
North-West	11.7	17.2	3.7	24.6	54	70.7	−5.9	26.3	−10.6	56.9	+5.6	10.5	−1.3	2.3	4.0 (4)	−8.1
South†	13.2	22.1	4.2	29.5	99	68.7	−8.7	29.0	−10.8	50.9	+16.2	9.2	+0.0	1.9	9.0 (4)	−13.5
Dudley North	11.2	17.1	4.5	34.1	69	69.3	−7.8	31.4	−12.3	51.2	+5.7	8.2	−1.5	2.5	6.7 (3)	−9.0
South	12.5	19.1	3.6	30.9	62	71.7	−7.8	29.4	−12.5	56.6	+9.6	10.9	−0.2	3.1	–	−11.0
Halesowen & Rowley R.†	12.9	18.3	3.6	28.5	87	73.6	−5.8	32.9	−11.9	54.1	+9.6	8.5	−1.4	2.6	2.0 (2)	−10.7
Meriden	17.4	28.9	4.0	7.2	0	71.6	−5.8	42.0	−13.1	41.0	+10.1	13.0	−1.0	4.0	–	−11.6
Solihull	21.3	31.1	2.0	27.0	0	74.4	−6.0	44.6	−16.2	24.3	+7.6	25.3	+4.3	4.7	1.1	–
Stourbridge†	16.0	24.2	3.2	33.0	83	76.4	−0.9	35.8	−13.0	47.2	+8.9	14.3	+2.5	2.7	–	−11.0
Sutton Coldfield	21.6	35.9	2.2	15.9	0	72.9	−5.4	52.2	−12.9	23.8	+8.9	19.3	+0.0	4.6	3.2 (2)	–
Walsall North	8.9	14.5	5.4	36.0	0	64.1	−10.6	27.5	−11.8	56.6	+9.9	9.4	−3.3	3.3	0.3	−10.9
South	10.7	18.5	5.7	28.9	0	67.3	−8.1	31.7	−10.1	57.9	+9.7	6.2	−2.0	3.8	–	−9.9
Warley	8.1	14.5	5.8	44.7	18	64.9	−6.6	24.1	−10.2	63.8	+10.7	9.7	−1.7	2.4	–	−10.5
West Bromwich East	10.3	15.0	5.4	31.8	16	65.4	−8.5	24.4	−13.5	57.2	+9.2	14.9	+1.6	3.5	–	−11.4
West	7.8	12.8	5.4	29.6	47	54.3	−15.1	–	–	65.3	+14.7	–	–	–	34.7 (2)	–
Wolverhampton N.E.	8.3	13.5	5.1	36.5	1	67.0	−11.2	27.9	−13.5	59.3	+10.3	5.3	−2.0	2.9	4.6 (2)	−11.9
South-East	7.5	12.5	5.6	35.3	0	64.1	−7.6	20.2	−11.6	63.7	+7.0	9.5	+0.0	2.8	3.8 (2)	−9.3
South-West†	15.0	23.9	4.4	34.6	0	72.0	−5.2	39.9	−9.4	50.4	+10.5	8.2	−0.3	–	1.5	−9.9

Employers/ managers %	Good income %	Unemployed %	Population density	Index of change	ENGLAND	% Voting	% Change in voting	% Con.	Con. change 1992-97	% Labour	Lab. change 1992-97	% Lib Dem	Lib Dem change 1992-97	% Referendum	% Other	Swing
					West Sussex											
21.6	30.1	1.3	1.5	104	Arundel & South Downs	75.9	-5.8	53.1	-9.7	18.3	+8.9	25.7	+0.6	–	2.9	–
15.4	21.2	2.3	16.2	17	Bognor R. & L'hampton	69.6	-6.4	44.2	-12.6	28.5	+15.0	24.0	-2.7	–	3.3	–
16.8	25.7	1.7	1.4	7	Chichester	74.6	-3.2	46.4	-12.9	17.2	+5.9	29.0	+2.4	5.9	1.4 (–)	-13.4
14.5	23.6	2.5	19.8	15	Crawley†	72.5	-5.0	31.8	-12.1	55.0	+14.7	8.2	-6.3	3.8	1.1 (2)	–
21.0	32.2	1.2	2.0	56	Horsham	75.8	-4.0	50.8	-11.5	18.7	+6.8	24.8	+2.0	4.0	1.8 (2)	–
22.3	33.0	1.4	6.0	15	Sussex Mid	77.7	-2.6	43.5	-15.5	18.6	+8.0	30.6	+2.4	5.9	1.4 (2)	–
16.1	23.6	2.2	16.1	71	Worthing E. & Shoreham	72.9	-5.2	40.5	-0.9	23.9	+10.6	30.6	-3.1	3.3	1.8	–
18.5	22.3	2.0	28.4	57	West	71.8	-6.6	46.1	-5.6	16.2	+7.6	31.1	+3.6	4.5	2.0	-7.4
13.6	17.6	3.6	18.5	16	West Yorks, Batley & Spen†	73.1	-5.4	36.4	-8.3	49.4	+6.4	8.8	-2.5	3.6	1.8 (2)	-7.4
10.7	16.2	6.2	29.9	0	Bradford North	63.1	-9.9	25.6	-6.6	56.1	+8.2	14.5	-4.1	2.9	0.9	-9.7
11.7	17.2	4.7	22.4	0	South	65.8	-9.4	28.0	-10.4	56.7	+9.1	11.3	-2.4	4.0	–	-9.5
10.8	19.6	6.7	27.0	0	West	62.9	-6.3	33.0	-0.8	41.5	-11.7	14.8	+4.3	3.0	7.7 (4)	+5.5
16.8	19.5	2.9	3.1	0	Calder Valley†	75.4	-6.3	35.1	-10.4	46.1	+8.7	14.7	-1.4	2.4	1.6 (2)	-10.4
16.2	21.1	2.8	5.2	0	Colne Valley†	76.8	-4.2	32.7	-9.3	41.3	+11.5	22.6	-4.4	3.4	– (4)	-6.0
12.8	17.2	3.3	16.4	51	Dewsbury	70.0	-10.2	30.1	-3.9	49.4	+2.1	10.3	+0.4	2.4	7.9 (3)	-10.9
18.2	27.7	2.5	4.5	0	Elmet†	76.7	-4.7	36.2	-11.3	52.4	+10.5	8.7	-1.9	2.7	–	-10.7
11.7	17.0	4.9	16.7	0	Halifax	70.5	-7.5	32.1	-10.5	54.3	+10.8	12.0	-0.8		1.5	-7.4
10.9	20.4	4.2	6.0	21	Hemsworth	67.9	-8.2	17.8	-8.0	70.6	+6.8	8.9	-1.5	2.8	–	-10.4
12.7	17.6	5.3	19.2	0	Huddersfield	67.5	-4.0	20.9	-13.0	56.5	+7.8	17.2	+1.2	3.3	2.1	-10.2
16.0	22.4	3.1	5.3	0	Keighley†	76.3	-5.9	36.7	-10.7	50.6	+9.7	9.8	-0.7	2.9	–	-7.3
8.7	14.3	8.1	25.3	18	Leeds Central	54.2	-8.1	13.7	-8.6	59.6	+5.9	11.3	-2.7	2.8	2.6 (2)	-9.7
10.3	17.7	7.2	26.2	0	East	62.8	-6.8	18.7	-5.6	57.5	+9.8	10.3	-3.7	3.5	–	-11.9
17.5	31.0	4.3	12.1	0	North-East†	71.8	-4.3	33.9	-11.5	49.2	+12.3	13.9	-2.8	2.1	1.0	–
16.2	28.0	2.8	12.1	0	North-West†	69.7	-3.8	32.1	-10.9	39.9	+12.6	23.7	-4.2	2.7	1.7 (3)	-10.1
10.0	15.8	4.7	28.9	0	West	62.7	-7.8	17.5	-8.6	66.7	+11.6	9.0	+0.1	3.0	3.8 (2)	

ENGLAND	Employers/ managers %	Good income %	Unemployed %	Population density	Index of change	% Voting	% Change in voting	% Con.	Con. change 1992–97	% Labour	Lab. change 1992–97	% Lib Dem	Lib Dem change 1992–97	% Referendum	% Other	Swing
Morley & Rothwell	13.4	18.9	2.9	11.2	44	67.1	-8.1	26.3	-10.6	58.5	+9.0	11.1	-1.9	3.0	1.2 (2)	-9.8
Normanton	14.7	20.9	3.1	12.7	41	68.3	-6.5	23.6	-12.0	60.6	+9.4	12.4	-0.9	3.4	–	-10.7
Pontefract & Castle.	8.7	15.6	4.5	12.9	0	66.4	-6.7	13.6	-7.4	75.7	+5.8	7.3	-1.8	3.4	–	-6.6
Pudsey†	17.0	23.6	1.8	16.3	0	74.3	-5.3	36.3	-7.3	48.1	+19.0	14.0	-12.4	1.6	–	-13.2
Shipley†	18.3	27.9	2.6	9.5	0	76.1	-5.0	37.8	-12.6	43.4	+15.0	15.1	-4.9	3.7	–	-13.8
Wakefield	15.3	22.2	3.9	6.1	69	69.0	-6.5	28.5	-12.0	57.4	+9.1	11.2	-0.1	2.9	1.4 (2)	-10.6
Wiltshire, Devizes	14.8	24.0	1.9	1.0	71	74.4	-9.6	42.8	-10.1	24.2	+12.2	26.5	-5.9	5.0	7.3 (4)	–
Salisbury	14.1	26.2	1.9	1.1	0	73.7	-5.9	42.9	-9.1	17.6	+8.5	32.2	-5.0	3.2	0.3	–
Swindon North	13.7	22.3	2.3	6.1	100	73.6	-3.6	33.9	-7.1	49.8	+7.1	12.9	-1.7	2.5	0.5 (2)	-7.1
South†	15.0	23.5	3.2	7.0	46	72.9	-9.0	35.8	-13.2	46.8	+16.0	14.4	-4.3	3.4	5.1 (3)	-14.6
Westbury	15.8	25.0	2.7	1.6	15	76.2	-5.6	40.6	-11.7	21.1	+10.5	29.9	-4.0	3.4	1.2 (2)	–
Wiltshire North	17.3	26.3	1.8	1.4	16	74.6	-9.3	43.8	-12.4	14.2	+4.1	37.8	+6.3	3.1	–	–

Employers/ managers %	Good income %	Unemployed %	Population density	Index of change	WALES	% Voting	% Change in voting	% Con.	Con. change 1992–97	% Labour	Lab. change 1992–97	% Lib Dem	Lib Dem change 1992–97	% Plaid Cymru	PC change 1992–97	% Other	Swing
12.5	22.5	2.8	4.7	6	*Clwyd,* Alyn & Deeside	72.1	−6.6	22.8	−14.1	61.9	+11.0	9.7	+0.0	1.7	+0.6	3.9	−12.5
11.4	18.1	2.9	0.8	67	Clwyd South	73.6	−5.4	23.1	−7.2	53.1	+8.4	9.4	−1.7	6.3	−1.6	3.1	−7.8
15.6	22.0	3.2	0.8	65	West†	75.2	−2.0	32.5	−16.0	37.1	+6.2	12.8	−2.9	13.4	+8.8	4.2 (2)	−11.1
12.3	23.8	2.7	2.4	20	Delyn	73.9	−6.4	26.7	−12.9	56.1	+9.3	10.5	−0.5	3.9	+1.3	2.8	−11.1
14.1	22.3	4.2	3.4	91	Vale of Clwyd†	74.6	−7.9	29.8	−13.9	52.7	+13.9	8.8	−3.7	5.8	+1.0	2.9 (2)	−13.9
12.1	21.8	3.3	6.3	32	Wrexham	71.8	−7.0	23.9	−8.6	56.1	+6.2	13.3	−1.7	3.2	+0.5	3.5 (2)	−7.4
12.4	19.0	3.2	0.4	39	*Dyfed,* Carmarthen E.& D.	78.6	−4.2	12.0	−8.3	42.9	+1.4	7.5	−1.6	34.6	+5.5	2.9	–
14.3	21.5	4.6	0.7	84	W. & Pembrokeshire S.	75.4	−1.3	26.6	−8.9	49.1	+10.6	8.2	−2.6	12.6	−2.4	3.4	−9.8
13.2	21.0	3.0	0.4	19	Ceredigion	73.7	−4.2	14.9	−9.1	24.3	+5.7	16.5	−10.0	41.6	+10.6	2.7	–
10.5	16.8	4.2	3.1	8	Llanelli	70.7	−6.5	12.1	−4.9	57.9	−3.4	9.2	−3.6	18.9	+3.2	1.8	–
13.9	20.5	4.7	0.6	62	Preseli P'shire†	78.2	−2.3	27.7	−11.8	48.3	+10.2	13.0	+0.7	6.3	−2.3	4.7 (2)	−11.0
7.5	11.4	4.8	6.7	0	*Gwent,* Blaenau Gwent	72.3	−5.1	6.6	−3.2	79.5	+0.5	8.7	+2.3	5.2	+0.3		–
9.8	14.3	3.2	6.6	0	Islwyn	71.9	−8.2	7.9	−7.0	74.2	−0.2	8.4	+2.8	6.2	+0.2	3.3	–
17.4	27.9	2.6	0.9	0	Monmouth†	80.8	−4.2	39.2	−8.0	27.7	+6.8	9.6	−1.4	1.0	+0.2	2.4	−7.4
12.6	20.6	4.8	5.8	0	Newport East	73.1	−8.2	21.4	−10.0	57.7	+2.7	10.4	−1.5	1.9	+0.1	8.6 (2)	−6.3
13.6	23.1	5.2	7.8	0	West	74.6	−7.6	24.4	−11.6	60.5	+7.4	9.7	+0.3	1.6	−0.1	3.8 (2)	−9.5
10.3	15.7	4.0	6.9	0	Torfaen	71.6	−5.1	12.3	−8.0	69.1	+4.9	12.1	−0.9	2.4		4.1 (2)	−6.4
13.9	19.0	5.3	0.7	0	*Gwynedd,* Caernarfon	72.6	−4.5	12.4	−6.7	28.4	+12.9	5.0	−0.8	51.7	−7.2	2.4	–
12.9	21.7	4.9	2.2	0	Conwy†	75.3	−2.3	24.3	−9.5	35.0	+9.3	31.2	−0.2	6.8	−0.5	2.7 (3)	–
14.0	18.4	4.5	0.2	0	Meirionnydd N. C.	76.0	−4.4	16.0	−10.5	23.0	+4.2	7.0	−1.9	50.7	+6.7	3.3	–
12.4	20.9	5.3	1.0	0	Ynys Mon	75.4	−4.1	21.5	−13.1	33.2	+9.7	3.8	−0.5	39.4	+2.3	2.0	–
15.3	24.2	3.1	5.4	0	*Mid Glamorgan,* Bridgend	72.3	−6.9	22.3	−12.9	53.1	+6.8	11.5	+1.2	3.8	+1.0	3.8	−9.8
11.1	18.0	4.4	6.9	0	Caerphilly	70.0	−6.7	10.7	−7.4	67.3	+4.2	8.2	−0.3	9.6	+0.0	3.5 (2)	−5.8
9.5	14.2	4.5	3.7	0	Cynon Valley	69.2	−6.7	6.3	−6.1	69.7	+0.6	10.3	+3.3	10.6	−0.3	2.5	–
8.5	12.7	4.8	4.8	0	Merthyr Tydfil & R.	69.2	−6.0	6.4	−4.7	76.7	+5.1	7.5	−3.8	5.9	−0.1	3.5 (2)	–
7.0	15.1	3.4	3.8	0	Ogmore	73.1	−5.8	9.8	−5.4	70.0	+2.2	9.2	+2.4	7.0	+0.6		−3.8

WALES

Constituency	Employers/ managers %	Good income %	Unemployed %	Population density	Index of change	% Voting	% Change in voting	% Con.	Con. change 1992-97	% Labour	Lab. change 1992-97	% Lib Dem	Lib Dem change 1992-97	% Plaid Cymru	PC change 1992-97	% Other	Swing
Pontypridd	12.8	22.8	3.3	6.4	0	71.4	–5.5	12.9	–7.4	63.9	+3.1	13.4	+4.9	6.4	–2.6	3.3 (4)	–
Rhondda	8.7	12.0	4.4	7.9	0	71.5	–4.5	3.8	–4.0	74.5	–0.1	5.7	+0.4	13.3	+1.5	2.7 (2)	–
Powys, Brecon & Radnor†	14.3	21.1	2.5	0.2	0	82.2	–2.2	29.0	–7.1	26.6	+0.4	40.8	+5.1	1.4	+0.5	2.1	–
Montgomeryshire	13.6	18.9	1.8	0.3	0	74.9	–3.5	26.1	–6.6	19.1	+6.7	45.9	–2.6	5.0	+0.2	3.8 (2)	–
S. Glamorgan, Cardiff C.	12.9	26.8	4.7	41.0	0	68.9	–4.1	20.0	–13.9	43.7	+1.7	24.9	+3.6	3.5	+1.8	7.7 (4)	–
North†	17.7	29.0	2.2	16.7	0	79.7	–3.7	33.7	–11.5	50.4	+11.5	10.9	–2.7	2.4	+0.5	2.5	–11.5
South & Penarth	11.5	19.7	5.6	21.3	0	68.3	–8.1	20.7	–12.9	53.4	–2.1	9.3	+1.5	3.1	+1.5	13.4 (4)	–5.4
West	12.8	23.3	5.7	24.2	0	68.9	–8.0	21.5	–11.4	60.3	+7.1	10.8	–0.1	4.8	+2.2	2.5	–9.2
Vale of Glamorgan†	16.0	28.2	4.1	3.2	0	80.0	–1.3	34.4	–10.0	53.9	+9.6	9.2	–0.1	2.5	+0.4	–	–9.8
W. Glamorgan, Aberavon	8.2	14.4	3.9	3.7	0	71.9	–5.1	7.9	–6.0	71.3	+4.2	11.3	–1.1	5.8	+1.0	3.6 (2)	–
Gower	15.9	27.0	3.0	2.4	0	74.9	–5.3	23.8	–11.3	53.8	+3.7	13.0	+3.0	5.1	+1.6	4.3 (2)	–7.5
Neath	10.3	18.9	3.6	2.7	0	74.3	–5.6	8.7	–6.6	73.5	+5.5	6.3	+0.9	8.1	–3.2	3.4 (2)	–6.0
Swansea East	9.1	18.3	4.4	16.3	0	67.2	–8.1	9.3	–7.9	75.4	+5.7	8.9	–0.6	3.3	–0.2	3.1 (2)	–6.8
West	13.6	24.7	4.7	22.0	0	68.2	–4.7	20.5	–10.9	56.2	+3.2	14.5	+4.0	6.6	+2.8	2.2	–7.1

SCOTLAND	Employers/ managers %	Good income %	Unemployed %	Population density	Index of change	% Voting	% Change in voting	% Con.	Con. change 1992–97	% Labour	Lab. change 1992–97	% Lib Dem	Lib Dem change 1992–97	% SNP	SNP change 1992–97	% Other	Swing
Borders, Roxburgh & B.	13.2	16.7	2.3	0.2	7	73.8	–3.1	23.9	–10.3	15.0	+6.2	46.5	+0.0	11.3	+0.7	3.3 (3)	–
Tweeddale, Ettrick & L.	14.4	22.1	2.1	0.3	41	76.4	–2.8	22.1	–8.6	27.4	+11.0	31.2	–3.8	17.1	–0.0	2.2 (3)	–
Central, Falkirk East	10.9	18.1	4.0	3.8	29	73.2	–3.3	14.0	–6.2	56.1	+12.0	5.2	–2.1	23.9	–4.4	0.8	–
West	9.8	18.2	4.6	6.4	14	72.6	–3.3	12.1	–6.8	59.3	+7.9	5.1	–1.0	23.4	–0.1	–	–
Ochil	13.2	21.5	4.1	1.6	43	76.9	–1.0	14.6	–9.4	45.0	+1.9	5.2	–1.7	34.3	+8.3	0.9 (3)	–
Stirling†	18.8	28.1	3.4	0.3	11	81.8	+0.2	32.5	–6.7	47.4	+8.8	6.2	–0.5	13.3	–1.1	0.4 (2)	–7.7
Dumfries & G'way, Dumfries†	11.1	19.5	4.0	0.4	2	78.9	–0.3	28.0	–15.1	47.5	+17.9	11.1	–0.6	12.0	–2.7	1.3 (2)	–16.5
Galloway & U. Nithsdale†	13.4	17.3	4.3	0.2	2	79.7	–1.3	30.5	–11.5	16.3	+3.4	6.4	–2.2	43.9	+7.4	2.8 (3)	–
Fife, Dunfermline East	9.8	16.8	5.0	3.2	3	70.2	–5.1	10.0	–6.3	66.8	+3.9	5.9	–0.2	15.5	+0.8	1.7	–
West	11.2	21.8	4.1	4.6	3	69.4	–6.5	12.6	–10.4	53.1	+11.6	13.6	–2.0	19.1	–0.6	1.5	–
Fife Central	9.9	15.6	5.2	7.2	2	69.8	–4.1	9.0	–8.4	58.7	+4.7	6.4	–0.5	25.0	+0.0	0.9	–
North-East	14.0	23.7	2.7	0.9	0	70.6	–6.6	26.5	–12.0	10.3		51.2	+4.8	10.8	+0.0	1.2	–
Kirkcaldy	10.3	18.0	5.8	6.6	2	66.9	–7.5	13.7	–8.4	53.6	+8.0	8.7	–1.0	22.9	+0.3	1.2	–
Grampian, Aberdeen C.	11.3	23.0	3.9	39.9	93	65.6	–1.9	19.5	–9.3	49.8	+6.7	13.2	+2.7	16.1	–1.3	1.3	–
North	10.4	19.5	2.5	7.5	87	70.7	+1.1	15.0	–3.6	47.9	+12.8	14.1	–9.7	21.8	–0.6	1.2	–
South†	13.9	28.0	2.6	9.3	90	72.8	–0.3	26.4	–11.0	35.3	+11.4	27.6	+1.0	9.7	–2.3	1.0	–8.0
Aberdeenshire W & Kinc.†	15.8	27.5	1.7	0.2	63	73.0	–3.8	34.9	–10.2	9.1	+2.3	41.1	+6.4	13.0	+0.5	1.9	–
Banff & Buchan	10.7	18.1	2.4	0.6	11	68.7	–1.6	22.8	–10.9	11.8	+3.2	6.0	+0.1	55.7	+4.9	2.6	–
Gordon†	16.2	23.3	2.0	0.4	64	71.9	–0.2	26.0	–21.9	10.3	+4.0	42.6	+15.4	19.9	+1.3	1.1	–
Moray	10.2	20.2	3.8	0.4	9	68.0	–3.6	27.6	–10.0	19.8	+7.9	8.9	+3.0	41.5	–3.0	2.1	–
Highlands																	
Caithness, Suth. & E.R.	12.4	18.9	5.7	0.1	32	70.0	–1.6	10.8	–10.8	27.8	+12.2	35.6	–8.8	23.0	+4.6	2.8 (3)	–
Inverness E, Nairn & L.†	14.2	24.3	4.3	0.1	12	72.5	+0.0	17.5	–6.0	33.9	+10.7	17.5	–9.2	28.9	+3.9	2.1 (3)	–
Ross, Skye & Inverness W.	13.2	20.9	5.5	0.1	33	71.6	–1.6	10.9	–10.9	28.7	+9.8	38.7	+0.0	19.5	+0.7	2.1 (2)	–
Lothian, East Lothian	13.2	21.2	3.0	1.1	16	75.6	–6.9	19.9	–10.2	52.7	–7.2	10.5	–0.5	15.7	+2.4	1.1	–8.7
Edinburgh Central	14.6	25.3	4.2	38.8	38	67.1	–1.1	21.2	–8.2	47.1	+8.6	13.1	–1.7	15.7	+0.5	2.8 (3)	–8.4

SCOTLAND	% Voting	% Change in voting	% Con.	Con. change 1992-97	% Labour	Lab. change 1992-97	% Lib Dem	Lib Dem change 1992-97	% SNP	SNP change 1992-97	% Other	Swing	Index of change	Population density	Unemployed %	Good income %	Employers/managers %
East & Musselburgh	70.6	-3.8	15.4	-8.6	53.6	+8.9	10.7	-0.8	19.0	+1.1	1.2	–	47	25.9	3.8	18.5	12.0
North & Leith	66.5	-5.0	17.9	-7.0	46.9	+12.0	13.0	+1.3	20.1	-0.2	2.1 (3)	–	43	45.7	5.8	23.6	12.4
Pentlands†	76.7	-0.6	32.4	-7.8	43.0	+11.8	10.0	-2.7	13.0	-2.6	1.6 (3)	-9.8	7	8.4	3.5	28.4	15.7
South	71.8	-0.2	21.3	-10.9	46.8	+5.3	17.6	+4.5	12.9	+0.0	1.3 (2)	-8.1	2	29.5	3.4	27.1	13.7
West†	77.9	-5.3	28.0	-10.2	18.8	+1.4	43.2	+13.3	8.8	-3.7	1.2 (3)	–	52	8.0	2.8	26.7	16.3
Linlithgow	73.8	-3.4	12.5	-1.2	54.1	+4.9	5.9	-1.1	26.8	-3.3	0.7	–	14	3.4	3.4	18.8	11.6
Livingston	70.9	-2.2	9.4	-8.7	54.9	+9.0	6.7	-2.4	27.4	+1.5	1.5 (2)	–	12	3.3	3.6	19.6	10.8
Midlothian	74.0	-0.1	10.9	-6.7	53.5	+5.3	9.2	-0.8	25.5	+2.2	0.9	–	21	2.3	3.1	19.1	10.2
Tweedale, Ettrick & L., (See Borders)																	
Orkney & Shetland	63.9	-0.9	12.2	-9.8	18.3	-1.6	52.0	+5.6	12.6	+1.5	4.8 (3)	–	0	0.2	2.7	20.6	13.6
Strathclyde, Airdrie & Sh.	71.4	-3.3	8.9	-6.0	61.8	-0.7	4.2	-0.3	24.3	+6.2	0.7	–	52	3.5	5.4	15.6	8.6
Argyll & Bute	72.0	-3.3	19.0	-8.8	15.7	+2.1	40.2	+5.3	23.1	-0.6	2.0	-5.2	0	0.1	4.6	19.1	14.4
Ayr	80.2	-1.7	33.8	-4.6	48.4	+5.8	4.7	-2.7	12.5	+1.4	0.4	-7.2	16	4.6	4.7	22.9	13.8
Carrick, Cumnock & Doon V.	75.0	-2.2	17.0	-8.7	59.8	+5.7	5.3	+0.1	16.6	+1.5	1.3	–	19	0.4	5.1	19.7	11.9
Clydebank & Milngavie	75.0	-2.3	12.5	-9.0	55.2	+5.0	10.5	+0.9	21.1	+2.6	0.7	–	7	10.2	5.0	21.5	11.7
Clydesdale	71.6	-5.0	16.3	-7.1	52.5	+7.9	8.4	+0.1	22.1	-0.9	0.7	–	0	0.6	3.9	20.9	13.8
Coatbridge & Chryston	72.3	-3.8	8.6	-7.0	68.3	+6.5	5.4	-0.5	17.0	+0.2	0.7	–	25	9.1	4.6	17.4	9.8
Cumbernauld & Kilsyth	75.0	-2.9	6.8	-4.5	58.7	+4.7	3.8	-2.0	27.7	-1.1	2.9 (3)	–	0	6.0	4.3	20.0	11.9
Cunninghame North	74.1	-3.2	23.5	-10.7	50.3	+9.3	5.5	-1.2	18.4	+0.2	2.3 (2)	–	0	0.9	4.6	20.6	13.5
South	71.5	-3.2	10.1	-6.2	62.7	+9.8	4.5	-1.7	20.7	-3.4	1.9 (2)	-10.0	0	5.8	5.8	15.9	8.6
Dumbarton	73.4	-2.8	17.6	-12.1	49.6	+6.0	7.6	-0.1	23.2	+4.8	1.9 (2)	–	0	1.5	5.4	21.1	9.7
East Kilbride	74.8	-4.3	12.0	-6.6	56.5	+9.2	7.2	-3.2	20.9	-2.6	3.3 (3)	–	2	2.9	3.6	20.7	12.7
Eastwood†	78.2	-1.7	33.5	-13.1	39.7	+15.6	11.7	-4.7	13.0	+0.5	2.0 (3)	–	2	4.9	2.5	33.3	21.1
Glasgow Anniesland	63.8	-6.4	11.5	-4.2	61.8	+8.8	7.2	-6.5	17.1	+0.0	2.4 (5)	-14.3	29	41.9	4.9	14.2	8.2
Baillieston	62.2	-4.5	7.7	-2.1	65.7	+2.5	3.8	-0.5	19.1	-3.4	3.6 (2)	–	93	23.2	6.8	13.6	7.0
Cathcart	67.6	-5.5	12.7	-8.8	57.4	+8.0	6.9	-0.3	18.5	-0.5	4.5 (3)	–	45	37.3	4.4	17.5	11.5

Employers/ managers %	Good income %	Unemployed %	Population density	Index of change	SCOTLAND	% Voting	% Change in voting	% Con.	Con. change 1992-97	% Labour	Lab. change 1992-97	% Lib Dem	Lib Dem change 1992-97	% SNP	SNP change 1992-97	% Other	Swing
13.0	18.0	6.7	36.2	123	Govan	64.5	-7.8	8.8	-10.9	44.1	+1.0	5.9	+0.4	35.0	+7.4	6.1 (6)	–
12.6	21.3	6.2	47.2	35	Kelvin	56.1	-11.4	10.8	-2.3	51.0	+4.1	14.2	-4.7	21.3	+2.0	2.6 (4)	–
8.0	11.7	8.5	33.0	16	Maryhill	56.4	-7.9	5.9	-3.8	54.9	+2.3	7.1	+0.5	16.9	-2.4	5.1 (5)	–
7.7	12.2	6.4	30.3	99	Pollok	66.5	-5.6	6.0	-2.1	59.9	+10.1	3.5	-0.9	17.8	-7.1	12.7 (3)	–
10.4	17.6	4.6	24.9	15	Rutherglen	70.1	-4.2	9.3	-9.9	57.5	+4.1	14.5	+2.9	15.2	-0.3	3.4 (3)	–
6.2	8.4	6.6	40.8	99	Shettleston	54.6	-9.6	5.5	-6.7	73.2	+7.7	4.0	-2.2	13.9	-2.1	3.4 (4)	–
5.3	8.8	7.4	34.9	44	Springburn	53.9	-6.7	6.0	-4.9	71.4	-6.4	4.3	-0.1	16.4	-3.3	1.9 (2)	–
9.0	15.9	3.9	10.0	54	Greenock & Inverclyde	71.1	-3.5	11.5	-9.6	55.2	+8.4	13.8	-0.1	18.5	+1.2	–	–
10.9	19.4	5.2	14.6	62	Hamilton N. & Bellshill	70.9	-5.2	10.4	-4.8	64.0	+5.7	5.1	-1.7	19.0	-0.6	1.5	–
11.6	17.8	4.5	9.9	24	South	71.1	-3.2	8.6	-7.4	65.6	+8.7	5.1	-1.5	17.6	-2.7	3.0	–
11.1	18.2	5.4	2.1	0	Kilmarnock & Loudoun	77.2	-1.8	10.8	-8.2	49.8	+5.0	4.0	-1.5	34.5	+3.8	0.9 (2)	–
9.8	15.6	4.9	16.1	5	Motherwell & Wishaw	70.1	-5.2	11.0	-4.6	57.4	+0.9	6.4	+0.3	22.4	+1.0	2.8 (2)	–
9.2	15.1	5.0	16.1	32	Paisley North	68.5	-5.3	9.6	-6.1	59.5	+7.6	6.9	-0.8	21.9	-1.5	2.1 (2)	–
10.1	16.3	5.4	17.3	15	South	69.5	-4.7	8.7	-6.7	57.5	+5.7	9.4	+0.5	23.3	-1.1	1.1 (2)	–
13.7	24.9	2.8	2.4	62	Renfrewshire West	75.9	-1.4	13.6	-9.2	46.6	+3.7	7.7	-0.8	26.5	+5.8	0.7	–
15.0	31.6	3.0	6.2	13	Strathkelvin & Bearsden	78.8	-2.0	20.1	-12.5	52.9	+6.8	9.7	+1.5	16.3	+3.4	1.0 (2)	-9.6
12.8	21.4	4.1	1.1	22	*Tayside, Angus*	72.1	-2.8	24.6	-13.5	15.6	+2.7	9.4	+0.6	48.2	+9.1	2.0	–
8.8	17.2	6.6	34.4	11	Dundee East	69.4	-4.0	15.8	-2.7	51.1	+6.8	4.1	-0.2	26.5	-5.5	2.4 (3)	–
7.5	16.2	5.8	32.1	9	West	67.7	-0.2	13.2	-5.7	52.8	+6.1	7.7	+0.2	23.2	-1.3	2.2 (2)	–
					Ochil, (See Central)												
14.7	23.1	3.6	0.5	20	Perth†	73.9	-2.8	29.3	-11.1	24.8	+11.6	8.0	-3.9	36.3	+1.9	1.5 (2)	–
15.0	19.9	3.1	0.1	21	Tayside North†	74.3	-1.8	35.7	-10.6	11.3	+4.3	8.2	+0.3	44.8	+6.0	–	–
10.3	20.1	5.5	0.1	0	*Western Isles*	70.1	+0.4	6.6	-1.8	55.6	+7.8	3.1	-0.4	33.3	-3.7	1.3	–

Table A1.4 Northern Ireland constituency results, 1997

Index of change		% Voting	% Change in voting	% UUP	% DUP	% Other U	Unionist ch. 1992-97	% APNI	APNI ch. 1992-97	% Con.	% SDLP	SDLP ch. 1992-97	% SF	SF ch. 1992-97	% WP	% Other
22	Antrim East	58.3	−4.3	38.8	19.5	5.1	−3.0	20.2	−5.0	6.8	4.6	−	1.6	−	.	3.5
0	Antrim North	63.8	−0.1	23.6	46.5	−	+1.2	6.2	−1.4	−	15.9	+1.6	6.3	+2.1	.	1.5
5	Antrim South	57.9	−1.6	57.5	−	8.7	−5.2	11.6	+0.7	−	16.2	+2.6	5.5	+2.5	.	0.5
22	Belfast East	63.2	−1.8	25.3	42.6	−	+13.5	23.8	−3.5	2.4	1.6	−	2.1	+0.4	0.6	1.6
24	Belfast North	64.2	+0.9	51.8	−	−	+0.1	5.4	−2.4	−	20.4	+2.1	20.2	+8.9	0.7	1.5
26	Belfast South	62.2	−6.2	36.0	−	14.4	−2.3	12.9	−2.7	2.4	24.3	+10.1	5.1	+2.6	0.7	4.1
21	Belfast West†	74.3	+2.3	3.4	−	−	−8.2	−	−	−	38.7	−5.5	55.9	+13.9	1.6	0.4
31	Down North†	58.0	−2.9	31.1	−	35.1	+17.1	20.7	+5.0	5.0	4.4	−	−	−	.	3.8
16	Down South	70.8	−6.7	32.8	−	−	−2.6	3.5	+1.0	−	52.9	−3.2	10.4	+6.8	.	0.4
13	Fermanagh & S. Tyrone	74.8	−1.1	51.5	−	−	−0.9	2.0	+0.3	−	22.9	+0.0	23.1	+4.0	.	0.4
17	Foyle	70.7	+3.5	−	21.5	−	−3.5	1.7	−0.3	−	52.5	−1.5	23.9	+6.6	.	0.3
27	Lagan Valley	62.2	−6.3	55.4	13.6	−	+2.1	17.2	+5.4	2.7	7.8	−1.3	2.5	+0.4	0.5	0.3
27	Londonderry East	64.8	+1.8	35.6	25.6	−	−3.6	6.4	−1.0	1.1	21.7	+1.8	9.1	+5.6	.	0.5
1	Newry and Armagh	77.9	+1.9	32.7	−	−	−3.5	1.8	+0.0	3.2	41.6	−7.7	20.4	+7.9	.	0.2
65	Strangford	59.5	−3.4	44.3	30.2	−	+5.6	13.1	−3.0	4.2	−	6.7	− 1.2	−	.	0.3
56	Tyrone West†	79.6	+8.3	34.6	−	−	−4.2	1.8	−2.9	−	32.1	+1.1	30.9	+10.9	0.5	0.2
106	Ulster Mid†	86.1	+3.6	−	36.3	−	−4.7	0.9	−1.7	−	22.1	−8.5	40.1	+15.9	0.5	0.1
0	Upper Bann	67.9	+2.0	43.6	11.5	−	−3.9	6.3	+0.7	0.9	24.2	+0.8	12.1	+6.0	1.2	0.2

Notes:

UUP: (Official) Ulster Unionist Party   APNI: Alliance Party of Northern Ireland   SF: Sinn Fein

DUP: Democratic Unionist Party   SDLP: Social Democratic & Labour Party   WP: Workers' Party

Other U: Other Unionist, viz. Progressive Unionist Party (Antrim East, Antrim South, Belfast South), United Kingdom Unionist (Down North)

'Unionist Change' is the change in the total vote for Official Unionists, Democratic Unionists and other Unionists.

Table A1.5   Outstanding results, 1997

12 Closest Results		
%	Votes	
0.0	(2)	Winchester (Lib Dem)
0.0	(12)	Torbay (Lib Dem)
0.1	(56)	Kingston & Surbiton (Lib Dem)
0.2	(77)	Dorset South (Con)
0.2	(130)	Somerton & Frome (Lib Dem)
0.2	(132)	Bedfordshire SW (Con)
0.3	(189)	Kettering (Lab)
0.3	(187)	Wellingborough (Lab)
0.4	(281)	Teignbridge (Con)
0.5	(240)	Milton Keynes NE (Lab)
0.5	(222)	Hexham (Con)
0.5	(238)	Lichfield (Con)

12 Highest Turnouts	
%	
86.1	Ulster Mid
82.2	Brecon & Radnorshire
81.8	Stirling
81.0	Wirral South
80.8	Monmouth
80.2	Ayr
80.0	Vale of Glamorgan
79.8	Leicestershire NW
79.7	Cardiff North
79.7	Galloway & U. Nithsdale
79.6	Tyrone West
79.1	Wansdyke

10 Biggest Majorities		
%	Votes	
74.4	(28,421)	Bootle (Lab)
71.6	(30,012)	Easington (Lab)
70.7	(28,035)	Blaenau Gwent (Lab)
69.2	(27,086)	Merthyr Tydfil (Lab)
67.2	(27,038)	Liverpool Walton (Lab)
67.2	(24,501)	Barnsley Central (Lab)
66.1	(25,569)	Swansea East (Lab)
65.7	(23,931)	Islwyn (Lab)
65.7	(22,906)	Tyne Bridge (Lab)
64.8	(26,741)	Neath (Lab)

10 Lowest Turnouts	
%	
51.9	Liverpool Riverside
52.2	Hackney N. & Stoke Newington
52.6	Manchester Central
53.0	Sheffield Central
54.2	Birmingham Ladywood
54.4	West Bromwich West
54.7	Leeds Central
54.7	Hackney S. & Shoreditch
54.7	Kensington & Chelsea
55.5	Vauxhall

10 Largest Conservative Share of Vote	
%	
55.3	Huntingdon
53.6	Kensington & Chelsea
53.1	Arundel & South Downs
52.2	Sutton Coldfield
51.6	Surrey Heath
50.9	Hampshire North-East
50.8	Horsham
50.6	New Forest West
50.4	Chesham & Amersham
50.2	Ruislip Northwood

10 Lowest Swings in Conservative Marginals	
%	
−5.2	Ayr
−5.6	Bristol North-West
−5.6	Forest of Dean
−6.4	Falmouth & Camborne
−7.1	Swindon North
−7.4	Batley & Spen
−7.8	Aldridge-Brownhills*
−8.7	Staffordshire Moorlands
−8.9	Loughborough
−9.3	Burton

* Retained by Conservatives

10 Lowest Changes in Conservative Share of Vote

%	
4.7	Bethnal Green & Bow
0.3	Greenwich & Woolwich
−0.8	Bradford West
−1.1	Antrim East
−1.2	Linlithgow
−1.3	Liverpool Riverside
−1.7	Liverpool Wavertree
−1.8	Western Isles
−2.1	Glasgow Pollok
−2.1	Glasgow Bailliestown

10 Greatest Falls in Conservative Share of Vote

%	
−29.7	Down North
−24.7	Tatton
−21.9	Gordon
−20.7	Woking
−19.0	Lewisham West
−18.6	Dulwich & W. Norwood
−18.4	Hastings & Rye
−18.3	Dagenham
−18.1	Newbury
−18.0	Wallasy

10 Largest Labour Share of Vote

%	
82.9	Bootle
80.2	Easington
79.5	Blaenau Gwent
78.4	Liverpool Walton
77.1	Knowsley South
77.0	Barnsley Central
76.8	Tyne Bridge
76.7	Merthyr Tydfil
76.4	Houghton & Washington E.
75.7	Pontefract & Castleford

10 Greatest Increases in Labour Share of Vote

%	
23.1	Liverpool Wavertree
22.4	Crosby
20.4	Brent North
20.2	Cambridgeshire NE
20.1	Hove
19.7	Stockton South
19.5	Wimbledon
19.4	Morecambe & Lunesdale
19.1	Erith & Thamesmead
19.0	Pudsey

10 Greatest Falls in Labour Share of the Vote

%	
−11.7	Bradford West
−7.2	Bethnal Green & Bow
−5.2	Christchurch
−4.9	Sheffield Hallam
−4.8	Harrogate & Knaresborough
−2.1	Cardiff South & Penarth
−1.6	Orkney & Shetland
−0.8	St. Ives
−0.7	Airdrie & Shotts
−0.6	Newbury

10 Largest Liberal Democrat Share of Vote

%	
54.5	Hazel Grove
53.2	Cornwall North
52.9	Newbury
52.0	Orkney & Shetland
51.5	Harrogate & Knaresborough
51.3	Sheffield Hallam
51.2	Fife North-East
50.7	Devon North
49.5	Cheltenham
48.7	Yeovil

10 Greatest Increases in Liberal Democrat Share of Vote
%

20.6	Sheffield Hallam
19.2	Christchurch
18.2	Harrogate & Knaresborough
15.8	Newbury
15.4	Gordon
13.3	Edinburgh West
11.4	Hazel Grove
10.7	Kingston & Surbiton
9.0	Cornwall South-East
8.5	Sutton & Cheam

10 Greatest Falls in Liberal Democrat Share of the Vote
%

−22.6	Greenwich & Woolwich
−14.6	Cambridgeshire NE
−13.8	Bethnal Green & Bow
−13.4	Erith & Thamesmead
−13.3	Wyre Forest
−13.2	Liverpool Wavertree
−12.4	Pudsey
−11.1	Blyth Valley
−10.4	Cotswold
−10.4	Stockton South

10 Highest Nationalist Vote Shares
%

55.8	Banff & Buchan (SNP)
51.8	Caernarfon (PC)
50.7	Meirionnydd Nant Conwy (PC)
48.3	Angus (SNP)
44.8	Tayside North (SNP)
43.9	Galloway & U. Nithsdale (SNP)
41.6	Ceredigion (PC)
41.6	Moray (SNP)
39.5	Yns Mon (PC)
36.4	Perth (SNP)

10 Highest Referendum Party Shares
%

9.2	Harwich
8.0	Folkestone & Hythe
7.6	Suffolk West
7.0	Reigate
6.9	St. Ives
6.7	Bexhill & Battle
6.6	Cotswold
6.6	Yeovil
6.6	Falmouth & Camborne
6.5	Truro & St. Austell

All 'Other' Saved Deposits

65.3	B. Boothroyd	West Bromwich West	The Speaker
60.2	M. Bell	Tatton	Independent
23.3	R. Silvester	West Bromwich West	Labour Change
11.4	S. Edwards	West Bromwich West	National Democrat
11.1	T. Sheridan	Glasgow, Pollok	Scottish Socialist Alln.
9.6	S. Radford	Liverpool, West Derby	Liberal
9.3	J. Foreman	Cardiff South	New Labour
7.5	D. King	Bethnal Green & Bow	Br. National Party
7.3	J. Tyndall	Poplar & Canning Tn	Br. National Party
7.2	T. Betts	Hackney South	New Labour
6.8	I. Kahn	East Ham	Socialist Labour
6.6	T. Milson	Bethnal Green & Bow	Liberal
6.1	B. Hughes	Billericay	New Labour
5.8	A. LeBlond	Jarrow	Ind. Labour
5.7	N. Farage	Salisbury	UK Independence
5.3	T. Burns	Cardiff Central	Socialist Labour
5.2	A. Scargill	Newport East	Socialist Labour

Table A1.6   By-election results, 1992–97

By-election	Date & Index of Boundary Change (%)	Turnout (%)	Con (%)	Lab (%)	Lib Dem (%)	Nat (%)	Other (%)
Newbury	1992	82.8	55.9	6.0	37.3	–	(1) 0.8
Lib. Dem. gain	6.5.93	71.3	26.9	2.0	65.1	–	(16) 6.1
(12)	1997	76.7	37.8	5.5	52.9	–	(4) 3.8
Christchurch	1992	80.7	63.5	12.1	23.6	–	(2) 0.7
Lib. Dem. gain	29.7.93	74.2	31.4	2.7	62.2	–	(11) 3.7
Con. recovery (4)	1997	78.6	46.4	6.9	42.6	–	(2) 4.1
Rotherham	1992	71.7	23.7	63.9	12.3	–	– –
	5.5.94	43.7	9.9	55.6	29.7	–	(2) 4.8
(0)	1997	62.8	14.8	71.3	10.4	–	(2) 4.0
Barking	1992	70.0	33.9	51.6	14.5	–	– –
	9.6.94	38.3	10.4	72.1	12.0	–	(3) 5.5
(10)	1997	61.4	17.6	65.8	9.5	–	(3) 7.1
Bradford South	1992	75.6	38.4	47.6	13.7	–	(1) 0.3
	9.6.94	44.2	17.8	55.3	23.9	–	(2) 3.0
(0)	1997	65.8	28.0	56.7	11.3	–	(11) 4.0
Dagenham	1992	70.7	36.3	52.3	11.4	–	– –
	9.6.94	37.0	9.9	72.0	8.4	–	(3) 9.7
(2)	1997	61.7	18.5	65.7	7.5	–	(5) 8.3
Eastleigh	1992	82.9	51.3	20.7	28.0	–	– –
Lib. Dem. gain	9.6.94	58.7	24.7	27.6	44.3	–	(3) 3.4
(26)	1997	76.6	33.7	26.8	35.1	–	(1) 4.4
Newham North East	1992	60.4	30.5	58.3	11.2	–	– –
(19)	9.6.94	34.8	14.6	74.0	4.2	–	(4) 6.3
(East Ham)	1997	60.3	16.1	64.6	6.5	–	(4) 12.7

Monklands East	1992	75.0	16.0	61.3	4.6	18.0	–	0.1
	30.6.94	70.0	2.3	49.8	2.6	44.9	(2)	0.4
(Airdrie & Shotts) (53)	1997	71.4	8.9	61.8	4.2	24.4	(1)	0.7
Dudley West	1992	82.1	48.8	40.7	10.5	–	–	–
Lab. gain	15.12.94	47.0	18.7	68.8	7.6	–	(7)	5.0
(Dudley South) (62)	1997	71.7	29.4	56.6	10.9	–	–	–
Islwyn	1992	81.4	14.9	74.3	5.7	3.9	(1)	1.3
	16.2.95	45.1	3.9	69.2	10.6	12.7	(3)	3.6
(0)	1997	71.9	7.9	74.2	8.4	6.2	(1)	3.3
Perth & Kinross	1992	76.9	40.2	12.5	11.4	36.0	(5)	35
SNP gain	25.5.95	62.1	21.4	22.9	11.8	40.4	(2)	1.5
(20)	1997	73.9	29.3	24.8	8.0	37.0		
Littleborough & S'worth	1992	81.6	44.2	19.9	35.9	–	–	–
Lib. Dem. gain	27.7.95	64.4	23.6	33.8	38.5	–	(7)	4.1
(Oldham E. & S'worth) (59)	1997	73.9	19.7	41.7	35.4	–	(3)	3.2
Lab. gain								
Hemsworth	1992	75.9	18.6	70.8	10.5			–
	1.2.96	39.5	8.8	71.9	6.9		–(6)	12.3
(21)	1997	67.9	17.8	70.6	8.9		–(1)	2.8
Staffordshire S. E.	1992	82.0	50.7	38.2	9.6		–(1)	1.6
Lab. gain	11.4.96	59.6	28.5	60.1	4.7		(10)	6.7
(Tamworth) (7)	1997	74.2	36.7	51.8	8.1		(3)	3.4
Barnsley East	1992	72.9	14.2	77.2	8.6	–	–	–
	12.12.96	33.6	7.3	76.4	8.4	–	(3)	7.9
(56)	1997	63.9	11.4	73.1	10.4	–	(3)	5.1
Wirral South	1992	82.3	50.8	34.6	13.1	–	(2)	1.5
Lab. gain	27.2.97	73.0	34.4	52.6	10.1	–	(9)	3.0
(0)	1997	81.0	36.4	50.9	10.4	–	(3)	2.3

Northern Ireland By-election

By-election	Date & Index of Boundary Change (%)	Turnout (%)	Pop U (%)	UK Unionist (%)	UUP (%)	DUP (%)	Alliance (%)	Con	Other
Down North	1992	65.5	42.9	–	–	9.8	14.7	32.0	(1) 0.6
	15.6.95	38.7	–	37.0	26.4	–	25.4	2.1	(4) 9.0
	1997 (31)	58.0	–	35.1	31.1	–	20.7	5.0	(4) 8.3

Note: New constituency names are given in parentheses.

Appendix 2 The Results Analysed

John Curtice and Michael Steed

As the results flowed in on election night, Labour's victory was widely hailed as a landslide. The overall total-vote swing of 10.3 per cent from Conservative to Labour across Great Britain[1] as a whole was the largest achieved by any party since 1945, and with 419 seats (including the Speaker), Labour secured more MPs than it had ever done before. In the litany of sweeping victories that brought left-of-centre governments to power after long periods of Tory rule, the 1997 election appeared to be at least the equal of both 1906 and 1945.

Yet when we take a slightly closer look at the result in terms of votes, a somewhat different picture emerges. First, at 44.4 per cent, Labour's share of the vote was lower than it had achieved in all elections from 1945 to 1966, including the three it lost in a row in the 1950s. Second, with the turnout across the United Kingdom as a whole at a record post-war low of 71.2 per cent, only 30.9 per cent of the electorate voted for the new government. Since 1945, only the Labour governments which emerged after the two 1974 elections won power after securing the active support of a lower proportion of the electorate.

The Liberal Democrats' performance also looked very different depending on whether one took account of seats or votes. Their share of the vote fell for the third election in a row; indeed at 17.2 per cent, it was the party's second worst performance since it started fighting elections on a nationwide basis in February 1974. Yet the party won no less than 46 seats, the largest block of third-party MPs since 1929, and twice as many as the Alliance secured at the height of its success in 1983.

Nonetheless, the Conservatives' performance looks poor irrespective of whether one focuses on seats or votes. At 31.4 per cent, their share of the vote was lower than in any parliamentary election since there was a mass franchise. With 165 seats, the party only just managed to beat its previous record low of 157 seats, the record set in the Liberal landslide of 1906. But even here the picture is not entirely straightforward. The Conservatives won 3 per cent more of the vote than Labour did in 1983. Labour's lead was two points lower than the Conservatives' was on that occasion too. Yet the Conservatives' tally of seats was 44 lower than Labour's 1983 total.

Moreover, if we were only to look at the outcome in terms of seats, we would miss one substantial new feature entirely: for the first time ever, a fourth party fought most of the seats in Great Britain. The Referendum Party, founded by the millionaire businessman Sir James Goldsmith, fought 547 of the seats in support of a single policy, demanding that there should be a referendum on whether the UK should remain within the European Union. It received no less than 2.7 per cent of the vote as its reward. In all, no less than 7.0 per cent of voters cast their ballots for someone other than a representative of the three main British parties, the highest total ever.[2]

The 1997 election result thus poses a number of important puzzles which this appendix tries to address. First, why did the Conservatives do so badly? Did disillusioned Conservatives remain at home? How far did Europe, the issue which dogged and divided the party throughout the period from 1992 to 1997, contribute to its downfall by encouraging a seepage of support to the Referendum Party? And what role if any was played by the state of the economy?

Second, why did Labour and the Liberal Democrats win so many seats on relatively unimpressive shares of the vote? What was the role of tactical voting, that is voters opting to vote for the party that was best placed to defeat the Conservative locally even if that party was not their first choice? How important were the opposition parties' attempts to concentrate their campaigning resources on key target seats?

Third, with the new Labour government committed to holding a referendum on its retention, what are the implications of the 1997 result for our understanding of the workings of the first-past-the-post electoral system? Has the election seen a restoration of the system's tendency to give the winner a bonus? Or was the result instead an indication of a new bias against the Conservatives that might hinder their ability to regain power? How different might the outcome have been under an alternative system?

There is, however, one methodological difficulty that we have to overcome before we can address any of these questions. A new set of constituency boundaries was introduced in the 1997 election. Although the changes were less radical than those of the previous review first implemented in 1983, only 165 seats were left completely unchanged. Fortunately we have available to us two sets of estimates of what the outcome of the 1992 election would have been on the new boundaries introduced in 1997 and these estimates enable us to calculate how far each party's support rose or fell in each constituency between 1992 and 1997.

The first set of estimates was produced by Colin Rallings and Michael Thrasher for the main broadcasting organisations, using, for the most part, local election results to estimate how the parties' support had been redistributed.[3] These are the estimates on which all the figures quoted in this book's appendices are based. A second set of estimates was produced independently by David Rossiter and his colleagues. These use the 1991 Census data on the social character of redrawn constituencies to estimate how they would have voted.[4] Encouragingly, these alternative estimates are within a percentage point or two of those produced by Rallings and Thrasher in most constituencies. However, in order to check that none of the patterns that we identify might be the artificial result of mis-estimates of what would have happened in 1992, we have repeated all of the analyses undertaken here using these alternative estimates as well as those of Rallings and Thrasher.[5]

Table A2.1   Measures of change since 1992

	Overall	Mean	Median	Standard deviation
Change in Conservative vote	−11.3	−11.4	−11.7	3.3
Change in Labour vote	+9.2	+9.6	+9.7	4.6
Change in Lib Dem vote	−1.2	−1.3	−1.4	4.1
Total-vote swing	−10.3	−10.5	−10.7	3.3
Two-party swing	−13.4	−13.4	−13.3	4.3

The following seats have been excluded from the calculation of mean, median and standard deviation: Tatton (no Labour or Liberal Democrat candidates in 1997); West Bromwich West (no Conservative or Liberal Democrat candidates in 1997); Greenwich & Woolwich (No Liberal Democrat candidate in 1992). These seats have been excluded from all analysis of party performance in the remainder of this appendix.

Total-vote swing is the average of the change in Conservative share of the vote and the Labour share of the vote. Two-party swing is the change in the Conservative share of the votes cast for Conservative and Labour only (that is, the two-party vote). In both cases a plus sign indicates a swing to Conservative, a minus sign a swing to Labour.

Just how party support changed across the country as a whole between 1992 and 1997 can be seen in Table A2.1. For each measure of change the table gives three statistics. The first, the overall change, is the change in the total of votes cast across the country as a whole. The second and third statistics are the mean and the median of the relevant measure of change in each of the 638 constituencies where the results at the two elections are comparable.[6] Although the first of these is the most widely quoted statistic when election results are reported, it is the latter two which are the more important when it comes to the distribution of seats. At this stage we should note that, on most of the measures, the mean and median measures of change were marginally worse for the Conservatives and better for Labour than the overall change.

Apart from measuring the level of the change since 1992, we also need to ask how much it varied from one constituency to another. British general elections used to be noted for the uniformity of the change in party support from one constituency to another.[7] Since and including the 1979 election, however, general elections have become notable for the amount of variation. Table A2.1 measures the amount of variation in each measure of change between 1992 and 1997 by calculating its standard deviation. However, some caution needs to be exercised in interpreting this measure at this election. As all of the figures have been calculated on the basis of the estimates by Rallings and Thrasher of what would have happened in 1992 in each constituency, some of the variation in the results will be the result of inaccuracies in those estimates rather than real differences between constituencies. Even bearing this in mind, the figures are still broadly similar to those for other recent elections. Yet again, the British electorate appears to have swung very differently in one part of the country from another.

As in all other recent elections, the performance of Labour and the Liberal Democrats' varied much more from one constituency to another than did that of the Conservatives. This suggests, perhaps, that their performance was influenced by one or more considerations that did not apply to the Conservatives. Table A2.2 examines this possibility further by showing the correlations between each of the three measures of party change. It shows that there was indeed a high correlation between Labour and Liberal Democrat performance: where Labour did relatively well, the Liberal Democrats did relatively badly – and vice versa. In contrast, there was little relationship at all between how well the Conservatives and the Liberal Democrats performed.

Table A2.2   Correlations between changes in party performance

Conservative and Labour	–0.41
Conservative and Liberal Democrat	–0.19
Labour and Liberal Democrat	–0.63

This overview provides us with some clear guidance about how best to set about our inquiry. We begin by looking at the variation in turnout, examining in particular whether the results suggest that Conservative supporters were more likely to stay at home. We then look more generally at the performance of the Conservatives, including the threat posed to the party by the Referendum Party. We then look at the performance of the main opposition parties. Finally, after a brief examination of the nationalists in

Scotland and Wales, we look at how the electoral system translated party performance into seats in the House of Commons.

TURNOUT

At 71.4 per cent, turnout was marginally lower than the 71.9 per cent recorded in 1970, the previous post-war low, when the election was held during the holiday season and when the rules on the availability of postal votes were tighter than they are now. It seems clear that the 1997 general election excited less interest than any other in living memory.

One obvious possible explanation is that this was caused by disillusioned Tory voters staying at home. If this were so we would expect to find that the Conservative vote fell most where turnout fell most, but, as Table A2.3 shows, there is no such relationship in the results. In Scotland, where turnout fell a little less (–4.1 per cent) than it did in either England (–6.9 per cent) or in Wales (–6.3 per cent), Conservative support actually fell less where turnout held up most. Elsewhere, Tory support fell by just as much where turnout dropped least as where it dropped most.[8]

Table A2.3   Turnout and Conservative performance

| Change in turnout | Change in % voting Conservative in | | |
	London & south-east	Scotland	Elsewhere
Fall less than 4%	–13.9 (34)	–9.0 (47)	–11.6 (39)
Fall 4–6%	–13.0 (51)	–6.2 (15)	–10.5 (133)
Fall 6–8%	–13.8 (71)	–8.1 (8)	–10.9 (119)
Fall more than 8%	–14.1 (34)	–4.5 (2)	–11.2 (85)

If Tory voters had been staying at home, then we would have also expected to find that turnout fell most in seats where the Conservatives were previously strongest, but in fact the opposite was true. Turnout fell on average by 1 per cent more in those seats that Labour was defending than in those that the Conservatives were. This was all the more surprising given that in 1992 turnout had failed to rise in Labour seats, whereas it had risen by more than 3 per cent in Conservative ones.[9] On average just 68 per cent turned out to vote in the average Labour seat, compared with 74 per cent in the typical Conservative one, a larger gap than ever before. Labour's heartlands, then, were distinctly lukewarm about their party's surge to victory.[10]

One partial explanation for the widening of the difference in the turnout between Conservative and Labour seats may have been changing perceptions of marginality. Turnout fell most heavily (−8.1 per cent) in those seats which Labour had captured from the Conservatives in 1992. In contrast it fell least (−5.2 per cent) where the Conservatives had only been less than 10 per cent ahead in 1992. Evidently voters in the former category took notice of the message of the polls and decided their local contest was no longer in doubt, or else the local parties themselves conveyed that message by slackening their campaigning efforts somewhat. Meanwhile the opposite forces were at work in those seats where the Conservatives were hanging on narrowly.

Even so, this is not a complete explanation of the continued widening of the turnout gap between Labour and Tory Britain. Turnout in safe Labour seats (that is, those with a 1992 majority of more than 30 per cent) fell by 0.6 per cent more than in safe Conservative ones. Despite the rapid growth of Labour Party membership over the last three years, the party still appears to have a significant problem in mobilising some of its traditional support into the polling station.

Nowhere was this more true than in the north of England (where turnout had already risen by less than in the south of England and the Midlands in 1992); it now fell again by more than in the south of England. Quite why this new North/South gap in turnout has appeared is one of the intriguing unanswered questions of recent British electoral behaviour; the fact that it has repeated itself means that certainly it can no longer be ignored.

Other variations in turnout are more readily accounted for. Turnout dropped much less in 1997 (in some cases it appeared to rise slightly) in university seats, where holding the 1992 election during the vacation had helped to depress it. Contrary to much press speculation beforehand, however, this was not accompanied by a higher than average swing against the Conservatives. Even more strikingly, some of both the biggest and the lowest falls were in London. For example, turnout rose in all three seats in the borough of Brent and either rose or fell by much less than average everywhere in Southwark, Newham and Hackney. Meanwhile there were above-average falls in Kensington & Chelsea, Wandsworth, Merton and Haringey. We noted after the 1987 election how turnouts had risen or fallen on that occasion by unusual amounts across whole London boroughs, and suggested that this reflected the impact of local changes in the practice of registration.[11] Such changes could have such an impact because, as the 1991 Census register check demonstrated, electoral registration was seriously deficient in London.[12] It is evident that the problem remains a serious one.

THE CONSERVATIVES AND THE ANTI-EUROPEANS

It has become commonplace in recent years to argue that rises and falls in support for the government can be accounted for by the state of the economy.[13] Voters are supposedly happy to re-elect the government if they feel that the economy is performing well. In contrast they swing against the government if the economy is performing badly. However, the Conservative defeat in 1997 came against the backdrop of low inflation, low interest rates and falling unemployment, all conditions which should have been conducive to the re-election of the government.

The geography of the Conservatives' performance in 1997 is also at variance with the idea of economic voting. If the economy were responsible for the Conservatives' downfall we would expect to find that the party's vote fell most in those regions or individual constituencies where the economy had been faring least well. In fact, what is notable about the Conservative performance in 1997 is the almost complete absence of any significant regional variation at all. The country deserted the Conservatives with one accord.

At first glance, Table A1.2 of Appendix 1 seems to contradict this assertion It shows, for example, that the Conservatives' vote fell particularly heavily in Outer London and in the South East outside the capital, while the party suffered below-average losses in Scotland, Wales, and to a lesser extent, the North of England, but much of this regional variation disappears once we take into account one important pattern, that is, the relationship between the Conservatives' performance and how strong they were beforehand.

This relationship is readily apparent from Table 2.4. The Conservative vote clearly fell more heavily in those seats where the party was previously stronger. Thus, for example, in those seats where the Conservatives started off with less than 15 per cent of the vote, its support fell by less than half the national norm. It might be thought that this was no more than should have been expected, especially when a party's vote was falling as heavily as the Conservatives' was in 1997. But in 1983 when Labour's vote fell precipitately to just 28 per cent, it actually went down most where the party was previously weakest.[14] And it has been demonstrated that there is no logical reason why a party's losses should be in proportion to its prior strength.[15] Indeed, even in this case the size of the fall in Conservative support was not proportional to the party's prior strength. There was little difference between the behaviour of those seats where the Conservatives started off with just one-third of the vote, and those where they had previously won two-thirds. It was only where the party had previously secured less than a third of the vote, that the size of its previous vote made a difference.

Table A2.4   Prior strength and change in Conservative support

1992 Con % vote	Change in % voting Conservative in			
	London	Rest of SE	Elsewhere	All
Under 15%	−5.0(1)	–	−4.2(21)	−4.2(22)
15–25%	−7.5(4)	–	−7.7(73)	−7.7(77)
25–33.3%	−12.6(12)	–	−10.2(66)	−10.6(78)
33.3–40%	−16.1(8)	−11.5(1)	−11.5(74)	−12.0(83)
40–50%	−15.5(16)	−13.1(26)	−11.7(122)	−12.3(164)
Over 50%	−15.0(32)	−13.2(90)	−11.7(92)	−12.8(214)

The Conservatives began the election in a much weaker position in Scotland, Wales and the North of England than elsewhere, so the pattern illustrated in Table A2.4 could therefore well be sufficient to account for much of the variation in Table A1.2. Indeed, as Table A2.5 illustrates, this is largely the case. If we look at just those seats where the Conservatives started off with a third or more of the vote, only London and, to a lesser extent, the rest of the South-East, stand out as regions where the Conservatives clearly did worse than the national average. Table A2.4 shows the Conservative performance was consistently worse in the South-Eastern corner of England in all but the least Conservative of constituencies.[16]

Table A2.5   Regional uniformity of Conservative performance[1]

Region	Change in % voting Conservative	
	(%)	(seats)
London	−15.3	(56)
Rest of South East	−13.2	(117)
South West	−10.9	(50)
East Anglia	−12.5	(22)
East Midlands	−12.2	(40)
West Midlands	−11.3	(51)
Yorks. & Humber	−11.6	(35)
North West	−11.9	(41)
Northern	−13.0	(14)
Wales	−11.7	(17)
Scotland	−11.2	(18)
Great Britain	−12.5	(461)

Table based only on those seats where the Conservatives won one-third or more of the vote in 1992.

Even this relatively poor Conservative performance in the South-East fails to provide any support to the idea that voters were influenced by the state of the economy. For, if the economy had mattered, then this should have been the area where the Conservatives turned in some of their best performances rather than their worst. Between the third quarter of 1995 and the first quarter of 1997, the price of the average semi-detached house had risen by 30 per cent in London, and by 15 per cent in the typical constituency in the South-East, compared with 12 per cent across the country as a whole. Equally, unemployment (defined as the total unemployed as a percentage of the electorate) fell on average by 1.9 per cent in the capital between January 1996 and March 1997 compared with 1.3 per cent across the country as a whole. In short, it is clear that the short-term state of the economy was not responsible for the Conservatives' misfortunes.[17]

One suggestion made after the election to explain why London and the South-East swung against the Conservatives[18] was that it was occasioned by an adverse public reaction to the privatisation of British Rail (completed in the months immediately prior to the election) together with concern at the prospect, if the Conservatives were to be re-elected, of the privatisation of the London Underground. It is undoubtedly true that, compared with most of the rest of the country, unusually large proportions of the electorate travel to work by rail in London and the South-East. If rail privatisation was the explanation for London's behaviour, we should expect to find that the swing against the Conservatives was higher the greater the proportion of rail commuters. Yet, if anything, the opposite proves to be the case.

However, it is noticeable that outside London there was a particularly large fall in Conservative support in a number of commuting constituencies on the edge of major conurbations. Thus in eight constituencies in that category where 6 per cent or more of those who are economically active travel to work by rail and where the Conservatives started off with more than a third of the vote, Conservative support fell on average by 14.2 per cent, two and half points above the national average.[19] Equally, in another eight such constituencies where the Conservatives started off with between a quarter and a third if the vote, Conservative support fell by 11.9 per cent, one and a half points above average. Meanwhile, other characteristics that these constituencies (and much of Outer London) also share in common, such as the fact that they contain relatively large numbers of owner-occupiers of semi-detached houses, are not generally correlated with Conservative performance. So we cannot dismiss the possibility that rail commuters may have had particular reason to be disaffected with the government.

What of the more general pattern that Conservative support fell most where the party had previously been strongest? One possibility that this suggests is that perhaps middle-class voters, who after all are more numerous in constituencies where the Conservatives are traditionally strong, were more likely to switch to Labour than were working-class voters. For many commentators, Tony Blair's attempt to fashion his party's image as 'New Labour' did indeed seem to be designed to improve his party's appeal to middle-class voters in particular (see Chapter 3). Perhaps here we have evidence that he succeeded.

Given the strong interrelationship between prior party strength and the class composition of a constituency, it is clearly difficult to disentangle the effect of one from the other. But if the pattern of Conservative performance were a reflection of class differences in behaviour, we should find that amongst the large body of seats where the Conservatives began with more than a third of the vote, Conservative support should have fallen more heavily in those seats with a larger proportion of middle-class voters. However, as Table A2.6 shows, there is no evidence that this is the case. If anything, Conservative support fell a little more heavily in those seats which were more working-class in character than in those which were predominantly middle-class.[20]

Table A2.6   Class composition and Conservative performance

| | Change in % voting Conservative in | |
	working-class seats	middle-class seats
London	−16.5 (12)	−15.0 (44)
Rest of south-east	−13.6 (22)	−13.1 (95)
Elsewhere	−12.1 (123)	−11.4 (165)

Table A2.6 is based only on those seats where the Conservatives won more than a third of the vote in 1992. Middle-class seats are those where the % of heads of households who are employers and managers (1991 Census) is greater than 19.0. Working-class seats are those where the % who are employers and managers is below that figure.

Another possibility that we might want to consider is that the pattern of Conservative performance is a reflection of the behaviour of the traditionally Conservative press both during the 1997 election campaign and indeed for much of the 1992–97 parliament. Many traditionally Conservative newspapers failed to endorse the Conservatives at this election, and most had provided highly critical coverage of the party over much of the previous five years (see Chapter 9). Perhaps these newspapers, which are generally more widely read in traditionally Conservative constituencies, and especially in London and the South-East, encouraged some of their readers to leave the ranks of the Tory faithful.

However, we can find little evidence to support this hypothesis either. For example, we can divide those constituencies outside London and the south-east where the Conservatives started off with more than a third of the vote into two groups of roughly equal size: those where the proportion of readers of traditionally Tory newspapers is above the national median, and those where it is below. The fall in Conservative support in the two groups was virtually identical at −11.6 per cent and −11.7 per cent respectively. It seems as though the Conservatives cannot blame their defeat on the behaviour of their erstwhile friends in the press.[21]

Almost every explanation of the Conservatives' performance which refers to political developments or social changes in the two or three years before the election seems to be found wanting. One key fact to bear in mind is that the tendency for Conservative support to fall more heavily where the party was previously strongest was also evident at every local election held from May 1993 onwards.[22] It was also apparent in the 1994 European elections when similarly it largely accounted for the apparent regional variation in Conservative performance.[23] This continued repetition of the same pattern of loss suggests that the Conservative defeat in 1997 was but yet another expression of a longstanding nationwide political disenchantment with the incumbent government, a disenchantment that almost undoubtedly set in the moment that the pound fell out of the European Exchange Rate Mechanism in September 1992.

The events of 'Black Wednesday' of course opened a wound within the Conservative Party that failed to heal thereafter as the party divided openly between its 'Euro-sceptic' and 'Euro-phile' wings. One of the reasons why it proved difficult to achieve an accommodation between the wings of the party was the pressure exerted by Sir James Goldsmith in establishing the Referendum Party. Many Conservatives, particularly those of a Euro-sceptic persuasion, believed that if the Referendum Party fought the election it could only succeed in taking votes away from themselves; thus they called for the party to adopt a more Euro-sceptic tone, particularly in respect of any single European currency, in the hope that this might persuade Sir James to stand down.

In the event the Referendum Party did contest no less than 547 constituencies, standing aside only in certain seats where the incumbent MP was known to be anti-European. On average its candidates secured 3.1 per cent of the vote in those constituencies where they stood, the strongest ever performance by a British minor party. It clearly outperformed its main rival for anti-European sentiment, the United Kingdom Independence Party (UKIP) which averaged only 1.2 per cent in the 194 constituencies where it stood and which trailed the Referendum Party in all but two of the 165 constituencies where both parties stood. Even in the 29 seats where a UKIP candidate stood and a Referendum Party candidate did not, only in one did the UKIP do as well as a Referendum Party candidate would have been expected to do.[24]

However, the Referendum Party's appeal tailed off noticeably north of the Scottish border where it secured an average of just 1.1 per cent of the vote. This may reflect the rather higher level of support for Europe in Scotland,[25] or more likely, a feeling that the party's anti-Europeanism was a form of English rather than British nationalism. The party also performed relatively weakly in both Merseyside and Inner London, with an average of just 2.1 per cent. Its best performances were all in those parts of England where Euro-scepticism is at its highest, the South of England outside inner London, and in East Anglia, where it averaged no less than 3.9 per cent. It tended to do particularly well in constituencies with a large agricultural or elderly population, the former doubtless a reflection of the controversy surrounding European agricultural policy.

One clear result of this pattern is that, overall, the Referendum Party on average scored more highly in seats that were being defended by the Conservatives (3.6 per cent), rather than by Labour (2.5 per cent). Moreover, the Referendum Party's share of the vote was greater than the Conservative majority in no less than 19 constituencies. But these facts alone are not sufficient evidence to demonstrate that Euro-sceptic Conservatives' fears about the damage that Sir James might inflict were in fact justified.

Ascertaining just how much damage was caused is much more difficult than is often realised. Some commentators have looked at how those who voted for the Referendum Party said how they voted in 1992. For example, amongst respondents to the BBC/NOP exit poll, over half of Referendum Party voters said they voted Conservative in 1992. Apart from the fact that most polls contained too few respondents who had voted for the Referendum Party to produce reliable estimates of their political origins, such information does not in any case tell us what damage, if any, the Referendum Party inflicted on the Conservatives. Perhaps those who switched from the Conservatives in 1992 to the Referendum Party in 1997 would simply have defected to another party if the Referendum Party had not stood. In other words, our aim should be to ascertain how Referendum Party voters would have voted in 1997 if the Referendum Party had not existed.

Looking at election results can help us to address that question. We can compare party performances in those constituencies where the Referendum Party did not stand with those where they did; and we can see whether one party suffered more than another where the Referendum Party did particularly well.

Table A2.7 addresses this by breaking down how each of the three main parties did according to the strength of the challenge posed by the Referendum and UKIP parties combined. In view of what we know already about the pattern of the Conservatives' performance, the table is confined to those seats where the party started with more than a third of the vote. We also look separately at seats in London, the rest of the south-east, and elsewhere.

Table A2.7   Impact of the anti-European parties

	Change in % voting			
Anti-European performance	Con	Lab	Lib Dem	No. of seats
London				
No candidate	−14.5	+14.0	+0.2	(6)
0–3%	−15.3	+13.8	−0.5	(31)
3–6%	−15.6	+12.0	−0.7	(19)
More than 6%	−	−	−	(0)
Rest of South-East				
No candidate	−12.2	+12.6	−1.2	(11)
0–3%	−13.7	+12.6	−0.7	(17)
3–6%	−13.1	+11.2	−2.4	(72)
More than 6%	−13.6	+9.9	−2.7	(17)
Elsewhere				
No candidate	−9.9	+10.5	−0.8	(27)
0–3%	−11.7	+9.4	−0.4	(118)
3–6%	−12.0	+9.5	−1.1	(124)
More than 6%	−11.6	+7.5	−2.2	(19)

The message from all three parts of the table is remarkably consistent. The presence or absence of an anti-European candidate clearly made a difference to how well the Conservatives performed, but the party's vote was largely uninfluenced by how well the local anti-European candidate(s) did. The two opposition parties in contrast were less substantially affected by the mere presence or absence of an anti-European candidate, but they were evidently the losers if that candidate were to do well locally. Further analysis which also takes into account the impact of the tactical situation on the performance of the two opposition parties (see further below) suggests that in fact it was the Liberal Democrats rather than Labour who were particularly likely to suffer from a strong anti-European performance.[26]

This pattern suggests that there were two parts to the appeal of the Referendum Party. First, it secured the support of a small band of strong anti-

Europeans, around two-thirds of whom might otherwise have been expected to vote Conservative: this source of support was much the same level across most of England and Wales. Second, and where it appealed most strongly, much of the Referendum Party's additional support derived from its use as a convenient vehicle of protest for voters who, even if they had voted for the Conservatives in 1992, would otherwise have opted for one of the opposition parties in 1997, and particularly the Liberal Democrats. For the most part the success of the Referendum Party was not so much a cause of the Conservatives' difficulties as a symptom.

Our findings clearly suggest that, contrary to what has widely been claimed, only a handful of the Conservatives' losses of seats can be blamed on the intervention of the Referendum Party. If we assume that where the anti-European parties won up to 3 per cent of the vote, two-thirds of that support was at the expense of the Conservatives, but that beyond that point their support came mostly at the expense of the opposition parties, then there are just six seats where the presence of an anti-European candidate can be said to have cost the Conservatives the seat, of which two were the result of a UKIP rather than a Referendum Party intervention.[27] At the same time there are up to three seats where a narrow Conservative victory coincided with a very strong anti-European vote; if that vote came disproportionately from the opposition, the anti-European intervention may well have helped avoid a Conservative defeat.[28] In so far as the objective of Sir James Goldsmith's campaign was to inflict losses on the Conservatives, it must largely be deemed to have been a failure.

A failure also were the attempts of some Conservative candidates to win support by openly opposing Britain's membership of the European Monetary Union (see Chapter 6). Those candidates who were reported in *The Times* and/or the *Daily Telegraph* as having taken an explicitly anti-EMU position suffered on average a 11.4 per cent fall in their vote, almost identical to the 11.3 per cent drop suffered by those who stuck to the party's official policy of 'wait and see'. If we take into account differences by region, prior strength or the presence or otherwise of an anti-European candidate, it only confirms the conclusion that taking an avowedly anti-EMU position did not help Conservative candidates save their seats. It is of course doubtful how many voters were aware of the particular position adopted by their local Conservative candidate.

In two constituencies, however, voters do appear to have been well aware of the attributes of their local Conservative candidate, namely their ethnic origin. In Bethnal Green & Bow where Conservative support rose by nearly 5 per cent, and in Bradford West where it fell by less than 1 per cent, the Conservative candidate was a Moslem while the Labour candidate was from a different ethnic minority. Both seats contain a significant Moslem minority who were evidently attracted into the Conservative camp by the religious affiliation of the local Conservative. Never before has such ethnic voting occurred on this large scale in Britain.[29]

THE OPPOSITION PARTIES

Many voters may well have been motivated by a longstanding dissatisfaction with the Conservatives in 1997. But they still had to decide who to vote for instead. We have already noted that there was a high correlation between the performance of the two main opposition parties, Labour and the Liberal Democrats. On the whole, where the Labour party did unusually well, the Liberal Democrats did badly, and vice versa. Evidently voters varied systematically between one constituency and another as to which of the opposition parties they decided to support.

Indeed, the source of that variation is very clear. Voters exhibited a striking tendency to opt for whichever of the two opposition parties appeared best placed to defeat the Conservatives locally. This can be seen in Table A2.8 which analyses the performances of the parties according to the tactical situation which pertained before the election (but excluding those constituencies where the Conservatives started off with less than a third of the vote). There are a number of important points to note.

First, on average Labour's vote rose by around three points more in those seats where they started off second to the Conservatives than in those where they were already in first place. This additional vote evidently came at the

Table A2.8   Tactical voting

	Change in % voting		
Tactical situation	*Con*	*Lab*	*Lib Dem*
Lab seats; Con over 33.3%	−12.6	+9.6	−0.3 (107)
Con/Lab seats	−12.6	+13.0	−3.0 (181)
Lib Dem seats; Con over 33.3%	−10.6	+9.6	+1.6 (8)
Con/Lib Dem; Con lead under 30%	−11.8	+6.5	+1.9 (80)
Con/Lib Dem; Con lead over 30%	−13.5	+10.0	−0.8 (60)
Three-way marginals[1]	−11.6	+10.9	−2.3 (18)

Three way marginals are where Con 1st, Lib Dem 2nd in 1992, but Labour within 6% of the Liberal Democrats.

expense of the Liberal Democrats whose support fell by three percentage points more where Labour began in second place rather than first. The Conservative performance in contrast was identical in both situations. This pattern is found consistently in seats where Labour started off second, even in those where they were a long way behind. Evidently around 3 per cent of voters who would otherwise have voted Liberal Democrat in these seats opted to vote tactically instead for Labour in order to defeat their local Conservative.

What of the seats where the Liberal Democrats started off second? Here it is possible to underestimate the extent of tactical voting. Table A2.8 shows that even in these seats Labour made significant progress, increasing their share of the vote by at least 6 per cent. The Liberal Democrats meanwhile struggled to make any advance at all. Undoubtedly Labour made net gains from switches from the Liberal Democrats since 1992. But, as in the case of our analysis of the impact of the Referendum Party, this is to ask the wrong question. We are interested not in the pattern of switching compared with 1992, but in ascertaining whether or not some voters behaved differently on account of the tactical situation in these seats than they otherwise would have done in 1997.

This means that we need to ask not whether Labour's vote went up more than the Liberal Democrats' vote did in these seats, but rather whether Labour's vote went up less in these seats than elsewhere, and whether the Liberal Democrats did better in these seats than elsewhere. In fact, this still gives us a conservative estimate of the extent of tactical voting because it takes no account of voters who may have already opted to vote tactically in 1992 or earlier and repeated that behaviour in 1997. Even so, the evidence that some voters made a tactical switch from Labour to the Liberal Democrats in many seats where the Liberal Democrats started off second is clear. The Liberal Democrat performance was on average a couple of points better in such seats, while Labour was up to three points worse off. Again, the Conservative performance showed little variation.

However, the extent of tactical switching varied much more in these seats than it did where Labour were the main challengers. In fact, where Labour started off not far behind the Liberal Democrats, then, as we can see from the results for the category labelled 'Three-way marginals' in Table A2.8, voters usually, though not invariably, appeared to regard Labour as better able to defeat the Conservatives. Moreover, the Liberal Democrats were more likely to benefit from a tactical squeeze the closer they started off to the Conservatives. Where the Liberal Democrats started off within 15 per cent of the Conservatives, the tactical vote nearly always swung in their direction, and, on average, their vote increased by no less than 2.7 per cent.[30] In seats where they started off between 15 and 30 per cent, their performance was more patchy; here, on average the Liberal Democrat vote rose by just 0.8 per cent. And where the Liberal Democrats started off more than 30 per cent behind, there was little evidence of radical voting at all. Labour clearly secured a tactical vote, and where the Liberal Democrats started off more than 30 per cent behind, there was little evidence of tactical switching at all.

This pattern clearly suggests that voters took the opinion polls into account in deciding what would be the most effective way of casting a tactical vote against the Conservatives. Where Labour started off second then, given that they were riding high in the opinion polls, there seemed little doubt in voters' minds that they were best able to defeat the Conservatives locally, and might even be able to do so in what were normally considered safe Conservative seats. In contrast with the Liberal Democrats running at below their 1992 level of support in the polls, voters took more persuading that they might be able to win locally, and the further the party started behind the Conservatives, the greater the persuasion needed. Indeed, in a few notable cases, such as Hastings & Rye and St Albans, whose well-publicised polls by the *Observer* on the weekend before polling day put Labour ahead locally, voters clearly decided that Labour were in fact better placed to win.

Just how were they persuaded? Here two things in particular seem to have mattered. The first was the Liberal Democrats' record in local government elections in the 1992–97 parliament. Within the south of England outside London, the Liberal Democrats had done particularly well in local elections to the south and west of a line running from Bristol to Oxford to Brighton. Labour, meanwhile, had made significant advances north and east of that line. The enhanced credibility that came from their performance to the south and west appears to have made it more likely that voters regarded the Liberal Democrats as a significant challenger in parliamentary elections. Thus in those seats in that area where the Liberal Democrats started between 15 and 30 per cent, their support rose on average by 0.4 per cent; elsewhere in the south where Labour had advanced, their vote fell on average by 1.9 per cent.

However, the second and more important factor appears to have been whether a seat was one which had been targeted nationally and was, as a result, the recipient of considerable resources from the party nationally for up to four years before the election. In recent years, a considerable amount of research has suggested that, contrary to what had hitherto been the conventional wisdom, local campaigning can make a difference to the success or otherwise of a party in a constituency.[31] It was in any case never clear that the conventional wisdom applied to the Liberal Democrats. In any event, the Liberal Democrats were far more successful in those seats which they targeted than elsewhere. Among those seats where the Liberal Democrats started off within 30 per cent of the Conservatives and which were not three-way marginals, the party's vote rose on average by 4.0 per cent in those seats it targeted, but fell by 2.3 per cent in those which it did not. The differential remains even if we allow for the fact that the party was more likely to have targeted seats where it started off closer to the Conservatives.

However, the 1997 election does not appear to support claims made that local campaigning can make a difference in respect of other parties' performances too. The Labour Party targeted 90, mostly marginal Conservative, constituencies. As in the case of the Liberal Democrats, these seats were in receipt of assistance from the centre long before the election campaign began, and activists from other constituencies were encouraged to travel there to lend their support. Yet, as Table A2.9 shows, the performance in these constituencies was very similar to that in other Conservative/Labour contests. In fact Labour not only won all but one[32] of its target seats, but as many as 68 that it had not targeted. In drawing up its list of target constituencies the party had seriously underestimated its electoral prospects.

Table A2.9   Failure of Labour targeting

	Change in % voting Labour in	
	Target seats	*Non-target seats*
London	+15.9 (7)	+14.6 (26)
Rest of south-east	+13.7 (12)	+14.2 (29)
Elsewhere	+11.8 (53)	+12.3 (54)

Table A2.9 is confined to those seats where Conservatives were 1st and Labour 2nd.

One other local factor which we have previously noted as being a feature of recent elections was evident once more: the tendency for incumbent MPs, especially those in marginal constituencies, to secure personal votes through providing a high-quality service to their constituent.[33] The effect was most apparent in those seats which Labour had captured from the Conservatives in 1992, where the previous Conservative MP did not stand again and where there was not a major boundary change. In these seats the Conservatives would have lost any personal vote that the previous MP had retained, while the new Labour MP had had an opportunity to develop his or her own personal support. On average Labour's vote rose by 2.5 per cent more in these seats than in comparable seats elsewhere.

However, if the evidence of a personal vote is not new, the scale and impact of tactical voting in the 1997 election was unprecedented. Until the 1992 election, Labour had never benefited significantly from tactical voting by

Liberal Democrat voters; if the Liberal Democrats were squeezed, the benefits had either gone evenly to both the Conservatives and Labour, or else slightly to the Conservatives' advantage. In 1992 Labour had benefited in marginal seats; on this occasion it benefited in supposedly safe seats as well. At least 15 and maybe as many as 21 seats were won by Labour from the Conservatives as a result of tactical switching, compared with between six and eight in 1992.[34] And while Labour voters have long shown a propensity to switch to the Liberal Democrats where they had a chance of winning, never before have their votes been worth at least 10 and maybe as many as 14 seats.[35]

Why did voters apparently find it easier to switch their support between the two main opposition parties than ever before? One possibility is that it was the result of the deep unpopularity of the Conservatives which meant that more voters than ever before were motivated by a desire to secure their defeat, but equally it may have been facilitated by the growing closeness of the two parties in terms of policy. This will be an important area of research when the British Election Study survey data become available.

SCOTLAND AND WALES

Nowhere were the consequences of the swing against the Conservative government more dramatic than in Scotland and Wales. The Conservatives lost all their seats in both these parts of the United Kingdom. The last time this had happened in Wales was in the Liberal landslide of 1906; it had never happened in Scotland. Already denuded of control of any local government in Scotland or Wales, and of representation in Strasbourg from the two countries, the result left the party of the Union looking more like an English than a British party. Moreover, in both cases the Tory disaster enabled the nationalists to strengthen their position.

In Scotland the Conservatives ceded second party in votes to the Scottish National Party (SNP). This was the first time this had happened since October 1974. However, this was more a reflection of the Conservatives' weakness than any SNP breakthrough; on average the nationalists' vote rose by just half a percent, and at 22.1 per cent, their support was no less than 8.3 per cent lower than in October 1974. But for the first time since 1979, the SNP performed better on average where it was previously stronger rather than where it was previously weaker, making its vote a little less evenly spread geographically. In part this was a result of tactical voting. The party's share of the vote fell in five of the seven seats the Conservatives were defending against a Labour or Liberal Democrat challenge.[36] In contrast it rose by 5 per cent or more in two of the three seats it had previously won in 1992 together with the two seats which it captured at the election;[37] Labour's vote on average rose by only 3.4 per cent in these four seats.

In Wales, second place in terms of seats was captured by Plaid Cymru simply by retaining the four seats it already held. Although the nationalists' vote rose on average by 1.0 per cent, at 9.9 per cent its support in the principality was still well below that achieved by the SNP in Scotland, or even what the party itself secured in 1970 (11.5 per cent). Its ability to win representation at Westminster on such a low share of the vote remained reliant on the heavy concentration of its support in Welsh-speaking north and west Wales. It won at least a third of the vote in all five seats where a majority of the population speaks Welsh. Nowhere else did it manage to secure as much as a fifth.

THE ELECTORAL SYSTEM

As we noted at the beginning, the impression that the 1997 election constituted a Labour landslide was very much a result of the operation of the electoral system. If the change in each party's share of the vote in each constituency had been the same as it was across the country as a whole, then Labour's majority would have been 131 rather than 179, and the Liberal Democrats would only have won 28 seats rather than their actual tally of 46. The Conservatives were the clear losers, winning no less than 43 seats fewer than they might otherwise have expected.

Moreover, this unfavourable treatment of the Conservatives came after the electoral system had already exhibited a considerable pro-Labour bias in the 1992 general election, giving the Conservatives an overall majority of only 21 despite having nearly an eight-point lead in votes.[38] True, the boundary review had removed some of the bias against the Conservatives caused by out-of-date boundaries, but it still left Labour needing a lower share of the vote to secure an overall majority than did the Conservatives.[39] So how was it possible for the system to have made the Conservatives' plight even worse in 1997?

One possibility might be that the first-past-the-post system has regained some or all of the ability it used to have to exaggerate the lead of the largest party over the second party, an ability that it almost lost completely in the 1970s and 1980s.[40] After all, we have seen that the Conservative vote fell less in seats where they were previously strong, whereas until 1992 at least the party had always performed best in those parts of the country where it had previously been strongest.[41] The 1997 pattern is precisely what would be required to increase the number of seats that are marginal between Conservative and Labour and thus increase the bonus the system gives to the winning party.[42]

But in fact the electoral system is still a long way from providing the kind of winner's bonus that the system regularly provided until 1974. Its operation then was sometimes likened to a 'cube law',[43] that is that if the two largest parties divided the votes between then in the ratio A:B, then the seats that they won would be divided in the ratio $A^3:B^3$. If this law had applied in 1997 (and assuming the Liberal Democrats and others won the number of seats that they actually did), then Labour's majority would have been as much as 229 rather than 179. True, the number of seats that are marginal between Conservative and Labour[44] rose from the 1992 figure of 97 to 114, but that is still well short of the 180 or so needed for the cube law to operate consistently.

Above all, if Labour's large majority were primarily the result of a restoration of the 'winner's bonus', then we should be able to demonstrate that the Conservatives would have won an equally large majority if they had been as far ahead in votes as Labour actually were. In fact nothing could be further from the truth. As Table A2.10 shows, if we assume that such a lead were achieved as a result of a uniform swing from the 1997 result, then the Conservatives would only secure a majority of 45. Labour's large majority was a reflection of a major bias in the electoral system in its favour, and is not an indication of a significant restoration of the winner's bonus.

Three benchmarks in Table A2.10 illustrate the degree of bias quite vividly. First, if the two parties were to have the same share of the vote, Labour would still be 79 ahead of the Conservatives in terms of seats. Second, in order to match Labour in terms of seats, the Conservatives need to be as much as 6.7 per cent ahead in votes. Third, Labour could still secure an overall majority even if they were as much as 1.5 per cent behind the Conservatives in votes; the Conservatives in contrast need a lead of ten points just to secure the same target. Never has the electoral system exhibited such a strong bias in favour of one of the two largest parties *vis-à-vis* the other. On this basis the only post-war elections that would have seen the Conservatives win an overall majority would have been those of 1983 and 1987.

Why has the system become so biased against the Conservatives? And can we necessarily assume that it will remain so biased in future? Two factors lie behind the bias. In part the explanation lies in the fact that fewer votes are cast in constituencies where Labour is strong than where the Conservatives are strong. But, more important is the fact that the Labour and the Liberal Democrat vote has become more effectively distributed, while at the same time the Conservatives' own support has become less efficiently dispersed.

Table A2.10   Relationship between seats and votes

	%Votes		Seats			
Swing to Con	Con	Lab	Con	Lab	Lib Dem	Other
0%	31.5	44.4	165	419	46	29
1%	32.5	43.4	175	413	42	28
2%	33.5	42.4	186	403	41	28
3%	34.5	41.4	198	393	39	28
4%	35.5	40.4	219	374	37	28
5%	36.5	39.4	236	359	34	29
6 %	37.5	38.4	251	345	33	29
6.5%	38.0	37.9	258	338	33	29
7%	38.5	37.4	263	334	32	29
7.2%	38.7	37.2	269	329	32	28
8%	39.5	36.4	279	320	31	28
9%	40.5	35.4	290	310	29	29
9.8%	41.3	34.6	300	300	29	29
10%	41.5	34.4	307	295	29	29
11%	42.5	33.4	320	280	29	29
11.5%	43.0	32.9	330	272	27	30
12%	43.5	32.4	340	263	26	29
13%	44.5	31.4	351	254	24	29

Others include 18 seats elected in Northern Ireland.

The main objective of the boundary review was to equalise, as far as possible, the size of parliamentary constituencies. On average, however, constituencies in both Scotland and Wales, where Labour dominates, are smaller than those in England, so even on the basis of the electorates being used by the various boundary commissions (1991 in England, 1992 in Scotland and 1993 in Wales), the average seat won by Labour in 1992 contained just over 4000 fewer voters than those seats won by the Conservatives. Meanwhile, the pattern of migration from the inner cities to more rural parts of the country, which for the last 40 years has meant that Labour constituencies have gradually become smaller as the boundaries have become older, meant that by the time of the 1997 election that gap had already widened to nearly 6500 voters.

However, the contribution that a constituency makes to the national vote total depends not just on the number of electors it contains, but also on the proportion of those voters that participate, and, as we saw earlier, turnout in seats being defended by Labour not only continued to be markedly lower than in those defended by the Conservatives, but the gap widened a little further. As a result, the 6500 gap in the number of electors widens to one of over 9000 when it comes to actual voters.[45]

The main reason why the bias against the Conservatives became more pronounced in 1997 lies in the changing geographical distribution of party strengths. First, as we have seen, the Conservatives lost support more heavily in seats where they already had a third of the vote, and thus where they had seats to lose. One way of evaluating the impact of this is to calculate what the Conservatives' national share of the vote would have been if its vote had fallen by as much in those seats where it started off with less than a third of the vote as it did in those seats where it started off with more than a third. If that had happened, the party's share of the vote would have been 1 per cent lower, sufficient to reduce our expectations of the number of seats that the party would have won on a uniform swing by at least a dozen seats.

Second, and in contrast, thanks primarily to tactical voting, both Labour and the Liberal Democrats did better in seats where they were challenging the Conservatives and thus had something to gain. Indeed, our estimate above that tactical voting might have cost the Conservatives between 25 and 35 seats would account for around two-thirds of the deviation of the Conservative performance from what would have happened under a uniform pattern of change.

The Conservatives' dilemma with respect to the electoral system is now very similar to that faced by the Liberal Democrats and their predecessors in post-war British politics. The Conservatives have become a relatively small party whose vote is geographically relatively evenly spread from one part of the country to another. The standard deviation of their vote across constituencies is, at 12.2, now only a little higher than that of the Liberal Democrats at 10.9, whose own support is now more geographically concentrated than ever before.[46] Both parties are at a clear disadvantage compared with Labour, whose vote is far more unevenly spread with a standard deviation of 17.9.

How far can we assume that this Conservative disadvantage would necessarily pertain in the event of a significant Conservative recovery at the next election and in the event that the existing electoral system is used once more? Would the Conservative Party necessarily be advised to reconsider its opposition to electoral reform because maintenance of the existing electoral system would put it at a severe disadvantage? There can of course be no definitive answer to such questions. Our judgement would be that Table A2.10 almost undoubtedly overestimates the extent to which the Conservatives would be disadvantaged, but even so, it is still likely that the electoral system could pose a significant barrier to a Conservative recovery.

Clearly one potential hope for the Conservatives would be that some of the tactical switching between Labour and the Liberal Democrats does not repeat itself at the next election. After all, voters will no longer have the motivation to vote against an unpopular Conservative government. On the other hand, a number of factors could militate against a full reversal of the tactical switching that occurred in 1997. First, we noted that the high level of tactical voting may also have been encouraged by the closer proximity between Labour and the Liberal Democrats; that motivation might still survive the Labour administration. Second, as far as switching from Labour to the Liberal Democrats at least is concerned, previous experience suggests that if the Liberal Democrats succeed in capturing a seat, they can often maintain a long-term squeeze on the Labour vote.

The Conservatives might also anticipate that in the course of any revival their gains might take on the reverse pattern of their losses between 1992 and 1997, and prove to be stronger in those seats where they are already stronger. But at the same time, many of the new incumbent Labour MPs will have the opportunity to generate personal votes which could well help depress any swing against them at the next election. Meanwhile, it is almost certain that the gap in the number of electors registered in the typical Conservative and Labour constituency will continue to grow, while the substantial gap in turnout between Conservative and Labour seats could also persist, especially if turnout in the north continues to be lower than in the south.

Yet whatever concerns the Conservatives might have about how the current electoral system might treat them in future, it cannot be assumed either that all of the alternatives on offer would have been equally attractive to them in the circumstances that prevailed in 1997. In particular, those systems such as the alternative vote and the single transferable vote, which take into account not only voters' first preferences, but also their second and subsequent preferences, could also have put them at a disadvantage. Unsurprisingly, surveys regularly find that a high proportion of Labour voters say they would support the Liberal Democrats as their second choice. However, Liberal Democrats have not always reciprocated. But the high degree of willingness of Liberal Democrat voters to switch tactically to Labour in 1997 suggests that a majority of Liberal Democrats may well have preferred Labour to the Conservatives on this occasion; indeed this is confirmed by the British Election Panel Study which, in the spring of 1996, found nearly a two to one majority of Liberal Democrat voters stating that Labour rather than the Conservatives were their second preference.[47]

Table A2.11   1997 result under different electoral systems

	First past post	Alternative vote	Single transferable vote in		Additional member system		Party list system
			small seats	large seats	75%	50%	
Con	165	103	193	195	196	207	208
Lab	419	436	340	317	326	303	300
Lib Dem	46	91	89	110	104	111	113
Others[1]	29	29	35	37	33	38	38

Note: 1. Others include 18 seats elected in Northern Ireland.

To illustrate what impact this might have had in 1997, we have used the distributions of second preferences in this survey to estimate how each party's supporters would have transferred their later preferences both under the alternative vote system and the single transferable vote (see Table A2.11). We have also estimated what the outcome would have been if the additional member system had been used, with the additional seats being allocated separately within each standard region.

In the case of both the single transferable vote (STV) and the additional member system (AMS), we have also explored two further options. In the case of STV we examine what might have happened if the constituencies used had been along the lines of existing Euro-constituencies and what might have occurred if they had been half that size.[48] Under the former option the average constituency would contain eight seats, whereas under the latter it would include just four. Meanwhile, as far as AMS is concerned, we show what would have happened if, first, three-quarters of the seats had been directly elected, and second, only half.[49] Note that in all cases we have assumed that voters would have voted the same way as they actually did under the current system. Clearly, given the evidence of tactical voting we have uncovered, this is unlikely always to have been the case.

As a benchmark against which to evaluate all these various systems we also show what could have happened if the election had been conducted under a national party list system without any constituencies at all, other than that separate elections were held in England, Scotland, Wales and Northern Ireland. In so doing we have preserved the existing over-representation of Scotland and Wales, a feature which is also retained by all the other simulations. We have also assumed that a party would need to win at least

5 per cent of the votes in a nation to win seats there, a condition we have also imposed in the allocation of additional seats in the case of AMS.

Two key points stand out from Table A2.11. First, thanks to the pattern of estimated second preferences, and particularly those of Liberal Democrat supporters, the Conservatives would have won even fewer seats under the alternative vote than they did under the existing system. Indeed, the alternative vote would have left them only narrowly ahead of the Liberal Democrats. The alternative vote clearly cannot be relied upon to ensure that the composition of the British House of Commons more accurately reflects the distribution of popular preferences than first-past-the-post.

Second, and again thanks to second preferences, Labour might well have secured an overall majority under STV despite winning only 43.2 per cent of the UK vote, so long as the constituencies used had been relatively small. This is because, with fewer seats per constituency, it becomes more difficult for smaller parties such as the Liberal Democrats to pick up seats. Labour has to date demonstrated a resistance to the use of STV even where, as in the case of the proposed Scottish and Welsh parliaments, they have agreed to the introduction of a system of proportional representation. However, if the 1997 election were to inaugurate a period of sustained good relations between the two parties, then Labour might in fact find the system to be more advantageous to it than AMS.

A point to note, however, is that even under the most proportional of systems – national party lists – Labour would have been in a commanding position in the House of Commons with 46 per cent of the seats, just 30 short of an overall majority, for even under this system, the 7 per cent of the vote cast for other parties in Great Britain would have been unrepresented thanks to the imposition of a 5 per cent threshold. At the same time, Labour would continue to benefit from the over-representation of Scotland and Wales.

CONCLUSION

The first-past-the-post system has long had a profound impact on British politics, and the 1997 election is no exception. The system turned a relatively modest Labour performance into a landslide in terms of Commons representation. After 18 years of Conservative rule, such a result might be thought to be maintaining a tradition of strong but alternating government. But at the same time, thanks to the weakness of the Conservative performance and the pattern of tactical voting, more third-party MPs were elected than for nearly 70 years. In addition, the outcome raises doubts about whether the system might make it significantly more difficult for the Conservatives to be returned to power in future. With the new Labour government committed to a referendum on the electoral system before the next election, the experience of 1997 suggests we would be unwise to rely on simple generalisations in judging its likely merits or otherwise in future.

ACKNOWLEDGEMENTS

This appendix has created a large number of debts. We are grateful to Martin Range of Oxford University and Sarinder Hunjan of Strathclyde University for invaluable computing assistance, without which nothing would ever have been written. Sean O'Grady of the BBC Political Research Unit demonstrated persistence beyond the call of duty in his pursuit of much of the data we have used. Richard Webber and Barrie Nelson of CCN Marketing compiled and generously made available to us data from the Mosaic database.

NOTES

1. This appendix confines its attention throughout to Great Britain, and all subsequent figures quoted in this appendix relate to Great Britain, rather than the United Kingdom. For the results in Northern Ireland see p. 288.
2. However, apart from Martin Bell's stunning victory in Tatton (the first victory by an Independent since 1945), none of the remaining plethora of mini-parties and Independents made a significant impact on the electorate. Details of the performance of other parties and the best individual performances by such candidates are given in Tables A1.1 and A1.5.
3. See C. Rallings and M. Thrasher (eds), *Media Guide to the New Parliamentary Constituencies* (1995). Appendix 1 also gives details of those cases where there is some doubt about the accuracy of these estimates in individual seats.
4. D. Rossiter, R. Johnston and C. Pattie, 'Estimating the Impact of Redistricting in Great Britain', *British Journal of Political Science*, XXVI (1997), pp. 319–31. We had available to us estimates produced by Rossiter et al. based on a slight revision of the method described in their article. We are grateful to David Rossiter for making his estimates freely available to us.
5. Note, however, that neither set of estimates provide a figure for the turnout in 1992 and thus enable us to calculate the change in turnout between 1992 and 1997 for each constituency. For details of how we have calculated change in turnout, see further below.
6. See the note to Table A2.1.
7. See, for example, R. Leonard, *Guide to the General Election* (1997); D. Butler and D. Stokes, *Political Change in Britain*, 2nd edn (1974), pp. 121, 140ff.
8. As noted above, neither Rallings and Thrasher nor Rossiter et al. provide estimates of the turnout in each new constituency in 1992 which can be used to calculate change in turnout between 1992 and 1997. We have simply estimated the 1992 turnout by taking the total number of votes that were estimated by Rallings and Thrasher to have been cast in 1992 in each constituency and divided that figure by the electorate used by the Boundary

Commissions in the course of creating the new constituencies. Only in Scotland is this a figure for the 1992 register; in England the figure is for 1991 and for Wales, 1993.

It should also be noted that the calculation of turnout in 1997 is also not without its difficulties. The law now permits persons to have their names added to the register after it comes into force on 16 February so long as they satisfy the original conditions for inclusion (namely, that they were resident at an address in the constituency on the previous 10 October). Any such additional names are not included in the electoral registration figures published by the Office of National Statistics (ONS). Electoral registration drives before the election are known to have resulted in the addition of several hundred names to the register in some constituencies, particularly in some inner city seats. In about half of the seats we have been able to secure via the Association of Returning Officers a statement of the exact number of persons eligible to vote on 1 May, taking into account late registrations. In other cases the electorate is simply based on the statistics published by ONS with an allowance made for the proportion of attainers likely to have come of age by May 1.

Both these considerations mean that the figures for change in turnout quoted for individual seats in Table A1.3 should be treated with some circumspection. We anticipate that our estimates are sufficient for the purposes of identifying broad patterns of association, as in Table A2.3, but should not be relied upon too heavily as a statement of what happened in any individual seat.

9. J. Curtice and M. Steed, 'Appendix 2: The Results Analysed', in D. Butler and D. Kavanagh, *The British General Election of 1992* (1992).

10. This is in sharp contrast with 1945 when Labour first swept to a major Commons victory. Turnout then was highest in Labour strongholds in northern cities, in Wales and in the mining and textile areas of Yorkshire and Lancashire.

11. J. Curtice and M. Steed, 'Appendix 2: Analysis' in D. Butler and D. Kavanagh, *The British General Election of 1987* (1988), p. 346.

12. S. Smith, *Electoral Registration in 1991* (1991).

13. See, for example, D. Sanders, H. Ward and D. Marsh, 'Macroeconomics, the Falklands War and the Thatcher government', in M. Lewis-Beck, H. Norpoth and J.-D. Lafray (eds) *Economics and Elections; The Calculus of Support* (1991); D. Sanders, 'Government Popularity and the Next Election', *Political Quarterly*, 62 (1991), pp. 235–61.

14. J. Curtice and M. Steed, 'Appendix 2: An Analysis of the Voting', in D. Butler and D. Kavanagh, *The British General Election of 1983* (1984).

15. I. McLean, 'The Problem of Proportionate Swing', *Political Studies*, 21 (1973), pp. 57–63.

16. Even this qualification would hardly be necessary if we were to exclude the deviant case of Bethnal Green & Bow from the table (see further below). In the remaining three seats in London where the Conservatives began with between 15 per cent and 25 per cent of the vote, the average fall in the Conservative vote was –11.6 per cent, clearly greater than in similar seats outside the south-east.

17. Figures for house prices are taken from the *House Price Index* published quarterly by the Halifax. Details are available separately for each county (in Scotland, region), and we have assumed that the price movement in each constituency has been the same as in the whole of the county of which it is part. Figures are unavailable for a limited number of very small counties/regions. Unemployment figures are based on counts for new parliamentary constituencies supplied by the Department of Education and Employment.

18. P. Hillmore, 'In the dock – and down the Cinque', *Observer*, 4 May 1997.

19. These are Crosby, Eastwood, Newcastle Central, Sutton Coldfield, Tynemouth, Wallasey, Wirral South and Wirral West.

20. See also J. Curtice, 'Class Dealignment Revisited', *CREST Working Paper No. 49* (1996); J. Curtice, 'Anatomy of a Non-Landslide', *Politics Review* (forthcoming).

21. See also J. Curtice, 'Is the *Sun* shining on Tony Blair? The Electoral Influence of Newspapers in Britain since 1992', *Harvard International Journal of Press Politics*, 2, pp. 9–26.
22. 'Tories out', *The Economist*, 15 May 1993; 'The Tories Revolt', *The Economist*, 14 May 1994; 'Tories out', *The Economist*, 13 May 1995.
23. J. Curtice and M. Steed, 'Appendix: An Analysis of the Results', in D. Butler and M. Westlake, *British Politics and European Elections 1994* (1995).
24. We undertook a regression analysis of support for the Referendum party in those seats where they stood where the independent variables were % people aged 65+, % employed in agriculture, % voting Conservative 1992, together with dummies for region. We then used the resulting equation to predict what the vote for the Referendum Party should have been in those seats where they did not stand, and compared this with the actual UKIP performance.
25. J. Curtice, 'One Nation Again?', in R. Jowell, J. Curtice, A. Park, L. Brook and K. Thomson (eds), *British Social Attitudes; the 13th report* (1996).
26. Thus, for example, if we look at those seats outside London and the South-East where the Liberal Democrats started off in second place and within 30 per cent of the Conservatives and at least 6 per cent ahead of Labour we find that Liberal Democrat support fell by 1.1 per cent where the local anti-European vote was greater than 6 per cent, compared with a rise of 2.8 per cent where the anti-European vote was less than 6 per cent. The equivalent figures for Labour were +5.7 per cent and +5.5 per cent respectively.
27. These are Kettering, Wellingborough, Milton Keynes North East, Winchester, Torbay and Kingston & Surbiton. Wellingborough and Torbay are the two seats where the UKIP rather than the Referendum Party intervened. Note that in Torbay the UKIP intervention was counter-balanced by a strong independent Liberal performance which may well have depressed the Liberal Democrat performance there. The total would probably have been one more if Sir Richard Body, who resigned the Conservative whip over Europe during the 1992–97 parliament, had been opposed in Boston & Skegness. Sir Richard's Eurosceptic credentials therefore probably saved his parliamentary career.
28. These are Totnes (won against the Liberal Democrats), Dorset South and Bury St Edmunds (won against Labour).
29. For further details see M. Le Lohe, *Muslim News* 25 April & 5 May 1997.
30. In this and the succeeding paragraphs we have excluded the four seats which the Liberal Democrats had won in a by-election during the 1992–97 parliament, together with Gordon which, although notionally a Conservative seat in 1992, was being defended by a Liberal Democrat incumbent, Malcolm Bruce.
31. See, for example, D. Denver and G. Hands, *Modern Constituency Electioneering* (1997); P. Whiteley and P. Seyd, 'Labour's Vote and Local Activism', *Parliamentary Affairs*, XLV (1992), pp. 582–95; C. Pattie, P. Whiteley, R. Johnston and P. Seyd, 'Measuring Local Campaign Effects: Labour Party Constituency Campaigning at the 1987 General Election', *Political Studies*, XLII (1994), pp. 469–79; C. Pattie, R. Johnston and E. Fieldhouse, 'Winning the Local Vote: The Effectiveness of Constituency Campaign Spending in Great Britain, 1983–92', *American Political Science Review*, LXXXIX (1995), pp. 969–83.
32. This was Brecon & Radnorshire, which was captured from the Conservatives by the Liberal Democrats.
33. See, for example, Curtice and Steed in *The General Election of 1992*, pp. 340–1; B. Cain, J. Ferejohn and M. Fiorina, *The Personal Vote: Constituency Service and Electoral Independence* (1987); P. Norton and B. Wood, 'Do Candidates Matter? Constituency-Specific Vote Changes for Incumbent MPs, 1983–87', *Political Studies*, XL (1992), pp. 227–38.
34. There are 15 seats captured by Labour which would not have been lost by the Conservatives if the movement of votes had been in line with the average movement in those seats which Labour were defending, but where the Conservatives won more than a third of the vote

in 1992 (treating London and the south-east separately), where the loss of the seat was not otherwise ascribable to a below average Conservative performance and where there was evidence of sufficient tactical voting to account for the outcome. These are Kettering, Northampton South, Harwich, Milton Keynes North East, Gillingham, Castle Point, Enfield Southgate, Harrow West, Hastings & Rye, Braintree, Hove, Wellingborough, Rugby, Norfolk North West and Sittingbourne & Sheppey. There are six seats where it is debatable whether the Tories would otherwise have lost the seat or where it is uncertain whether there was sufficient tactical voting to account for the outcome: Eastwood, Shipley, Stroud, Romford, Chatham & Aylesford, and Thanet South.

35. Using the equivalent criteria to those in the previous note 34 above, the 10 seats are Winchester, Northavon, Harrogate, Carshalton & Wallington, Eastleigh, Sutton & Cheam, Kingston-upon-Thames, Lewes, Richmond Park and Taunton. The four possible seats are Torbay, Aberdeenshire West, Newbury and Sheffield Hallam.

36. This calculation excludes both Gordon, notionally defended by the Conservatives but where the old seat was won by the Liberal Democrats in 1992, and Ayr, notionally defended by Labour but where the old seat was won by the Conservatives in 1992.

37. This excludes Perth, won by the SNP from the Conservatives in a by-election.

38. J. Curtice, 'The Hidden Surprise: The British Electoral System in 1992', *Parliamentary Affairs*, XLV (1992), pp. 466–74; Curtice and Steed, *The General Election of 1992*, pp. 347–54.

39. Rallings and Thrasher, op cit.; Rossiter et al., *op cit*.

40. J. Curtice and M. Steed, 'Electoral Choice and the Production of Government: The Changing Operation fo the Electoral System in the United Kingdom since 1955', *British Journal of Political Science*, XII (1982), pp. 249–98; J. Curtice and M. Steed, 'Proportionality and Exaggeration in the British Electoral System', *Electoral Studies*, V (1986), pp. 209–28; J. Curtice, 'The British Electoral System: Fixture without Foundation', in D. Kavanagh (ed.), *Electoral Politics* (1992).

41. Curtice and Steed, 'Proportionality and Exaggeration'.

42. G. Gudgin and P. Taylor, *Seats, Votes and the Spatial Organisation of Elections* (1979).

43. M. Kendall and A. Stuart, 'The Law of Cubic Proportions in Election Results', *British Journal of Sociology*, I (1950), pp. 183–96.

44. As defined in Curtice and Steed, 'Proportionality and Exaggeration'.

45. This figure does, however, exaggerate the Conservatives' disadvantage *vis-à-vis* Labour. This is because the Liberal Democrats perform better in Conservative constituencies, reducing the difference in the size of the two-party vote in Conservative and Labour seats.

46. Despite the increased concentration of their vote, the Liberal Democrats' ability to win seats is still heavily dependent on the level of support for the Conservatives, as Table A2.10 shows. After 1997 there are only seven seats where the party is second to Labour and less than 30 per cent behind, so the party can profit little from any fall in Labour support. In contrast the Conservatives are second to the Liberal Democrats in all but seven of the 46 seats they hold, clearly leaving the party vulnerable to a rise in Conservative support.

47. In this survey, 52 per cent of Liberal Democrat supporters in England and Wales said they would give a second preference vote on a ballot paper to Labour, while only 29 per cent opted for the Conservatives. Meanwhile 78 per cent of Labour supporters named the Liberal Democrats as their second preference while only 9 per cent opted for the Conservatives. Conservative supporters in contrast divided 56 per cent Liberal Democrat and 19 per cent Labour. For further details of the British Election Panel Study, see L. Brook and B. Taylor, 'British Election Panel Study: Interim Technical Notes', *CREST Working Paper No. 41* (1996). Thanks to oversampling in Scotland, separate estimates are available and are used for the distribution of second preferences there. Unfortunately details of the results to a similar question asked of respondents to the 1997 British Election Study were not available at the time of writing.

48. We have used the recommendations that had been issued after 1996 by the Boundary Commissions for the redrawing of European constituencies to bring them in line with the new Westminster constituencies by the time of the general election. In Scotland these were final recommendations, and in England and Wales provisional recommendations. The smaller constituencies are subdivisions of those Euro-constituencies into two undertaken by the authors.

49. Here we have simply assumed that the proportion of directly elected seats won by each party would be the same as the proportion of seats that they actually won in each region in 1997. In practice the results are likely to have been more disproportional. This may mean that we have somewhat overestimated the ability of the allocation of additional seats to overcome the disproportionalities created by the results in the directly elected seats. Additional seats are allocated using the D'Hondt highest average method.

Select Bibliography

Austin, T. (ed.), *The Times Guide to the House of Commons May 1997* (Times Books, 1997).

Baker, D., Gamble, A. and Ludlam, S., 'Whips or Scorpions? The Maastricht Vote and the Conservative Party', *Parliamentary Affairs*, 1993.

Baker, D., Gamble, A. and Ludlam, S., 'The Parliamentary Siege of Maastricht 1993: Conservative Divisions and British Ratification', *Parliamentary Affairs*, 1994.

Balen, M., *Kenneth Clarke* (Fourth Estate, 1994).

Barnet, A., Ellis, C. and Hurst, P. (eds), *Debating the Constitution: New Perspectives on Constitutional Reform* (Polity Press, 1993).

Bennie, L., Brand, J. and Mitchell, J., *How Scotland Votes: Scottish Parties and Elections* (Manchester University Press, 1997).

Blackburn, R., *The Electoral System in Britain* (Macmillan, 1995).

Blair, T., *New Britain: My Vision of a Young Country* (Fourth Estate, 1996).

Bonefeld, W., Brown, A. and Burnham, P., *A Major Crisis? The Politics of Economic Policy in Britain in the 1990s* (Dartmouth, 1995).

Brook, L. and Taylor, B., 'British Election Panel Study: Interim Technical Notes', *CREST Working Paper No. 41* (Centre for Research into Elections and Social Trends, 1996).

Broughton, D., *Public Opinion Polling and Politics in Britain* (Harvester Wheatsheaf, 1995).

Broughton, D., Farrell, D., Denver, D., and Rallings, C. (eds), *British Elections and Parties Yearbook 1994* (Frank Cass, 1995).

Butler, D. and Kavanagh, D., *The British General Election of 1992* (Macmillan, 1992).

Butler, D. and Ranney, A. (eds), *Electioneering: A Comparative Study of Continuity and Change* (Clarendon Press, 1992).

Butler, D. and Stokes, D., *Political Change in Britain* (2nd edn, Macmillan, 1974).

Butler, D. and Westlake, M. (eds), *British Politics and European Elections* (Macmillan, 1995).

Cain, B., Ferejohn, J. and Fiorina, M., *The Personal Vote: Constituency Service and Electoral Independence* (Harvard University Press, 1987).

Coleman, S., *Television Debates: An Evaluation and a Proposal* (Hansard Society King-Hall Paper, March 1997).

Commission on Social Justice, *Social Justice: Strategies for National Renewal* (Vintage, 1994).

Conservative Party, *The Campaign Guide* (Conservative and Unionist Central Office, 1997).

Cowley, P. et al., *Blair's Bastards: Discontent within the Parliamentary Labour Party* (Centre for Legislative Studies, University of Hull, 1996).

Cowley, P. and Norton, P., *Are Conservative MPs Revolting? Dissention by Government MPs in the British House of Commons 1979–1996* (Centre for Legislative Studies, University of Hull, 1996).

Crewe, I., 'Electoral Behaviour', in D. Kavanagh and A. Seldon (eds), *The Major Effect* (Macmillan, 1994).

Crewe, I., 'The Opinion Polls: Confidence Restored?', *Parliamentary Affairs*, 1997.

Crewe, I. and Gosschalk, B. (eds), *Political Communications: the General Election Campaign of 1992* (Cambridge University Press, 1995).

Crewe, I. and King, A., *SDP: The Birth, Life and Death of the Social Democratic Party* (Oxford University Press, 1995).

Crick, M., *Michael Heseltine: A Biography* (Hamish Hamilton, 1997).

Curtice, J., 'The Hidden Surprise: The British Electoral System in 1992', *Parliamentary Affairs*, 1992.

Curtice, J., 'Class Dealignment Revisited', *CREST Working Paper No. 49* (Centre for Research into Elections and Social Trends, 1996).

Curtice, J., 'Is the *Sun* shining on Tony Blair? The Electoral Influence of Newspapers in Britain since 1992', *Harvard International Journal of Press and Politics*, 1997.

Curtice, J., 'So how well did they do? The polls in the 1997 election', *Journal of the Market Research Society*, 1997.

Curtice, J., 'Anatomy of a Non-Landslide', *Politics Review* (forthcoming).

Curtice, J. and Jowell, R., 'The Sceptical Electorate', in R. Jowell et al. (eds), *British Social Attitudes* (1995).

Curtice, J. and Steed, M., 'Electoral Choice and the Production of Government: The Changing Operation of the Electoral System in the United Kingdom since 1955', *British Journal of Political Science*, 1982.

Curtice, J. and Steed, M., 'Proportionality and Exaggeration in the British Electoral System', *Electoral Studies*, 1986.

Denver, D., *Elections and Voting Behaviour in Britain* (Harvester Wheatsheaf, 1994).

Denver, D. and Hands, G. (eds), *Issues and Controversies in British Electoral Behaviour* (Harvester Wheatsheaf, 1992).

Denver, D. and Hands, G., 'Constituency Campaigning', *Parliamentary Affairs*, 1992.

Denver, D. and Hands, G., *Modern Constituency Electioneering* (Frank Cass, 1997).

Denver, D., Norris, P., Broughton, D. and Rallings, C. (eds), *British Elections and Parties Yearbook 1993* (Harvester Wheatsheaf, 1993).

Dunleavy, P. et al., 'Sleaze in Britain: Media Influences, Public Response and Constitutional Significance', *Parliamentary Affairs*, 1995.

Dynes, M. and Walker, D., *The New British State: The Government Machine in the 1990s* (Times Books, 1994).

Evans, B. and Taylor, A., *From Salisbury to Major: Continuity and Change in Conservative Politics* (Manchester University Press, 1996).

Evans, M., *Charter 88: A Successful Challenge to the British Political Tradition* (Dartmouth, 1995).

Farrell, D., Broughton, D., Denver, D., and Fisher, J. (eds) *British Elections and Parties Yearbook 1996* (Frank Cass, 1996).

Field, F., *Making Welfare Work* (Institute of Community Studies, 1995).

Fielding, S., *Labour: Decline and Renewal* (Baseline Books, 1995).

Franklin, R., *Packaging Politics: Political Communications in Britain's Media Democracy* (Edwin Arnold, 1994).

Garner, R. and Kelly, R., *British Political Parties Today* (Manchester University Press, 1993).

Gavin, N. and Sanders, D., 'The Economy and Voting', *Parliamentary Affairs*, 1997.

Gudgin, G. and Taylor, P., *Seats, Votes and the Spatial Organisation of Elections* (Pion, 1979).

Halfacre, K. and Flowerdew, R., 'The Relationship between inter-constituency migration and postal voting', *Electoral Studies*, 1993.

Halloran, P. and Hollingsworth, M., *A Bit on the Side: Politicians – Who Pays Them?* (Simon and Schuster, 1994).

Hayes, B. and McAllister, I., 'Marketing Politics to Voters: Late Deciders in the 1992 British General Election', *European Journal of Marketing*, 1996.

Heath, A., Jowell, R. and Curtice, J. (eds), *Labour's Last Chance? The 1992 Election and Beyond* (Dartmouth, 1994).

Heffernan, R. and Marqusce, M., *Defeat from the Jaws of Victory: Inside Kinnock's Labour Party* (Verso, 1992).

Hogg, S. and Hill, T., *Too Close to Call: Power and Politics – John Major in Number 10* (Little, Brown, 1995).

Hutton, W., *The State We're In* (Cape, 1995).

Jenkins, S., *Accountable to None: The Tory Nationalisation of Britain* (Hamish Hamilton, 1995).

Johnston, R. and Pattie, C., 'The Impact of Spending on Party Constituency Campaigns', *Party Politics*, 1995.

Jones, N., *Election 92* (BBC Books, 1992).

Jones, N., *Sound Bites and Spin Doctors: How Politicians Manipulate the Media – and Vice Versa* (Cassell, 1995).

Jones, N., *Campaign 1997* (Indigo, 1997).

Jowell, R. et al., '1992 British Election: The Failure of the Polls', *Public Opinion Quarterly*, 1994.

Jowell, R. et al., (eds), *British Social Attitudes: Twelfth Report* (Dartmouth, 1995).

Jowell, R. et al., (eds), *British Social Attitudes: Thirteenth Report* (Dartmouth, 1996).

Kavanagh, D. (ed.), *Electoral Politics* (Clarendon Press, 1992).

Kavanagh, D., 'New Campaign Communications: Consequences for British Political Parties', *Harvard International Journal of Press and Politics*, 1996.

Kavanagh, D., 'Speaking Truth to Power? Pollsters as Campaign Advisors', *European Journal of Marketing*, 1996.

Kavanagh, D., *Election Campaigning: the New Marketing of Politics* (Blackwell, 1997).

Kavanagh, D., *The Reordering of British Politics* (Oxford University Press, 1997).

Kavanagh, D. and Seldon, A. (eds), *The Major Effect* (Macmillan, 1994).

Kay, J., *The Foundations of Corporate Success* (1995).

Kellner, P., 'Why the Tories were Trounced', *Parliamentary Affairs*, 1997.

Kendall, M. and Stuart, A., 'The Law of Cubic Proportions in Election Results', *British Journal of Sociology* I, 1950.

King, A. (ed.), *Britain at the Polls 1992* (Chatham House, 1992).

Leonard, R., *Guide to the General Election* (Pan Books, 1997).

Lewis-Beck, M. et al. (eds), *Economics and Elections: The Calculus of Support* (University of Michigan Press, 1991).

Linton, M., *Money and Votes* (Institute for Public Policy Research, 1994).

Linton, M., *Was it the Sun wot won it?* (Nuffield College, Oxford, 1995).

Linton, M., 'Maybe the *Sun* won it after all', *British Journalism Review*, November 1996.

Ludlam, S. and Smith, M. J. (eds), *Contemporary British Conservatism* (Macmillan, 1996).

McLean, I., 'The Problem of Proportionate Swing', *Political Studies* 1973.

McLean, I. and Butler, D., *Fixing the Boundaries: Defining and Redefining Single Member Electoral Districts* (Dartmouth, 1996).

McNair, B., *News and Journalism in the UK* (Routledge, 1994).

McSmith, A., *John Smith: Playing the Long Game* (Verso, 1993).

McSmith, A., *Kenneth Clarke: A Political Biography* (Verso, 1994).

Mandelson, P. and Liddle, R., *The Blair Revolution. Can Labour Deliver?* (Faber, 1996).

Market Research Society, *The Opinion Polls and the 1992 General Election* (July 1994).

Marr, A., *Ruling Britannia: The Failure and Future of British Democracy* (Michael Joseph, 1995).

Miliband, D., (ed.) *Reinventing the Left* (Polity Press, 1994).

Nicholson, E., *Inside – and Outside – the Conservative Party* (Indigo, 1996).

Norris, P. and Lovenduski, J., *Political Recruitment: Gender, Race and Class in Britain since 1979* (Cambridge University Press, 1995).

Norton, P. and Wood, B., 'Do Candidates Matter? Constituency-Specific Vote Changes for Incumbent MPs, 1983–87', *Political Studies*, 1992.

Norton, P. (ed.), *The Conservative Party* (Harvester Wheatsheaf, 1996).

O'Muircheartaigh, M., 'Election 97: a Triumph for the Pollsters?', *Journal of the Market Research Society*, June 1997.

Pattie, C., Whiteley, P., Johnston, R. and Seyd, P. 'Measuring Local Campaign Effects', *Political Studies*, 1994.

Pattie, C. et al., 'Winning the Local Vote: The Effectiveness of Constituency Campaign Spending in Great Britain 1983 1992', *American Political Science Review*, 1995.

Rallings, C., Farrell, D., Denver, D., and Broughton, D. (eds), *British Elections and Parties Yearbook 1995* (Frank Cass, 1996).

Rallings, C. and Thrasher, M., *Britain Votes 5* (Dartmouth, 1993).

Rallings, C. and Thrasher, M., *Media Guide to the New Parliamentary Constituencies* (BBC, ITN, PA News, Sky, 1995).

Rentoul, J., *Tony Blair* (Little, Brown, 1995).

Riddell, P., *Honest Opportunism: The Rise of the Career Politician* (Hamish Hamilton, 1993).

Ridley, F.F. and Doig, A. (eds), *Sleaze: Politicians, Private Interests and Public Reaction* (Oxford University Press, 1996).

Rose, R., 'Structural Change or Cyclical Fluctuation?', *Parliamentary Affairs*, 1992.

Rose, R., 'On the Crest of a Wave', *Parliamentary Affairs*, 1997.

Rosenbaum, M., *From Soapbox to Soundbite: Party Political Campaigning in Britain since 1945* (Macmillan, 1997).

Rossiter, D., Johnston, R. and Pattie, C., 'Estimating the Impact of Redistricting in Great Britain', *British Journal of Political Science*, 1997.

Sancho-Aldridge, J., *Election '97: Viewers' Responses to the Television Coverage* (Independent Television Commission, 1997).

Sanders, D., 'Government Popularity and the Next Election', *Political Quarterly* 1991.

Scammell, M., *Designer Politics: How Elections are Won* (Macmillan, 1995).

Seymour-Ure, C., 'The British General Election of 1997: Editorial Opinion in the National Press', paper presented at APSA Convention, Washington D.C., 1997.

Shaw, E., *The Labour Party since 1979: Crisis and Transformation* (Routledge, 1994).

Smith, M.J. and Spear, J. (eds) *The Changing Labour Party* (Routledge, 1992).

Smith, S., *Electoral Registration in 1991* (HMSO, 1991).
Smith, S., *The Electoral Register* (HMSO, 1993).
Sopel, J., *Tony Blair: the Moderniser* (Michael Joseph, 1995).
Sparrow, N., 'Improving Polling Techniques Following the 1992 Election', *Journal of the Market Research Society*, 1993.
Spencer, P. and Curtice, J., 'Flexibility and the Feel Good Factor', *Kleinwort and Benson Securities*, November 1994.
Stark, L.P., *Choosing a Leader: Party Leadership Contests in Britain from Macmillan to Blair* (Macmillan, 1996).
Stephens, P., *Politics and the Pound* (Macmillan, 1996).
Tunstall, J., *Newspaper Power: The National Press in Britain* (Clarendon Press, 1996).
Wallace, W., *Why Vote Liberal Democrat?* (Penguin, 1997).
Waller, R. and Criddle, B., *The Almanac of British Politics* (5th edn, Routledge, 1996).
Whiteley, P. and Seyd, P., 'Labour's Vote and Local Activism', *Parliamentary Affairs* XLV, 1992.
Whiteley, P., Seyd, P. and Richardson, J., *True Blues: The Politics of Conservative Party Membership* (Clarendon Press, 1994).
Willetts, D., *Blair's Gurus* (Centre for Policy Studies, 1996).
Willetts, D., *Why Vote Conservative?* (Penguin, 1997).
Williams, J. and Stoddart, T., *Victory: with Tony Blair on the Road to a Landslide* (Bookman, 1997).
Wright, T., *Why Vote Labour?* (Penguin, 1997).

Index